Lights and Shadows of Spiritualism

LIGHTS AND SHADOWS

OF

SPIRITUALISM

LIGHTS AND SHADOWS

OF

SPIRITUALISM

By D. D. HOME

" Light—more light ! "—GOETHE

SECOND AND CHEAPER EDITION

LONDON
VIRTUE & CO., LIMITED, 26, IVY LANE
PATERNOSTER ROW
1878

TO MY WIFE,

Whose loving sympathy and constant care have soothed me in many hours of trial and pain, and whose superior counsels have aided me in composing a work, the end and aim of which is to place a much-insulted Truth on a plane where honest lovers of such Truth would not have cause to blush in avowing themselves to be what she is, a Christian and a Spiritualist,

I, IN AFFECTION AND ESTEEM,

Dedicate

THIS BOOK.

CONTENTS.

PART I.

ANCIENT SPIRITUALISM.

PART II.

SPIRITUALISM IN THE JEWISH AND CHRISTIAN ERAS.

***

CHAPTER I.

THE SPIRITUALISM OF THE BIBLE.

CHAPTER II.

THE SPIRITUAL IN THE EARLY CHRISTIAN CHURCH.

CHAPTER III.

SPIRITUALISM IN CATHOLIC AGES.

CHAPTER IV.

THE SHADOW OF CATHOLIC SPIRITUALISM.

CHAPTER V.

THE SPIRITUALISM OF THE WALDENSES AND CAMISARDS.

CHAPTER IV.

CHAPTER V.

PEOPLE FROM THE OTHER WORLD.

CHAPTER VI.

SCEPTICS AND TESTS.

CHAPTER VII.

ABSURDITIES.

CHAPTER VIII.

TRICKERY AND ITS EXPOSURE.

CHAPTER IX.

TRICKERY AND ITS EXPOSURE (*continued*).

CHAPTER X.

THE HIGHER ASPECTS OF SPIRITUALISM.

CHAPTER XI.

THE HIGHER ASPECTS OF SPIRITUALISM (*continued*).

LIGHTS AND SHADOWS OF SPIRITUALISM.

PART I.

ANCIENT SPIRITUALISM.

CHAPTER I.

THE FAITHS OF ANCIENT PEOPLES.

THERE descend to us, among the fragmentary records which, with shattered temples and decaying cities, form the only remaining proofs that such nations as the Assyrian and the Egyptian were once great upon the earth, many evidences of the vividness with which light from another world broke in upon man during the earlier ages of our own. Every spiritual phenomenon which has in the present day startled the Christians of the West was, centuries ago, familiar to the Pagans of the East. On the common foundation of a belief that spirit visits were neither few nor far between every mythology of those far-back times was based. The most superhuman virtues, and abominable crimes, of Chaldean, Phœnician, Egyptian, Hebrew, Greek, and Roman, are traceable to a spiritual source. For then, as since, the good of the truth that man cannot " die, to live again," but, living once, lives eternally, was at times largely perverted to evil. Side by side with noble natures, made yet higher and purer by communion with high and pure minds that no longer tenanted the flesh, were demons doing the behests of demons—evil creatures of both sexes, and all ages and conditions, who, instigated by spirits still fouler, worked ceaselessly to fill the earth with bloodshed and uncleanness. By intercourse with spirits the cheerful assurance of immortality was perpetuated through all times and nations, and the dark vestibule of the grave brightened with a glory from beyond. Through intercourse with spirits also the awful rite of human sacrifice—men seeking to appease imaginary deities by the murder of their brethren—had birth. It was natural that when, at the touch of the departed, the clouds that veil our hereafter shrank away, man, gazing on the newly revealed morning-land, should imagine he saw gods walking there. Thus the power of the spirits for good and evil became immeasurable. The valiant phalanx of the Greeks rushing down upon the Persian multitude at Marathon, every breast thrilling with the thought that around thronged the spirits of their ancestors, and the deities of their nation, inspiring and encouraging them to the combat, supplies an example of the best phase of spiritual influence. The same Greeks, solemnly hewing in pieces or burying alive unhappy captives, whose torments would, they supposed, win them favour in the sight of evil beings erringly exalted into deities, may stand as an instance of the worst.

But the dark and the bright phases alike witness to the intensity of faith which primæval man had in the invisible. Even when we know little else of a nation we know generally that the corner-stone of its mythology was a belief in the return of the departed. Heroes and sages were not, when death snatched them, lamented as having for ever passed away. Their spirits hovered still above the land they had loved and served : at times visibly appearing to the posterity by whom they were adored, counselling them in the moment of danger, or leading on their hosts to victory. If a spirit were frequent in his appearances and mighty in the services he rendered, he speedily became worshipped as a god. Again, when it was discovered that only in the presence of certain persons could spirits manifest themselves, these mediums were set apart, and priesthood had its origin. Immortal man is immortally ambitious—peculiarly liable also to mislead and be misled. The priest speedily aspired to be the founder of a sect—the builder up of some system of theology or government. He walked among men as one with them but not of them; clothed with distinctive garments; hedged round by the sanctity of mysterious rites. From among the invisibles who surrounded him he selected as his peculiar guardians and guides those whose counsels were agreeable to his soul. It leaves a dubious impression of the majority of spirits and mediums in ancient days, that in every land of which we have knowledge we find altars dripping with human blood; prisoners of war butchered ruthlessly, as acceptable offerings to the gods; temples polluted with licentiousness; the most unblushing vice; the most systematic cruelty. These things all sprang from the abuses of communion between world and world; abuses for which spirits alike with men were blamable. Were the beings anciently worshipped as gods in reality devils? If by devils we understand human beings depraved to the lowest pitch, then many probably might be accounted so. It is not to be doubted that then, as now, the messengers of God—high, holy, and pure spirits—constantly watched over and communicated with the better children of earth. But to that end mediums were necessary, and the mediums were usually ambitious and often depraved. Loth to be but the servants of the spirits, they foolishly and uselessly aspired to govern them. The entreaties and admonitions of their good angels were neglected and contemned, until these in grief held aloof, and seemed to have forsaken the earth. The dangerous beings who counselled pleasant things, and, while seeming pliant to the slightest wish, held their victims firmly to the service of evil, reigned almost unchecked. Dwellers in darkness, they desired, with the malignity of unrepentant wretchedness, that souls yet on earth should enter the spirit-realm tainted with a leprosy deep as their own. Through their fancied masters and real tools, the priests, nation after nation was led away from faith in the One God to worship his creatures. What these deities were, the records that have descended to us irrefragably prove. Resembling men, they are depicted as possessing the passions and attributes of fiends. In every mythology it was a cardinal point that to

avert their wrath blood was necessary. Fearful penalties were
denounced against such as offended these pseudo-gods. Among
the light lively peoples of the South of Europe the idea of punishment after death took the shape of confinement in silence and
eternal night; with sterner nations it was a vision of unhappy
faces looking up from a burning tomb. The infamous doctrines
that have disgraced our own age—doctrines which seek to sap the
very foundations of society, and, taking from love all that is
beautiful and endearing, leave only its filthy and debasing mockery
—were inculcated by these deities; enforced in their temples by
precept and example, and disseminated through nations with the
effects of a pestilence. What society was two thousand years ago
history witnesses but too well. Good, and good spirits, seemed
almost to have fled from the earth. The servants of evil were
everywhere. All temples of all deities had become offences to the
eye of heaven—plague-spots of bloodshed and licentiousness. The
many accepted, as they have in all ages done, the deities offered to
them, and, obedient to their behests, cultivated the evil of man's
nature and carefully repressed the good. The intelligent and
gifted perceived that, living or fabled, the beings to whom the
nations erected temples were assuredly not gods, and the creators
of the universe; but either monsters of the imagination, or
creatures of a scale somewhat beneath that on which they
themselves moved. They sought refuge accordingly in epicurean
negation, and attention to the things of this life. At length the
evil grew to an unendurable height. That period when the Roman
power had attained its zenith, was the nadir of the morality and
happiness of man. Then the forces of good in the invisible world
began once more to stir. Upon an earth enervated with wickedness and convulsed with strife; upon nations where the most
hideous vices stalked the land openly and unashamed; upon
nations where the stake, the cross, and the scourge were in hourly
use, and where man plotted how to be most inhuman to his fellow-
man; upon the century of Tiberius, Caligula, and Nero, of
Messalina, Agrippina, and Locusta,—the great awakening of the
Christian gospel dawned. Founded in miracle, attested by prodigy,

spread by apostles whose touch healed the sick, whose words caused the maimed to become whole, and the cripple to arise and walk, and to whose eyes was revealed the whole radiance of the Unseen, it conquered rapidly region after region, setting at defiance the possible and the common, and discovering by burning proofs that the ladder which Jacob beheld was but faintly typical of that immortal one stretching. from earth to heaven by which multitudes of the departed have in all ages continually ascended and descended.

I have said that since the founding of our world communion with another has existed, and that in every fragmentary history of an ancient nation its tokens peep through. Among the very few legends that Time has floated down to us respecting the mysterious Etruscans is one which ascribes to them devotion to magic, and the power of raising the dead. Their cognate race, the almost equally mysterious Phœnicians, had in the highest degree the belief both in evil and beneficent spirits; and in their evocation by means of wild and complicated rites. Other nations, of whose mythologies but the most slender scraps have been handed down—the Scythians for example, the Gauls, the Teutons and the Sarmatians—appear also to have cherished this universal faith. In France and our own isles the Druids were acquainted with the phenomena of clairvoyance and animal magnetism; they cultivated the trance, and through visions sought for an insight into futurity. The histories of Egypt, Assyria, Chaldea and Persia, of Greece and Rome, of India and China, are steeped in spiritualism. In a later portion of this work I shall dwell upon the Hebrew annals. It will be sufficient that at present I, under the head of ancient spiritualism, devote my attention to the countries already named; that I bring from the storehouse of history the best-attested incidents illustrating the communion of men and spirits, and make clear their relation to the phenomena witnessed in our own age. I confess that it is impossible to construct from the imperfect relics of ancient chroniclers narratives of such weight and authenticity as are available from the rich materials of more modern times; but enough remains to amply illustrate and verify whatever I have already asserted in this introduction to my task. I shall seek to show that the occurrences received with stubborn incredulity in the nineteenth century were familiar to the first, and perhaps equally familiar to centuries long anterior to the Christian era. I shall point to the belief in the supermundane entertained by the mightiest minds of these ancient ages, and rank as spiritual believers such giants as Homer, Hesiod and Pindar; as Alexander and Cæsar; as Virgil and Tacitus; as Cicero, Seneca, Pliny, Plutarch, and a hundred more. Finally, having pointed out the vivid resemblance which the spiritual phenomena of the past bear to the spiritual phenomena of to-day, I shall call attention to the fact that the outbreaks of evil which of old convulsed the earth, were heralded by just such clouds as, at first no bigger than a man's hand, have rapidly come to overcast the present spiritual horizon.

CHAPTER II.

THE uncountable years that have elapsed since Ninus shared his sceptre with Semiramis, and the first sage watched on the summit of the Tower of Belus, have all but whirled away with them into oblivion the history of the Assyrian realm—the mightiest of the ancient world. From the scanty fragments of Berosus, and the more copious remains of Herodotus, together with the Hebrew scriptures, do we chiefly glean what is known to us of this remarkable people; unless we dare trust the Greek historian who recounts that Semiramis invaded India with an army of two millions of men. The researches of Layard and Smith, indeed, have of late greatly added to our knowledge of this antique race. From disinterred Nineveh come to us the pictures, the picture-writings, and the sculptures of the mighty Assyrian warriors—the scourges of all neighbouring nations. We have by their own hands portraits of the men who devastated Egypt, and carried the Ten Tribes of the Hebrews into captivity. And, formidable as was the Assyrian soldiery, the priests wielded a yet more terrible power over their fellow men. Of the most ancient among them we know little; save that they were devoted soothsayers, and respected by all men for their gift of looking into the future. With the period of the division of the Assyrian empire our information begins to increase. Pre-eminent is that awful instance of spiritual power recorded in the Hebrew annals, and apparently confirmed by late researches—the passing above the Assyrian camp of an angel who destroyed silently, and in a single night, Sennacherib's army of a hundred and eighty thousand men.

We know from Herodotus and others that when the Babylonian empire was in the glory of its power, the influence of the Chaldean sages had also attained its zenith. Every secret of nature which man had unveiled, the whole knowledge then acquired respecting the visible and the invisible, was locked in the bosoms of these famous philosphers. They held in the Babylonian commonwealth a station equally dignified with that held in a neighbouring country by the powerful magicians of Egypt. They guided the footsteps of the young just entering upon this present life—they smoothed the passage of the old just departing to another. Futurity was their especial study, and, by diligent comparing and interpreting of dreams and prodigies, they had established what they believed to be a complete system of divination. Especially were they famous for their watchings of the stars. The astronomers of the eighteenth and nineteenth, and the astrologers of the sixteenth and seventeenth centuries A.D., alike recognise predecessors in those inquiring spirits, who from the summit of the Tower of Belus nightly searched the Assyrian heavens. Even when the Babylonian empire fell before the shafts of the Mede the magi survived. They flourished in Babylon in unchecked power, from the era of Cyrus to that of the Darius whom Alexander subdued, and they made one of their most remarkable prophecies to the Macedonian hero himself.

At the distance of three hundred furlongs from the great city Alexander was encountered by a deputation of the most famous magi. These warned him that he should on no account presume to enter Babylon, as the gods had decreed that once within the walls he must assuredly die. So deeply was the conqueror of Asia moved by this prediction that, while sending his chief friends into Babylon, he himself encamped at a distance of two hundred furlongs from the walls. But the Grecian philosophers who accompanied him, the doubting disciples of Anaxagoras and others, went into the King's presence, and by their lively ridicule temporarily effaced from his mind all respect for the wisdom of the Chaldeans. Alexander entered Babylon, and in a few months was gathered to his fathers. Various other omens had foreboded the disappearance of this royal meteor from the earth which he astonished. Shortly after the magnificent obsequies of his favourite Hephæstion, a Babylonian who had been placed in confinement was found by the King dressed in the royal robes and seated on the throne. Alex·ander, amazed, demanded of the man who had advised him to this act. The intruder answered simply that, "he knew not how he found himself there." By the advice of the soothsayers he was put to death ; but the omen sank deeply into the conqueror's mind.

Not long afterwards he sailed forth, accompanied by a small flotilla, to view the harbour of Babylon. A storm arose, and Alexander's vessel was parted from the rest. After tossing on the waters for several days refuge was found in a narrow creek choked with overhanging shrubs. The King's diadem was plucked from his head by a projecting bough, and flung into the waves. A sailor swimming from the vessel recovered the crown, and placed it on his own brow the more speedily to reach the ship. Both by Alexander and the Chaldeans this second prognostic was considered ominous, and he was counselled to offer sacrifices to the gods. At the feast which accompanied the proposed rites the great conqueror quaffed at a draught a huge goblet of wine, sighed, appeared smitten with an overwhelming sickness, and was assisted forth to his deathbed. Two days before, Calanus, an Indian philosopher, had, on ascending his funeral pyre, announced to Alexander that the latter must prepare to speedily follow him to the Shades.

The philosophy of Egypt divides with that of Chaldea the honour of being the most ancient of which we moderns have knowledge. So many centuries have been numbered with the past since even the decay of either of these civilisations, that it almost ranks with the impossible to decide on which nation the light of learning first dawned. The preponderance of evidence, such as that evidence is, inclines to the side of Egypt. Zonaras, indeed, asserts that the Egyptians derived their mythology from the Chaldeans, but this modern researches contradict. It is, in any case, incontestible that the Egyptian priesthood was the wisest and the most magnificent of the ancient earth. In dignity they were equal to their brethren of Chaldea, in wisdom they even surpassed them. What their temples were, the awful ruins of Karnac, the city of shrines, even now witness. The avenues of sphynxes extend for miles; the desert is crested with columns whose massiveness no other nation can equal. In these stupendous recesses was once hived that wisdom a few fragments of which, despite the sleepless jealousy of its guardians, Greek sages bore back to their own land, and embodied in Greece's sublimest philosophy. The splendour of the little that remains causes us the more to regret that mass of knowledge which, by the erring system of the Egyptians, is irrecoverably lost. For here, as in each of the great empires of the East, the few enlightened ones in whose keeping was the wisdom and the science of the age, far from striving to disseminate the seeds of knowledge among the great body of the people, jealously restricted that knowledge to themselves and their descendants, leaving the outer world in hopeless darkness. The mass of the nation were estimated as cattle, the puppets of the nobles and the magi, fit only for contemptuous abandonment to the worship of apes and beetles. In the temples, on the contrary, the utmost striving after discovery was apparent—an intellectual activity that never ceased. The paintings which Denis and Montfaucon have copied from their walls make manifest that mesmerism and clairvoyance were familiar things with the magicians of Egypt; that through these or other means they obtained communication with the world of spirits, and practised with spirit-aid the art of healing. In the temples were placed representations of the more miraculous cures. These seem to have been chiefly procured by aid of the trance or mesmeric sleep, in which, without doubt, spirits no less than men usually operated. To induce this sleep incense was used. Its influence was assisted by the soft music of lyres. Elevated thus above its material prison, the soul for a space held free communion with the spiritual world. King Rhampsitimus, the magi of Egypt asserted to Herodotus, descended by such means to the mansions of the dead, held converse with the gods, and returned after awhile to the upper day.

Into Egypt went Pythagoras, to increase from the greater stores of that country the wisdom which he had acquired in Greece. But so rigidly did the magi restrict all learning to their own caste, that not until he had passed from temple to temple, and had undergone disciplinary initiations more and more severe, was the philosopher, after twenty-two years of patience, admitted to the inner mysteries. Returning to Greece, he became the martyr of the spiritual truths with which he astonished his countrymen. Delos, Sparta, Elis, and Crete, in turn cast him out. Everywhere derided as a madman, he passed over into Italy and wandered through the magnificent colony of Magna Græcia, teaching and working miracles in Crotona, Rhegium, and Metapontus. The fate of the prophets of all ages pursued him. At Crotona the mob burned down his school, and forty neophytes perished in the flames. Hunted by enemies thirsty for his life, he immured himself in the Temple of the Muses at Metapontus, and was there suffered to die of want. But his doctrines, the fruits of the painful years passed in Egypt, endured after him—the error with the truth. From the Egyptians he had acquired the theory of transmigration, as inculcated in the sacred books of Hermes Trismegistus. At death, according to these strange metaphysics, the soul of man passed into another body. Sometimes the spirit reappeared as a human being—sometimes as an animal. The nature of the new receptacle was determined by the purity or wickedness of the former life. Three thousand years were passed in this manner, and if then sufficiently purified, the spirit ascended to the immortal gods. During the latter centuries of this curious species of purgatory, the soul was supposed to reside in those animals which the Egyptians held peculiarly sacred. Thus a cat represented a being particularly close to eternal felicity : a beetle was perhaps still nearer. A modification of this marvellous religion was taught by Pythagoras, exaggerated after his departure by his disciples, and finally extinguished in the grossness of its own absurdities. Our own century, strange to say, has witnessed the resurrection of this ancient folly. I shall take occasion in a later portion of this work to treat of the belief of those apers of antiquity who, discarding the animals, have unearthed from their dusty receptacle the remaining relics of the Pythagorean system, and, clothing these with the fantasies of their own imaginations, have submitted to the notice of a bewildered world the identity-confounding chimæra of re-incarnation.

Our information respecting the Egyptian oracles, falls far short of the ample knowledge accorded to us of the Grecian. The most famous—can it, however, be held an oracle of Egypt?—was that renowned temple buried in the solitudes of the Libyan Desert, and consecrated to Jupiter Ammon. Alexander of Macedon, in the plentitude of his power, visited it to interrogate the deity on some subject near to his heart. Question and answer were alike kept secret; but the magnificence of the conqueror's offerings intimated that he was satisfied with the response accorded him. A very few predictions of less celebrated oracles have been preserved by the Greek historians. Among such, two singularly-fulfilled prophecies deserve notice.

Whilst Sethon, formerly a priest of Vulcan, held the Egyptian sceptre, he was dismayed by the approach of that Sennacherib whose invasion of Judæa heaven so terribly frustrated. Deserted by the warrior tribe, he betook himself to the temple of Vulcan, and implored against the Assyrians the aid of the deity whom he had served. As he stood before the image a vision came upon him. Vulcan, he dreamed, spoke, and bade him be of good cheer, for that he himself would fight in his worshipper's behalf. Hereupon Sethon, gathering courage, marched to encounter Sennacherib. He was followed only by a rabble of tradespeople and mechanics; at sight of whom the Assyrian laughed, accounting himself certain of victory. On the morning of the battle, however, Sennacherib found that he was overthrown before the strife commenced. During the night myriads of field-mice had entered the Assyrian camp, and devouring the bowstrings and quivers of the warriors, had left them almost defenceless. The victory of the Egyptians was easy and complete.

Herodotus tells us that after the death of this Sethon twelve kings reigned in the different provinces of Egypt. An oracle announced that he who, in the temple of Vulcan, poured a libation from a brazen vessel, should expel his fellows and reign as sole monarch. On the occasion of a certain sacrifice, Psammeticus, one of the twelve, having found himself without the accustomed golden cup, filled a brazen helmet with wine and made his libation. On this the remaining kings banished him to the marshes of the coast. Burning with indignation, he consulted the oracle as to how he might best avenge the injury. It was replied that vengeance would be accorded him when brazen men arose from the deep. The answer was naturally held by Psammeticus a mockery. Shortly afterwards, however, certain pirates clad in brass armour appeared in Egypt from Ionia and Caria. These strangers Psammeticus took into his pay, and having, by their aid, become sole ruler of the Egyptians, the oracle's prediction was most curiously accomplished.

From the dim magnificences of the race who reared the pyramids we pass to Persia and Zoroaster. Even before the time of that mighty iconoclast the history of his country bears interesting traces of intercourse with another sphere. Cyrus, the subduer of Asia, was heralded and attended by prophecy, both in Persia and among the Jews. Astyages, his grandfather, saw in vision a vine proceed from his daughter Mandane, by which the whole of Asia was overshadowed. The soothsayers explained this to mean that Mandane would be delivered of a son who should conquer all the kingdoms of the East. Fearing lest he himself might be among the rulers deposed, the jealous monarch wedded his daughter, not, as was the usage, to a prince of the Medes, but to Cambyses, a native of the subject kingdom of Persia. He again dreamed of the vine that overshadowed Asia, and again received the explanation of its pointing to the coming of a conqueror who should tread all nations under foot. On this the King determined to destroy the fruit of the marriage the instant that it saw the light. The fruit was Cyrus, whom Astyages commanded Harpalus, his chief captain, to take with him and put to death. Harpalus, reluctant to execute the foul mandate, sent the babe to be reared far from the court, in the rude Highlands of Persia. Arrived at manhood, Cyrus

speedily approved the truth of the prophecy, and, deposing Astyages, reigned over Persia and Media in his stead. He conquered
Crœsus of Lydia, and, overthrowing the Babylonian empire, permitted the captive Jews to return to Palestine. According to
Josephus this favour was won by the Jews at Babylon displaying
to Cyrus the prophecy wherein Isaiah alludes to him by name. The
forty-fifth chapter of the prophet thus opens :—" Thus saith the
Lord to his anointed, to Cyrus, whose right hand I have holden,
to subdue nations before him ; and I will loose the loins of kings
to open before him the two-leaved gates ; and the gates shall not
be shut ; I will go before thee, and make the crooked paths
straight : I will break in pieces the gates of brass, and cut in
sunder the bars of iron : And I will give thee the treasures of darkness, and hidden riches of secret places, that thou mayest know
that I, the Lord, which call thee by thy name, am the God of
Israel. For Jacob my servant's sake, and Israel mine elect, I have
even called thee by thy name, though thou hast not known me."

Cyrus, continues Josephus, on being shown this prediction, and
the equally remarkable one contained in the twenty-eighth verse of
the preceding chapter, acknowledged that the Jehovah of the
Hebrews was indeed the God of nations, and that from Him he
received the sceptre of the world.

Nor was the close of the mighty conqueror's career unaccom-
panied by prodigy. Invading Scythia, he dreamed that Darius, the
son of Hystaspes, stood before him with wings springing from his
shoulders ; of which the one overshadowed Europe, the other
Asia. Believing that the gods had thus warned him of a plot
against his throne, he sent Hystaspes back to Persia, to watch over
Darius until he should himself return. But, although the son of
Hystaspes was in reality destined as his successor, no conspiracy
had been implied. The vision given to Cyrus was an admonition
of his own approaching death. He was vanquished and slain in a
battle with Tomyris, queen of the Massagetæ ; and the sceptre of
Persia descended to Cambyses, his son. On the death of that
monarch anarchy distracted the empire, and Darius Hystaspes,
inspired by various omens, stood forth as a competitor for the

throne. Overpowering his rival Smerdis, he assumed that imperial purple to which he had not been born, and began a reign of prosperity almost unequalled in his country's annals.

In the time of this Darius, Zeréthoschtro, the " Golden Star " of Persia, dawned upon the world. His name, softened into Zoroaster, is familiar to us as that of the mightiest religious reformer of the ancient East. By both lines of ancestry, as well through his mother Dogdo, as his father Poroschasp, could he boast of descent from the remote kings of Persia. Poroschasp, says tradition, was descended from that Djemschid, the fabulous embellisher of Istakhar, whom Ormuzd gifted with creative powers ; and who was, according to Persian legends, fifth in line from Noah. Of omens vouchsafed immediately before and after the birth of Zoroaster, the Easterns have many most marvellous tales. His mother, being pregnant, saw in vision a being glorious as Djemschid, who assailed the djins or devs — the Persian evil spirits—with a sacred writing, before which they fled in terror. The interpretation of the magian to whom she applied, was that she should be favoured among women by bearing a son to whom Ormuzd would make known his laws ; and who should spread them through all the East. Against this son every power of evil would be in arms. Tried by afflictions and perils innumerable, the prophet would ultimately drive his foes before him like chaff, and receive even in his own country the utmost honour. A king should be raised up who would accept his sacred writings as the word of truth, and make them the law of Persia : everywhere the new religion would prevail : Zoroaster would ascend to the side of Ormuzd in the highest heaven, and his foes sink to Ahriman and hell.

Alarmed lest the prophet whose advent was thus heralded should prove the destroyer of their order, certain among the magi conspired to slay him immediately upon his birth. Darius, whose ear they had gained, becoming possessed with an evil spirit, rode off in search of the babe. Less fortunate than Herod, he discovered the object of his hatred, and, on lifting his sword to hew in pieces the infant Zoroaster, the arm that grasped the weapon was withered to the shoulder, and the King fled convulsed with terror and agony. Disappointed in their opening plot, the magi speedily took heart a second time to attempt murder. On this occasion they were themselves the agents of their evil wishes. A fire having been kindled, the embryo reformer was stolen from his mother's dwelling, and cast into the flames. Dogdo, seeking on all sides for her son, found him at length lying peacefully on his fiery couch, as if in a cradle, and carried him home uninjured. As he grew to manhood numerous other efforts were made to compass his death. He was placed in the way of savage bulls, was cast to wolves, and fed with victuals in which poison had been mingled. Through all this the spirits to whose service Zoroaster had been consecrated supported him unhurt. At thirty years of age his mission began. Quitting his native place he journeyed towards the court of Iran; but being warned in a vision of an attack which the magi and devs combined waited to make upon him, he turned aside into the mountains of the Albordi. There the things which "eye had never seen" were revealed to his gaze. He was lifted up to the highest heaven, and beheld Ormuzd in his glory, encircled by the hosts of the angels. Food sweet as honey was given to him, on eating which his eyes were opened to all that passed in the heavens and the earth. The darkness of the future was made to him as day. He learned the inmost secrets of nature; the revolutions of worlds; the influences of the stars; the greatness of the six chief angels of God; the felicity of the beatified; the terrible condition of the sinful. He went down into hell and there looked on the evil one face to face. Finally, having received from Ormuzd the Divine gospel which should illumine the East, he was bidden to return to earth, and teach it to all conditions of mankind. Celestial fire was given to him, to be kept burning as a symbol of the glory of God in every city where his teachings were received. Placed again upon the mountains of Albordi or the Balkan, Zoroaster reared in a cavern an altar to the Creator, and kindled upon it the first sparkles of the sacred flame. As he resumed his journey a host of furious devs and magi beset him, and sought to destroy the Zend-avesta—the gospel which Ormuzd had committed to his care.

These the prophet put to flight by pronouncing some verses from the sacred book. . He continued his course to Balkh, and, being denied admittance to the King, cleft the roof of the palace, and descended into the midst of the court. All save the monarch himself fled in terror. The King caused them to re-assemble, and Zoroaster, encircled by a ring of courtiers and magi, expounded with vehement eloquence the doctrines he had been sent upon earth to spread. The magicians present then endeavoured to confound him with the learning of which their minds were the repositories; but the prophet solved with the utmost ease the most abstruse problems of their science, and broke through every mental net that could be spread. Hereupon the monarch declared himself a convert to the new religion, and was followed by others of his court. Many Persians, however, including the whole body of the magi, were stirred to rage by the thought that a single daring and successful reformer should succeed in subverting beliefs which had endured from an antiquity almost immemorial. For years the prophet's history is that of attempts on the part of enemies to destroy his life and credit, and of the miracles by which he put their rage at defiance. At length the good cause triumphed. Opposition was beaten down, and Zoroaster became to the Persians whatever, at a yet more ancient date, Moses had been to Israel.

His law, like that of the Hebrew prophet, was at once theological and civil. The portion remaining to us of the Zend-avesta, or Living Word, has three grand divisions: the Izeschné, the Visfered, and the Vendidad. These again are parted into sections too numerous to be here mentioned. A Litany, a Liturgy, and a general code of laws, are among the matters included. Prayers are drawn up for even the most trifling occasions. On cutting hair or nails; before making pastry; after sneezing; on seeing a leprous person, mountains, a cemetery, a city, the sea; on killing cattle; on killing vermin; and at a thousand other times, verbose petitions are to be reiterated by the devout.

The theology of Zoroaster is far more tolerant than that of the Calvinistic section of Christendom. The eternal hell to which all but the elect are to be consigned, makes no appearance in his religion. Even Ahriman and his devils are in the end to be pardoned and restored. The Creator, he teaches, formed together with the world Ormuzd and Ahriman, the good and the evil principle. These, with their respective hosts, shall contend on the battle ground of the universe for a space of twelve thousand years. At the end of this period comes a conflict like the Christian Armageddon, in which Ahriman and his subordinates are utterly overthrown. The evil one hereon repents, and, in presence of the Eternal, enters into a solemn league of amity with Ormuzd. Hell itself is purged, and through all creation sin and sorrow are annihilated. I may mention that Zoroaster condemns all men, even the best, for a space to his inferno; but none are to be chastised beyond their deserts, and not even the vilest eternally.

Such a revelation was of a truth spiritual and sublime. Zoroaster's place is high above that of Mahommed in the ranks of the founders of faiths. The disciples of the Koran did, indeed, vanquish and subvert to a newer creed the disciples of the Zend-avesta, but the event was no miracle. When, in the seventh century after Christ, this conquest took place, the Zoroastrian system had endured for near twelve hundred years. As shaped by the founder its moral teachings were pure and beautiful, and its idea of the Divine One high and just. But with the passing of centuries abuses began, like foul parasites, to cling to and mar the noble structure. As with all other systems of the ancient world, the evil portion of the unseen beings around us, having undermined with malignant patience, at length succeeded in overthrowing the work of the good. Aided by the unworthy servants to be found before all altars, they defaced with vice after vice the temples where constantly burned the sacred fire. Sensual indulgence, against which Zoroaster had launched his sternest anathemas, made foul the lives of his descendants. The adoration given at first to the unseen Creator, was lavished in process of time on the visible objects He had created. The sun, the stars and the sacred fire were the gods of this new idolatry. Thus the great decay went on. The evil influences without worked mightily and with success. Licentiousness desecrated the temples; human sacrifices began to make foul the altars. At last, when hypocrisy had replaced piety, and sensuality and sloth stood in the place of spiritual zeal, there poured down on Persia that ardent multitude of fanatics whom Mahommed's intolerant enthusiasm had inflamed. The choice was the Koran or the sword. Sapped already at all points by internal corruption, the edifice Zoroaster had reared hasted to its fall. The few who refused to abjure their religion fled from Persia for ever, or, remaining, were relentlessly put to death. At the present day the numerous Parsees scattered through Hindostan and other countries of the far East are tho dispersed relics which remain of that once mighty and united brotherhood which revered the teachings of the " Golden Star."

CHAPTER III.

INDIA AND CHINA.

"I HAVE seen," says Apollonius of Tyana, "the Brahmins of India dwelling on the earth, and not on the earth, living fortified without fortifications, possessing nothing, and yet everything." The "dwelling on the earth, and not on the earth" alludes to their being frequently levitated. Apollonius had journeyed into Hindostan to seek admittance to the treasury of Indian wisdom. The supermundane attainments of the Brahmins were displayed to him immediately that the object of his mission became known. He was brought into the presence of the chief sage of the caste, who addressed him in the following words:—"It is the custom of others to inquire of those who visit them who they are, and for what purpose they come; but with us the first evidence of wisdom is that we are not ignorant of those who come to us." Thereupon this clairvoyant recounted to Apollonius the most notable events of his life; named the families both of his father and of his mother; related what the philosopher had done at Ægae; described by what means Damis had become the companion of his journey, and repeated all that they had heard and talked of by the way. Awed and humbled by knowledge so unearthly, the astonished Greek earnestly besought to be admitted to its secrets. After the usual length of waiting he became duly illuminated, and returning, astonished Europe with his piercing clairvoyance and wondrous powers of healing. Lecturing at Ephesus the words suddenly died upon his tongue. He bent forward amazedly, and, gazing into space, exclaimed, "Strike! *strike* the tyrant!" Then, turning to the bewildered audience, he continued, "Domitian is no more;

the world is delivered from its bitterest oppressor." In the very day and·hour when Apollonius beheld this vision at Ephesus was the despot assassinated at Rome.

If a stranger acquired such gifts chiefly from a sojourn in the temples of the Brahmins, what must have been the spiritual wealth of those Brahmins themselves? The aim of their religion was to lift the soul above the thraldom of the senses and place it in unity with God. Like the Platonists, they judged that the spirit is enveloped by a form of luminous ether—as the Vedas have it, " sûkshonas-arira," a finer body. A multitude of sensations perplex us, and these " buddhi," or reason, was created to command. Sent into earthly life, the soul migrates from body to body in a most marvellous and truly Pythagorean manner. These incarnations ended, the spirit appears before Yamas, the Minos of the Brahminical theology. As its actions have been righteous or unjust, so is it translated to the paradise of Indra, or condemned to various of the purifying hells. Final beatitude, according to the ideas of both Brahmin and Buddhist, consists in absorption into the Divine nature and eternal union with God. By Europeans this creed is commonly regarded as betokening a species of annihilation ; but although violent pains and pleasures would seem to be immortally banished from these Eastern " just spirits made perfect," the individuality of each is unchangeably preserved. To the heavenly felicity of " Nirvana " but one path conducts—unceasing mortification of the spirit and the body. The laws of Manu minutely prescribe the inflictions which the devotee must endure. To scorch in summer before the hottest fires ; to shiver naked in running streams in the depth of winter ; to pass hours buried in ant-nests, or writhing on couches studded with numerous spikes ; to be clad in the bark of trees, and have for food leaves and roots, and for drink impure water; to deny the tongue its use ; to swing suspended by hooks passed through the flesh of the back : these are some of the torments in which from immemorial antiquity Hindoo existences have been spent. In the day of Alexander of Macedon such penances flourished in full rigour, and they have continued unremittingly popular down to the present time.

Brahmins and Buddhists alike teach that the Deity has repeatedly descended in human shape to purify the world. The Brahmins, however, decline to recognise Buddha as one amongst these avatars. They describe the deity whom the Buddhists worship as a species of demon permitted, at a time when the earth was filled with evil, to arise and lead the wicked astray. Thus an irreconcilable enmity exists between the followers of the two great creeds. "By their fruits ye shall know them." Despite the holy horror of the Brahmins, the faith of the Buddhists is vastly more spiritual and elevated than their own. If a demon inspired it he had undeniably forgotten his condition, and was for the nonce masquerading as an angel of light. His teaching Christians cannot but recognise as wise and pure. The wasting of life in sacrifice is strictly forbidden, and even the blood of animals may not, on any pretext, be spilt. The faithful are earnestly entreated to live at peace with their fellow-men, and to keep themselves in the words of St. James, "pure and unspotted from the world." The eating of flesh is prohibited, and the doing injury to even the smallest creature which God's hand has formed held a sin. The Vedas and Puranas of the Brahmins Buddha altogether rejects, and reprobates these writings for their unholy advocacy of living sacrifices. By so stern a denunciation of the darker among its doctrines the more ancient sect of the Brahmins was moved to fury. They drove the converts of the new heresy from Hindostan Proper, and relentlessly persecuted all who dared re-enter that peninsula. But beyond the Ganges, and east and north of the Himalayas, Buddhism waxed mightily. Overspreading, and becoming the state religion of Nepaul, Thibet, and Affghanistan, of Burmah China, Mongolia, and Japan, it stands at the present day foremost, as regards the number of devotees, among the great religions of the earth. That this splendid fabric is more imposingly vast than solidly real; that in various of these lands—China and Burmah in especial—systems of unblushing foulness and hideous cruelty usurp the pure name of Buddhism, are incontrovertible facts. But a faith that has had so unequalled an influence on the destinies of the East well deserves notice, and the space can hardly be wasted that is accorded to a brief *résumé* of the beliefs prevalent among this mighty family of spiritualists.

An article of faith constantly iterated in the Buddhist writings is that departed souls have in all ages returned to our world. Like Milton in his thousand times quoted avowal, these scriptures say that

> " Millions of spiritual beings walk the earth
> Unseen, both when we wake and when we sleep."

Countless numbers are continually ascending and descending on the missions of the gods. Some are the guardians of cities, others of individuals; others again haunt by night caverns, forests, and all solitary spots. In describing these unseen beings every resource of the glowing imagination of the East is expended. They pass to and fro among men wrapped with an ethereal veil, and thus conceal from earthly eyes their forms, a thousand times more beautiful than those of mortals. They are crowned with unfading flowers, and brilliant with all the glories of Paradise. The brightest of the stars are less clear and radiant than their eyes, and the white garments in which they are robed emit the most delicious perfumes. Some are kindly, others fierce; but all wield the mightiest influence over the destinies of mankind.

As was natural in the case of beings so attractively depicted, and whose presence it is probable that spiritual tokens were continually making manifest, the mass of the people have in process of time come to adore them as divinities. At this day there are probably some hundreds of millions of deities set up in the niches of the Buddhist Pantheon. By the kindred sect of Brahma three hundred and thirty millions of these false gods are computed to be adored.

We find in Thibet, where Buddhism flourishes in the fullest vigour, a startling copy of the ritual and ceremonies of the Roman Church. The priests are tonsured. The faithful have their rosaries for prayer, and tell the beads as zealously as any Spaniard. Monasteries have multiplied to such a degree that monks and priests are held to be in number almost a moiety of the population.

The priesthood, magnificently robed, sometimes in yellow, sometimes in purple and gold, pass on festival days to the temples, attended by bursts of barbaric music, canopied with banners, and surrounded by censers heavy with incense; the faithful as the procession moves by prostrating themselves in the dust. Holy water is abundant throughout the temples, baptisms continually occur, and relics of saints are to be found everywhere. The priests are permitted housekeepers, " around whom," says Mr. Howitt in his " History of the Supernatural" " families unaccountably spring up, and are styled nephews and nieces." Indeed, so parallel are the customs, social and ecclesiastical, to those of the Catholic Church, that, when first her emissaries obtained entrance to Thibet, two of their number, Fathers Grüber and Maffie, indignantly wrote home to accuse the devil of having " set up in that far land a most blasphemous mockery of the rites and paraphernalia of the true faith."

In China of old the worship of a single Supreme Being seems to have obtained. Gradually falling from this original Theism, the adoration of the visible objects of creation, and of a host of invisible powers, became in process of ages the theological taints of the Celestials. Spirits presiding over the elements were recognised, and temples erected to each. Ancestors, too, were deified, and annual festivals instituted at which the progenitors of the reigning monarch received the homage of that mighty empire which in former days their sceptres had swayed.

With the increase of idolatry abuses of every kind grew and multiplied, until, in the seventh century before Christ, China was eaten up with all imaginable error and corruption. In the latter years of that century the reformer Lao-tse appeared. Spiritual faith had been almost extinguished, and this present world was the only one of which the Chinese took heed. Lao-tse drew around him the few inquirers into the problems of futurity who still remained, and strove with their aid to awaken a longing after spiritual things in the bosoms of his countrymen. Persecuted vehemently, as all prophets of all eras and kingdoms have been, he fell into a disgust with his mission, and, shaking the dust of cities from his feet, retired to pass the remainder of his life in religious calm. Yet, although the labourer had turned back from the sowing of the seed, the harvest of such efforts as he had already made was in no long time reaped. A religious awakening took place, and the sceptical and vicious public mind was stirred to its inmost depths. Then appeared Confucius, the great purifier of the morals of the empire, as Lao-tse had been of its metaphysics. He inculcated the necessity of honouring parents, of being truthful in every business of life, of actively fulfilling all social and natural duties, of keeping faith with others, and of rendering obedience to the laws of man and God. In his writings the most striking of the ancient Chinese legends are transmitted to modern times. These traditions speak like the Hebrew Scriptures of the fall of man, and the hurling down into misery and darkness of an angelic host who had rebelled against the Supreme.

Lao-tse and Confucius are alike in their deep belief in the nearness of the spiritual world. All truth respecting the future state, says the former, has been brought down to man by the messengers of God. Prayer and self-denial are the charms which open the eyes of the mind to the spiritual beings around us. Apparitions have occured since the creation of the globe. Invisible to the dim eyes of the flesh, spirits, evil and good, constantly hover above the earth, checking or aiding the advancement of man. The limitless universe constitutes but one family; earth, heaven, the spirits yet in the flesh, the spirits of the dead, form a single empire ordered by the eternal reason of Schang-ti. The beings ever near man watch constantly his deeds. Do we give way to evil, the evil spirits enter, and become strong within us, by reason of their affinity to the darkness of our souls. If, despising temptation, we drive from us these demons, ministering angels constantly attend us, and cherish within our bosoms. a light that gleams brighter and brighter unto the perfect day.

Such were the high and wise teachings of the two chief prophets of the Celestial Empire. They so far succeeded in their mission as to implant in Chinese bosoms a faith in the supermundane which, if anything, has grown stronger with the lapse of ages. Inter-

course with the world of spirits is daily sought after in every temple
of the greatest empire of the East. But, whatever the state of
spiritual health may have been] when the teachings of Lao-tse
and Confucius had yet the eloquence of novelty, the present
degradation of this unfortunate race appears almost irremediable.
Guardian angels seem for a space to have abandoned the Chinese,
and the whispers of demons tempting to evil are the only messages
from the invisible listened to to-day. In China itself opportunities of observation are almost denied to Europeans, and
the corruptions of the empire, though known to be extreme, are
in great measure hidden. But in the cities of the Pacific sea-
board of America—inundated of late years by uncountable
thousands of the race I at present treat of—the whole measure of
their gigantic wickednesses and dwarfish virtues may be observed.
The most rapidly enlarging portion of San Francisco consists of a
rookery of wretched dwellings styled the Chinese Quarter. There
the vices which chroniclers shudder to name, and which among
even the most fallen of European races, lurk but by stealth in the
darkest and foulest dens, walk abroad openly and unashamed.
Murder is too common to excite more than the attention of a
moment. Truth in man, and chastity in woman, are virtues equally
unknown. The filth of the dwellings is such that hogs or pole-
cats could scarcely be at ease within them. Children die in frightful numbers, or are placidly put out of the way should the parents
find them inconvenient to keep. And with all this the Chinaman
is frugal, gentle, industrious, and prepossessing in appearance and
manners. But beneath the varnished outside crust a sink of
iniquity is concealed. The refuse of Europe and America has been
drawn to Califormia and Utah by the thirst of gold, yet the veriest
wretches among the white men stand amazed at the depths of
iniquity to which their yellow rivals can, without compunction,
descend.

CHAPTER IV.

GREECE AND ROME.

I PASS now from Asia to Europe, and from the faint grandeur of
the traditions preserved respecting the empires which were the
mistresses of the ancient East to the fuller and more reliable
information possessed respecting those civilizations of the West
enthroned by the Egean and upon the Tiber. The "glory that was
Greece" is indeed irrecoverably extinct, and the "grandeur that
was Rome," fallen into an almost hopeless decay. Empires have
been founded, have flourished, and have perished, since the last of
the Delphian Pythonesses drew a last response from the spirits
whom she was appointed to serve. It was centuries anterior to
the birth of Mahommed that the last public reading of the books of
the Cumæan Sibyl took place in the temples of Rome. But the
array of mighty spirits who shone with so immortal a lustre on
the City of the Violet Crown, the City of the Seven Hills, and
other cities and commonwealths of the Grecian and Roman dominions, have bequeathed to us works in whose undying pages the
actions and the thoughts, the worship and beliefs of the Italians
of two thousand and the Greeks of almost three thousand years
ago, are as undyingly preserved. These great writers were with
few exceptions believers in the return of the departed. Scarcely
a poet or philosopher amongst them but, whilst busied with the
things of this present world, had as active a faith in, and was as
anxiously inquisitive respecting, the things of the life to come.
And the great historians of Greek times—Herodotus and Xenophon
in especial—when giving account of apparitions or marvellously
fulfilled prophecies, do not present them as paradoxes which are to-

be received with wonder and distrust; but rather relate them as
truisms known and accepted from time immemorial by the race for
whom they wrote. Let me, in support of the views I have
advanced, select some proofs of the extent to which belief in the
presence of an eternal and invisible order of things side by side
with this temporal and visible creation, prevailed amongst the
Greeks. I shall open with the poets: in all nations the voices of
the popular faith.

"The gods," says Homer, "like strangers from some foreign
land, assuming different forms, wander through cities, watching
the injustice and justice of men. There are avenging demons and
furies who haunt the ill-disposed, as there are gods who are the
protectors of the poor."—(*Odyssey*, xvii. 475). Says Hesiod :—

> " Invisible the gods are ever nigh,
> Pass through the mist, and bend the all-seeing eye.
> The men who grind the poor, who wrest the right
> Aweless of heaven's revenge, stand naked to their sight ;
> For thrice ten thousand holy demons rove
> This breathing world, the delegates of Jove ;
> Guardians of man, their glance alike surveys
> The upright judgments and the unrighteous ways."
>
> *Works and Days.* Elton's Translation, p. 32.

It is Sophocles who supplies me with the following beautiful
passage :—"I fondly thought of happier days, whilst it denoted
nothing else than my death. To the dead there are no toils.
They drink purer draughts and continually ascend higher."

Can we term this aught but the spiritual teaching of the nineteenth century anticipated. And hearken to Pindar :—"But the
good, enjoying eternal sunshine night and day, pass a life free
from labour ; never stirring the earth by strength of hand, nor yet
the crystal waters of the sea in that blessed abode, but with the
honoured of the gods all such as lived true lives, and took
pleasure in keeping their faith, spend in the heavens a tearless
existence."

"Spirits," says Pythagoras, "announce to man secret things,
and foretell the future." The doctrine of Socrates was the same.

"Socrates thought that the gods knew all things—both what is said, what is done, and what is meditated in silence—are everywhere present, and give warnings to men of everything."—*Memorab.* i. 1.

The fragments that remain to us of Æschylus are throughout instinct with the mysteries of another world. Strange and appalling beings—the Titans and the Furies—move in shadowy procession across his pages. He loves to contemplate the supermundane; but it is the supermundane in its gloomiest guise: "a land of darkness, as darkness itself, and where the light is as darkness." From the grim sublimity of such tragedies as the Prometheus, it is pleasant to turn to the more truly Greek beliefs preserved in the plays and poetry of Sophocles, Euripides, and Homer, and in the philosophy of Plato. Homer and Sophocles have been already called as witnesses to the intensity of the Greek conviction of the nearness of spiritual things, and I shall content myself with describing, by the aid of these, and other great brethren of the guild of poets, the faiths which they represent as having prevailed in their age and land.

The Greeks, then, saw gods everywhere. The eternal snows of Parnassus; the marble temples of Athens glistening in the rays of a Southern sun; the thousand isles nestling in the blue waters of the Egean; the fragrant groves where philosophers disputed; the fountains shadowed by plane-trees; the solemn fields of Platæa and Marathon: each and all of these had their attendant sprites. A thousand deities received homage in a thousand temples. Yet amidst this error the form of that One God, the Uncreated and the Supreme, whom Christianity adores, was by the higher minds of the nation perceived "as in a glass, darkly." Socrates taught that a single deity governed the universe. "To [the Unknown God," said the inscription which Paul found at Athens. The people, it is true, were not disposed to receive such a doctrine. To the light, lively Greek a pantheon of divinities was a mental necessity. From the picture of a single mighty spirit controlling the destinies of creation; everywhere present, yet everywhere unseen; knowing all, yet known of none; eternal, invisible, and incomprehensible,—the multitude shrank in disgust. Gods who mingled visibly in the actions of man; who clothed themselves with material forms to lead on to victory the hosts of the countries they cherished; who shared the passions of humanity and sympathised with its infirmities; who, while controlling the present, gave omens of the future of nations and individuals: these were the beings to whom, in love or fear, the Greek bowed down. His poets represented one god as appearing angrily in the clouds, and hurling down thunderbolts into the midst of armies contending on the earth; another as wandering in the shape of a beardless youth from city to city, and challenging men to contend with him on the lyre which he loved: this goddess as snatching from out the midst of the battle an endangered warrior, of whose] stately form she had become enamoured; that, as urging her celestial steeds from capital to capital to stir up the surrounding nations against a commonwealth that was the object of her hate. And the' legends of these gods, which with the vulgar were objects of devout credit, were by the philosopher made the vehicles of a higher purpose: allegories for the delicate shadowing forth of spiritual things. The sage had been struck by the thought that the soul perhaps came from an existence in some distant and different world to be incarnated here, and he hid his idea in the lovely myth of the love and union of Cupid and Psyche. He saw that the great benefactors of mankind—the increasers of the world's stock of mental or physical power—were uniformly tormented by that world in life, and worshipped by it after death. Thus the legend of Prometheus and his theft of fire from heaven for the benefit of man; of his torture on Mount Caucasus, and unconquerable defiance of the deity who oppressed him; of his ultimate deliverance and triumph, arose. So with all the fables of the Greeks. Through this beautiful mythology constantly breaks the radiance of the spiritual world; even as the eyes of Athenian actors gleamed through the openings of their masks. We learn from a hundred master-pieces of the intellect how untiring was that spirit of restless inquiry with which every people of Hellas searched into the secrets of the unseen. No city was founded; no army marched forth to battle; no vessels laden with emigrants set sail for Italy or Asia Minor without consulting the oracles of the gods. The fiery imagination, and the intellect at once subtle and vigorous of the Greeks, peculiarly fitted them for the reception of impressions from the invisible world. To the profounder realities of such intercourse, indeed, they seem never to have penetrated. The secrets hived in those imperishable temples where were celebrated the rites of the mystic Isis, entered not into the philosophy of Hellas, or entered only through such men as Pythagoras, who, scoffed at and persecuted in life, were revered and imitated by their countrymen after death. But, although the more startling of spiritual phenomena were not among the Greeks things of daily occurrence, no race more generally impressionable to spiritual influence existed in the ancient world. It is through the Grecian nature that the Grecian name has become immortal. Knowledge was not here, as in the great Asiatic empires, regarded as a lamp of inestimable rarity, to be carefully reserved for guiding the footsteps of a few, while the mass of their fellows wandered in darkness. Like the rain, it fell everywhere. The philosopher or poet, inspired consciously or unconsciously by the whispers of attendant spirits, hastened to publish to all men the ideas which fermented in his brain. Inspired by the whispers of attendant spirits? Are not poets, philosophers, and indeed all geniuses, knowingly or unknowingly the subjects of inspiration from another world? To what but the promptings of numerous spirits influencing a single mighty imagination can be ascribed the marvellous creations which glow in the dramas of Shakspeare? From whence but the sphere of all light could proceed the Divine gleams that crossed the brain of a Raphael? And the citizen of Attica was in respect of supremely gifted countrymen peculiarly fortunate. For him the inspirations of a hundred minds had taken imperishable shape. " He saw," says Lord Macaulay, " the plays of Sophocles and Aristophanes ; he walked amidst the friezes of Phidias and the paintings of Zeuxis ; he knew by heart the choruses of Æschylus ; he heard the rhapsodist at the corner of the street reciting the shield of Achilles or the death of Argus." And Homer, Æschylus, and Zeuxis—

Phidias and Sophocles, alike inculcated with all the strength of their magnificent genius the constant interference of spirits in the affairs of men! Had the Greeks missed being a nation of spirit-ualists it had indeed been a miracle. But, save with such philosophers as those of the Atomic school, the belief in the immortality of the soul and the return of departed spirits to watch over those yet on earth was, as I have endeavoured to show, deep and universal. Every nature fitted to be the instrument of the spirits was secluded with jealous care from influences pre-judicial to such a mission, and consecrated as the life-long servant of a shrine of more or less renown. The majority of such media were of the fairest portion of the fairer sex. A succession of virgins presided over the most renowned oracle of Greece, that of the Delphic god, and received from another world the messages of prophetic import destined, now for commonwealths, now for individuals. And besides that of Delphos a hundred oracles of lesser fame were scattered through Hellas. Even the smallest of these shrines blazed with jewels and gold ; the gifts of crowds of anxious devotees. This ceaseless hunger for communion with the unseen, and constant exposure to spiritual influence, had, as in all lands and ages, its dark no less than its glorious side. Human sacrifices sometimes made horrible Grecian altars ; departed spirits were frequently elevated into imaginary gods. But the corruption of the Greeks was not as the corruption of Nineveh, Babylon, and Memphis. Brilliant virtues redeemed it : magnificent acts of heroism were inspired by this intercourse with the unseen. "To-night," said Leonidas to the three hundred of Thermopylæ, "we shall sup with the immortal gods." "On, sons of the Greeks ! " was the battle-cry of Marathon, "above you the spirits of your fathers watch the blows which, to preserve their tombs from desecration, you strike to-day."

Hundreds of well-attested instances have been handed down to us of the manner in which the oracles of Hellas were fulfilled. From these I shall select such as are not only most striking in themselves, but best supported by outward evidence. As has been already mentioned, the Delphic oracle far outstripped all com-

petitors in the importance and truthfulness of its prophecies.
Says Plutarch :—"It would be impossible to enumerate all the
instances in which the Pythia proved her power of foretelling
events; and the facts of themselves are so well and so generally
known, that it would be useless to bring forth new evidences.
Her answers, though submitted to the severest scrutiny, have
never proved false or incorrect." And he relates, amongst other
proofs of his assertions, that she predicted the eruption of lava and
ashes with which Vesuvius overwhelmed the cities of Pompeii and
Herculaneum.

To Delphi sent Crœsus of Lydia, when uneasy at the rapid
growth of the Persian power. He had previously despatched ambassadors to the most renowned shrines of the age; bidding them
demand of the oracles on a certain day in what work the King was
at the moment employed. The replies from other temples are
unknown, but that from the Delphic god ran as follows :—

"See! I number the sands; I fathom the depths of the ocean;
 Hear even the dumb; comprehend, too, the thoughts of the silent.
 Now perceive I an odour, an odour it seemeth of lamb's flesh;
 As boiling it seetheth; commixed with the flesh of a tortoise;
 Brass is beneath, and with brass is it covered over."

The divination was in all respects complete. At the appointed
hour Crœsus had retired alone into an inner apartment of his
palace; and there had, indeed, cut to pieces a lamb and a tortoise;
afterwards cooking the flesh in a vessel of brass. Awed by the
proof of superhuman knowledge which the Delphic oracle vouchsafed, he sought by magnificent gifts to obtain the favour of the
god. The embassy which bore his second question had in charge
three thousand oxen, numerous gold and silver vessels, a golden
lion, a hundred and seventy ingots of the same metal, and a statue
also in gold, and adorned with girdle and necklace of incredible
value. Depositing these before the shrine of the god, the ambassadors of Crœsus demanded whether it were well that he
should march against the Persians. The oracle's response ran
thus :—

" If Crœsus pass the Halys he shall destroy a great empire."
Unconscious that the empire indicated was his own, Crœsus already
exulted in the thought of subjugating Persia, and at once prepared
for war. A third and yet more magnificent embassy, bore from
him a gift to every inhabitant of Delphi, and a demand whether his
rule should long continue. The oracle replied, " When a mule
becomes the ruler of the Persian people, then, O tender-footed
Lydian, flee to the rocky banks of the Hermos ; make no halt, and
care not to blush for thy cowardice."

Crœsus smiled at a pleasantry which appeared to him to confirm
the impossibility of any interruption to that success which had
attended the earlier actions of his life. At the head of a vast host
he crossed the Halys, and, encountering the Persians under
Cyrus, was made captive, his army annihilated, and his kingdom
reduced to the condition of a province of the Persian empire. In
despair he reproached the Delphic god for luring him to ruin by
predictions utterly false. But the oracle replied that, through his
own carelessness in not seeking the name of the empire over which
destruction impended, was he brought low ; and that, with regard
to the last of its responses, Cyrus, the son of a Median princess
and a Persian of humble condition, was the ruler prefigured under
the type of a mule.

Xerxes, the monarch whom the combined fleets of Greece vanquished at Salamis, crossed the Hellespont at the head of the
mightiest host Europe had ever seen. Dismayed by the myriads
who marched under the orders of the Persian king, the Athenians
sent to beg counsel from the chief oracle of Hellas. The Delphic
god replied :—" Unfortunates, wherefore seat yourselves ? Fly to
the verge of the earth : forsake your houses and the lofty crags of
your wheel-shaped city. For neither does the head abide firm ;
nor does the body, nor the lowest feet, nor therefore the hands,
nor aught of the middle remain—all is ruined. For fire and guiding
Mars, driving the Syriac car, overturn her, and destroy many other
towering cities, not yours alone ; and to the devouring flame
deliver many temples of the immortals, which even now stand dripping with sweat ; shaken with fear. Down from the topmost roof

trickles black blood : token of woe unavoidable. Begone then from the shrine, and pour the balm of courage into the wound of calamity."

This prediction, and the counsels which accompanied it, reduced the Athenians to despair. No city, ancient or modern, was ever more beloved by its inhabitants than that of the Violet Crown. To die, sword in hand, in its defence, seemed a doom far preferable to a flight, the citizens knew not whither. They sent a second embassy; humbly beseeching that the immortal gods would not command them to leave to destruction and desecration their hearths, and the tombs of their fathers. But the Pythoness replied that Heaven knew not how to change its purpose, and that the decrees of the deities were as adamant. Yet for the comfort of the suppliants she was inspired to add : "When all is taken; that Cecrops' hill in itself contains, and the fastnesses of sacred Cithæron, wide-knowing Jove gives unto the goddess Triton-born a wooden wall alone to abide inexpugnable ; this shall save you and your children. Await not quietly the throng of horse and foot that invades your land ; but turn your backs and withdraw ; the time shall be when you too will stand against the foe. Godly Salamis ! thou shalt see the sons of women fall, whether Ceres be scattered or collected."

Never was prediction more exactly fulfilled. The mighty host of the Persians, having disembarked from their ships at the nearest point available for an attack, marched against Athens. As the heads of the enemy's columns came in sight the Greek galleys put to sea. The city was deserted, save by a few desperate patriots who, knowing that the Acropolis had once been encircled by a hedge, and vainly imagining that this might be the wooden wall of which the god had spoken, determined to defend that portion of Athens to the last, They fell to a man ; fighting with the valour common to the Hellenes of the age. Athens was entered by the Persians, and, after having been plundered, destroyed by fire. Then the invading host returned through Attica, burning and pillaging whatever lay in the way. Expeditions were despatched for the sacking of distant towns ; and finally the Asiatics returned to their ships. Off Salamis, in accordance with the prophecy of

the oracle, the combined navies of Greece encountered them ;
and, by reason chiefly of the burning valour which animated the
Athenian portion of the fleet, and the skill with which Themistocles,
the Athenian admiral, manœuvred his ships, a complete victory
was obtained, and the freedom of Greece achieved. An oracle of
Bœotia had, we learn, predicted this event in equally clear terms
with that of Delphi.

I have mentioned that expeditions were despatched by Xerxes
for the destroying of towns distant from the line of march adopted
by the main body of his army. Amongst other squadrons, one of
four thousand men marched to pillage the shrine of Delphi, and
bring into the treasury of the Persian King the vast riches collected
there.   Unprepared for any effectual defence, the alarmed priesthood demanded of the oracle whether they should flee with the
treasures of the temple to some more secure spot, or bury those
treasures in the precincts of the shrine itself.   The deity replied
that he would himself preserve his property, and forbade even
the least of the offerings consecrated to him to be moved.   On
this all, save the Pythoness, and a few of the boldest dwellers in
Delphi, departed to seek refuge in the mountains.   Speedily the
Persian legion came in sight, and pressed forward exultingly to the
pillage of the wealthiest fane of the ancient world.   The temple at
first remained silent as the grave.   When, however, the barbarians
sought to ascend the crag on which it stood, clouds suddenly
gathered overhead, from which unceasing flashes of lightning
broke forth, accompanied by deafening thunders.   Then a superhuman voice was heard to proceed from the shrine, and huge
rocks, loosened from the summits of Parnassus, crashed through
the ranks of the invaders, and levelled them like grass.   Appalled,
the remnant turned and fled.   On this the Delphians gathered
heart, and hastily snatching weapons, descended from their
hiding-places, and pursued the fugitives for miles.   Such was the
slaughter occasioned in the Persian ranks by lightnings, falling
crags, and the spears of the Greeks, that of the whole four thousand scarcely a man escaped.

The foregoing instances are gathered from Herodotus.   I have chosen them because, occurring (save in the case of Crœsus, the narrative of whose intercourse with the Delphian oracle other historians confirm) at no great distance from his own time, the Father of History was well qualified to judge of the truth or false-hood of these portions of his work. And, when not deceived by evidence merely hearsay, no ancient author adhered more rigidly to facts. Says Professor Gaisford, his translator:—"It can hardly be doubted that one who took such pains to ascertain the truth would be equally scrupulous in offering nothing but the truth to his reader; and, indeed, strange as it may sound to those who have been in the habit of hearing Herodotus stigmatised as a liar by persons who ought to know better, there is probably no author, ancient or modern, the inspired writers excepted, who deserves to be placed before him in the scale of truth and accu-racy."—(Introduction, p. xxxi.)

Pausanias, Plutarch, and a somewhat less trustworthy writer, Diodorus Siculus, are equally full of the supermundane, and equally emphatic in asserting the veracity of the narratives they give. In the Laconics of Pausanias is to be found one of the weirdest and most picturesque stories of pagan times: that of his namesake the King of Sparta, who commanded the Greeks at the battle of Platæa, and Cleonice the Byzantine maid. Cleonice, slain unknowingly by the monarch who had enslaved her, was thence-forward the haunter of his life; appearing when any great evil menaced Pausanias, and predicting the woe that was about to happen. Plutarch also has the tale. In modern times it has furnished the groundwork for one of the noblest passages of Byron's "Manfred:"

> "The Spartan monarch drew
> From the Byzantine maid's unsleeping spirit
> An answer, and his destiny. He slew
> That which he loved, unknowing what he slew,
> And died unpardoned—though he called in aid
> The Phyxian Jove, and in Phigalia roused
> The Arcadian evocators to compel
> The indignant shadow to depose her wrath,
> Or fix her term of vengeance : she replied
> In words, of dubious import, but fulfilled.

The prediction to which the poet refers was that in which Cleonice indicated the ghastly manner of her slayer's death. Pausanias, after rendering many eminent services to the state, was detected in a conspiracy against it, and fled to a temple for sanctuary. In Lacedæmon the kings were merely elective magistrates, such as in more modern times have been the doges of Venice. The oligarchy of Sparta assembled, and, having deposed and outlawed their monarch, caused every opening of the temple in which he had taken refuge, to be hermetically closed. Thus entombed alive, the unhappy Pausanias perished of want.

Space forbids that I should quote more than a very few of the instances to be gathered from Plutarch and Diodorus. The remarkable narrative which succeeds is given by the former writer.

"PAN IS DEAD."

In the reign of Tiberius certain mariners had set sail from an Asiatic port for one in Italy. As they lay becalmed off the Echinades, an unearthly voice was heard thrice to call upon one Thamus, an Egyptian of the company, and, after the third time, to bid him that as the ship passed Palodes, he should declare loudly that " the great Pan was dead." Thamus, having consulted with his fellows, resolved that, should a steady gale be blowing when the vessel reached Palodes, he would journey on silently; but that if becalmed there, he would speak that which the voice had commanded. As the mariners gained the charmed spot the wind again died away, and the bark lay idly on a smooth sea. Then Thamus, looking forth towards Palodes, cried with a loud voice 'Ομεγας Πὰν τεθνηκε—" The great Pan is dead." This he had no sooner done than there broke forth the sound of many voices, uttering mighty lamentations, intermingled however, as it seemed, with shouts of triumph. Then a breeze sprang up, and the sails of the vessel filling, Thamus and his companions were borne rapidly away. The date assigned to this occurrence is that of Our Saviour's death.

Tiberius, says Plutarch, was extremely concerned to discover the truth or falsehood of this narrative, and, having made searching inquiries, fully satisfied himself that these events had taken place exactly as described.

According to Diodorus, Althæmenes, the son of a king of Crete, was warned by the oracle that he would unknowingly slay Catreus his father. Dreading the fulfilment of the prophecy, he quitted his country, and settling at Rhodes, hoped to escape so horrible a fate. In course of time, his father became extremely old, and longing to see his son once again before he died, set sail for the place of his exile. Having landed during the night, a fray commenced between his attendants and some persons of the town. The unhappy Althæmenes, coming angrily forth to end the riot, slew one of the strangers in the heat of passion, and looking on the face of the dead man perceived his father.

From the same writer we learn that Philip of Macedon, when he consulted an oracle respecting his ambitious design of attacking Persia, was bidden to remember that the ox being crowned and garlanded implied his end to be at hand, and that men stood prepared to sacrifice him. This enigma Philip's wish made father to the thought that he should seize and slay the monarch of the Persians. He began, therefore, mighty preparations for war. But the death foreshadowed was in reality his own. As, clothed with more than royal magnificence, and having his image borne before him in company with the statues of the gods, he entered the theatre at Ægea, Pausanias, an esquire of his body-guard, suddenly drew a dagger, and struck him to the heart.

I cannot better close this portion of my subject than with a reference to the spiritual guidance vouchsafed to the noblest mind of all pagan antiquity. Socrates, as every one in the slightest degree acquainted with Grecian history must be aware, was from his earliest youth the object of unearthly monitions. A " Divine voice " (as he himself terms it) attended him, not to urge to good, but to restrain from evil. It was equally busy in the most momentous and the most trifling actions of life. At Athens, at Corinth; when he lifted a spear against the enemies of his country; when he bore with meekness the revilings of the shrewish Xantippe; when in the height of his success he stood surrounded by Plato, Alcibiades, and others of the noblest youth of Greece ; when old, feeble, and persecuted, he calmly prepared himself to die—the voice was ever with him. It did not advise respecting the conduct of any action in which he was engaged, but it uniformly warned him against taking any step which might have proved prejudicial or evil. This has been made the ground for interpreting the history of the unearthly monitor as nothing more than an allegorical representation of conscience. But the conscience of Socrates was unlikely to warn him of unknown dangers awaiting himself or his friends, nor, when any of those friends meditated a crime, was it probable that it would perceive and endeavour to prevent it. Yet Xenophon testifies that Socrates obtained from the voice and imparted to his intimates many foreshadowings of perils which awaited them, and was never convicted of error. Yet Plato relates that Timarchus, a noble Athenian, being at a feast in company with Socrates, and rising to depart, was peremptorily bidden by the latter to reseat himself. " For," said he, " the spirit has just given me the accustomed sign that some danger menaces you." Some little time after Timarchus offered again to be gone, and was again stayed by Socrates, who had heard the warning repeated. Taking advantage, at length, of a moment when the philosopher was absorbed in earnest discourse, Timarchus stole off unobserved, and a few minutes afterwards committed a murder, for which being carried to execution, his last words were, " that he had come to that untimely end by not obeying the spirit of Socrates."

As the *Quarterly Review* once remarked, it is impossible to avoid being struck by the extreme similarity between certain points of the careers of Socrates and Joan of Arc. The Greek sage and the French heroine were alike accustomed from early childhood to be controlled by heavenly voices, which none but themselves could hear. Both rendered to those counsellors the most implicit obedience. In either case the voices approved their unearthly origin by undeniable tokens. The subject of such monitions saw at times in vision the radiant beings by whom he or she was guided. Each demonstrated by a noble and blameless life the heavenly nature of those beings, and the purity of their teachings. Both were warned by the invisibles who guarded them that their careers would close in the reception of the crown of martyrdom. Both, amid the execrations of the mob, passed by roads terrible to travel from a world that was not worthy of them. Here the parallel ends. How immeasurably beneath the Greece of two thousand three hundred years ago was the Europe of the fifteenth century after Christ! Socrates, though execrated as the attempted overturner of his country's religion, was suffered to pass away in the gentlest manner consistent with a sudden end. Indeed the death he died can hardly be described as a violent one, or bitter to be endured. Surrounded by attached friends, he took from a weeping executioner the cup of poison, and draining it, departed calmly, and almost painlessly, to be with the immortals. Joan—reviled, tormented, and immodestly used—endured for months a bitterness deeper than the bitterness of any death, and in death the utmost agony of which the human frame is capable. Lied to and abused; mocked by enemies with false hopes of life, and by pretended friends with false hopes of succour, her torment of suspense was only ended by that other agony of the stake of which even to think is to sicken with horror. From the fate of Socrates no less than that of the French heroine may we reap the lesson of the blindness of man in all ages to spiritual light! But no other narrative in the world's repertory reveals so mournfully and awfully as that of the saintly maiden of Domremy the unrelieved darkness of those depths to which, when it misconceives the origin of that light, humanity can descend.

In Rome we find reproduced the spiritual beliefs prevalent among the Greeks, but darkened and made more severe, to accord with the darker and severer natures of the masters of the ancient world. The poets, like the poets of Greece, crowd their pages with portraits of the dwellers in the invisible. Virgil is as rich in the spiritual as Homer; Ovid, Horace, and Lucan deal throughout in miracle. As in Hellas, the gods descend among men, and are described as displaying passions akin to the passions of man. But love—which was in Greece the chief motive for the visits of these deities, who, like their brethren described in Genesis, "saw the daughters of men that they were fair,"—was in Rome altogether absent. To wreak their wrath on nations which had offended them; to lead on to conquest peoples that stood high in their favour; to enjoy the tumult and carnage of the battle-field—these are the motives by which the Italian poets represent the truly national among their gods as invariably actuated in their descents to earth. The lust of pleasure is supplanted by the lust of blood. It is such a difference as exists between the good-natured amorous Zeus worshipped by the Greeks, and the stern majesty of the Jupiter of the Roman people.

Yet from Greece came the whole of the philosophy and arts of Rome. The oracles of Greece were revered in Italy, and up to the very time of their becoming finally silent did emperors and senates send to consult them. As Horace tells us :—"Capta ferum victorem cepit." Greece, enslaved by the swords of the Romans, ruled yet by supremacy of mind.

Nor should we forget the peculiar connection between the civilisation of Italy and that far more ancient one whose almost immutable relics slowly moulder by the Nile. The metaphysics of Rome were those of Egypt, brightened by a sojourn in Greece. The mesmeric treatment of the sick practised in Roman temples was but an apish reflex of that deep knowledge of magnetic and spiritual phenomena possessed by Egyptian priests. Nay, the most celebrated of all Roman miracles, the extraordinary cure by the Emperor Vespasian of a blind man and a paralytic, was wrought on Egyptian ground. This event, which two great contemporary historians—Pliny, and the sceptical Tacitus—have described from the narratives of eye-witnesses, and which David Hume, in his "Essay on Miracles," declares the best attested instance of the supermundane in all history, took place in that magnificent Egyptian city named after Alexander the Great. I quote the story :—

"Vespasian spent some months at Alexandria. During his residence in that city a number of incidents out of the ordinary course of nature seemed to mark him as the particular favourite of the gods. A man of

mean condition, born at Alexandria, had lost his sight by a defluxion on
his eye. He presented himself before Vespasian, and, falling prostrate
on the ground, implored the Emperor to administer a cure for his blindness. He came, he said, by the admonition of Serapis, the god whom
the superstition of the Egyptians holds in the highest veneration. The
request was that the Emperor with his spittle would condescend to
moisten the poor man's face and the balls of his eyes. Another who
had lost the use of his hand, inspired by the same god, begged that he
would tread on the part affected. Vespasian smiled at a request so
absurd and wild. The wretched objects persisted to implore his aid.
He dreaded the ridicule of a vain attempt ; but the importunity of the
men, and the crowd of flatterers, prevailed upon the prince not entirely
to disregard their petition.

"He ordered the physicians to consider whether the blindness of the
one, and the paralytic affection of the other, were within the reach of
human assistance. The result of the consultation was, that the organs
of sight were not so injured but that, by removing the film or cataract,
the patient might recover. As to the disabled limb, by proper applications and invigorating medicines, it was not impossible to restore it to its
former tone. The gods, perhaps, intended a special remedy, and chose
Vespasian as the instrument of their dispensations. If a cure took
place the glory of it would add new lustre to the name of Cæsar, if
otherwise, the poor men would bear the jests and raillery of the people.
Vespasian, in the tide of his affairs, began to think that there was
nothing so great and wonderful, nothing so improbable or even incredible,
which his good fortune could not accomplish. In the presence of a
prodigious multitude, all erect with expectation, he advanced with an air
of severity, and hazarded the experiment. The paralytic hand recovered
in functions, and the blind man saw the light of the sun. By living
witnesses who were actually on the spot both events are confirmed at
this hour, when deceit and flattery can hope for no reward."

The hour alluded to was that at which Tacitus wrote. Vespasian was dead, and the imperial tiara had passed for ever from
his family.

Nothing remained to impede the exposure of deception, if
deception there had been ; nothing could make those witnesses
with whom the historian conferred fear to speak the truth, or hope
to profit by a lie. It deserves to be mentioned that Strabo and
Suetonius, as well as Pliny, confirm this narrative of the greatest
of the Roman annalists.

A species of apparition of which I have myself been made the
subject occurred to this same Emperor. He saw in a temple at

Alexandria the double of one Basilides, then living, and known to have been at a considerable distance from the place. Here is the tale as Tacitus relates it :—

"Vespasian was now determined to visit the sanctuary of Serapis, in order to consult the god about the future fortune of the empire. Having given orders to remove all intruders, he entered the temple. While he adored the deity of the place he perceived, in the midst of his devotions, a man of principal note amongst the Egyptians advancing behind him. The name of this person was Basilides, who, at that moment, was known to be detained by illness at the distance of many miles. Vespasian inquired of the priests whether they had seen Basilides that day in the temple. He asked a number of others whether they had met him in any part of the city. At length, from messengers whom he despatched on horseback, he received certain intelligence that Basilides was not less than fourteen miles distant from Alexandria. He therefore concluded that the gods had favoured him with the preternatural vision, and from the import of the word Basilides (royal), he inferred an interpretation of the decrees of heaven in favour of his future reign."

Pliny the Younger has preserved to us numerous accounts of apparitions, among which stories that respecting the philosopher Athenodorus is the most remarkable. Athenodorus, having occasion on his arrival at Athens to purchase a house, a large and fair one was shown to him. The lowness of the terms demanded being out of all proportion with the size and beauty of the mansion, he perceived that there was some mystery in the case. He inquired, and received the history of the events which had driven all former tenants from the house. At midnight a noise was heard, and the ghastly figure of a skeleton passed through the various apartments, dragging with it a rusty chain. Athenodorus, undaunted by the story, philosophically bought the mansion, and installed himself therein. As, at midnight, he sat writing, the spectre appeared, and clanking its irons, motioned that he should follow. The philosopher calmly signed to it to wait, and proceeded with his task. At length, when the entreaty had been several times repeated, he rose, and intimated himself ready to follow where it desired. On this the spirit preceded him to an inner court of the mansion, and there vanished. Athenodorus laid some leaves and grass to mark the spot, and returned to his studies. The next morning he sought the magistrates of the city. A search was instituted, and a skeleton loaded with rusty chains discovered beneath the place marked. This having been interred in a proper spot, the philosopher placidly pursued his labours in the house he had purchased, unvisited for the future by such grisly guests.

Trajan, says Macrobius, previous to his invasion of Parthia, was invited to consult the oracle of Heliopolis, where the method of inquiry was by sealed packets. Incredulous as to the power of the deity, he forwarded a packet and desired a sealed reply. This arriving, and being opened, a blank paper only was found. The courtiers expressed amazement, but the Emperor confessed that, being sceptical as to the wisdom of the oracle, he had placed nothing in his own packet but a blank sheet. The response was therefore apt, and Trajan now confessed his curiosity and mystification by sending ambassadors to demand whether from his war in Parthia he should return safely to Rome. A vine cut in pieces and wrapped in a linen cloth was sent him, as symbolising the manner of his return. He died in the East, and even so were his remains brought back to Italy.

I shall cite now some instances of phenomena strikingly similar to the phenomena occurring in our own day. The handling of live coals without injury—a manifestation which has frequently occurred to myself—was witnessed also in these ancient times. Strabo and Pliny unite in assuring us that in the reign of Augustus the priests of a temple at the foot of Mount Soracte dedicated to the goddess Feronia, had been known to walk bare-footed over great quantities of glowing embers. The same ordeal, says Strabo, was practised by the priestesses of the goddess Asta Bala in Cappadocia.

That a mode of conversing with spirits by means of the alphabet was known and used in Roman times, the historian Ammianus Marcellinus proves by the following narrative:—

"In the days of the Emperor Valens, A.D. 371, some Greek cultivators of theurgy, who in those days usurped the name of philosophers, were brought to trial for having attempted to ascertain the successor to the throne by means of magical arts. The small table or tripod which they had used for this purpose was produced in court, and on being submitted to the torture, they gave the following account of their proceedings :—

" ' We constructed, most venerable judges, this small ill-omened table which you behold, after the likeness of the Delphian tripod, with wood of laurel, and with solemn auspices. Having duly consecrated it by muttering over it secret spells, and by many and protracted manipulations, we succeeded at last in making it move. Now, whenever we consulted it about secrets, the process for making it move was as follows. It was placed in the centre of a house which had been purified by Arabian incense on every side ; a round dish composed of various metallic substances, being, with the needful purifications, set upon it. On the circular rim of this dish the four-and-twenty characters of the alphabet were cut with much art, and placed at equal intervals, which had been measured with perfect exactness. A person clad in linen garments, in slippers also made of linen, with a light turban wreathed about his head, and carrying branches of the sacred laurel in his hand, having propitiated the deity who gives the responses, in certain prescribed forms of invocation, according to the rules of ceremonial science, sets this dish upon the tripod, balancing over it a suspended ring attached to the end of a very fine linen thread, which also had previously undergone a mystic initiation. This ring, darting out, and striking at distant intervals the particular letters that attract it, makes out heroic verses, in accordance with the questions put, as complete in mode and measure as those uttered by the Pythoness or the oracles of the Branchidæ.

" ' As we were, then and there, inquiring who should succeed the present Emperor, since it was declared that he would be a finished character in every respect, the ring, darting out, had touched the syllables ΘΕΟ, with the final addition of the letter Δ (making Theod), some one present exclaimed that Theodorus was announced as appointed by fate. Nor did we pursue our inquiries any further into the matter, for we were all satisfied that Theodorus was the person we were asking for.' "

It is amusing to note the pedantic minuteness with which these ancient theurgists detail the rites and invocations through which their intercourse with another world was, as they supposed, obtained. Of the fact that their intense desire for communion with spirits alone attracted spirits to them they seem to have been blissfully ignorant.

It is quite within the limits of probability that genuine messages from the spirit world would be obtained by a circle which should repeat with the same solemn faith the "derry down" chorus of the Druids, the nursery rhyme of "Mother Hubbard," or the theosophical nonsense of the present day.

The story has a tragical and remarkable sequel. The tyrant Valens, fearing for his throne, caused Theodorus, though a man eminent for his virtues and attainments, to be at once put to death. Nor was his jealous alarm satisfied with a single victim. The pagan philosophers were also judicially murdered, and as many whose names commenced with the letters "Theod" as the emperor could get into his power. Yet the prediction was, in · spite of all, fulfilled. Theodosius, whose name was similar to the letters of the answer so far as that answer had been suffered to proceed, succeeded Valens upon the throne of the West. The story of Marcellinus, I may add, is confirmed by the early Church historians—Socrates, Scholasticus, Sozomen, &c.

In view of that similarity of phenomena, as an instance of which the foregoing narrative is given, a passage to be found in Tertullian is very striking. The Christian father thus reproaches the pagans of his age: "Do not your magicians call ghosts and departed souls from the shades below, and by their infernal charms represent an infinite number of delusions? And how do they perform all this, but by the assistance of evil angels and spirits, by which they are able *to make stools and tables prophesy!*" The object of Tertullian's book, like that of his whole life, being to destroy paganism, it was natural that he should represent these things as the work of fiends. Whether evil spirits or good were concerned, the fact that fifteen centuries ago séances were held with tables remains a most remarkable one.

Space fails me to describe the omens that attended Cæsar's death; and how the apparition of that Cæsar was beheld by Brutus at Philippi; how Caracalla was foreshown his assassination in a dream; and Sylla, the night before he died, saw in a vision the manner of his end. These, moreover, are things that have a thousand times been described. Nor can I find room to tell of the spiritual in the lives of Scipio, Marius, Cicero, Antony, Augustus, and other famous Romans. I have now depicted intercourse with

another world as it existed in the various ancient nations, and
have given the principal and best-authenticated instances to be
found in the history of each people; but, were the whole of the
supermundane occurrences that old historians relate to be collected
and commented upon, we might suppose with the apostle that the
world itself could hardly contain the books which should be
written. With some remarks on Roman spiritualism in its relation
to the social condition of the people, I shall therefore close.

The worst and most frightful time of heathen misgovernment,
was that of the twelve Cæsars. During the whole of this period
the foulest vices and the most hideous cruelties stalked abroad
arm-in-arm. Nothing in the nineteen centuries of the Christian
era—neither the Italy of Alexander VI., nor the England of
Charles II., nor the France of the Regent Philip—has yet been
found to equal the Rome of Nero and Tiberius. The hard,
systematic, unblushing vices and ferocities of the Italians of that
age remain unapproachable. As the Christian revelation is the
highest of all gospels; so the time of the dawning of that light
was the darkest in the history of the world. And why had earth
fallen so low? An impartial student of history will answer, as I
answer, Because of the corruptions of those who served as instruments for intercourse with spiritual beings. "Ye are of your
father the devil, and do his works," said Christ to the Judæan
priesthood of His day. The same reproach might be applied to
the priesthood of imperial Rome, and more or less, as I have
already endeavoured to show, to every hierarchy of the ancient
world. Only spirits yet more evil than themselves could manifest
through beings so corrupted as these consecrated mediums gradually became. Every wickedness that can be committed by beings
merely human, was on the head of the wretched *sacerdos* of
the Roman Empire. It had been found in a long course of ages
that the true spiritual phenomena were exhaustive, infrequent, and
difficult to obtain. Attention was therefore directed to simulating
them by falsehood, and priest after priest toiled with a misdirected
ingenuity to invent or perfect the machinery of imposture. By the
time of Augustus this system of deceit was in full flow. It con-

tinued so for centuries, decaying only with the decay of the
Roman power itself. Exposures, doubtless, were less frequent
than in our own age. The medium power of the ancient world was
chiefly to be found in the ranks of the priesthood ; it is chiefly to
be found outside those ranks at present. Thus the whole weight
of sacredness and authority might of old be allied with fraud.
But, although fewer and further between, exposures did come,
and their effect was exceedingly great. The lives and teachings of
the priests, too, were causes of endless scandal and demoralisation.
What were the intelligent to think of a man whose life was one
long career of hypocrisy and vice, interrupted only when he was
asleep or drunk; whose temple was filled with contrivances for
palming off the vilest impostures on a credulous public ; and who,
from a succession of false pretences to medial powers, had come at
last almost to disbelieve in their existence ? What were they to
think of the deities whom these priests were appointed to serve :
deities who cried constantly for human sacrifices ; who saw their
temples made receptacles for the foulest vice, and smiled
approvingly ; who gave teachings inciting to every form of
immorality and bloodshed ? The intelligent stigmatised the priests
as utterly worthless impostors, whose deities were the hideous
creatures of their own foul minds. They cried, as so many in our
own day have done, that religion was from first to last a lie ; that
there was no God, neither any immortality for man. Suddenly,
from out this chaos rose the foundations of the first Christian
Church. It was founded, as in the succeeding part of this work I
shall seek to show, by men to whom spiritual signs and wonders
were as their daily bread, and whose pure minds held communion
only with the beneficent portion of the dwellers in another world.
To the spiritualism of the Christian era will my next chapters be
devoted. · It suffices to say, in concluding this description of communion with another sphere as practised in pagan times, that the
corruptions, through which the pretensions to mediumship of the
Roman and other priesthoods ultimately came to be received with
such derision, are rampant among the mediums of our own age.
How often do we see men—ay, and women—who, although

E

possessed of medial powers, have degraded themselves and the noble cause to which they should be devoted, by the vilest and most unblushing fraud! How often, too, do we perceive a still lower class of impostors who, destitute of the slightest pretensions to mediumship, earn a shameful livelihood by the simulation of certain forms of spiritual phenomena! And what among the lives and teachings of the flamens who consented to deify Nero, could surpass in foulness the antic filthinesses of a few creatures of our own age, who have introduced themselves like ghouls into the spiritual ranks, disgusting and repelling the pure-minded and the thoughtful? Is modern spiritualism a Divine revelation given for the elevating and brightening of the world? Then how are we to estimate the impostors mentioned above, whether they mingle medial gifts with their deceit, or confine themselves to falsehood unrelieved by any gleam of truth? How are we to regard the vile and foolish teachings which have of late years been produced in such plenty, through these and their kindred harpies? Above all, in what manner may we regard the weak-minded enthusiasts by whom these evils are encouraged and perpetuated; who accept the most absurd and vicious doctrines with a kind of inspired idiocy of belief, which, if not able to remove, can at least gulp down, mountains; who, as regards spiritual phenomena, display a folly almost unparalleled in ancient or modern times; whom any boy can delude with imposture, and any madman with absurdity; and who, whether that boy or madman were willing or unwilling, would exalt him to the rank of a prophet, and revere him as a spiritual guide? It is these who will accept "explanations" of whose supreme ridiculousness an Australian savage might be ashamed, rather than admit that a medium can deceive. It is these who reject the admonition to "try the spirits" as a needless insult, and thus bar the door at once on scientific research. Finally it is from these and the knaves whom they encourage that modern spiritualism emphatically requires to be delivered.

PART II.

SPIRITUALISM IN THE JEWISH AND CHRISTIAN ERAS.

———◆———

CHAPTER I.

THE SPIRITUALISM OF THE BIBLE.

I HAVE separated the Hebrews from the peoples dealt with in the former portion of this work because it has appeared to me that the spiritualism of the Testaments, Old and New, would best be treated of as one great whole. The signs and wonders recorded by the prophets and apostles of Israel, from Moses to St. John, are indubitably the mightiest and most famous which the Creator has vouchsafed to mankind.

I do not, however, propose to devote to them any very great proportion of these pages, and my reasons will, I trust, be held sufficient. Ninety-nine out of every hundred of my readers are as familiarly acquainted with the histories of the signs accorded to Abraham, and the miracles wrought through Moses, as with any of the chief events of their own earthly lives. The commentaries on the prophecies of Isaiah, Jeremiah, Ezekiel, Daniel, and others would require a lifetime to number. The sermons preached on the miraculous events recorded in the lives of Christ and his apostles might, if collected and printed, fill a hundred libraries as large as the Alexandrian. Were I to quote the chief wonders of Hebrew times, as recorded in our own noble version of the Scriptures, I should be simply deluging the reader with histories, magnificent indeed, but the tritest of the trite.

Were I to attempt in my own language a description of these occurrences, how poor would such efforts seem beside those of the inspired writers   I shall confine myself to the citation of certain remarkable instances, and to an inquiry into their influence, and the circumstances of their origin. The few incidents dwelt upon at any length will be found incidents bearing more or less upon the phenomena of to-day.

We find the foundation stone of the Biblical writings to be everywhere miracle. The assumption which, since the mighty discoveries of Newton, has been constantly becoming more rooted among scientific men, that the physical laws of the universe are eternal and immutable, here has no place. Such an assumption indeed, if admitted, reduces the Hebrew Scriptures to a collection of fables,—and not even "fables cunningly devised." The present condition of the scientific world affords a striking example of its effects. In no other age has research into the mysteries of creation been so diligently pursued. In no other age has the disposition to set up the "laws of nature" as a species of idol, appeared so strong. The natural consequence has been that our scientific men have progressed from a disbelief in miracle in general to a disbelief in the particular miracles recorded in the Bible, and from a disbelief in the Bible appear rapidly progressing to a disbelief in God. In 1874 we had Professor Tyndall's Belfast address. It appears likely that in a very few years this minute and studied oration will be openly received by the school which the Professor represents, as an able exposition of their articles of faith. I search it in vain for any indication of a belief in a Personal God. The deities to whom this scientist would appear in secret to bow down, are known to him and his fellow-adorers by the awe-inspiring titles of Atom and Molecule. Not yet, however, are the penetralia of the temple to be unveiled to the outer world. Such a casting of pearls unto swine would utterly misbecome a man of the Professor's acumen. For the uninitiated he has a kind of convenient shadow known as "Nature," which he interposes between their gaze and the inmost secrets of his philosophy, and respecting which he discourses in a most excessively mystic jargon. Nature appears to

serve him as she served the Arbaces of Lord Lytton's novel. On
her shoulders may be laid the burden of all that does not accord
with the philosopher's idea of the fitness of things. It would be
unjust to say that the whole of the scientific men of the age are at
one with Professor Tyndall in his peculiar theology. But, although
the law of the physical sciences is progress, the law governing the
ideas of devotees to those sciences respecting religion, both natural
and revealed, would seem to be as undoubtedly retrogression. The
deity whom even the the most religious of such men worship is
nothing more than an imitation of the Zeus of the Greeks; as
limited in power as that Zeus, and governed like him by an
inexorable Fate. The Omnipotent God of Christianity they totally
reject. That this is so, quotations from a hundred authorities
would prove. I shall content myself with citing part of a critique
directed, in the early years of the spiritual movement, against
certain phenomena occurring at Ealing, I being the medium
through whom they occurred :—

"These are strong facts, and it is allowing a great deal to say that we
think Mr. Rymer to be in earnest in stating his belief in them. For
ourselves we entirely disbelieve them, and shall gladly give anyone the
opportunity of convincing us.

"In the meanwhile we venture to recommend to Mr. Rymer's attentive
study an old-fashioned college text-book, which we suspect he has never
opened : Pratt's 'Mechanical Philosophy.' He will there learn of
those immutable laws which the unchanging God has impressed once
and for ever on creation ; and, reading of the wondrous harmony and
order which reign by their operation throughout the wide bounds of creation, he may perhaps come to share our doubt and disbelief of those
imaginings which tell us of their violation in moving tables and shaking
lamps and dancing chairs, and he may, perchance, should his study
prosper, catch also a sense of the pitying scorn with which those nurtured
on the strong meat of the inductive philosophy within the very courts
and halls that a Newton trod, view these sickly spiritualist dreamers,
thus drunk with the new wine of folly and credulity."

Such is a fair specimen of the mode in which these Sir Oracles
discourse on subjects not in accordance with their own systems of
philosophy. I may answer them through the mouths of their own
gods. It is tolerably certain that, nigh two hundred years ago,

Newton was to Descartes and others of the renowned scientists of
the age " a sickly dreamer drunk with the new wine of folly and
credulity." It· is still more certain that Francis Bacon was, by
many philosophers of the time of James I., allotted a place in
that " Ship of·Fools" to which this admirer of Bacon's inductive
philosophy so calmly consigns the spiritualists of the era of
Victoria.

As regards any and every system of Christianity, is not the
friendship of such men more dangerous than their hostility ? They
diligently search for and remove from between the covers of the
Bible whatever the scientific mind cannot grasp. They gravely
assure us that the laws of the universe are not to be altered or
superseded even by the Deity who instituted them—thus at once
depriving that Deity of his attribute of Omnipotence, and reducing
the Creator to be subject to the created. Did Elisha cause iron to
float on water ? Was the shadow of the sun turned back on the
dial of Hezekiah ? Was Aaron's rod, on his throwing it down,
changed into a serpent ? The worshippers of " the laws of
Nature" would consider themselves besotted did they credit any
such absurdities. They are not as the early Christians were. They
are assuredly not followers of the Christ who, taught that " with
God all things are possible." The theory that there are everywhere throughout the universe wheels within wheels ; laws by
which that of gravity may be modified or temporarily set aside ;
invisible forces which exert power over matter : such a theory is
to the scientific Christian what the creed he professes was to the
Greeks of the first century—foolishness. He calmly assumes
that the whole of the ways of God in the governing of the worlds
which He has made are now known to man, and he stops his ears
against any evidence to the contrary. He dismisses, as I have
said, from that Bible which he professes to reverence as the Word
of God, whatever may be considered as savouring of miracle. To
what extents this demolition proceeds I shall now endeavour to
show. Christianity, deprived of all but what may be explained by
the *known* laws of creation, and exposed in such a condition to the
assaults of sceptics, resembles a vessel which, having been·care-

fully denuded of rudder, masts, and compass, and pierced with innumerable holes, is sent to sea to encounter a storm.

We are told frequently in the Old Testament of God appearing visibly to man, and speaking with him face to face. Yet we read in Exodus that, when Moses desired to behold the Lord in all His glory, He replied, "Thou canst not see my face; for there shall no man see me and live." How are the apparent contradictions to be reconciled? Spiritualists reconcile them by their knowledge of the countless ministering spirits which constantly watch over earth, and ceaselessly pass to and fro on the errands of the Master of spirits. Such, clothed in a material form, may have executed God's commands regarding Adam. Such wrestled with Jacob, and were seen by him, in trance, ascending and descending between heaven and earth. Such appeared to Abraham as towards evening, he sat in the door of his tent. Such delivered Lot from the destruction which impended over the Cities of the Plain. Such carried the commands of God to his servant Moses, guided that Moses to the presence of the Egyptian King, and wrought, by means of the powers accorded to them, the whole of the wonders related in the Pentateuch. By spirits like these was Gideon prompted to his mission of deliverance. By such spirits was the mighty host of Sennacherib destroyed. To the beholding of these spirits were the eyes of Elisha's servant made equal when the Syrians sought the life of his master. "And when the servant of the man of God was risen early, and gone forth, behold, a host encompassed the city both with horses and chariots. And his servant said unto him, Alas, my master! how shall we do? And he answered, Fear not: for they that be with us are more than they that be with them. And Elisha prayed, and said, Lord I pray thee open his eyes that he may see. And the Lord opened the eyes of the young man; and he saw: and, behold, the mountain was full of horses and chariots of fire round about Elisha."

We have here a striking proof that the human eye can be made to perceive spirits. I see no room for sceptical cavilling, or explaining away. The prophet prayed that his servant's eyes

might be opened, and God opened them, so that this Israelite saw
the glories of the spiritual beings around. "Clairvoyant" he would
have been termed in our own day, and as such, ridiculed by the
scientific men with whom that word is another term for dreamer.
But the particular story I have quoted is from writings all
European Churches hold to be sacred. It requires to be accepted
or rejected in its entirety: Professing Christians must admit that
the eye of man can occasionally behold spiritual beings, or
condemn the Hebrew chronicler as the narrator of a circumstantial lie.

That spirits can, in the present day, operate upon matter with
powers similar to those possessed by human beings still in the
flesh is an assertion received with derisive incredulity by myriads
who profess every sabbath their belief that such occurrences were
common from two to four thousand years ago. The tens of
thousands of clergymen who have preached against such facts of
modern spiritualism as the moving of material objects without visible
agency, and the millions of listeners who have agreed with their
sermons, would doubtless be indignant were it asserted that they
disbelieved in the loosing by an angel of the chains of Peter, or the
rolling away by another angel of the stone which secured the
sepulchre of Christ. With what intense scorn, too, are the
testimonies regarding that levitation by spirit power of which I
and others have in modern times been the subjects, received
by Christians of Europe and America who may read on one page
of their Bibles how the apostle Philip was suddenly snatched up
from out the sight of the eunuch whom he had baptized, and
conveyed from Gaza to Azotus, a distance of thirty miles; in
another place the verses in which Ezekiel tells how the hand of
the Lord lifted him, and carried him into the midst of the valley
which was full of bones. Again, the appearances of spirit forms
and hands which have so frequently occurred in the present age,
are heard of with absolute incredulity, and the vouchings of
witnesses of the highest standing, intellectual and social, calmly
set aside. Yet one of the most picturesque chapters of the
Old Testament is that wherein Daniel recounts how the "fingers

of a man's hand," at the impious feast of Belshazzar, were seen
by the monarch himself and a thousand of his satraps, to write in
fiery characters upon the wall of the palace an intimation of the
approaching doom of Babylon. And Ezekiel recounts how he
beheld a spirit-hand, and the roll of a book therein, and that, when
the hand spread out the book before him, it was written within
and without. As to the human body being made insusceptible to
the action of fire, have we not Daniel's history of the three Jewish
youths who walked unhurt in the midst of the flaming furnace?
If such mighty works were done two thousand five hundred years
ago, why should not lesser wonders be witnessed in our own time?
Is the arm of God grown less mighty? The question has often
been asked, but never responded to. Science cannot, and religion
dare not answer in the negative.

How science treats spiritual phenomena in general, I have
already endeavoured to show. How she behaves with regard to
the particular phenomena of which I have just spoken was
instanced in the *Quarterly Review*, of October, 1871. The article
on spiritualism contained therein has been praised as logical and
able. Yet the argument it was written to enforce is simply
this:—B, the author of the essay, has never witnessed certain
phenomena which have occurred in the presence of A, and to
whose occurrence A has testified. It is highly improbable that
such phenomena should occur. The premise that such events are
unlikely to happen, and the premise that B has never known
them to happen, when put together produce the inference that
their occurrence in the presence of A is an utter impossibility, and
his narrative therefore worthless. And has the inductive philosophy come to this! Were such arguments to be advanced by a
man of science on the opposite side, would not his hostile
brethren have re-discovered that " many dogs can arrive at more
logical conclusions?"

I return to the examination of miracle as contained in the
Bible. The first passage on which I light (1 Chron. xxviii. 19)
is a remarkable illustration of the inspirational writing and drawing
of the present day. David had given to Solomon his son the

patterns of the temple, and all with which it was to be furnished. " These things," said he, " the Lord made me understand in writing, by His hand upon me, even all the works of this pattern."

It would seem that a species of divination practised in the East to this very day was known of old among the Hebrews. How are we to understand Gen. xliv. 15—" Is not this it by which my Lord drinketh, and whereby, indeed, He divineth " —unless as an intimation that the obtaining of visions by looking stedfastly into a cup filled with wine or other liquor, was a species of clairvoyance practised in the days of Joseph ?

Had I space, and did the patience of the reader permit, I might proceed to minutely analyse the prophecies contained in the writings of Isaiah, Jeremiah, Ezekiel, Daniel, and the lesser seers. The chief of these prophecies related to the coming of Christ, and all who have ever searched the Scriptures know how exact were the forebodings of his advent. Of lesser interest are those mystical predictions given by Daniel and others, on which the ingenuity of theologians of all nations and ages has been fruitlessly expended. Perhaps the terrible attractiveness with which the prophecies relating to the last siege of Jerusalem are invested, may excuse my lingering over them for a moment. The most awful is that description given by Moses of the calamities which should befall the Hebrews when they had utterly forsaken the God of their fathers, and space for repentance was no longer allowed. This denunciation, the bitterest ever spoken by a prophet, occurs in the twenty-eighth chapter of the book of Deuteronomy. Before Jerusalem was taken by Titus every item of its horrors had come to pass. And the words of Christ, though they shock us with no such literal presentment of the miseries to be endured by the doomed race, are solemnly significant of the wrath to come. " When ye shall see the abomination of desolation, spoken of by Daniel, stand in the holy place, then let them which be in Judæa flee unto the mountains. . . . And woe unto them who are with child, and who give suck in those days. . . . For then shall be great tribulation, such as was not from the beginning of the world to this time, no, nor ever shall be " (Matt. xxiv.). Again,

"And when ye shall see Jerusalem compassed by armies, then know that the desolation thereof is nigh. . . . For these be the days of vengeance, that all things which are written may be fulfilled. . . . And they shall fall by the edge of the sword, and shall be led away captive into all nations; and Jerusalem shall be trodden down by the Gentiles, until the times of the Gentiles shall be fulfilled" (Luke xxi.).

Seventy years after the Crucifixion came this great woe. The legions of Titus marched into Palestine. Rome still reigned as mistress of the world; indeed, her power had scarcely attained its zenith. The conquests of Trajan lay yet in the womb of the future, when those of the son of Vespasian were made. Yet the Jews for long deemed themselves secure of triumph. Their city was the strongest of all cities; and false prophets were not wanting to delude them. Thus encouraged, they fiercely defied the power of the Empire, and vowed to recover that independence which the Maccabees had died, to preserve, or like those heroes fall fighting to the last. Did not the whole Christian world regard the miseries of Jerusalem as chastisements sent of God, how frequently would the superhuman endurance of her children be quoted to instance what can be borne by nations striving to be free! In no other siege was the valour displayed so frantic. In no other siege did the attacked seem so completely to have triumphed over death. The Romans were at first disposed to make captives of such as fell into their power. But these, in nearly all cases, preferred death in defence of the Holy City to a life of ignominious servitude, and fought desperately to the last. And what they so stoically endured, they were no less ready to inflict. Such of their enemies as they captured they remorselessly put to death. Enraged by this, and the determined resistance of the besieged, the Romans proceeded to display in its most refined form, the cruelty seldom absent from their wars. All Jews who came into their hands alive were crucified in view of the city, and perished in torment, with their dying eyes fixed on home and friends. Even as their fathers had done unto Christ, was it done unto them. At length came the end. Wall after wall had been carried, until the last stronghold of the Jews was reached. Within the city no food remained save human flesh. Even mothers, as Moses had prophesied, slew and ate their children in the madness of hunger. Many Jews had frantically endeavoured .to break through the Roman lines, and, being taken, were crucified in such numbers, that wood became scarce, and no more crosses could be made. Then followed the capture of the temple. As if inspired with a sudden frenzy, the Roman soldiers rushed forward, flinging in firebrands from every side. Titus, who desired the preservation of so magnificent a shrine, in vain ordered his guards to beat them off. The fabric consecrated to Jehovah was burnt to the ground, and over against what had been its eastern gate did the Roman legionaries set up their standards, and, offering sacrifices to them, hail Titus as Imperator with " acclamations of the greatest joy." The most awful siege recorded in the world's history was at an end. Eleven hundred thousand of the Jews had been slain. So many were carried into captivity that the markets became glutted, and the Roman soldiery sought in vain to find purchasers for their slaves. I think none who read of these events but must endorse the pathetic assertion of Josephus : " It appears to me that the misfortunes of all men, from the beginning of the world, if they be compared to these of the Jews, are not so considerable as they were." So fearfully had the predictions of Christ and Moses been fulfilled.

In quitting the Old Testament for the New let me say that there is to be noticed a remarkable similarity between the miracles recorded of the Jewish prophets and those afterwards performed by Christ.

The rendering inexhaustible by Elijah of the widow's cruse of oil and barrel of meal, is a parallel on a lesser scale to the miracle of the loaves and fishes. So with the means by which Elisha fed a hundred men. The restoration to life of an only child by each of these prophets recalls the raising from the dead by Jesus of that young man of Nain, " the only son of his mother, and she was a widow." Naaman, who was healed of leprosy upon having faith sufficient to obey Elisha's mandate of washing in the Jordan, reminds us of several of the miracles of Christ. And, finally, the narrative of the man whose dead body was cast into the tomb of Elisha, and sprang up revivified on touching the prophet's bones, is a marvel almost equalling anything that the New Testament contains.

One other incident in Old Testament spiritualism deserves to be noticed. Although such marvellous tokens of spiritual power were vouchsafed to the Jews, the Levitical law forbade them to seek intercourse with the spirits of the departed. The reason is not difficult to find. Jehovah feared that, like the nations around them, his people would be drawn from the worship of the One God to adore a multitude of the beings whom He had created. Nor were restrictions unnecessary. On a hundred occasions do we hear of the Jews hastening to this and far grosser forms of idolatry. As Macaulay with great justness remarks, their whole history "is the record of a continued struggle between pure theism, supported by the most terrible sanctions, and the strangely fascinating desire of having some visible and tangible object of adoration." I know that the European mind of to-day and the Hebrew mind of three thousand years back have little in common. That childish savagery which could satisfy the craving for some outward symbol of spiritual things with the image of a calf, has disappeared from among civilised men. But for a few weak minds the danger out of which all idolatry springs still exists. There are not wanting enthusiasts to say to the spirits, "Ye are gods," and revere, as something more than human, those through whom tokens of their presence are given. It was against this great evil that the Levitical law was directed. With the Jews of old almost a whole nation was at all times ready to fall into error; with the spiritualists of to-day comparatively few are led into such folly. Yet it behoves all who wish well to our cause to raise their voices earnestly against these things, and, impressing upon their weaker brethren that mediums and spirits are alike but fallible, urge that to neither should this unreasoning faith and baseless reverence be accorded.

It is from the abuse of the faculty of veneration that such things in great part spring. By minds in which that faculty was exceed-

ingly strong, and caution and judgment correspondingly weak, the
wildest extravagances of religious history have been perpetrated.
The sceptical type of intellect, which can perceive nothing beyond
this present world, and rejects with the greatest disdain all
testimony relating to a future life, may be accepted as a character
whose weakness is the antipodes of that just described. The mass
of mankind hold a course equally distant from the two extremes,
and are neither disposed to accept without testimony nor to reject
without investigation. Yet there come periods when almost the
whole world seems to be infected with one or other of these
diseases. Just at present the second is rampant, and is the
deadliest foe by which Christianity can be menaced. For the
essence of the religion of Jesus is miracle, and signs and wonders
accompanied him throughout his career. The account of His birth is
the chief marvel in all history, yet it is almost matched by what
occurred at and after His death. From the commencement of His
mission until the final agony of the cross He continued to enforce
the tidings He had come upon earth to proclaim by the mightiest
works that earth had ever seen. And the power that was His He
kept not to Himself. In His name the apostles whom He sent out
were made to do many marvellous works. "And when He had
called unto Him His twelve disciples He gave them power against
unclean spirits to cast them out, and to heal all manner of
sickness, and all manner of disease. . . . . And He commanded
them, saying: Heal the sick, cleanse the lepers, raise the dead,
cast out devils; freely ye have received, freely give." Yet, as
Christ prophesied, these men were hated of all the world for His
name's sake; and to Himself the nation whom His mission
particularly concerned gave only death. They saw Him raise the
dead, and cleanse the leper; give sight to the blind, and cause the
lame to walk. They received from Him teachings such as ear had
never before heard, and they rewarded Him with the crown of
thorns and the cross. For their condition was worse than that
of the man who sat by the wayside as Christ went out from
Jericho. Bartimeus, through all his darkness, could recognise his
Lord; but the chiefs of the people, though spiritually blind,

desired not that their eyes might be opened; and, unable to comprehend the Light of the World, they sought to extinguish it.

Had the high-priest Caiaphas, when, with his acolytes, he mocked the victim stretched upon the cross, saying : "He saved others—himself he cannot save ; "—had this man been told that there should come a day when his victim would be worshipped as the Son of God in almost every country over which the Roman sceptre extended; and in yet vaster regions, of whose existence those Romans had never dreamed ; that in the very city from whence then went forth the fiats of Cæsar, would be set up the authority of pontiffs who deemed it their all on earth to be revered as vicegerents of this Christ ; that the ancient glory of Jerusalem should be extinguished, and even the foundations of her temple almost pass from view; and that a scanty remnant of the once mighty and flourishing nation of the Jews should wander from city to city of realms possessed by the triumphant Christians, ever expecting to behold the Messiah who should deliver them from their woes, and ever disappointed : would he not have scorned the prophecy as a madman's dream ? Had Lucian, when, in the reign of Trajan, he wrote with pitying wonder of that contempt of death which the Christians displayed, been informed that the statue of that very Trajan would be one day hurled from the noble column erected as its pedestal, and an effigy of a chief among these Christians take its place, with what a display of lively ridicule would he have laughed down such a tale ! And could the incredulity of either have been held matter for surprise ? Was it probable in the days of Caiaphas that the teachings of Christ would ever spread beyond Judæa ? Was it probable in the days of Lucian that this carpenter, and son of a carpenter, would be adored as God by all the nations of the Gentiles ? How comes it then that at his name the heads of such uncountable millions bow ?

The Protestant will answer that, Christ being God, the Christian religion was of God, and that, therefore He has nourished and preserved it. But how has it been nourished and preserved ? By miracle, all history replies. It is an easy thing now that men

should accept the faith which their fathers have from time immemorial accepted. The matter was far otherwise in the days of
Nero, Trajan, and Diocletian. Then, Christianity was professed
only in secret, and by a few; being held by the many an abomination or a foolishness. Its ethics were as noble as at present; but
with those ethics was inseparably connected the rejection of the
hundreds of deities whom Greek and Roman worshipped, and the
acceptance of Christ as God; and he or she who did so accept
Him, became thereby immediately exposed to inflictions such as
human nature faints but to contemplate. The renunciation
of the pomps and vanities of this world was then no vain form.
With the embracing of the Christian religion the certainty of a life
of privation and suffering was also accepted, and the peril of a
death of agony dared. To encounter the constant opposition of
those they loved, and provoke the hatred of their nearest and
dearest; to be in continual danger of denunciation to the
authorities; to meet for worship only in deserts and catacombs:
these were some of the things which all Christians endured.

It was well if at a meeting for praise and prayer the little congregation were not broken in upon by bands of fierce soldiery, and
minister and hearers involved in one common massacre; if an
assembling to celebrate the supper of the Lord did not end in those
who had partaken of that love-feast being thrown to the beasts of
the arena; if from the funeral rites of some brother or sister
departed, the mourners were not snatched away to be smeared
with pitch and set up as torches in the garden of Nero. How
many Christians perished by these, and modes of death equally
dreadful, in the three centuries that followed the Crucifixion, it is
impossible to compute. However great the number of martyrs,
their agonies were insufficient to check the progress of the new
faith. Nay, these agonies were even coveted by many converts
as the most glorious mode of finishing their earthly career.
Numbers denounced themselves to the authorities, and passed to
deaths of lingering torture with triumphant joy. The whole population of a small town in Asia, we learn from Tertullian, sought
such a fate. Having heard that the emperor had issued an edict

commanding all Christians to be put to death, they flocked in a body to the proconsul, and acknowledged themselves adherents of the new faith. On this the Roman deputy executed a few of the chief men, and dismissed the others to their homes. And they departed; not lamenting that their friends had come to so terrible an end, but that they themselves had been deemed unworthy to receive the solemn crown of martyrdom; not rejoiced because they had escaped dying in unutterable torture, but because a select few of their number had obtained admittance into the noble host of those whose blood was shed in the service of God. The words of St. Paul express the sentiment with which every martyr seems to have met death: "I am now ready to be offered, and the time of my departure is at hand. I have fought a good fight; I have finished my course; I have kept the faith: henceforth there is laid up for me a crown of righteousness, which the Lord, the righteous judge, shall give me at that day."

And why were the Christians of the first century so much more devoted to their creed than those of the nineteenth? How came it that, in spite of the most bloody and unsparing persecutions men had ever groaned under, the new creed spread with rapidity over the whole of the then civilised world? What was it by which zealot and atheist—the prejudices of men bigoted in favour of their old religion, and the prejudices of men bigoted in favour of their no-religion—were alike so speedily and so thoroughly conquered? Was it not in great measure by the continual working of signs and wonders?—by the impetus which the unceasing intervention of spiritual beings gave to the advancement of the Christian religion? Could a creed whose high teachings were supported by such striking miracles be likely to fail? The internal evidences, indeed, were alone sufficient to prove this faith to be of God. But those internal evidences were recommended to such men as Paul, John, and Peter, by the power which they themselves possessed of working mighty things, by the marvels which many of them had seen the great Founder of their belief accomplish, by the frequent descent upon them of the Spirit of God, by the gift of miraculously healing, by the

ability of understanding many and diverse tongues. Nor was it
to the apostles alone that spiritual things were brought so close.
The faith of such of their successors as Polycarp, Ignatius, and
Justin Martyr, as Tertullian, Cyprian, Ambrose, Augustine, and
a hundred others, was strengthened by signs and wonders almost
equally great. Nor are these signs and wonders yet extinct.
The noblest Christians of all ages have sought for and received
them. It may be affirmed, without danger of the assertion being
disapproved, that there never was a truly great man of any church—
one distinguished by the intensity of his faith and the nobility of
his life—but knew himself to be attended constantly by ministering
spirits. Such was the faith of Savonarola, of Loyola, of Bunyan, of
Fénelon, of Wesley, and of numerous others whom I have not
space to name. Nor is it probable that such men as Calvin and
Torquemada were unsupplied with spiritual guides ; though, doubtless, spiritual guides of an exceedingly undeveloped class. I
purpose in my next chapters to point out how a constant vein
of miracle runs through the history of the early Fathers, and
how traces of miracle have continued down to the present day
in every Church worthy the name of Christian. Not now, indeed,
does faith "subdue kingdoms, stop the mouths of lions, quench
the violence of fire, escape the edge of the sword." By these
things were the early Christians " out of weakness made strong."
Those countless thousands who in the time of the power of
the Romans went to death as to a bridal, did not *believe* that
the faith they professed was the truth—they *knew* it to be such.
Spirits had spoken with them face to face ; they had been permitted
while yet on earth to catch a glimpse of the glories of the hereafter. It mattered not what men might do against the body ; for
the soul an incorruptible crown was laid up in heaven. Such
Christians would have heard with mute amazement the assertion
that death is a "bourne whence no traveller returns." By a
thousand incidents of their lives were such teachings disproved.
Signs that a Thomas could not have doubted were continually
afforded them of the watch which those who had gone before kept
over the disciples of the true faith yet on earth. Some, like

Stephen, saw in the hour of death the heavens open, and the Son
of Man stand at the right hand of God. Others, like Peter, were
delivered from bondage and the peril of death by spiritual hands.
Like Polycarp they stood in the midst of flames and were not
harmed. Like Polycarp, too, voices whispered to them to be
strong, and quit themselves like men. As Ammon, they were
borne by spirits through the air. With Montanus, they were
thrown into ecstatic trances, and delivered messages from another
world. With John, they were circled at times by the glory of
the inner heaven, and those that looked on them saw their faces
"as the faces of angels." It was by men like these—men strong
with an unshakable certainty of the truth of what they taught—that
Christianity was carried to the farthest ends of the earth. It was
thus that the philosophy of Greece and the pride of Rome were
overthrown, that incense ceased to smoke on the altar of Jupiter,
and Poseidon and Isis were laid prostrate in the dust.

I do not advance these views as theories. They are facts,
as every genuine Christian will be ready to admit. But there
are numbers of men, professing to be Christians, who, denying
that such things have happened, will stigmatise these great truths
as dreams of the most baseless kind. For Christ is now, even
more than of old, uncomprehended by many who call themselves
his disciples. They "understand not the sayings which He speaks
unto them." It was thus, as every Evangelist proves to us, in
Judæa. Upon the earth to which he came to bear tidings of
peace and goodwill the Son of Man walked alone. Mary understood Him not, nor Joseph, nor they who, according to the belief
of the Jews, were the sisters and brothers of this Jesus. He
began his mission, and the nation to whom He preached understood him not. Even the most beloved of his disciples could but
faintly comprehend and sympathize with their Master. They
perceived his miracles, and "being afraid, spoke among themselves, saying, 'What manner of man is this?'" They listened
to his teachings, and "wist not of what He talked." They
approved their charity by forbidding others to cast devils out in
the name of Christ, and the extent of their faith by failing to do

so themselves. Whether Christ walked in Jerusalem or in the desert, surrounded by his disciples, or absent from all men, He was, as regards this world, equally alone. The love that He bore to man, not even John or Peter could understand. The spirit in which He taught none could perceive. When, in the garden of Gethsemane, He became "sorrowful even unto death," He withdrew to endure that mighty agony alone. The afflictions that tormented Him were not trials into which the twelve could enter. Whilst He suffered, his disciples slept. So was it before Pilate. So when passing from the judgment-seat to the cross. So when on that cross He cried: "My God, my God, why hast Thou forsaken me?" So when, having bowed his head, He said "It is finished," and, as He gave up the ghost, the earth quaked and the veil of the temple was rent in twain. And equally solitary does Christ remain unto the present day. Never have his teachings been truly understood of men. The master is still alone. "The light shineth in the darkness, and the darkness comprehendeth it not."

Had it been better comprehended how different would have been the history of the whole Christian world! Then Athanasius and Arius would not have cursed each other both for this life and the next. Then Constantine would not have been accepted as a fitting head for the Church of Christ. Then Julian would not have been driven in despair to the worn-out philosophies of pagan times. Then religion would not have been found throughout the dark ages uniformly on the side of might, and ever straying further from what was right and true. The career of Becket could never have been lived. Dominic would not have believed in burning the bodies of men to save their souls from eternal fire. Religious wars would never have desolated the world. The Inquisition would not have been established. Such natures as those of Torquemada and Calvin would have been viewed with abhorrence by men of all climes and creeds. In the pages of history we should read of no such laws as those established in the sixteenth century at Geneva; of no such reigns as those of Henry VIII. of England, and Charles IX. of France. The touch of Borgia or of Leo would not have defiled the papal tiara. Instead of sects too numerous to be counted, there might, at this day, be seen a single Church embracing all Christendom. Instead of brethren inflamed against each other by causeless hatred there might be found that unity which the Psalmist tells us it is so pleasant to see. Instead of gigantic wars, and rumours of wars, we might be living in the midst of the reign of universal peace, the "federation of the world." Controversy would be a name forgotten, and the pens and works of polemical divines moulder in oblivion and dust. But these speculations are indeed dreams.

It is time that this chapter should conclude. I have done my best to prove how intimately miracle is bound up with each of the many books of the Bible, and how total would be the ruin effected by tearing all miracle away. I have sought also to point out the resemblance between certain phenomena of Jewish times and the phenomena of the present day. Want of space, indeed, has prevented me from doing the subject justice. Besides the instances adduced, there are numerous others scattered through every book, from Genesis to the Revelation of John. But these any searcher of the Scriptures can readily find for himself. He will also, I think, find sufficient evidence to make plain to him that the shadow of Hebrew spiritualism was the tendency which, even more than Assyrians, Egyptians, or Persians, the race chosen of God had to listen to the whispers of evil spirits, and exalt those spirits into deities : a tendency which the most terrible threats and chastisements proved insufficient to restrain. He will agree with me that solely against this tendency were the terrors of the Levitical law directed. He will also agree with me that by rejecting whatever in the Testaments, Old or New, is inexplicable by known laws, or apparently opposed to those laws, men make the prophets and chroniclers liars and the teachings of Christ of no authority. If we are to believe that so much of Scripture is false, what security have we that the rest is true ? A single error admitted injures Holy Writ : what then of this mass of error ? It is but cold truth to say that those who, professing to be worshippers of Christianity, would either totally deprive the Bible of miracle or accept only the miracles attributed to Christ, treat the chief of religions as of old the soldiers of Pilate treated her Founder. They deprive her of the vestments that so well become her. Having plaited a crown of thorns and shaped a sceptre from a reed, they adorn her with these. Then, bowing the knee before her, they expose her in this state to the derision of the nations.

CHAPTER II.

A FAVOURITE dictum with many divines is, that miracle ceased with the apostolic age. We have no certain evidence, say they, that signs and wonders occurred after the last of the twelve had departed from earth. Learned bishops have not been ashamed to employ the whole force of their ecclesiastical eloquence in endeavouring to prove this hypothesis a certainty.

Yet the fáct undeniably is that, as regards external evidence, certain miraculous occurrences recorded by Athanasius, Augustine, and others, are better supported than anything the New Testament contains. The internal evidence which in the Bible carries such weight is, of course, weaker in the case of the Fathers. Yet, conjoined with the historical testimony, it has proved sufficient to induce such men as Locke and Grotius to admit the authenticity of these narratives. The first tells us that we must allow the miracles, or, by denying that they occurred, destroy the authority of the Fathers, and even] their reputation for common honesty. The second not only warmly defends the spiritual in the early Church, but avows his entire belief that such things had continued down to his own day. Milton, Cudworth, Bacon, Addison, Dr. Johnson, and a host of men equally distinguished, have held one or other of these opinions. Indeed, it is difficult to see how Christians can do otherwise. The words used by Christ are, " He that believeth on me, the works that I do shall he do also, and greater works than these shall he do." If Protestant divines deny that such works are now done, is not the inference plain ? They are of opinion that men have ceased to believe in Christ.

Not such was the faith of early and fervent members of the Church.   How hardy seem the expressions of Tertullian on the subject! So earnestly did he hold to the text above quoted, that men asserting themselves to be Christians, who yet could not expel a demon, were in his judgment, worthy of death.   "Let some one be brought forward here at the foot of your judgment-seat, who, it is agreed, is possessed of a demon.   When commanded by any Christian to speak, that spirit shall as truly declare itself a demon, as elsewhere falsely a god.   In like manner let some one be brought forward of those who are believed to be acted upon by a god. . . . Unless these confess themselves to be demons, not daring to lie unto a Christian, then shed upon the spot the blood of that most impudent Christian." (Apol. 23.)

The words of St. Paul to the Corinthians are :—" Concerning spiritual gifts, brethren, I would not have you ignorant. . . . For to one is given by the Spirit the word of wisdom. . . . to another the gifts of healing by the same spirit ; to another the working of miracles ; to another prophecy ; to another discerning of spirits ; to another divers kinds of tongues." As regards the last but one of these gifts, a curious passage is to be found in the " De Animâ " of the Tertullian above quoted :—

" We had a right," says the great orator, " after what was said by St. John, to expect prophesyings ; and we not only acknowledge these spiritual gifts, but we are permitted to enjoy the gifts of a prophetess. There is a sister amongst us who possesses the faculty of revelation. She commonly, during our religious service on the Sabbath, falls into a crisis or trance. She has then intercourse with the angels, sees sometimes the Lord himself, sees and hears Divine mysteries, and discovers the hearts of some persons ; administers medicine to such as desire it, and, when the Scriptures are read, or psalms are being sung, or prayers are being offered up, subjects from thence are ministered to her visions. We had once some discourse touching the soul while this sister was in the spirit. When the public services were over, and most of the people gone, she acquainted us with what she had seen in her ecstasy, as the custom was ; for these things are heedfully digested that they may be duly proved. Among other things, she told us that she had seen a soul in a bodily shape, and that the spirit had appeared unto her, not empty or formless and wanting a living constitution, but rather such as might be handled : delicate, and of the colour of light and air—in everything resembling the human form."

Thus, in the early Christian Church, we have an exact counterpart of the clairvoyance, the trance speaking, and the healing mediumship of the present day. It is also noteworthy that what Tertullian calls the "corporeal soul," or "soul in bodily shape," minutely coincides with the spirit-form as beheld in the visions of ancient and modern seers. Pythagoras and Plato speak of it as a "luciform etherial vehicle," St. Paul calls it the "spiritual body," Swedenborg the "spiritual man," the seeress of Prevorst the "nerve spirit," and Davis the "inner being." All genuine clairvoyants, in short, convey, under different forms of expression, the same idea.

At the age of eighty-six took place the martyrdom of Polycarp. A few nights previous, whilst praying in his bed, the aged saint had perceived his pillow wrapped in fire, without being consumed. This he knew to be an omen of approaching martyrdom. On the day of his departure a number of Christians attended to the place of execution one who had been the disciple and friend of the Apostle John. As they went a spirit voice was heard by all to cry loudly: "Be strong, O Polycarp, and quit thyself like a man." When the pile was lighted the flames refused to touch him, and curved outward on all sides from his form. A fragrant scent, as of aromatic drugs, was diffused around, and the martyr, with a glorious countenance, stood quietly in the midst of the fire, appearing to the beholders like a figure of burnished gold. In dismay, the executioner thrust him through with a sword. There died with him other believers, respecting whom the Church of Smyrna says:—"While they were under torments the Lord Jesus Christ stood by, and, conversing with them, revealed things to them inconceivable by man." Such were the experiences of the early saints.

Sozomen and Socrates, the Church historians, relate two striking instances of information obtained from the departed respecting matters which had troubled the living. Irene, the daughter of Spiridion, Bishop of Trimithon, had been entrusted by a member of her father's flock with the keeping of a large sum of money. Shortly afterwards she died; and the owner came to Spiridion for

the return of the deposit. Spiridion, knowing nothing of the
matter, searched in vain every spot where his daughter might
have placed such a trust, and was forced to inform his visitor that
the money could not be found. On this the man tore his hair,
and exhibited the greatest distress. His pastor bade him be calm,
and proceeding to the grave of Irene, solemnly called upon her
spirit to appear. She at once responded to the summons, and
informed her father that she had buried the money for greater
security in a certain corner of the house. There it was found
by Spiridion, and immediately restored to the rightful owner.

But the second narrative is yet more interesting. Evagrius, a
Grecian philosopher, had been, with much difficulty, converted to
Christianity by Synesius, Bishop of Cyrene. Even after his conversion he would appear to have felt doubts as to the certainty of
a future life, and these doubts he, on his death-bed, expressed in a
peculiar manner. He gave to Synesius a bag containing a very
large sum in gold, which sum he requested him to apply to the
benefit of the poor of the city, and desired, moreover, that the
Bishop would give him an acknowledgment of the debt, and a
promise that Christ would repay him in another world. Synesius
willingly subscribed to these terms, and the poor were made happy
with the legacy. But Evagrius had no sooner passed away than
his heirs brought an action against the Bishop for the recovery of
the debt, a memorandum of which they had discovered among the
papers of the deceased philosopher. In vain did Synesius plead
the circumstances of the case; and, proving that the gift was for
the poor, relate the expectation of his creditor that Christ would
repay him in another world. Judgment was about to be given for
the heirs, when a visit from the spirit of the departed relieved the
Bishop of their claims. At dead of night Evagrius appeared, and
with a joyful voice, confessed that the Lord had satisfied the debt
in full. He further bade Synesius go to his sepulchre, and told
him that he would there find a quittance for the sum. Next day,
the Bishop, accompanied by the heirs of Evagrius, and the
authorities of the city, proceeded to the grave, and caused it to be
opened. In the hand of the corpse was found a paper, subscribed

as follows, in the undoubted handwriting of the departed:—
" I, Evagrius the philosopher, to thee, most holy Sir, Bishop
Synesius, greeting. I have received the debt which in this paper
is written with thy hand, and am satisfied; and I have no action
against thee for the gold which I gave to thee, and by thee,
to Christ, our God and Saviour." The bill upon which this
appeared was the acknowledgment made by Synesius, at the time
of receiving the gold. It had been placed within the tomb, as the
heirs of Evagrius admitted, in accordance with their father's dying
request. But they solemnly denied that the extraordinary words
by which the debt was cancelled had then been present on the
paper. The receipt thus remains, like the sentences interpreted by
Daniel, an instance of that direct spirit-writing so much cavilled at
in the present day.

Numerous other miracles occurred in the early ages of the
Church which I have only space to name. Pre-eminent are those
of Anthony, Martin, and Ambrose, the second of whom is reported
to have raised the dead. The cross seen in the heavens by Constantine and his army, is a spiritual sign with the history of which
the reader is probably familiar. So with regard to the discovery,
by the Empress Helena, of the sepulchre wherein Christ had lain.
Marvels equally deserving of notice are to be found scattered
through the pages of Irenæus, Origen, Tertullian, Eusebius,
Athanasius, Theodoret, and Evagrius. Amongst these are the
narratives of miraculous incidents which occurred during the relentless persecutions of Maximian and Diocletian, and the history of
those Christians of Carthage whose tongues were cut out by Hunneric
the Vandal, and who yet continued to speak with all their former
fluency. Regarding this last event, the testimony is as perfect as
that concerning any incident in modern history. Bishop Douglas,
feeling too much embarrassed by the weight of evidence to deny
the occurrence of this wonder, and yet anxious to reconcile it with
his pet theory of the confinement of miracle to apostolic times, had
the pleasing audacity to assure his readers that nothing was more
common than that men who had lost their tongues should retain
their speech. The right reverend father in God was unfortunate

in living a century or so too soon. His statement would have formed a fitting pendant to the theories of certain scientists of the present day.

" We might easily prove by citations from the fathers," says a writer in the " Encyclopædia Metropolitana," " that one object of the experiences to which the Christian neophyte was subjected, was his introduction to a lawful communion with the spirits of the departed." In this assertion I heartily concur. Indeed, nothing can be more amazing than the ignorance displayed by those divines who at the present day inform us that the Mosaic law forbidding men to seek communion with the departed, has, in all ages, been observed by the Christian Church. Have they the slightest acquaintance with the writings of the fathers of that Church? If so, are they not aware that, besides the instances cited from Tertullian in the opening of this chapter, a score of others might be given to prove that, while vehemently condemning spiritualism as practised by the Pagans, the early Christians were themselves devoted to spiritualistic practices? They anathematized the mediums of the heathen because they believed that the spirits manifesting through them were uniformly evil. They sought earnestly for communion with another world by means of their own mediums, because they perceived the spirits who gave token of their presence through these to be departed friends, and believed them, without exception, angelic beings : natures glorified and happy.

The outpouring of this " gift to discern spirits," was coveted by every congregation of Christians, whether Asiatic or European, of the East or of the West. Even when occurring amongst those whom the orthodox deemed heretical brethren it was not the less rejoiced in. Montanus, though the body of the Church held his teachings in the highest degree pernicious, was connived at by many on account of his spiritual gifts. Two of his female followers, the ladies Maximilla and Priscilla, were held in such esteem as prophetesses and clairvoyants, that the protection of the Papacy itself was granted them against their enemies.

The Montanists, it is true, appear to have been far worthier of reverence than the majority of those who persecuted them. The great purposes of their leader were to put down the follies and vices of the period, and to reform the discipline of the Church. Wherever a church of Montanists arose, there appeared numerous energumens, or, as we now say, mediums. In the midst of the congregation these would pass into an ecstatic state, and deliver addresses whilst entranced. Such a speaker was the sister alluded to by the most eminent disciple of Montanus, the great Tertullian.

Nothing can better express the confidence which the early Christians had in the continual protection of guardian spirits than the beautiful words of St. Augustine :—

"They watch," says the son of Monica—"they watch over and guard us with great care and diligence in all places and at all hours, assisting, providing for our necessities with solicitudes; they intervene between us and Thee, O Lord, conveying to Thee our sighs and groans, and bringing down to us the dearest blessings of Thy grace. They walk with us in all our ways; they go in and out with us, attentively observing how we converse with piety in the midst of a perverse generation, with what ardour we seek Thy kingdom and its justice, and with what fear and awe we serve Thee. They assist us in our labours; they protect us in our rest; they encourage us in battle; they crown us in victories; they rejoice in us when we rejoice in Thee; and they compassionately attend us when we suffer or are afflicted for Thee. Great is their care of us, and great is the effect of their charity for us. They love him whom Thou lovest; they guard him whom Thou beholdest with tenderness; they forsake those from whom Thou withdrawest Thyself; and they hate them that work iniquity, because they are hateful to Thee."

So living was the faith of Christians from fourteen to eighteen centuries ago! Disputes on other points of faith might distract the Church in these early ages—Homoiousians rage against Homoousians, Gnostics anathematize Sabellians, the Arian Constantius persecute the followers of Athanasius, the Athanasian Theodosius persecute the Arians; but to one strong stay the devotees of either creed equally clung: that of the nearness of the spirit world, and the possibility of communion between those still on this side the grave and those who had known the change called death. Origen might differ from Cyril as to whether the condition of the devil were hopeless or not; but he could agree with him that multitudes of spiritual beings, benignant and malevolent, continually surrounded his brother Christian and himself. The certainty of a continual spiritual presence—the consciousness of the ceaseless watching of spiritual eyes—were common to every flock of believers, from the Pillars of Hercules to the shores of the Persian Gulf, and from the cornfields of Sicily to the forests of the Grampians. It mattered not whether their condition in this world were one of happiness or pain. In the first century or the fourth, as well in the reign of Nero as in that of Constantine, the same angelic whispers upheld the believer in life and strengthened him in the hour of death; the same Christ stood ready to bid the faithful servant welcome to the glory of his Lord. Such men could say with Paul, that neither principalities nor powers might wrest from them the great joy of their faith. To live was Christ, and to die gain. The pleasures and pains of earth they equally despised. All their hopes were concentred on the glorious mansions wherein was prepared for them a place; all their ambition was devoted to the brightness of an eternal crown. In honour or in lowliness, they saw only the mighty mark towards which they pressed. Whether surrounded by the gloom of the catacombs or the glory of the palace, they lived less in this world than in the next. Already the heavenly things which by other men were seen faintly, or not at all, were to them more real than the turmoil of that Vanity Fair wherein for a space their lot was cast. That this might be, a hundred miracles were wrought. Lest they should forget that God is mighty to save, they were snatched from the mouths of lions, and protected amidst the violence of fire. Lest their faith should wax weak, the spirits who had gone before gave to them continual tokens of their nearness and their love. When "afflicted, destitute, tormented," they wandered in a world unworthy of them, their vision was withdrawn from the things of earth, and fixed on the glories awaiting all who should hold fast to the end. Before the judges, in the arena, at the stake, voices whispered to them of the realm where God should wipe away all tears, and in the ecstasy of the mind the body's agonies were forgotten. Triumphant over death, serene amidst the extremity of pain, their radiant countenances witnessed to their enemies of how little avail against those to whom the spiritual had been brought so close was the fiercest malice of man. Upon such the splendours of the world of light could not break with a brightness altogether unconceived. Whilst yet on earth they tasted of the joys to come. Their eyes were opened to the glories of their future home. Their ears were filled with its music. Their spirits enjoyed its peace. Thus supported, they encountered victoriously all the obstacles of their pilgrimage, and, "faithful unto death," passed to enjoy the crown of life which, throughout that pilgrimage, had been ever before their gaze.

I am not sure that in a chapter respecting spiritualism in the early ages of the Christian Church the Alexandrian school of philosophy should find a place; but the inexorable limits of space forbid my devoting to Plotinus, Iamblichus, and the rest of the Neo-Platonists a full chapter, while it is certain that such men must not be passed unnoticed. Of all Pagan systems theirs most nearly approached the religion of Christ. Doctrines, indeed, which Neo-Platonism still more intimately resembles, are those of Buddha and Brahma; and it was imperative that this should be, since from India much of the philosophy of the school was confessedly drawn.

The teaching of Nirvana was held by Ammonius and his successors in its sublimest form. To the lessons drawn from the East they added the noblest portions of the wisdom of Plato, and mingled with the whole fragments both of the truth and error of Pythagoras. The philosophy thus formed flourished long in the schools of Greece, and became, by reason of the nobleness of its ethics, the grandeur of its speculations, and the extent to which spiritual gifts were possessed by its first teachers, a formidable rival to the Christian faith. It was not until the reign of Justinian, when the men who had been its chief glories had long departed, that Neo-Platonism finally fell from its high estate.

The prophet of the school was Apollonius of Tyana. As

mentioned in a former chapter of this work he acquired his theurgic wisdom almost wholly in the East. He was a native of Tyana, in Asia Minor, and nearly contemporary with Christ.

Numerous miracles of the highest class are attributed to him. He cured by spiritual means the most violent diseases, and gave frequent predictions of future events. Meeting a funeral procession, where a bridegroom in an agony of despair followed the bier of his young wife, he caused the procession to stop, and succeeded in recalling the dead girl to life. At Corinth he became the hero of that legend which has formed the subject of Keats's "Lamia." Apollonius was greatly attached to a young Greek named Menippus, who persisted, contrary to the wishes of the philosopher, in marrying a rich and beautiful woman of the city. When the guests were assembled for the wedding, Apollonius, unbidden, walked into their midst, and commanded the demon which animated the body of the bride to come forth. After a fruitless struggle, it is said, the spirit complied, and confessed itself an *empuse* or vampire, whose intention was to have destroyed Menippus in his sleep.

By temperance and purity the earthly life of this sage was prolonged to almost a hundred years. " My mode of living," he wrote, " is very different to that of other people. I take very little food, and this, like a secret remedy, maintains my senses fresh and unimpaired, as it keeps everything that is dark from them, so that I can see the present and future, as it were, in a clear mirror. The sage need not wait for the vapours of the earth and the corruptions of the air to foresee plagues and fevers ; he must know them later than God, but earlier than the people. The gods see the future, men the present, sages that which is coming. This mode of life produces such an acuteness of the senses, or some other power, that the greatest and most remarkable things may be performed. I am, therefore, perfectly convinced that God reveals his intentions to holy and wise men." By " acuteness of the senses or some other power " Apollonius evidently implied clairvoyance. How wonderfully this attribute was developed in him numerous events in his history prove. At

Ephesus, as related in my chapter on India, he perceived and made known the assassination of Domitian in the very hour when that event occurred at Rome.

Unlike many beings less highly gifted, this philosopher never sought to assume a dictatorship over the souls of men. He was totally undesirous to become the founder of a religion. His mission was to bring nearer to man the glories of the spiritual world, and the only preparation for that world which he felt himself empowered to inculcate was purity, physical and moral. He lived revered by all Greece and Italy, and after his death was regarded with yet higher veneration. At Tyana a temple was built in his honour—a species of memorial which he could scarcely have expected or desired. The Emperor Hadrian collected his letters, and every authentic document which existed respecting his life. These, having long been carefully preserved, were finally delivered by the Empress Julia, the mother of Severus, to Philostratus, who constructed from them his life of the great theurgist—a work which all well-informed critics have agreed in regarding as authentic.

Long after the death of Apollonius arose Ammonius Sacchas, the true founder of the Neo-Platonic school. His successors, each of them more famous than Ammonius himself, were Plotinus, Porphyry, Proclus, and Iamblichus. By these men Neo-Platonism was rapidly carried to its highest development. As I have said, this school professed extreme respect for the deeds and writings of the philosopher of Tyana. He had, however, left nothing behind him which could justify his being exalted into a Messiah, and no such attempt was made. Indeed, high as was the admiration of the Neo-Platonists for Apollonius, they appear to have felt an equally high, perhaps higher, admiration for Christ. They admit his miracles, and show no trace of antagonism to his teachings. It was chiefly the fault of the Christian Church itself that it failed to absorb the Alexandrian philosophers. Even in those early ages intolerance had sprung up and become strong. Nor need we wonder at this, since, once rooted in any religion, it is a weed that attains maturity as rapidly as Jonah's gourd.

G

Plotinus and Iamblichus were now libelled as deadly enemies to the Church of Christ. They claimed to have purified the soul so that they could perceive spirits, and, by the help of these spirits, perform miracles. The Christians, perceiving that irrefragable proof of spiritual gifts existed among the Neo-Platonists, adopted the priestly tactics of all ages and faiths. Without showing that the spirits who communed with Ammonius and his followers were evil, they denounced the mediums of Alexandria as sorcerers. Forgetting the reply of Christ to that reproach, they hurled against them the cry of the Pharisees, "Ye cast out devils by Beelzebub, the prince of the devils!" Nay, even this did not content them. At the head of a rabble of such bigots as have in all ages defiled the pure name of Christian, a Bishop of Alexandria (Cyril, if I remember aright), succeeded in seizing and murdering a beautiful and saintly maiden named Hypatia, whose teachings were esteemed throughout the city. The outrage was attended by circumstances of the foulest horror. Cyril, and his fellow-disgracers of the human form, having stripped their victim, hewed her almost in pieces, and dragged the mangled remains in triumph through the streets. No worse crime was ever perpetrated by Calvin! Yet there can be little doubt but that the ecclesiastical monster and his satellites returned thanks to God for the great work He had permitted them to accomplish, and, with the blood of the victim yet fresh on his hands, Cyril may have found matter for a very eloquent sermon in the command, "Thou shalt not suffer a witch to live." Happily, such crimes as this were rare in the early ages of the Church. Not until that Church had ceased to struggle for existence, and was become in her turn dominant, did murder assume a clearly defined position amongst the duties of her servants.

Plotinus, the successor of Ammonius Sacchas in the leadership of Neo-Platonism, was as deeply tinged with asceticism as any Christian hermit of ancient ages. He lived sparely, held fasts whose length and frequency tasked to the utmost his bodily powers, and displayed clairvoyance in its highest form. The minds of men, he repeatedly proved, were to him as open books.

As recounted by Porphyry, his teachings resembled exactly those of the Indian Brahmins and Buddhists. He held God to be not only without but within us. He is present to all, yet men flee from Him. *Spirits released from the body are not divided by space, but by the difference of mental and moral qualities. If such difference cease they are immediately near to each other.* In the words I have italicised the great Neo-Platonist expresses a truth which the revelations of all modern spiritualism go to confirm. Plotinus taught, moreover, that a perfect union with God might be attained by resembling Him in quality and disposition. Withdrawn from the sensual attractions of earth the spirit became filled with light from the Source of all light. Out of that source flow increasing shapes and spirits—the *eidolen* of Heraclitus. To community with these we arrive by despising the things of earth. Such communion is obtained in ecstasy—ecstasy being almost invariably the work of spirits. Plotinus possessed this ecstatic sensitiveness, and drew from it all his theurgic power, working thus signs and wonders, predicting future events, and healing the most hopeless diseases. Like Socrates, he knew himself to be constantly attended by a guardian spirit, who warned him from evil and inspired him to good.

Porphyry, the disciple of this Plotinus, naturally clung to the doctrines of so enlightened a master. He industriously collected materials from which the life of Plotinus might be written, and compiled an account of it with the greatest care. Himself distinguished less by medial power than by intellectual gifts, he was succeeded in the direction of Alexandrian philosophy by a man the most truly spiritual of all the Neo-Platonists. This was Iamblichus, one of the greatest seers of the ancient earth. Albeit clinging still to some of the errors of Pythagoras, he lived a blameless and exalted life. So famous was he for his learning and power of healing that, in process of time, he came to be styled the "divine." It was this Iamblichus who, according to Eunapius,

> "From out their fountain dwellings raised
> Eros and Anteros at Gadara."

Indeed, no magian of Egypt appears to have had a closer intercourse with the world of spirits. He was, above all his brethren,
familiar with the phenomena of clairvoyance. Divine music frequently resounded in his ears. He endured unhurt the blows of
weapons and the touch of fire. His life was passed in a total
abstraction from the things of earth. He displayed in the highest
perfection the three cardinal virtues, faith, hope, and charity,
and his remarks on prayer are worthy of the noblest Christian.
With those remarks I shall conclude the present chapter :—

"Prayer constitutes a portion of the sacred service, and confers a
universal advantage on religion, by creating an unerring connection
between the priests and God. It conducts us to a perfect knowledge of
heavenly things. It procures us that inexpressible devotion which
places its whole strength in God above, and thus imparts to our souls a
blessed repose. No act prospers in the service of God, where prayer is
omitted. Daily repeated prayer nourishes the understanding, and prepares our hearts for sacred things ; opens to man the Divine, and
accustoms him by degrees to the glory of the Divine light. It enables
us to bear our sufferings, and the weaknesses that are human ; attracts
our sentiments gradually upwards, and unites them with the Divine ;
enkindles whatever is holy within our souls. It purges away all way-
wardness of mind; it generates true hope and faith. In a word, it helps
those to an intimate conversation with spirits who exercise it diligently
and often. How effectual it is! How prayer and sacrifice mutually
invigorate each other, impart the sacred power of religion and make it
perfect! It becomes us not therefore to contemn prayer, or only to
employ a little of it, and throw away the rest. No ; wholly must we use
it ; and above all things must they practise it who desire to unite themselves sincerely with God."

CHAPTER III.

I HAVE now to deal with that portion of the world's history in which the light kindled in the early Christian Church was constantly becoming dimmer by reason of the gross vapours that surrounded it. No record is written in blacker characters than that of the seven centuries which followed the assumption of the crown of the West by Charlemagne. The demon of Intolerance, driven forth for a space by the pure teachings of Christ, seemed to have returned, bringing with him seven other devils worse than himself. Hypocrisy was there, and murder, and crimes and vices which men shudder to name. The chair of St. Peter was filled by a succession of degraded pontiffs—each more worthless than his predecessor. The profligacy of churchmen became appalling. "Viler than a priest" was one of the common expressions of Southern Europe in the twelfth century. Those who styled themselves the keepers of the Gospel sneered in secret at the teachings which that Gospel contained. Nay, they appeared, with the perverseness of profligacy, to pride themselves upon shaping their conduct in diametrical opposition to the rules laid down by Christ and the Twelve. Because the Messiah was meek and lowly, the prelates of his Church displayed themselves through a succession of ages the proudest of the proud. Because He had blessed those who hungered after righteousness, they plunged defyingly into the foulest vice. Because He had praised the merciful, these corrupted servants made their hearts hard as the nether millstone. Because Paul had said that a bishop should be blameless, just, and temperate, able with sound doctrine to exhort and convince, they made a mock of the episcopal dignity by bestowing it on children just able to speak, and men fallen beneath the brutes. Nor was this the worst. For dogmas in which they put no faith, for ethics that they did not reduce to practice, the rulers of the Church were yet ready to inflict death in its most horrible form. And in the infliction of such death they contrived to unite with the most hideous cruelty the blackest hypocrisy. Because the Christian kingdom was not of this world, they handed over to secular execu- tioners the victim whom they had sentenced, with a jocular request that all possible tenderness might be shown. The mode of slaying was already determined. Since the Gospel forbade the shedding of blood, its ministers thought it well to substitute for a short and easy death the unendurable agony of the stake.

To such men it was impossible that beneficent spirits should manifest themselves. Accordingly, in numerous instances, the miracles of the Catholic Church were accomplished through the undeveloped beings whom the evil natures of its priests attracted, or, if such resources failed, were simulated by means of accom- plished fraud. Few readers of history need to be reminded of the exposures made in our own country at the time of the Reformation. The winking Madonnas, the roods of grace, the talking heads, and bending images, were dragged into the light of day and their concealed machinery exposed to the disgust and derision of men. And the inner secrets of monasteries and convents were exposed with equal ruthlessness and found equally foul. To take one instance, and that extremely mild, in that beautiful Abbey of Furness, from which Thomas Cromwell ejected the monks by the summary process of demolishing the roof, strange things were brought to light. The magnificent pile lies low in a charming valley, nestling amidst ancient trees, and so situated as to be well shielded and hidden by rising ground. Like the architects of Newstead, its holy founders

> " Preferred a hill behind
> To shelter their devotion from the wind."

This earthly paradise, about the meridian of Henry VIII.'s

reign, was inhabited by numerous men outwardly saintly. Presumably each was as Adam during his first days in Eden, but,
unlike him, cut off from all expectation of an Eve. Yet what did
Cromwell and his subordinate iconoclasts discover ? They learned
that the society they came to disestablish had long been one of
the wealthiest in England. Tired of the literal interpretation put
by dull predecessors on the vows of fasting and silence, the abbots
and brethren had hit on means whereby to render those vows
agreeable. Fasting they found compatible with an immense
expenditure on wine and provisions, and their solitude was
enlivened by the introduction of the fair sex into the abbey. Nay,
to such lengths had they gone that, unsatisfied with paramours,
they had ventured the introduction of their necks into the forbidden noose of matrimony. Rogerus Pele, the then abbot, had
two wives, although for a priest to have even one was, according
to Church canons, a deadly sin. A holy subordinate, fired with
the ambition of surpassing his superior, had encumbered himself
with fair helpmeets to the number of no less than five. Such, in
the sixteenth century, were some of the *milder* abuses of the
Church.

I have alluded to the prevalence of mock miracle in the days
when Catholic power was at its height. It was disgust at this
rank growth of tares which caused the Reformers of the sixteenth
century to reject the whole spiritual harvest as worthless. Yet
reason might have discovered to them that with so much imposture
there was assuredly mingled a certain proportion of truth. In
nations destitute of a coinage the counterfeiting of money is
impossible. Where a coinage exists base money is certain to be also
in circulation. The more esteemed the products of the true mint,
the more numerous will the spurious imitations become. It is
thus with the occurrences that come under the definition of
miracle. Were real miracles impossible the world would never
have been vexed with false. Had not miracle been found a
mighty engine for upholding a faith and extending its limits, the
Romish Church would scarcely have played the cheat to such an
extent. Why the counterfeit signs and wonders so greatly out-

numbered the true may easily be shown. An undetected imposture was equally advantageous to the Church with a work really wrought by spiritual hands, and the imposture was the more readily obtained of the two. Rome, therefore, received under her protection a number of coiners of spiritual phenomena, and ordered that their production should pass current as genuine miracle. Such a policy, of course, proved suicidal. It was one of the broad and easy ways that in the end lead to destruction. Were a government to collect secretly the most skilful counter-feiters among its subjects, and keeping them, unknown to the rest of the community, employed in the constant manufacture of base coin, send forth large quantities of spurious money mixed with a certain proportion of genuine, how great would be the amazement of all civilised men when the deed was brought to light! The idea seems too wild for the wildest fiction. Yet such was, in spiritual matters, exactly the course which the Papacy of old adopted, and even since the Reformation has, in a modified degree, continued to follow. As was natural, a tremendous retribution followed when things had reached their worst. Laymen who perceived the chicanery that was sought to be practised on them, and priests disgusted with the chicanery they were required to practise, joined in the mighty outbreak of the sixteenth century. From all countries' ripe for Protestantism the false prophets of Rome were expelled with contumely and disgust. The tools of their nefarious trade were publicly exposed and destroyed. And, as in the vehemence of reaction against such a government as I have imagined, its injured subjects might, when they had brought to condign punishment the corrupters of their coinage, resolve that, to prevent the recurrence of an event so disastrous, even the issue of genuine money should be made illegal, so Protestantism has ordered that wherever its rule extends miracle shall cease. The natural result has followed. Those whose faith demands imperatively the support of the spiritual seek that Church where the spiritual is to be found. They may know that Rome is still often guilty of fraud, but they prefer running the risk of false money to wanting money altogether. The Church which manufac-

tures miracle is in their eyes far preferable to the Church in which
no pretensions to miracle are made. Thus, while Protestantism
languishes everywhere, new converts are daily flocking to that
hierarchy which claims to hold unceasing intercourse with another
world,—which, when better-attested phenomena fail, discovers
ignorant peasant boys to whom the Virgin has revealed herself,
and enthusiastic country maidens marked with the five wounds of
Christ. Supported by these and nobler aids, the Church of Rome
may, in the words of a great critic, "exist in undiminished vigour,
when some traveller from New Zealand shall, in the midst of a
vast solitude, take his stand on a broken arch of London Bridge to
sketch the ruins of St. Paul's." This is not a consummation
devoutly to be wished, but it is decidedly one to be feared. If
Protestantism be not in its turn reformed, Protestantism is
doomed. A Church cannot long make head against such scepticism
as that of the present day, which, when assailed on all sides for
proofs of its doctrines, answers only that those doctrines prove
themselves. We see in countries like Germany and England a
constantly growing inclination to separate the ethics of Christianity
from its dogmas. That which men want to-day is a foundation for
their faith.

Such a foundation many have had in even the darkest ages of
the Roman Church. Dominic, Torquemada, and Borgia might be
" damned to everlasting fame "—pilloried in the pages of history
for the scaring of future generations from the Catholic faith,—but
coeval with these workers of iniquity, whose evil deeds have lived
for centuries after them, were doers of the noblest good. Among
the chief of these was St. Bernard. His life is one continual
record of the marvellous. Wherever he went he approved the
literal exactness of Christ's words, " He that believeth in me, the
works that I do shall he do also." At his prayer the blind saw and
the lame walked. A biography of this great man has been compiled by a Mr. Morison. His prejudices against the spiritual seem
inveterate, but he is nevertheless staggered by the facts which, as
a faithful biographer, he is bound to record. .

He relates how visions of the future were granted to Bernard,

and how he thus predicted with the most marvellous accuracy that
which should come to pass. He describes how the saint's journey
through the Rhine country was glorified by a constant exhibition
of miraculous powers. In one day at Constance his prayers, and
the imposition of his hands, restored sight to eleven persons totally
blind, and acquired for eighteen cripples the use of their limbs.
At Cologne he healed twelve lame citizens, besides causing three
who were dumb to speak, and ten deaf persons to hear. Nor
were these things done secretly, and in a fashion that left room for
suspicion to enter. It was before mighty multitudes, and under
the scrutiny of innumerable eyes, that Bernard worked. The
testimony of ten of these eye-witnesses remains to what they saw.
Herman, Bishop of Constance, and nine others, kept a diary of the
miraculous cures accomplished before them. This account, as Mr.
Morison remarks, would seem to have been drawn up with the
express purpose of avoiding cavil, whilst attracting attention. The
names and the condition of these witnesses are given, and they
solemnly make oath that they witnessed with their own eyes the
miracles recorded. They describe how the halt, the blind, the
deaf, and the dumb were brought from all parts to be touched
by Bernard. When the patient was presented to him he simply
prayed, made the sign of the cross upon the part affected, and the
cure was perfect. The following extract contains the wonders
wrought in a single day :—

"In the Church of St. John, at Cambray, after the mass, a boy deaf
and dumb from his mother's womb received his hearing and spoke, and
the people wondered. He had sat down beside me deaf and dumb, and
having been presented to Bernard, in the self-same hour he both spoke
and heard. The joyful excitement was scarcely over before a lame old
man was raised up and walked. But now a miracle occurred which,
beyond all others, filled us with astonishment. A boy blind from his
birth, whose eyes were covered with a white substance—if, indeed, those
could be called eyes in which there was neither colour nor use, nor even
so much as the usual cavity of an eye—this boy received his sight from
the imposition of Bernard's hand. We ascertained the fact by numerous
proofs, hardly believing our senses that in such eyes as his any sight
could reside. In the same place a woman who had a withered hand
was healed. In the town of Rosnay they brought to him in a waggon a

man ill and feeble, for whom nothing seemed to remain but the grave. Before a number of the citizens and soldiery Bernard placed his hands upon him, and immediately he walked without difficulty, and, to the astonishment of all, followed on foot the vehicle in which he had just before been carried."

Next year, in France, the same marvels were wrought wherever Bernard passed. I venture to quote the narrative by an eye-witness of one among the most striking of these miracles :—

" At Toulouse, in the church of St. Saturninus, was a certain regular canon named John. John had kept his bed for seven months, and was so reduced that his death was expected daily. His legs were so shrunken that they were scarcely larger than a child's arms. He was quite unable to rise to satisfy the wants of nature. At last his brother canons refused to tolerate his presence any longer among them, and thrust him out into the neighbouring village. When the poor creature heard of Bernard's proximity he implored to be taken to him. Six men, therefore, carrying him as he lay in bed, brought him into a room close to that in which we were lodged. . . . . Bernard mentally prayed to God, ' Behold, O Lord, they seek for a sign, and our words avail nothing unless they be confirmed with signs following.' He then blessed him and left the chamber, and so did we all. In that very hour the sick man arose from his couch, and running after Bernard, kissed his feet with a devotion which cannot be imagined by any one who did not see it. One of the canons meeting him nearly fainted with fright, thinking he had seen a spectre. John and his brethren then retired to the church, and in a Te Deum gave praise to God."

I might describe many other marvellous cures which Bernard performed, but the above notable and strongly attested instances are sufficient. They will carry conviction of his spiritual gifts to any unprejudiced mind. Of later events of the kind the cure of Mademoiselle Perrier, niece to the celebrated Pascal, is a marvellous and invulnerably well-attested case. The miracles also, wrought in 1731, and subsequent years, at the tomb of the Abbé Paris, are equally well-attested, and still more marvellous. The first of these wonders occurred in 1656. Mademoiselle Perrier was, at the time, between ten and eleven years old. Since the age of three years and a half, her left eye had been consumed by a lachrymal fistula, the malignant humour of which had decayed the bone of the nose and that of the palate. So offensive was the disease, that the nuns of Port Royal, in which famous institution she had become a boarder, were forced to keep her strictly apart from the rest of their young charges. As a forlorn hope it was determined to try the actual cautery, and for this purpose the girl's father came, accompanied by a surgeon, to Port Royal. But, immediately before the time fixed for the operation, the nuns were inspired to touch the eye of the sufferer with a thorn, held in high veneration as a professed relic from the crown of Christ. To the awe and amazement of all present the decayed bones became instantly firm and sound, the effusion of humour ceased, and all trace of disease vanished in an instant. The father beheld the miracle, and wept for joy. The surgeon who had come to operate upon this apparently hopeless case, scarcely dared trust his sight. Eleven other surgeons and physicians of eminence afterwards examined Mademoiselle Perrier, and confessed, without exception, the miraculous nature of her cure. The court, though it bore to Port Royal a deadly hate, and had ordered the destruction of that seminary of Jansenism, was compelled also to admit the authenticity of the marvel. A mass in music was instituted by the parents of the young girl, to be celebrated for ever in the Cathedral of Clermont, on March 24th of each year, the anniversary of their daughter's instantaneous recovery. A picture of the event was placed in the church of Port Royal. Racine drew up a narrative of the case, which Pascal, Arnauld, and Felix attested. The Archbishop of Paris, and the doctors of the Sorbonne, investigated with the severest scrutiny of malice the whole of the circumstances, and were forced, in their sentence of October 22nd, 1656, to admit that "this cure was supernatural, and a miracle of the omnipotence of God." Benedict XIII. forever consecrated the case in Catholic eyes by quoting it in his printed Homilies as one of many proofs that miracles had not ceased. Finally, during the twenty-five years which Mademoiselle Perrier lived after being thus suddenly healed, the malady showed no signs of return.

A volume would be required to treat in detail of the miracles wrought at the grave of the Abbé Paris. Douglas, Bishop of Salisbury, employed great part of a dull work in simply seeking to weaken the credit attached to them. Destitute of facts to support his theory—that the cures were in some instances performed by ordinary means, in others merely pretended to be performed—he strove, by suppressing various authentic narratives, and mis-stating the remainder, to show how dishonest a sceptic a Christian divine may be. He employed against these particular miracles the very arguments which David Hume had previously employed against all miracles : strange weapons for a Churchman to use! The two chief axioms of his work are : 1. That we must suspect as false asserted miracles which are not published at the time when, and in the place where, they are said to have occurred. 2. That we must suspect them to be false if in the time when, and at the place where, they are said to have occurred, they might be supposed to pass without examination. Were the authority of these rules conceded they have yet absolutely no bearing on the cases the Bishop designs to attack. The miracles at the tomb of the Abbé Paris took place chiefly in 1731, and the three or four years next in sequence. They were published at the time when and in the place where they happened. The Abbé had been a Jansenist. Far therefore from allowing them to pass without examination, the mis-named Order of Jesus, with whose tyranny France was still cursed, strove by every means, allowable or iniquitous, to cover these alleged miracles with disgrace, and their upholders with confusion. Yet the solemn truth of the facts resisted the utmost efforts of calumny. If Douglas succeeded in making them doubted in England, it was by shameless perversion and suppression of testimony. The most unscrupulous of Jesuit casuists might have been proud to own the Bishop's work : the least candid of Protestant divines should have blushed to write it. It is sufficient, in the judgment of all who know the facts, to pillory the author on " infamy's high stage " forever.

Carré de Montgeron was a dissipated courtier of the " siècle de Louis Quinze." His father had been Master of Requests under Louis XIV.; his mother was a daughter of Field-Marshal Diery. Wealthy and idle, M. de Montgeron plunged headlong into all the sensuality of the court. His conscience was the sole thing which troubled him, and this he stifled by educating himself into a determined Deist. He became a *conseiller au Parlement* whilst the final life and death struggle of the long war between the Jesuits and [the Jansenists was raging. The Jansenists had right with them, but might was on the side of the Order of Jesus. Port Royal fell, and the supporters of the bad cause rejoiced. That cause had, however, received deadly wounds in the conflict, and after languishing long, succumbed to the first attack of a new foe. It does not appear that M. de Montgeron took more than a languid interest in the struggle and its issue; but he drew from it the inference that the doctrines which the Jesuits and their supporter, Pope Clement XI., condemned as heretical, were among the chief foundations of the Christian religion. Thus he became convinced that the professedly orthodox thought secretly as he did himself, and that religion was only a cloak with which hypocrites covered vice. He went on confirmed in his own immorality and infidelity until the year 1731. In that year he heard, like all Parisians, of the miracles performing at the tomb of the Abbé Paris, in the cemetery of St. Medard. At first he ridiculed them, then the mass of evidence advanced in favour of their reality troubled him with a fear lest, after all, the teachings of the Christian faith were true. He determined to visit the scene of these alleged wonders, and by calling to his aid the chief medical men of Paris, unmask completely the imposture, if an imposture were being practised. He first went to the churchyard alone. The extraordinary scenes which greeted him, the multitude of afflicted, and the fervour of their prayers, touched his heart for the first time in many years with a sentiment of religious awe. Perplexed, he fell on his knees by the edge of the tomb, and petitioned that, if there were indeed an immortality for man, light from that future world might shine in upon the darkness of his mind. Immediately, he tells us, reasons for crediting the teachings of Christ poured upon him in vivid succession with a force he had never felt before. He rose a changed man. For four hours had he remained kneeling beside the tomb, heedless of the pressure of the crowds around. Day after day, he now returned to the churchyard, and investigated the miracles there wrought. By this time all Paris was stirred with these events. The Jesuits, maddened that such works should be wrought at the tomb of a Jansenist, had recourse to the civil power. All avenues of access to the tomb were ordered to be closed. It was then, says Voltaire, that some wit inscribed on the churchyard wall :—

> " De par le Roi,—défense à Dieu
> De faire miracles en ce lieu."

The remark of the great infidel that God obeyed is contradicted by the fact that miracles still continued to be performed for a space of at least twenty years.

Meanwhile M. de Montgeron had selected from above a hundred well-authenticated cases nine in which the injuries or diseases had been of so terrible a character that the physicians had adjudged a cure hopeless, and in which the cure by means of prayer at the tomb had been widely published, and put past doubt by medical and other evidences. He sought with indefatigable industry all the attestations available on the subject. He procured the testimony of the miraculously healed sufferers themselves, of their friends, of their enemies, of celebrated physicians and surgeons, of magistrates, notaries, courtiers and priests. The whole he published in a quarto volume] dedicated to the King. He personally presented a copy of the work. It was received with apparent favour, but the same night M. de Montgeron was rewarded for his fearless advocacy of the cause of truth with a lodging in the Bastile.

I shall now attempt to give in a brief compass the history of seven of these nine cases. The first on our author's list is that of Dom Alphonse de Palacios, a young nobleman of Spain, son of Dom Joseph de Palacios, councillor of state to the Spanish King. He was in Paris to seek relief for his right eye. His left had been destroyed six years before by a fluxion succeeded by inflammation. The right had been since injured by a blow, and another cause had now made its state apparently hopeless. This was the withering up of the optic nerve of the lost eye. The nerve of the remaining eye, being in conection with it, began to wither also. Sight by rapid degrees disappeared. The famous oculist, Gendron, examined the right eye, and pronounced recovery not to be hoped for; the sufferer must submit to total blindness for the rest of his days. At this stage, according to the narrative penned by Dom Alphonse himself, the eye more resembled a crushed mulberry than an eye; a ray of light falling on it caused intolerable pain; the unhappy youth was driven to sit in darkened rooms with his eye carefully bandaged. For seven days before the miracle he was without sight.

He heard of the marvellous cures wrought in the cemetery of Saint Medard, and besought to be taken there. The fear of bringing down on his family the wrath of the Pope and the Inquisition caused his attendants and his tutor, the celebrated Rollin, to hesitate. At length his agony and unceasing prayers wrung forth a consent. He was carried to the Abbé's tomb. The journey was not made in vain. On the instant the sight of the right eye returned, and he could cast away his bandage and in full daylight give thanks to God. He went two days after to the great oculist whose fiat had doomed him to a life of darkness. On seeing his late patient Gendron desired in amazement to know what had happened. The story was told, and the surgeon declared that no man on earth could have restored Dom Palacios to sight, and that a startling miracle had been accomplished. A full statement of the facts was drawn up, and deposited with the notary public. At once the clergy began to persecute all concerned. Dom Palacios returned to Spain, and the terrors of the Inquisition were let loose on him. It was at one time asserted by the Archbishop of Paris that he had signed a statement denying the miracle. Inquiry being made, the highest Church dignitary in France appeared to have deliberately lied. To the last, in spite of menaces, imprisonment, and the ruin of his worldly prospects, the grateful young nobleman continued to avow that he had been cured by the hand of God, and that his recovery of sight was in no way owing to the skill of man. Numerous witnesses supported him. Gendron, the oculist, Rollin, Rector of the University of Paris, Sir Edward Aston, the celebrated surgeons Demanteville and Souchay, Linguet, a physician who had attended the young Spaniard, and his relation M. Linguet of the College of Navarre, publicly attested the veracity of Dom Alphonse's statements, and made depositions as to their knowledge of the case before and after the cure. Priestly power, though used with more than priestly intolerance, was as a reed against the truth.

The sixth of M. de Montgeron's cases is also one of blindness. Pierre Gaultier was a saddler's apprentice in a village of Languedoc. The small-pox had left scars on the pupil of his left eye which weakened its power of vision. Whilst busied one day with a knot in some harness, it yielded unexpectedly, and an awl which he held was plunged into the other eye. It pierced even to the retina, and left him with no vision but that of the defective eye which disease had injured. The surgeons could do nothing. By the advice of his confessor Gaultier journeyed to Paris, and visited the famous tomb. He returned with the sight of that eye which the awl had blinded perfectly restored. The two small-pox scars of the left eye still remained.

At once the priesthood was in arms. Famous oculists were consulted, who examined the eyes and declared that had the scars of the other been removed, the miracle would have been past doubt. These scars could not be obliterated by any mortal skill. Again the confessor advised Gaultier to go to Paris, and again he followed the advice. This second journey to the tomb resulted in perfect restoration; the scars totally disappeared. The sight of both eyes was fully regained.

A new method of attack was now adopted by the Jesuits. At the instance of his father, a baker to the army of Italy, the young man had gone to join him. It was reported that the disappearance of the scars was merely pretended, and that the Bishop of Montpellier, a warm defender of the miracle, had caused Gaultier to be hidden from observation lest the truth might become known. The fact was that, on hearing of the cure, the Bishop had made careful investigation, and only when perfectly satisfied of its reality had he attested it in a letter to the Archbishop of Sens. His superior now reproached him with lending himself to an imposture. The accused, a man whose noble character was esteemed throughout the South of France, caused a search to be instituted, and soon had the satisfaction of discovering Gaultier amongst the forty thousand soldiers at the time in Italy. He was brought back, and his sight was demonstrated to be perfect.

The Order of Jesus, though beaten at all points, was not to be put down. The arrest of Gaultier was procured for the crime of being healed by miracle. Once in prison, he was threatened with a dungeon for life. In terror, he consented to sign a statement that he still saw but very imperfectly. The statement was published. All his relations denied its truth. His father proved to the intendant the reality of the miracle, and obtained his son's release. The Jesuits now turned their attention to the confessor who had advised the journey to Paris. He and another priest who affirmed the miracle, were dismissed from their benefices. The plea was, that they had lent themselves to imposture. In grief, their congregations, by whom they were greatly beloved, appealed to the Bishop of Agde. He took up the case, and demonstrating the innocence of the deprived clergymen, procured their restoration. They returned amidst the exultations of their flocks. The Jesuits were now humbled effectually. Gaultier, freed from his dread of their power, publicly recanted the statement fear had wrung from him, and described by what menaces and cruelties the pretended confession had been obtained. .

In the fifth of these cases the Jesuits once more demonstrated the truth of the assertion contained in M. de Montgeron's dedicatory preface, that they had used the most unscrupulous means to suppress the proofs of the miracles. The case was that of a woolcarder named Philippe Sergent. Having become paralyzed in all his limbs, he was admitted to the Hôtel Dieu as incurable. His friends, hearing of the miracles, demanded his discharge from the hospital, and took him in a cart to the Abbé's grave. Instantly recovering the use of his limbs, he sprang on the tombstone unassisted, and sang a Te Deum. After showing himself at the hospital he took a cellar, and recommenced his business. A stranger called on him, and offered a hundred pistoles if he would sign a declaration that he had not been cured. Sergent refused indignantly, and a persecution at once commenced. He was driven from Paris, and settled at Rheims. Still enemies were on his track. After fleeing successively to Dinant, Namur, Mons, and Liege, he returned in despair to Paris. There, finding that the priesthood were circulating lying statements respecting his case, he boldly proceeded to make a public deposition as to the miraculous circumstances of the cure. Besides this testimony the evidence of the doctors who attended him is given by Montgeron.

I have gone at such length into these three instances that I can do little more than allude to the remaining miracles. Two of the sufferers, Mesdemoiselles Thibault and Courronneau, laboured under fearful complications of paralysis and dropsy. Despite that famous physicians had pronounced their disorders incurable, they were wholly healed by visits to the tomb. The case of the eighth patient, Marie Cartin, resembled that of the Mademoiselle Perrier before alluded to; she also was pronounced incurable. Not only, however, was the disease which consumed her face eradicated, but one half of her body, after being paralysed for twelve years, recovered fully its vigour. I shall mention one more miracle; in some respects the most extraordinary of the nine.

Mademoiselle Coirin had been twelve years afflicted with a cancer in the left breast. The affected part was destroyed, and came away in a mass; and the disease had tainted the blood of the whole system. The effluvium was horrible. When medical science had abandoned the case as hopeless, a single visit to the tomb obtained an entire cure. Most wonderful of all, the breast and nipple were perfectly restored, and left free from even the slightest scar. The royal physician, with others of the profession, inquired into the miracle. Their testimony was decisive. They admitted that they had known the case, and had pronounced it incurable by any merely earthly skill. It was now cured, and the cure was perfect. No human hand had accomplished the marvel— it was to be ascribed to the hand of God. "The restoration of a nipple absolutely destroyed, and separated from the breast," said

M. Goulard, the King's physician, "is an actual *creation;* for a nipple is not merely a continuity of the vessels of the breast, but a particular body, which is of a distinct and peculiar organization."

I may here take my leave of the Abbé Paris. If the wonders wrought at his tomb are to be rejected, there is an end of all the miraculous healing in history. No such evidence supports the miracles of Scripture. In favour of the reality of these cures, we have the attestations of the sufferers themselves, the depositions unwillingly wrung from some doctors and frankly granted by others, the reluctant testimony of the clergy and the court. Against all these are set only the unscrupulous fabrications of Jesuit malice—the calumnies of an order which yet more than that of Dominic has disgraced the Catholic Church. It is on such testimony as the last that the dishonest Bishop of Salisbury would persuade us the assertors of these miracles were yet more dishonest than himself. *Credat Judæus!*

The "Lives of the Saints" are one and all ridiculed by Protestant minds. The Pharisee of England or Prussia looks with pitying contempt on the devotee who believes that St. Martin restored the dead to life, and that St. Gregory turned a lake into dry land by his prayers. It is not my business to take up the cudgels on behalf of a Church so well able to defend itself as that of Rome. I shall content myself with quoting from the work of Mr. Howitt a few of the more remarkable miracles attributed to her saints.

St. Francis Xavier raised various people from the dead. St. Winifreda healed numbers of diseases at her miraculous well. St. Gregory stayed a flood by striking his staff into the ground, which staff thereon took root and became a tree. St. Martin, like the poet Horace, was miraculously protected from the falling of a tree. Such protection, as described in the first volume of my "Incidents," I have myself been favoured with. St. Charles Borromeo was fired at whilst performing mass, but the bullet merely struck upon his rochet, and fell harmless to the ground. Dominic, the evil enthusiast who founded the Inquisition, is asserted to have by prayer restored a nobleman to life. One would think that if the prayers of such a nature were heard, it could only be by spirits equally dark. St. Hyacinth crossed the Vistula, when because of a flood no boat dared venture, by walking on the surface of the waves. St. Francis of Assissium bore in his hands, feet, and side the five wounds of Christ.

The last phenomenon has occurred in all ages of the Church, and never more strikingly than at the present day. I need only refer to Louise Lateau, the Belgian stigmatist, to mention a case which has baffled medical science. Equally celebrated in their own times were such stigmatists as Saints Catherine, Hildegarde, Brigitta of Sweden, and Pasithea. More recent cases are those of Catherine Emmerich, Maria von Morl, and Dominica Lazari. Catherine bore the mark of the crown of thorns, and was besides clairvoyant. Her attendant physician published a description of the case in the year 1815. Maria had the stigmata. Dominica also bore them, and more prominently. Her marks, says Ennemoser, bled on the Friday of every week.

It is natural that I should be deeply interested in a 'particular manifestation, of which abundant instances are given in the lives of Catholic saints. I refer to the being raised from the ground by spirit-power, and held, without any physical support, floating in the air. Such a phenomenon is denied and derided in our own days by persons who have had no opportunity for observation of the facts, but whose illimitable conceit prompts them to imagine that all things in heaven and earth are known to their philosophy. The most convincing evidence is dismissed as worthless. The most unimpeachable witnesses are reviled as not to be trusted. A few sneers, and the usual parrot jargon regarding " the violation of known physical laws," end the matter, and the reviewer retires amidst the plaudits of his brethren. Yet such violations of physical laws are reported as having occurred since the age of Enoch, and may have occurred for unknown thousands of years before. As I have said, they were frequent amongst those on whom the canonical honours of Rome were conferred. St. Theresa was many times the subject of such experiences. She relates that frequently during her devotions an unseen power raised her, and held her suspended above the ground. A bishop, a Dominican, and the sisterhood of her convent attest as witnesses her rising in the air. In the year 1036, Richard, Abbot of St. Vanne de Verdun "appeared elevated from the ground as he was saying mass in presence of Duke Galizon and his sons, and a great number of his lords and soldiers. Savonarola, of whom I shall have occasion to speak in the following chapter, was beheld, a short time before his martyrdom, to rise slowly from the ground, and "remain suspended at a considerable height from the floor of his dungeon, absorbed in devotion." Mr. Madden in his life of this great man, most truly observes, "To any one conversant with the lives of the saints it will be well known that similar phenomena are recorded in numerous instances, and that the evidence on which some of them rest is as reliable as any human testimony can be." In the case of Savonarola, the evidence, as Elihu Rich points out, is peculiarly authentic. Those who recorded the phenomenon were the very men who condemned him to the flames. Was it probable that they would seek by a circumstantial lie to glorify the object of their hate ?

Calmet tells us that he "knew a good monk who rose sometimes from the ground, and remained suspended without wishing or seeking it, on seeing some devotional image, or hearing some devout prayer, such as ' Gloria in excelsis Deo.' " Also he claims to have been acquainted with a nun " to whom it has happened in spite of herself to be thus raised up in the air to a certain distance from the earth ;—it was neither from choice nor from any wish to distinguish herself, for truly she was confounded at it." The same thing happened in the cases of St. Philip Neri, St. Catherine Colembina, and St. Ignatius Loyola, which last was "raised up from the ground to the height of two feet, while his body shone like light." It may be remarked that this luminosity of the human form—a not uncommon manifestation of modern spiritualism—has also been noticed from extremely ancient times. Iamblichus rose frequently to the height of ten feet from the earth, and his body and dress on such occasions assumed the colour of gold. But the most striking narratives of the kind are to be found in Scripture. I need cite but few other instances of ecclesiastical levitations. St. Dunstan, a little before his death, was observed in the presence of several persons to rise from the ground, and, whilst all who witnessed the phenomenon were yet astonished at it, he spoke, and predicted his approaching end. St. Albert of Sicily, during prayer, was elevated to a height of three cubits. St. Cajetanus, St. Bernard Ptolomei, and St. Philip Benitas were also seen frequently thus to rise from the earth. To end with two cases not clerical and somewhat nearer to our own time, the celebrated Anna Maria Fleischer was beheld during the period of the Thirty Years War in Germany to be frequently lifted by invisible means " to the height of nine ells and a half, so that it appeared as if she would have flown through the windows." In days still more modern similar phenomena were reported of the Seeress of Prevorst.

It cannot be said that the whole, or even the half of the miracles claimed by the Catholic Church, are worthy the faith of reasoning men. He who puts credence in all she asserts to have occurred is equally foolish with the man who believes that all calling themselves mediums in our own times have spiritual gifts. But he who disbelieves that any "signs and wonders" can ever have come out of Rome is the very one who will denounce the spiritualism of the present day as nothing more than a gigantic imposture, and will, sometimes openly, but more often in secret, hold all miracle impossible, and look upon every record of spiritual phenomena, whether contained in Scripture or elsewhere, as untrue. To such natures historical evidence is nothing, and less than nothing. Sceptics so pronounced may indeed be at times converted to a belief in the truth by wonders occurring in their own presence; but they are far more difficult than Thomas to convince. The absurd inference drawn in the present day is, that such men should be shunned by every good spiritualist, and zealously excluded from all séances; because they are ever on the watch for trickery in the medium, and when successful in discovering such trickery immediately set up a shout of triumph, and call the attention of the general public to the imposture they have unmasked. Would not the better course for spiritualists be to set

their faces as one man against fraudulent mediums, and to send after
the "reveries of Jacob Behmen" and the gospel according to Joe
Smith those wretched "explanations" of the simulation of spiritual
phenomena which just now it is sought to make pass current as
articles of faith ?   But for the discussion of such matters the concluding portion of this work will be more in place.

I shall pass now to the darkest phase of Catholic spiritualism—
dark in the sense of its having left the deepest stain on the Roman
Church.   In ending this chapter of less tragical occurrences a most
remarkable prophecy, delivered and fulfilled a little above a century
ago, deserves to be given.   It is recorded, says Mr. Howitt, by the
Abbé Proyaid, in his "Louis XVI. détroné avant d'être Roi," and
was confirmed by an inquiry which Cardinal Maury caused to be
set on foot in 1804.

Bernardine Renzi, a simple peasant girl of Valentano, predicted
with much confidence, in the year 1774, the approaching death of
Ganganelli, who then filled the chair of St. Peter.   On hearing of
the prophecy his Holiness caused its utterer to be arrested and
cast into prison.   With her was seized the curé of Valentano—
the confessor of the girl.   Neither manifested the slightest surprise or alarm when the arrest took place.   Bernardine quietly
remarked "Braschi will liberate me ; " and the curé informed the
officer who made him prisoner that this seizure had been three
times predicted by the young prophetess.   At the same time he
delivered up some papers in which were set down not only the
prophecy of the Pope's death and the date when it should occur,
but the day of his own arrest, the duration of his imprisonment,
and the date when he should be released.   The day fixed as Ganganelli's last on earth was September 22nd, 1774 ; but this
approached, and still the Pope felt no sickness.   At ten o'clock on
the morning of the 22nd of September, however, Bernardine
accosted the superior of the convent of Montefiascone, in which she
had been placed as a prisoner, with the words, "You may order
your community to offer up prayers for the Holy Father.   He is
dead." By the first courier came a confirmation of these startling
tidings.   The Pope had died suddenly at eight in the morning,

that is to say, some two hours before the girl's intimation of her prophecy having been fulfilled ¸was delivered. And the accomplishment of her second prediction was, if possible, still worthier of notice. Cardinal Braschi, although none, when the conclave met, had dreamed of making him pontiff, was found when it parted to have been elected to the vacant seat. Yet his success seemed to hold out no hope of Bernardine's liberation. Angered by the pasquinades circulated on his owing the tiara to the influence of a village girl, Braschi determined to render her second prophecy a lying one, and prove that she would not be freed through him. He appointed as her judges men on whom he thought he could rely, and instructed them to condemn her. The case was tried, and still Bernardine triumphed. So manifest had been the fulfilment of her prediction regarding Ganganelli that even partisanship could do nothing. The girl and the confessor were both acquitted, as innocent of any evil design. Thus the second prophecy was as accurately accomplished as the first, and Braschi and his tools were driven to console themselves by pronouncing that Bernardine had been under the influence of a fiend.

CHAPTER IV.

To that convenient accusation of working miracles by the help of
demons, we owe the blackest crimes which disgrace the annals
of the Church of Rome. It was a weapon misused alike by the
just and the unjust; mighty for evil, but impotent for good.
Was it desired to ruin a man on whom the stigma of heresy could
not be fastened? Then the charge of sorcery speedily sent him
to the stake. Did a sudden outbreak of spiritual manifestations
excite the inhabitants of any particular region? As the occurrences
were useful or injurious to the temporal power of the Church, so
did that Church act. If the phenomena could be made subservient
to her purposes, she canonised the mediums as saints: if they
appeared to militate against those purposes, she burnt the mediums
as wizards. Nay, so entirely was her recognition of the spiritual
governed by worldly policy, that the same man might be at one
time extolled as inspired by the angels of God, and a little later
denounced as in league with the powers of darkness. The Papacy,
as I have shown, had recognised that miracle is a mighty weapon
for the advancement of a faith. When she found a servant of the
spirits who was also content to be her slave, she, to borrow a
metaphor from the language of Scripture, clothed him with a robe
of pride, and set him in a high place, proclaiming that thus should
it be done to the man whom the Church delighted to honour. So
that he faithfully devoted his medial powers to the advancement
of the Catholic religion, it mattered not what his character in
other respects might be. [An arch-fiend of cruelty such as
Dominic, and a nature gentle as St. Bernard's, a pure creature

like St. Catherine, and a brutal wretch like Francis, were equally prized. Their names were glorified during life, and all but worshipped after death. The magnificent sepulchres that enshrined their bones witnessed daily the prayers of the faithful. But was the man who formed the link between this and the future world a high-minded and free-spirited being, disposed to become neither the serf of spirits nor of men; taking from the Catholic religion only what was good, and making manful war on the innumerable abuses which defaced it,—such a one as Savonarola in short? Then the Vatican let loose on him its terrors. He might perhaps be barely tolerated, while his line of conduct did not diverge too widely from the line of policy marked out by the Church; but on the instant that he raised his voice against her wrong-doing there were made ready for him the faggots and the stake. Another victim was added to the long list in which are enrolled such names as Savonarola and Jeanne D'Arc; and Rome took hypocritical credit to herself for having punished one more servant of the devil. Doubtless, among the millions of unhappy beings destroyed as wizards and witches, there were numbers really under the influence of evil spirits. Nothing else can explain the frantic outbreaks which so often dismayed Europe during the Middle Ages. Our fathers, having greater faith than ourselves as regards spiritual things, were both better qualified to judge of the phenomena and more ready to admit their reality. Their eyes were not carefully closed against light from another world, but anxiously strained to perceive its faintest gleams. They often, however, committed the deadly error of mistaking the origin of that light, and such mistakes were made excuses for the most frantic cruelty and intolerance. The great criminal was the Catholic Church, though as I shall have occasion to point out in a future chapter Protestant Churches also deeply burdened themselves with the crime of murder. But it is against Rome chiefly that the blood shed during the Dark Ages in torrents throughout Europe cries out for vengeance. She denounced all spiritualism outside her own pale as magic, and its adherents as workers of wonders by means of the power of Satan. Yet she had a kind of magic of her own, and that same " Satan " was the word with which she conjured.   It was laid aside or brought into play, as circumstances commanded.   A miracle which benefited the Church was ascribed to God.   A miracle which embarrassed or injured the Church was laid to the account of the Prince of Evil.   But this was not the worst: we may detest the cruelty which is founded in bigotry and misplaced zeal ; but a far deeper detestation should be reserved for the cruelty which is the effect of cold worldliness and calculating hypocrisy.   Such was, in perhaps the majority of instances, the cruelty of the Church of Rome.   She lighted her pyres and launched her anathemas, not because she really believed burning the bodies of men to be for the advantage of their souls, but because she considered persecution a necessary means of preserving her temporal power.   Her two battle-cries were " Heresy " and " Sorcery," and whenever the first failed the second was unsparingly used.

Of the demoniac fury with which the Church of Rome formerly persecuted heretics much has been written.   The eloquence of Protestant authors of all sects and every age has been employed in painting such martyrdoms as those of Huss, Oldcastle, Anne Askew, and Coligni ; in describing how Torquemada ruled over Spain like a subordinate fiend commissioned by the Prince of Darkness to make that fair country hideous in the sight of God and man; and how the burning of Latimer and Ridley lighted a flame in England which has never been put out.   Such diatribes are praiseworthy : the effects of a revolt of the best principles contained in human nature against inhuman cruelty.   It is not, in truth, easy to be too vehement in attacking the Catholic treatment of heretics.   That treatment was, over and over again, such as Nero would have shuddered at.   But of the yet more frightful scenes enacted under the pretence of punishing sorcery strangely little has been said.   This indifference is puzzling, in view of the history of the past.   It is scarcely too much to assert that the persecutions for witchcraft were to the persecutions for heresy as the Catholic Hell to the Catholic Purgatory—as a whip of scorpions to a whip of cords.   Nine millions of persons are computed to

have been burned, hanged, or drowned for sorcery under the
auspices of the various Churches of Christ. Protestantism is
responsible for some hundreds of thousands of these deaths, but
immeasurably the greater number of the victims were victims of
Rome. In every country of Europe witchcraft was of old the
charge which committed the hugest number of sufferers to the
hands of the executioner. To quote a few lines from Leckey's
chapter on the subject in his " History of Rationalism," " Seven
thousand victims are said to have been burnt at Treves. Decrees
were passed on the subject by the parliaments of Paris, Toulouse,
Bordeaux, Rheims, Rouen, Dijon, and Rennes, and they were all
followed by a harvest of blood. The executions which took place
in Paris were, in the emphatic words of an old writer, 'almost
infinite.' In Italy a thousand persons were executed in a single
year in the province of Como, and in other parts of the country,
the severity of the inquisitors at last created an absolute rebellion." Multiply the instances similar to these almost to infinity,
and, taking into consideration the hundreds of years for which the
devilish work went on, that total of nine millions, which I have
quoted from a German authority on the subject, will no longer
appear difficult of credence.

It is worthy of remark that the years in which persecution for
witchcraft raged most wildly were years in which Europe was
distracted by great calamities. During the period of the Black
Death the excesses wrought in Christendom were beyond anything
heathen history contains. A single instance will suffice :—at one
of the French towns—Chinon, if I remember aright—the populace
rose on their usual victims, the Jews, and accused them of having
caused the pestilence by magic spells. It is not to be supposed
that, in proportion to their numbers, the Jews suffered less from
the Black Death than the Christians ; but popular fury knows
nothing of logic. The whole of the doomed race within reach, to
the number of two hundred, were seized. A vast trench was dug.
In this trench straw, fagots, and other combustibles were heaped ;
fire was put to the mass, and the captives bound and brought
close. Then, when the flames were at their fiercest, the unfor-

tunates were raised one by one and cast upon the pyre. Infants and old men, mothers, husbands, and children, young men and maidens, perished together. The eloquence of Cicero could add nothing to the horrors of the bare description. " I command ye," said Christ, " that ye love one another." Thus did certain, defiling the name of Christian, execute that command.

Some may object that the persecutions for sorcery were the outcome of an unenlightened age, and that the Church, unable to arrest the movement, was forced to be content with directing it. But all history testifies that the fury of the popular mind against witchcraft was the sequence, and the inevitable sequence, of certain teachings which the Papacy had adopted and exaggerated from that Levitical law Christ came to supersede, and of other laws which she had invented for herself. " Thou shalt not suffer a witch to live," commanded Moses. " All workers of spiritual signs and wonders, save those stamped with my approbation, are wizards and witches," was the decree of Rome. She promulgated the two teachings, as requiring the obedience of all who owned her supremacy, and horrors such as earth had never before witnessed were the result.

The learning of Europe was, until the invention of printing, almost wholly confined to the cloister. The ecclesiastical power represented the brain, and the civil the arm which that brain moves. To the priesthood men of the law and men of the sword were alike subservient. Rome, therefore, had at her command the two powers which move the world, and which, in almost all ages of the world, have been found at war—brute and intellectual force. Ahriman and Ormuzd had for a space ceased their battles, and were united in common subjection to a mighty mistress. Until the printing-press of Guttenburg overturned this condition of things the Papacy was, for good or evil, omnipotent. It will scarcely be denied that, as regarded intercourse with the world of spirits, she perverted her limitless power steadily to evil. Her pontiffs and priests were, in unnumbered instances, the most detestable of mankind—creatures whom every possible crime had polluted. Their lives are inconceivable on the supposition that they put the least credence in the Scriptures committed to their charge. Heaven, Hell, and Purgatory were to them the various parts of a cunningly devised fable, invented for the purpose of bringing money into the coffers of the Church. In Satan and his subordinate fiends they put not the slightest faith; they knew that Christ nowhere expressly inculcates the dogma of a personal devil. They were aware that the devil, such as the multitude believed him to be, was a gigantic shadow, manufactured to suit the purposes of Rome. The Prince of Darkness then, if they did not exactly, like one of Shakspeare's characters, pronounce him a gentleman, was in their eyes a useful though a rather ugly puppet, who could be made available for a variety of evil purposes. They wondered at the fear the multitude had of the figure, and jested much over that fear among themselves; but they did not hesitate to turn the awe of the vulgar to account, and in a way that has blackened their names everlastingly. Under cover of a charge of sorcery they wreaked private grudges without number. If they believed anything, it was that the making a compact with Satan was as impossible as the making a compact with the forms one sees in a dream. Yet for this impossible crime they consigned millions to the executioner. Did space permit my passing from the general to the particular, I could show, by hundreds of examples, that the Catholic law condemning sorcerers to the flames was but an engine by which the priesthood defended their temporal power from attack, stayed the reform of vile abuses and the march of intellect, and satisfied their malice on those they hated. A genius surpassing that of ordinary men had perfected some great invention which the Church thought it to its interest to suppress. "A compact with the devil" explained the matter, and inventor and invention perished in the same fire. A reformer had arisen who witnessed with indignation the evil lives of the clergy, and sought to end such scandals. His own pure life had, perhaps, brought him into a fit state for communion with the better dwellers in the spirit world. At once the Church seized on him as a wizard, and his projected reforms ended at the stake. A prelate desired pretext

for robbing some wealthy layman of his property or his life—
perhaps of both; what easier to contrive than a charge of
sorcery? A priest had in vain endeavoured to lead astray some
fair member of his flock; what more thorough revenge could
disappointed lust imagine than to procure her punishment as a
witch? Such infamies are not dreams. They were the every-day
facts of existence three or four centuries ago. Mixed with them
were other causes predisposing to the waste of life. There were
the ignorant passions of the multitude, there was the furious
bigotry of those who sincerely believed witchcraft a possible
crime. There were continual outbreaks of strange and hideous
phenomena, such as only the most degraded spirits, working
through congenial media, could have produced—phenomena sufficient to fill even the most liberal of men with horror and disgust.
By means of these instruments the more astute and unimpas-
sioned persecutors worked. They dragged the worst phases of
spiritualism conspicuously into the light, and in this and other
ways stimulated popular fury to a more ungovernable pitch.
They encouraged their brethren who persecuted from zeal, and
pretended a similar zeal, if they had it not. Europe was filled
with bloodshed, from Lisbon to the confines of Muscovy, and the
authors of this bloodshed contemplated their work with satisfied
complacency, as a masterpiece of polity. By means of stake and
halter they had tamed the spiritual. Lawful miracle was to be
found only within the bounds of the Church, and under such conditions ranked among the mightiest of her weapons. Outside the
Roman pale all miracle was illegal. Intercourse with the spirit-
world, which, properly directed, would have speedily delivered the
human mind from the thraldom of Papal error, was classed as of
the works of the devil. Industriously drilled by the priesthood
to that belief, the idea of a suppositious supervision constantly
exercised by a suppositious Satan over mundane affairs became
at last a chief article in the creed of the vulgar. To the Prince
of Evil every event in the least uncommon was ascribed. If a
Roger Bacon discovered gunpowder, or an old woman hit upon a
method of butter-making superior to that practised by her

neighbours, if a Guttenberg invented the art of printing, or a cow produced a five-legged calf, Bacon and the old dame, Guttenburg and the cow, were equally denounced as emissaries of hell. Nay, the faith in miracles from Satan would appear to have been stronger than the faith in miracles from God. The Protestant separatists rejected Rome's teaching of the continuance of celestial signs and wonders, but belief in infernal marvels was too ingrained to be destroyed. Ministering angels were repudiated by Luther and Knox, but tempting demons were solemnly recognised, and their supposed servants on earth persecuted with a fury born of antipathy and unreasoning fear. In a certain company where Luther was present, the talk fell on witches spoiling eggs. "I would have no compassion on these witches," remarked the great reformer, "I would burn all of them. Yet he was one of the most enlightened Protestants of his day. The first winnowing-machine introduced into Scotland was denounced from many pulpits as a demoniac invention which brought with it literally "blasts from hell." One reverend Calvinist refused the communion to all who had accepted this gift of the devil to man. And the folly of rushing to Satan for an explanation of anything unusual or miraculous, which folly it was the policy of Rome to inspire and foster, still continues. In what a number of ridiculous sermons, Protestant and Catholic, have the spiritual phenomena of the present day been attributed to the direct agency of the fallen Son of the Morning and his myrmidons! The notion that all media not clerical have given themselves over to Beelzebub is evidently still strong among peasants and priests —that is to say, with the two most unenlightened classes of mankind.

A famous tale of horror among the many accounts of trials for witchcraft which history has preserved, is the burning of the noblest virgin of the Middle Ages—Jeanne d'Arc. Joan, an angel of light, was condemned as a fiend of darkness by a mixed tribunal of soldiers and priests : the former inspired to their cruelty by hatred, the latter by policy. The reproach of England, she is at once the glory and the shame of France. Churchmen of her own

I

country sat among the judges who decided on her murder; the king and the nobles whom she had saved, the army which she had led to victory, stirred not a step to save her. For the chieftains of England and France were equally enraged against the inspired shepherdess. Talbot, Bedford, and Burgundy were wrathful that, before this girl they, the successors to the victor of Agincourt, should have been forced to flee like sheep; Charles and Orleans chafed to think that they had approved themselves more timid soldiers, and less skilful generals, than a simple peasant girl. French and English alike knew, indeed, that she had done these things by a power not her own. They had witnessed her penetrating clairvoyance, they had beheld her every prophecy fulfilled; and when the brief and brilliant mission of the wonderful maid was accomplished; when, after advancing almost to the Mediterranean, the invaders were beaten back to the shores of the English Channel, her foes, having seized her, condemned and slew her, as in league with devils, and her false friends appeared, by their inaction and silence, to acquiesce in the truth of the verdict and the justice of the sentence. Neither party thought of recognising in the deliverance of France the hand of God. The doubtful sort of halo which hung around Joan prevented her recognition as a saint. Instead of wasting her existence in a convent she rode at the head of armies. Instead of the sable garments of a nun, she wore the glittering armour of a knight. She was no tool of the Papacy, but an instrument shaped by Heaven to accomplish the deliverance of her fatherland. It was scarcely possible that a corrupted Church could recognise in her one of the noblest of the daughters of God; and the Church held true to its traditions. At first it denounced her as a servant of the Evil One, and when the sure changes of time had rendered this policy unsound, and English and French were alike busy in "gleaning up into the golden urn of history" the ashes of her whom their forefathers slew, the Church of Rome stood sullenly aloof, and lent neither aid nor countenance to the work. A bishop of that Church had been one of the foremost among the murderers of Joan, and by Romish ecclesiastics the perjuries were sworn, and the indignities and cruelties planned and put in action, of that long agony, worse than death, which preceded the fiery ascent of the Virgin of Domremy to the place prepared for her on high. These churchmen acted after their kind. It would have been strange indeed, when so much of the infamy of persecution was to be obtained, if the priesthood had not contrived to come in for the largest share.

Joan belonged to the village of Domremy, in what is now the department of the Vosges. In early childhood unearthly voices sounded in her ears whilst she tended sheep in the fields. Soon majestic forms, which she believed to be those of St. Margaret and St. Catherine, appeared to her in all the glory of another world. They were sent to prepare the little peasant maiden for her appointed task. During the next few years Joan lived the happiest and most spiritual of lives ; a life that could scarcely be considered of earth. She drank in the lessons of her guides, and gazed with reverent delight on their glorious forms. She was clasped in their arms, and felt the loving kisses and embraces of these sisters gone before. Were they absent from her, she passed the hours in an expectant longing for their presence, and kissed frequently the turf whereon they had appeared to stand. Her every thought was of her guides ; her single prayer to be for ever with them in the land where there are no more tears. "When I saw my saints," said she to the tribunal which murdered her, "I wished to follow them to Paradise."

At length this happy existence ceased. Henceforth her life was to be one of action and endurance, of glory, agony, despair. A voice like a trumpet announced to her one day that the work was ready, and the hour for attempting it at hand. By her means the banner of St. Denis was to advance to victory, and that of St. George to fall from its high estate. She was appointed by Heaven the deliveress of France. Great renown would be hers, but still greater pain. Yet, in the darkest as the brightest hour, ministering spirits would be by her side, and voices, not of earth, would whisper comfort. And the example of the Man of Sorrows must be ever in her mind. As Christ had expired in agony, mocked and insulted by all around, so a martyrdom equally terrible was appointed to be her lot. She would fall into the power of enemies; her body they might destroy, but the spirit no malice could harm. As was her cross, so hereafter would be her crown. She might be tried with agonies such as human nature shudders to conceive, but she should assuredly pass from those agonies to be one of the greatest in the kingdom of heaven.

How she accomplished her mission is written with imperishable characters in the history of the world. The importance of that mission it is difficult to over-estimate. Without Jeanne d'Arc Charles VII. would never have been crowned at Rheims, and the English Henry VI. might have reigned peacefully at Paris. In the conquest of France, England, alike with her victim, would have been ruined. All the miseries which usually attend the conquered would have fallen on the conqueror. The desire of a yet further aggrandisement would have occupied the sovereigns of the unwieldy empire which, at first that of Great Britain and France, must speedily have become that of France and Great Britain. Constantly forced to visit the continent, Henry VI., or some succeeding monarch, would have ended by fixing the seat of government there. His descendants would have become more and more alien from England, and more and more attached to France. The larger country would have been exalted at its neighbour's expense. Another war would have arisen. The English, disgusted with the injuries of their country, and ill-disposed to recognise as its princes men born and bred in a land which the valour of their fathers had conquered, would have sprung to arms. After years of desolation and bloodshed the conflict would have ended, as such conflicts must of necessity end, in the separation of the two realms. England would have been again the England of Henry IV., and, as consolation for a ruined commerce, a depopulated territory, and an empty treasury, would have had the miserable boast that statues of the victor of Agincourt had been erected within the walls of Paris, and that for a space Englishmen had trodden on the necks of their neighbours. The miseries of an unnatural and sickly union between two kingdoms intended to flourish apart from each other, and the still sharper miseries with which the violent dissolution of that union would have been attended, Joan's deeds averted. For this great benefit to the two nations she was rewarded with the stake. England burned her, and France stirred not a finger to avert her death.

. With the various stages of her career every schoolboy is familiar. She made known her mission. Undaunted by threats, unimpressed by ridicule, she pressed her suit for an interview with the Dauphin until that interview was obtained. At a glance she selected him from the crowd of courtiers, amongst whom, in a dress that had about it no indication of his rank, Charles had purposely hidden himself. She proclaimed to him that through her should he be crowned at Rheims, and that by her would the city of Orleans be relieved. She declared to him a secret which he had thought known to himself alone. She spoke of her mission in a tone of lofty faith. . " No one upon this earth, neither king nor duke, nor the daughter of the King of Scots, no one but myself, is appointed to recover this realm of France. Yet I could more willingly remain to spin by the side of my poor mother; for war seems no work for me. But go I must, because the Lord my Master wills it." "And who is the Lord your Master?" "The King of Heaven," Joan replied.

After long and tedious examinations, and after giving various proofs of knowledge more than mortal, the Virgin of Domremy was permitted to clothe herself in armour, to place at her side an ancient sword which spirits had directed her to take from the church where it was preserved, and to depart at the head of a brigade destined for the relief of Orleans. This city, the single stronghold of note which yet held out against the English, was at its last gasp. The besiegers had confidently announced that they would capture it by a certain day. It was the crisis of the fate of France.

. Joan arrived before the walls of Orleans. She succeeded in conveying food to the beleaguered and starving garrison. At the head of a small body of troops she threw herself within the city.

She purified the morals, and revived the fainting courage of the soldiery. By the evidences she gave of her inspiration from another world she gradually roused them to enthusiasm. When their minds were prepared for battle she led them against the invaders. The English were defeated, and forced to raise the siege. In that victory Joan's country was saved.

Until now the men of Agincourt had been considered invincible. When the forces of England and France met, the latter fought half-heartedly and were beaten almost before the battle began. The relief of Orleans dissolved the spell. Before a city which they had disdainfully vowed to take within a certain time, the English had met with sudden and striking disaster; they had suffered defeat at the hands of a foe inferior in strength, and had been driven to raise the siege with ignominy. Thenceforth the tide of fortune ran strongly in favour of France. Among her armies there was no more of the old panic fear. Occasional reverses might cause anxiety, but in the main things went well. Wherever Joan commanded, and her counsels were implicitly followed, England strove in vain. The skill and valour of Talbot and Bedford were turned to foolishness before a country maiden of nineteen. At length all which her guides had commanded her to promise was accomplished. The invaders were beaten back to the provinces of the extreme north. At Rheims, in the old cathedral of Notre Dame, Charles was solemnly crowned king of France, the holy maid standing by his side.

Joan threw herself at the feet of the new-made sovereign, and earnestly implored that she might be allowed to retire. Her mission, she said, was accomplished, and in token of this, the voices by which she had been guided in her career of victory had suddenly become silent. She could no longer be of use, and awful misfortunes threatened her. In violation of the duties of gratitude Charles refused the desired permission to depart. The English were still in France. It was necessary that the holy maid should drive them forth. Sadly and reluctantly, but overpowered by the warmth of her patriotism, Joan suffered herself to become pledged to the attempt. She went forth, knowing that it was to certain death. Her spirit-counsellors had left her, and with them had departed success. The worst speedily came. Deserted by her troops, she was made prisoner, and placed in confinement whilst her captors deliberated as to what should be her fate. Her treatment henceforth until death, has stamped all concerned in it as blots on the human species. Now she was threatened with the rack; now forced to assume male attire, and exposed to the brutal insults of the English and Burgundian men-at-arms. She was one day told that the morrow should see her led to the stake, the next soothed with lying oaths that her life should be spared. At length the fiends around her were weary of their sport. They determined, with one crowning deed of cruelty, to release their victim from the earth, whereon they had caused her to suffer horrors equalling anything in the Inferno of Dante, and in that deed to hold themselves up to the detestation of all posterity. A stake was fixed in the market-place of Rouen. Weeping bitterly, and clasping a crucifix to her breast, the unhappy maiden of nineteen passed to the scene of death. She was chained to the post, and brushwood heaped around her. The captains of England and Burgundy, and certain churchmen of France, looked on with the implacability of a cold and unmanly hate. The pile was kindled, and the flames rose. Speedily the dense smoke hid for ever from sight the form of the noblest martyr of the dark ages; the most unhappy heroine of all time. The last cry heard to issue from Joan's lips was the one word "Jesus." Her ashes were collected, and thrown into the Seine.

The man or woman is little to be envied in whose breast the name of Jeanne d'Arc excites no sentiment of interest or compassion. The author has irremediably blackened his fame who stoops to assail her memory with ribald sneers, and unprincipled distortion of facts. Such a stigma attaches to Voltaire. In a lesser degree it soils even the great name of Shakspeare. The principal fault of the poet of all time was a ready pandering to the passions of the multitude. Where his audience had a strong prejudice respecting an historical character he depicted that character to suit, indifferent whether the portrait were a likeness or a caricature. In the present instance the English detested the memory of Joan as that of a strumpet and a witch; as such Shakspeare drew her. History gives the slander the lie. She was pure in every respect, and the purest of spirits ministered to her. The misdirected genius of even the prince of dramatists cannot sully her fame, far less the ribald calumnies of Voltaire. In everything she approved herself sent of Heaven. She declared that spiritual beings had commissioned her to save Orleans, and cause Charles VII. to be crowned at Rheims. She persisted in her task until the prophecy was fulfilled. She then declared that her guides had departed, warning her to return at once to her quiet village home, if she would avoid a hideous fate. The king overruled her wishes, and victory at once went and death came. Whilst spirits guided her she triumphed over obstacles that according to human calculations were insurmountable. When those counsellors were gone she attempted a less difficult task, and perished. Historians have termed her an enthusiast, and have sought to account by her enthusiasm for her success. An enthusiast she truly was; but there are two species of such natures: the one wonderfully useful to human progress, the other in the highest degree pernicious. There is the noble and unconquerable enthusiasm which is founded on the certainty of inspiration from another world; there is, moreover, the irrational and flighty enthusiasm which is attributable to the unstable fancies of a diseased mind. It is easy to discern that Joan's inspiration was of the former sort. Nothing of her prophecies remained unfulfilled; but the wild vaticinations of madness are not thus accomplished. A simple country girl, she led to battle the armies of France. Herself possessed of not an acre of ground, she gave to Charles VII. a kingdom. At an age when most girls are just beginning to be occupied with affairs of love, she was busied with affairs of state. At an age when such conquerors as Cæsar and Napoleon were yet obscure citizens, she had covered herself with imperishable renown. The angel of the Lord was as visibly with her as when he shone, a pillar of fire, on the night journeys of the astonished Israelites. Not less than Enoch did she walk with

God. Like Moses she led a nation out from the house of bondage, and the translation of Elijah pales before the tragic grandeur of that flaming chariot in which she was whirled away to hear the words, " Well done, good and faithful servant ! " and to receive the diadem of unspeakable brightness promised to all who in the cause of truth endure steadfastly unto the end.

Jerome Savonarola was born at Ferrara in the year 1452. He took orders as a Dominican friar, and became speedily the best and greatest man of that corrupt order. The time when Savonarola commenced his mission was one of those which are the reproaches of history. The priesthood with few exceptions wallowed in a sea of vice. An abnormal monster, having every vice of Belial without his graces, and the cruelty and craft of Lucifer without his courage, had foisted himself into the chair of St. Peter under the title of Alexander VI. His son, Cæsar Borgia, was astounding Italy with his genius and his crimes. Savonarola became " mad for the sight of his eyes which he saw." He stood forward to attempt a reform of discipline and morals. Spiritual counsel was not wanting. He had in great measure the gifts of mediumship, and listened constantly to voices not of earth. At first his design prospered. The citizens of Florence were awed by the eloquence of a man who denounced their sins with the energy of an Ezekiel, or one of the witnesses foretold in the Apocalypse. The most spacious buildings were too small for the crowds that listened with tears and cries of repentance when Savonarola preached. The gay Capua of the Arno seemed rapidly becoming purified from all taint of frivolity and vice. He whose eloquence had wrought these marvels contemplated them with astonishment and joy. The desire of still greater triumphs arose in his mind. He would be to Rome, her prelates and her pontiff, as Jonah had of old been to the princes of Nineveh. He would make of Italy a land pure in the sight of God. Armed with spiritual weapons, surrounded by the heavenly host, he would arrest the progress of those myriads of invaders who were descending from the Alps on the fertile plains and rich cities of Tuscany, Lombardy, and Venetia. The attempt was made. He journeyed to the camp of Charles VIII.,

and rebuked him with the authority of an apostle. He supported
by striking predictions the warnings which he believed himself
commissioned to deliver. The king was so far influenced by
the speedy fulfilment of one of these prophecies as to abandon
his projected siege of Florence, since Savonarola was the master-
mind of that city. But his army, and the companion vultures of
Spain and Switzerland, still retained their grasp on Italy, and still
battled for possession of the prey on which they had pounced.
Disappointed in his patriotic hopes, Savonarola turned more
ardently than ever to his religious projects. He denounced the
Pope, and called on all true servants of Christ to join in hurling
him from the throne which he disgraced. He lashed with vehement
eloquence the vices of the priests. A storm arose such as at a
later day broke upon the head of Luther. Like Luther, Savonarola
faced it with the most dauntless fortitude. With two of his chief
disciples he was seized and imprisoned. It was impossible that
against so devout a Catholic a charge of heresy could be sustained.
The Church had recourse, therefore, to its other and yet more
terrible weapon. There was ample proof that Savonarola held
intercourse with the dwellers in another world. He had uttered
prophecies and they had been fulfilled. He had a miraculous
power of reading the thoughts of men. In his dungeon he had
been seen to rise slowly from the ground, and remain without any
support suspended in the air. Evidence not a hundredth part as
strong had procured the deaths of countless thousands. Savonarola was condemned as a sorcerer, and in company with his two
adherents died at the stake.

The one other martyrdom I think it necessary to quote is that
of Urban Grandier. In the career of Joan of Arc we behold
illustrated the apparently inadequate means with which heaven
sometimes accomplishes its mightiest designs; in the fate of
Savonarola the entire success that had attended the efforts of the
Papacy to imbue the mind of Christendom with an unreasoning
belief in the omnipotence of the devil. A monk, learned, pious,
accepting fervently every doctrine of the Catholic Church, blameless
in morals, and powerful throughout the north of Italy, is accused

of being a wizard. The evidence on which he is condemned as a servant of the Evil One exactly resembles that on which Theresa and Loyola were pronounced saints of God. But the Church saw reason for the distinction. Ignatius and Theresa were the submissive tools of the pontiff for the time being : Savonarola attacked his vices. The Papacy decided that manifestations which in the one case were produced by angels, were in the other the work of devils. Reduced to its simplest form, the decree was that, in the matter of spiritual manifestations as in every other, the Catholic Church was infallible, and that when she pronounced white to be black it must be accepted as such. And for centuries all Europe did so accept it !

Grandier's case instances the ease with which, when ecclesiastics high in the Church desired to crush an enemy, a lying accusation of sorcery might be fastened on a man absolutely destitute of medial powers. This victim was, during the reign of Louis XIII., parish priest of Loudun, in the diocese of Poitiers. His success in the pulpit induced the jealousy of other priests, and a conspiracy was formed to ruin him. In Loudun was a convent of Ursuline nuns. These women were instructed to feign themselves possessed by devils, and to charge Grandier with having brought about the possession. The Archbishop of Bordeaux investigated the case, and acquitted the accused of all the charges. He advised him, however, to resign his benefice, and remove from the neighbourhood of his implacable enemies. Grandier obstinately refused. Another plot was formed. Some unknown wit had produced a satire on Richelieu, then the real ruler of France. It was declared that the priest of Loudun was the author. The malicious cardinal resolved on an action worthy any devil of heathen or Christian theology. Grandier was tried once more on the old charge, and, in defiance of all justice, condemned. Nothing in the least approaching evidence was offered. The martyr, after being racked repeatedly, became the victim of that infernal torture of the boot which the last and worst of the evil Stuart dynasty afterwards watched inflicted on the Scottish Covenanters. When bones and flesh had been crushed into a mangled mass, Grandier was carried to the place of execution, and burnt alive. At the instant the pile was lighted he summoned Father Lactance, a chief amongst his murderers, to meet him in a month before the judgment-seat of the Eternal God. Lactance, perfectly well when the summons was delivered, died at the prescribed time. The nuns who had been tutored to act the possessed continued to behave as though inspired by Beelzebub himself. Of the various ecclesiastics concerned in the murder of Grandier, Richelieu alone would appear to have known neither repentance nor remorse. The cardinal's punishment was reserved for the hour when, in another world, he and his victim should again be brought face to face.

These three narratives may be accepted as striking illustrations of the crimes done by Rome under cover of the charge of sorcery. Yet the instances I have given can by no means be put forward as the worst. The blood of millions of other victims cries from the ground against the Papacy. In whatever market-place the symbol of the cross was upreared during the Middle Ages a stake and a gallows appeared on either hand. The number of victims handed over by the priesthood to the secular arm, with a charitable prayer that all possible tenderness might be shown, would about equal the united populations of Scotland and Ireland at the present day. Demons more cruel than Richelieu may have inflicted on many of these doomed ones tortures even surpassing the tortures endured by Grandier. Natures as noble as that of Jeanne d'Arc may have perished and made no sign. We have the history of the persecution as a whole, but of particular agonies we know little. There are indeed hideous records of these ancient horrors scattered through various cities of Europe ; into which records few have the wish or the opportunity to penetrate. Fortunately, the moral of history lies usually on the surface. The lessons to be deduced from what I have described as the Shadow of Catholic Spiritualism are, that the inhumanity of a priesthood surpasses that of other men as the malice of a fiend might be supposed to surpass the malice of an elf, and that never has the Church of Rome known respect for the rights of men or sympathy with their sufferings when the advancement of her power, temporal or spiritual, was to be obtained by increasing those sufferings or disregarding those rights. The Greek Church, more truly Christian, and at least equally rich in spiritual gifts, exercises, and has for centuries exercised, a tolerant and nobler policy.

CHAPTER V.

FEW churches have been more evidently protected of God than that little band of brothers whose sufferings inspired Milton to the cry—

> "Avenge, O Lord! Thy slaughtered saints, whose bones
> Lie bleaching on the Alpine mountains cold!"

The Waldenses were justly designated "The Israel of the Alps." They preserved through centuries their independence and their faith, albeit surrounded on all sides by hostile nations, the weakest of whom had a hundred times their resources. Against the power and the cruelty of France and Savoy they bore up unyieldingly, supported simply by spiritual aid.

They were neither to be exterminated nor subdued. In the darkest hours of their fortunes light from another world cheered them, and when they seemed fallen to the very earth spirit-hands raised them up. As in the Hebrew scriptures, we read of a few men driving armies before them. As in Palestine, the deliverances of the oppressed were frequently so miraculous that the oppressors cried in astonishment, "This is the hand of God!"

The Vaudois, or Waldenses, are sometimes asserted to have originated in the twelfth century, and to have had for their first leader a Peter Waldo of Lyons. The truth seems to be that, far from these ancient Protestants taking their designation from Waldo, he drew his own from the Waldenses. It was during the fourth century that their schism from Rome took place. At first they disclaimed the desire of a total separation, and contented themselves with strong protests against abuses. The Church, with the lapse of time, departed yet more widely from apostolic traditions, whilst the Waldenses had become but the more strongly attached to them. ` The split gradually widened. At length the little Piedmontese congregation withdrew wholly from communion with Rome, and was thenceforth persecuted with unrelenting fury.

The separatists sought refuge in one of the most romantic of nature's strongholds. They peopled the higher valleys of the Piedmontese Alps, and there vowed to defend their religion to the last. We may imagine them, as Mrs. Hemans has imagined, exclaiming—

> "Thou hast placed our ark of refuge
> Where the spoiler's foot ne'er trod ;
> For the strength of our hills we bless Thee,
> Our God, our fathers' God ! "

For above ten centuries the attack and defence continued. Rome gave no quarter. Her desire was to extirpate these heretics—not to convert them. With all the forces of Europe at her command, the attempt failed. The Waldenses were a Church when Charlemagne sat on the throne of the West, and they were a Church when Napoleon surpassed the conquests of Charlemagne. They beheld the kindred heresy of the Albigenses arise, menace the supremacy of the Papacy, and become extinguished in the seas of blood shed by De Montfort and Dominic. They were battling for existence when Wickliffe thundered against the corruptions of Rome—when his bones were torn with ignominy from their sepulchre—when his disciples were hunted with fire and sword. Whilst Savonarola was raising his voice against Papal abuses, the Papacy was hounding on France and Savoy to lay waste the valleys where the Vaudois had so long dwelt. Whilst Luther was crying for all who truly worshipped Christ to come out from the Roman Babylon, and range themselves by his side, the devil of persecution was doing his worst among the Piedmontese Alps. Then came the Huguenot wars of France, and the fierce religious struggles in Germany. The attention of Rome was directed to a

greater schism, and an immensely more imminent danger. For a
space the Waldenses tilled their fields and celebrated their worship
in peace.   But the storm which had menaced the very existence
of the Catholic Church blew over.   Protestantism, after progressing to the shores of the Mediterranean, was driven back almost to
the Baltic.   The Papacy could turn its attention again to the little
community which had been a thorn in its side for ages.   The
flames of persecution once more raged furiously amongst the
mountains of Northern Italy.   In those Eden-like recesses scenes
of the wildest horror were perpetrated.   The Catholic princes not
actively engaged in the devilish work looked approvingly on.   At
length the news of maidens dishonoured; of children tossed on
spears; of women ripped up, or hurled down rocks; of men slain
in defence of their homes witnessing with their last glance their
wives and daughters exposed to horrors worse than death; of
whole families burned in their burning dwellings, reached and
roused the heroic usurper who then controlled the destinies of
England.   Cromwell stood forth as the champion of the Vaudois.
The voice of the first soldier of Europe was not one against
which Rome might stop her ears.   Sullenly the mandate
was given that persecution should cease.   As sullenly was it
obeyed.   The ruler of Savoy retired from the valleys which he
had devastated, and, like a wolf overawed by the interference of
some more lordly animal, remained watching the moment when
he might with impunity rush once more on the coveted prey.   In
no long time the opportunity was granted.   Death struck down
the English Protector; his throne passed to a debauchee and
a coward; his wise and magnanimous policy was abandoned.
France and Rome hastened to give the signal to their tool, the
Duke of Savoy.   An army was once more marched into the fastnesses of Northern Piedmont.   The last and most merciless of the
Waldensean persecutions commenced.

Nothing in modern history, unless it be the triumphs won a few
years later by the Protestants of the Cevennes, can equal the
marvels which the Vaudois now accomplished.   Of their former
wars we have but scanty accounts.   Judging by the disproportion

between their strength and that of their enemies, even the first of these crusades should have ended in the extirpation of the Waldenses. Yet century after century passed by, and beheld them still resisting. We turn to the histories of that great struggle in which they were occupied during a portion of Louis XIV.'s reign, and can no longer wonder that the little Piedmontese community was enabled to defend itself so long and so well. Of these narratives, some are given by the Vaudois themselves, some by their persecutors, some by their friends. In almost every page occur traces of spiritual aid. We read how seventeen of the persecuted encountered and defeated a force of near nine hundred men. We read how the little hamlet of Rora, containing but fifty houses, was held for a while against ten thousand regular troops, and how, when its smoking ruins were no longer tenable, the gallant handful of defenders made good their retreat. It is told us that when their implacable enemies had closed with heaps of brushwood the mouths of the caverns wherein certain Vaudois had taken refuge, and had endeavoured by lighting the piles to suffocate them or burn them alive, the imprisoned mountaineers, bursting suddenly through the fiery barrier, chased before them fifty times their number of French and Savoyards, who cried, as they fled, that the heretics were aided by the powers of hell. The precipices which in the darkest night they traversed without hurt; the hardships they endured without succumbing; the miraculous way in which they were sometimes supplied with food; the fervour with which they thanked God for victory; the serene enthusiasm with which they triumphed over death,—all are there. "I have witnessed," said Arnaud, their pastor and leader, "prodigies beyond the course of nature, or the natural strength of man."

In April, 1686, came the crisis. As Savoy was unequal to the conquest single-handed, the vast resources of France were joined to hers. The allies, having united their forces, made a final swoop on the doomed race. After two days of desperate fighting the Waldenses laid down their arms. Fourteen thousand were cast into various prisons; of whom eleven thousand perished. The extremes of cold, heat, hunger and thirst, were the ills which slew these unhappy captives. Such unconquerable spirits as had disdained submission betook themselves to Switzerland or the Protestant States of Germany.

Among these last was a chosen troop of between eight and nine hundred men, headed by the great Waldensean pastor, Henri Arnaud. Three years later this band resolved to attempt a return to their Piedmont valleys. They crossed Lake Leman on the night of August 16th, 1689. It was the commencement of a march in some respects more marvellous than that of Xenophon. The little band of brothers succeeded in baffling the united forces of France, Savoy, and the Catholic cantons of Switzerland. In ten days eighteen battles were fought. The allies lost several thousand men; the Waldensean killed amounted to seventy. At the bridge of Sababertran, they forced a passage against two thousand five hundred well-entrenched troops. Of the Vaudois, fourteen were slain. The enemy's loss was at least six hundred. " Who is so dull," cries Arnaud, " as not to see that God alone could give victory to a mere parcel of men, without money, and almost without arms, against the King of France, before whom all Europe trembled ? " For the heroic achievers of these marvels were a few hundreds of fainting wretches, clothed in scarcely decent rags, and sleeping usually on the earth. Their drink was water, their food roots and herbs. Against them were arrayed over twenty thousand of the finest troops of France and Northern Italy; abundantly provided with arms, ammunition, and provisions, and accompanied by mules burdened with ropes for the hanging of captured Vaudois. No balance could have been more unequal; but the sword of Heaven was cast into the lighter scale, and it sufficed for the outweighing of the other. The halters remained unused. The best soldiers of Europe fled before a handful of ill-armed starving peasants. In passes where a few men might have held thousands at bay, thousands were dislodged by a few. At length the Italian Alps were reached. With tears of joy and exulting hymns the Waldenses entered the familiar valleys. Their brethren who had been spared in the persecution eagerly welcomed them. It was expected, however, that the endeavours to crush the little congre-

gation would speedily recommence. Fortunately the fear proved
groundless. Discord arose between France and Savoy, and Duke
Amadeus allied himself with the English. At the request of
William III. he grudgingly conceded to his Waldensean subjects
certain rights over their lives and properties. The grateful Vaudois
enlisted by thousands under his banner, and did excellent service
against the French. The war ended in the discomfiture of Louis.
Immediately the Duke hastened to oppress his Protestant subjects
once more. Three thousand persons not born in the valleys
were banished. The remaining Vaudois endured the weight of
numerous oppressive edicts. But the worst of the persecution was
past. Catholic princes dared no longer gratify their appetite for
intolerance with the murder of women and children, or the whole-
sale massacre of defenceless men. The Duke of Savoy might still
occasionally venture on the burning of a Waldensean pastor or two,
but laymen were not now robbed of their lives. By slow degrees
their rights over their property came also to be recognised. The
persecution which exterminates had ceased, and the persecution
which irritates also in process of time drew to an end. It was
not, however, until late in the present century that the government
of Piedmont finally ceased from vexing that little Alpine Israel in
whose behalf such great things were done of old.

In the extreme South of France lies the beautiful region of the
Cevennes. Mountains green with vines, delightful valleys, a
cloudless sky, and a delicious climate, combine to create one of
the most charming of European paradises. From the summits of
the higher peaks the magnificent expanse of the Mediterranean is
visible. Roads are few, and often of the rudest character. The
dwellers in this primitive region mostly hold the Protestant faith.
The villages are old and picturesque. Sometimes, in the remoter
recesses of the mountains, a congregation assembled in a solitary
nook surprises the eye of the traveller. The pastor stands on a
fragment of rock under the shadow of some ancient tree. The
little flock gathered round him listen reverently to his eloquence,
or join in the simple and monotonous psalmody of the district.
Minister and hearers belong to some village nigh at hand that is

destitute of a church. It was destroyed probably during the war of the Cevennes.

Nothing in the annals of France can interest a spiritualist more than the events of that wonderful struggle. The evidences of spiritual intervention are still more complete than those afforded by the persecution of the Vaudois. There were men among the little Camisard army of three thousand whom fire would not burn nor bullets pierce. There were clairvoyants to whom the most hidden secrets of the enemy were as an open book. Through these seers spies and ambushes were detected, the route and numbers of the royal army revealed, and the words which its leaders spoke in their tents carried to the leaders of the Protestant host. In battle the patriots seemed transfigured. They were endowed with a strength and a bravery far surpassing those of their calmer hours. Out-numbered a hundred to one, they disdained the defensive and pressed eagerly on to the attack. Yet a more incongruous rabble than the Cevennois heroes never moved the laughter of regular troops. Boys of twelve fought in their ranks side by side with men in the prime of life. The Samson of the Camisards was an under-sized slender youth of seventeen. The commander-in-chief was a vine-dresser. His associates in authority were bakers and carders of wool. There was but one leader who had previously seen anything of war. Yet in the counsels of these strange gene-ralissimos nothing but harmony and wisdom prevailed. Before their spiritually directed movements the craft of the oldest marshals of France was turned to foolishness.

Amongst the peasants who adored and followed Rowland the vine-dresser and Cavallier the baker, the strangest diversities existed. At the beginning of the war the majority were in want of everything. A few had guns; of the remainder most were armed with swords or scythes. The others contented themselves with such weapons as David employed in doing battle with Goliath. Like David too they endowed themselves with the arms of the enemy and clothed themselves in his spoil. Every new field made more soldierly the appearance of the Camisards. Rags were replaced by coats, and staves by muskets. The chiefs adorned

themselves with the broad and feathered hats and the scarlet uniforms of slain king's officers. They glittered with gold chains and
rings of ruby and diamond. They charged the ranks of Montrevel
and Villars mounted on magnificent chargers, the mementoes of
their prowess on former fields of fight. Gaps were to some degree
made in the Protestant ranks. The recruits who filled these gaps
exhibited all the squalor which had characterized their brethren at
the commencement of the war. Thus the motley appearance of
the little army was never wholly effaced. Beside men splendid
with uniforms torn from the dead captains of Louis the Great
fought hungry peasants clad in little more than a tattered blouse,
who mowed at the legs of the horses with weapons that had
formerly served to reap their fields. And the Camisards were unquestionably less formidable when their means of defence became
apparently increased, than when, naked, half-armed, and starving,
they charged desperately upon the foe. Their mightiest victories
were achieved by little bands of undisciplined and almost weapon-
less men. The power of another world went with them, and those
whom a single company of dragoons might have seemed sufficient to
scatter, defied successfully the whole might of France.

It is to the revocation of the Edict of Nantes that we are to look
for the cause of the rebellion. The Catholic priesthood owed to
the influence of Madame Maintenon that coveted increase of power,
and Protestant France owed to her the expatriation or slaughter of
half a million of citizens, and the letting loose of tens of thousands
of soldiers on a peaceful and inoffensive race. The government
chiefly directed its crusading efforts to the Cevennes. That portion
of Languedoc offered an enticing field for attempts at conversion.
The heretics were numerous, and enthusiastically attached to their
faith. Accordingly Louis dispatched to them missionaries in the
shape of regiment after regiment of his best troops. These armed
apostles showed themselves as benevolently zealous in proselytiz-
ing as their master could have desired. They quartered themselves perforce on the objects of their solicitude. They commenced
industriously to furnish materials for that page of history infamous
as the "Dragonnades of the Cevennes." The Inquisition it se

might have taken lessons from them in the art of cruelty. Some of their catechumens they rolled naked over floors covered with broken glass. Some they anointed with oil, and held before fierce fires until half-roasted, in the vain hope of thus indoctrinating them in the mysteries of the Eucharist. They impressed on women the necessity of attending mass by tearing the dresses from their backs, and flogging them until their shoulders streamed with blood. Men who were mutinous they shot. Maidens who were good-looking they dishonoured.

The prisons overflowed with victims. Although the captives died by thousands; although their dungeons were hideous depths into which the sun never penetrated, choked with filth and alive with snakes and toads; although malaria, insufficient and impure food, cold, dampness, and want of light, were constantly at work destroying life, sufficient room could not be found. A happy few were placed under hatches, and shipped off to reach America, or find a grave in the depths of the ocean. The gibbet and the wheel disposed of others. The residue were condemned to the galleys or imprisonment. Some toiled for life at the oar; some were let down with ropes into the filthy pits which were to be their places of captivity; some pined in cells where they could neither lie down nor stand upright. Carrion and the garbage of cattle were flung to them for food. Their bodies swelled to an incredible extent; their skin peeled off; such as were liberated issued like living corpses from the hideous dens in which they had been caged. The features of many were unrecognisable; others had lost their hair or teeth; others again had become imbeciles or raving mad-men. It seemed that even a few weeks' confinement in one of these Infernos was enough to take from the immured wretch all semblance of humanity.

Yet the Cevennois remained unconquerable, and patiently endured whatever the ingenious malice of their tormentors could inflict. Imprisonment, torture, pillage, the rack, the gallows, the wheel—all were in turn tried, and all proved insufficient to tame the noble obstinacy of the oppressed race. The missionaries of Louis reported the failure of their efforts. It was owing to no lack of zeal that such a failure had to be confessed. They had destroyed villages by the score, and taken lives by the thousand. Yet, although so many heretics had perished, scarcely a convert could be shown. It was necessary that decisive measures should be authorised. The true course for a Catholic king evidently was, to treat his Protestant subjects as Israel had treated the inhabitants of Jericho and Ai: exterminate the heretics, and their places could be supplied by a colony of the faithful.

Extermination was resolved upon. Marshal Montrevel and the Intendant Lamoignon de Baville received orders to divide the doomed territory into sections, and to distribute to each its troop of soldiers, who should rase every house, lay waste every field, and slay every man, woman, and child who refused to embrace Catholicism. The diabolical work began, and the Cevennois at length rose in rebellion. A brigade of between two and three thousand men was organized, and this little army, without experience, and almost without weapons, ventured to take the field against a host of sixty thousand veteran troops, trained in the most approved discipline of the time, and seasoned by more than one war.

For ten years the struggle went on ; for ten years the deeds wrought by the Cevennois continued to astonish Europe. The oppressed had cried to heaven, and the cry was heard. Every day some new spiritual manifestation occurred amongst them. Many became mediums, and thus served as channels for communications from another world. They spoke, whilst in the trance, not the ordinary patois of the district, but the purest French. They revealed the plans of the enemy ; they warned their brethren of approaching battles, and named those of the Camisards who would fall. Such invariably went forth in triumph to their martyrdom, assured that death would bring to them a glorious reward. The Camisards who issued from the conflict unhurt frequently owed their preservation to miracle. Bullets were found within their shirts which had flattened against the skin. The swords of those who struck at them flew from their bodies as from a coat of mail. And, whilst the weapons of the persecutors thus failed to hold, the

sword of every Camisard carved through the royal ranks like that
of a destroying angel. In battle the inspired knew nothing of
fatigue. The veteran soldier of France might faint beneath the
heat and burden of the conflict; but his peasant adversary fought
on steadily to the end. Spirits were at hand to strengthen the arm
of every patriot. Often, in the fiercest of the fight, the Camisard
seers looked up, and saw that the space around was filled with an
angelic host, who imparted to the onset of the oppressed a strength
not of earth. The patriots, as I have said, never at any one time
exceeded in number three thousand men. They slew in the ten
years that the war lasted, one-third of the royal army.

Laporte was the brain of the Camisards, and Cavallier their
right arm. The former was a man of forty, endowed by nature
with a considerable share of intelligence, which constant intercourse with spirits brightened gradually into astonishing wisdom.
Through his exertions all was orderly in the Protestant ranks, and
each man had his fitting place. He exhorted continually the
troops of whom he was commander-in-chief; he prayed and
prophesied in their midst. He caused magazines to be constructed
in the caverns of the rocks and in the depths of the forests.
Here abundant stores of provisions and clothing, of cattle, corn
and wine—all taken from the enemy—were laid up. The wisdom
of the precaution was speedily apparent. Before the war had
lasted long, every Cevennois town and village was in ashes.
Save for the store-houses, whose existence was owing to the
wisdom of Laporte, the insurgents must have surrendered or
starved. Nor was it only in the matter of provisions that, through
the spiritually directed genius of this extraordinary man, the
persecutors were, against their will, compelled to be of service to
the persecuted. The patriots, like the Christ whom they worshipped, had not where to lay their heads. Laporte gave them
for abodes the castles and châteaux of their enemies. Retreats
had been constructed for the wounded; but beds, surgical appliances and medicines were wanting. He forced the Catholics to
furnish all. At times the royal generals sought to entrap, by
means of negotiation, the patriots whom they could not crush.

But to oppose to the commanding sagacity of Laporte the craft of diplomacy, was seeking ·to entangle an eagle by means of à cobweb. The first disdainful exertion of his strength broke through all.

Cavallier had a weaker head, but a yet stronger heart. In battle his brandished sword was the principal; standard of the Camisards. Where the chosen troops of the enemy clustered thickest round their banners, there that sword was ever seen carving for itself a terrible path. At the right hand of the young hero rode his friend Ravenel, a man of gigantic stature; at his left a boy still younger than himself, his brother Daniel. Behind came the cavalry of the Camisards, almost every man mounted on a horse that had formerly been backed by some soldier of the king. Cavallier himself rode a noble charger, which he had torn in battle from its royalist master, Colonel La Jonquière. This successful single combat was but one of many similar exploits. Whatever opponent he selected was as certainly doomed to death, as though the sword were already in his throat. The royalists whom he and his followers charged, if not above three to one, were scattered as with the shock of a thunderbolt. As a cavalry leader Cavallier seems to have excelled both Rupert and Murat. Their exploits were achieved against foes seldom more numerous, often less disciplined, and never better armed than their own squadrons. The force that the Camisard hero led was a mob of undisciplined peasants, unskilled in the science of war, and unacquainted with the use of the weapons they wielded. To remount themselves, or equip recruits, they had only the horses which they captured from the enemy. It was a fortunate circumstance for these raw countrymen, when each patriot had opposed to him only two of the best soldiers of the age. Such was the force which, under the command of Cavallier, achieved exploits more astounding than those attributed to any fabulous hero of old romance. Out-numbered, sometimes seven to one, they yet remained masters of the field of battle. Dismounted, they, without artillery, captured fastnesses which might have withstood a regular siege. For ten years they continued to prove themselves superior to the

fiercest efforts of the whole chivalry of Catholic France.   It was
not until disunion rose amongst them, till puffed up with success
they despised the counsel of their spiritual guides, till luxury and
corruption supplanted piety and abstemiousness, till their leaders
proudly styled themselves dukes and counts, till Cavallier was
outwitted, and Rowland Laporte suffered himself to be betrayed,
that their glory departed.

And the hero under whose guidance they achieved their most
terrible triumphs—he whom every foe dreaded, and every friend
adored,—was not this Cavallier one in whom, if strength of body
were wanting, skill in arms might to some degree explain the
marvellous way in which he fought ?   The only verdict which a
candid inquirer into his history can return, is, that never was
warrior so apparently incapable of the marvels attributed to him.
He was but nineteen when his career of glory ended.   A peasant,
and the son of a peasant, he had received not the slightest education ; he knew nothing of the management of any weapon; his
stature was low, his frame slender, his countenance simple and
almost child-like.   Save during his career in the Cevennes, he
accomplished no exploit which, in the slightest degree, deserves
to be termed striking.   And how came it then that, whilst unedu-
cated, and still a boy, he led armies to battle with all the skill of
Clive, with more than the valour of Murat ?   I answer, as he
himself would have answered, and as every unprejudiced student
of the Camisard war must answer, because he was veritably a
"heaven-born general," an instrument controlled by spirits and
chosen of God.   While he listened to the voices of his guides he
was invincible.   When he came to rely on his own strength he
fell.

In common with many of his followers Cavallier was clairvoyant.
Once, at a place between Nair and La Cour de Creviez, he started
as from a dream, and cried that he had seen Marshal Montrevel at
Allez, who gave to a messenger, to carry to Nismes, letters containing important plans against the Camisards.   He described the
dress and features of the courier, the colour of his horse, and the
numbers and appearance of the escort which attended him.

"Ride full speed," said he, "and you will encounter them at the ford of the Gardon." At once a number of Camisards sprang to the saddle, and the messenger was captured at the place indicated. His appearance and surroundings were as Cavallier·had seen them in his vision. The letters found upon him contained a complete exposition of Montrevel's plans. These the Cevennois could now take steps to baffle.

But the most wondrous manifestation recorded of the Camisards is the well-attested power which some among them possessed of resisting the action of fire. I select as an instance the ordeal undergone at Serignan, by a medium named Clary, in the presence of Colonel Cavallier and many spectators, some time in August, 1703. Whilst entranced, he was commanded by his guides to place himself in the midst of a large fire. A spot was selected. Around rose a natural amphitheatre of low hills, where the crowds assembled could arrange themselves to behold the event. A large pile of dry branches having been collected, Clary placed himself upon it. The pyre was kindled; the flames speedily shot up above the head of the apparent martyr, and he stood enwrapped with fire. In this position he remained until all the wood was consumed. When the last flicker had died away, he walked forth unhurt. All rushed to congratulate him on the wonderful justifi-cation of his faith. "I was one of the first to embrace him," writes an eye-witness; "his white blouse was not in the least injured by the action of the fire. I examined his hair, and it was not singed." Having satisfied themselves that Clary was wholly unscathed, the Camisards around burst forth into a Huguenot version of the hundred and fourth Psalm :—

"Bénis le Seigneur, O mon âme !
Seigneur ! maître des dieux, roi de l'éternité,
Sur ton trone éclatant, ceint d'un manteau de flamme,
Tu règnes, couronné de gloire et de beauté !"

In 1704-5, came the fall of the Camisards. Marshal Villars, some years later the antagonist of Marlborough, was dispatched to cope with Laporte and Cavallier. After the defeat of Blenheim

the presence of the troops hitherto employed against the Cevennois had become imperatively necessary outside France. Fortune
favoured the arts of the new royalist commander. He induced
Cavallier to appoint a meeting at Nismes, and gave hostages for
the safety of the young hero. The conference duly came off.
The marshal exerted his utmost subtlety. In presence of the
dangers menacing France, it was time that this fratricidal war
should cease. The king had empowered him to offer liberty of
conscience to the brave Cevennois. His majesty desired, moreover, to form of them a regiment for service against the English.
Who was so fit to be the commander of this battalion as the
hero Cavallier, whose sword had a hundred times led the way
to victory, whose name was famous from Lisbon to Vienna ?
Cavallier listened and wavered. He demanded other privileges ;
more certain guarantees. Villars responded that, by a gentleman
and loyal subject the word of a king was always accounted sufficient guarantee. Besides, his majesty's goodness was infinite.
He had expressed himself willing that the Cevennois should pray
in their own fashion, but not that they should rebuild their
churches. Could Colonel Cavallier doubt, however, but that,
when Louis the Great found his brave Protestant subjects ready to
march against Marlborough and Eugene, he would accord them
whatsoever privileges they desired ?

Laporte and the spirit-guides of Cavallier were alike absent.
The weak youth yielded. He signed the contract binding the
Camisards to lay down arms, and departed to summon to other
fields of glory the heroic few who had so long followed him as a
deliverer sent of God. A roar of execration greeted his statement
of the treaty. He announced that liberty of conscience was
henceforth to be granted. At once Laporte started forward.
" What liberty ? " cried the indignant chief. " No ! unless the
Camisards have liberty to worship God, not in deserts and caverns
only, but in their own churches, with all the rights and guarantees
of citizens, they will live and die with arms in their hands."

The rage of the Camisards grew frantic. " Traitor ! "
" Betrayer ! " shouted the thousands whom, until now, the voice

of Cavallier had stirred like a trumpet, who had again and again followed him cheerfully to apparently certain death. He strove to explain. Fresh clamours instantly drowned his voice. Then Rowland again made himself heard. "Though we cannot agree with our deluded brother," said he, "let us not part in anger." Silently, and for the last time, he embraced his fellow-chief. The hearts of the Camisards melted. They thought of the days when to follow Cavallier was to rush on to victory; when his sword had been as the sword of Azrael, and the charges that he led had scattered armies. With sobs and tears the little host crowded round to bid adieu for ever to its beloved leader. The unfortunate Cavallier seized the moment: "Let all who love me follow me!" he cried. Forty came forth from the ranks, the rest remained with Rowland. The pity of the Camisards was with their former hero, but no longer their obedience.

Cavallier and his melancholy troop sought the camp of Villars. They were instantly sent under guard to Versailles. Thence Louis destined them to a life-long captivity in the fortress of Brisac. On the way thither they escaped, and crossed the frontier in safety.

A few words will relate the subsequent history of the Camisards. Laporte, having become proud, despised the warnings of the spirits, and did what was agreeable in his own sight. He styled himself Duke of the Cevennes, and boasted that the country was his, won by his sword. His guardian angels left him, and with them went victory. Lured into an ambush by a traitor, the unfortunate hero died, fighting to the last. Two subordinate chiefs, Ravenel and Catenat, were burnt alive at Nismes, almost within sight of the battle-field where, two years before, the Camisard patriots had triumphed over the royal forces commanded by the Comte de Broglie.

Cavallier had gone to Holland. There he collected a regiment of Huguenot refugees for service against the French in Spain. The war over, he betook himself to England, and died in 1740, governor of the island of Jersey. It is scarcely necessary to add that he never returned to the Cevennes.

With Laporte and Cavallier departed the independence of the Cevennes. The army split itself into numerous petty bands, which were overpowered and slaughtered in detail. Some Camisards quitted the country, some were made prisoners and hanged, burnt, or broken slowly on the wheel. For nearly a century the renewed martyrdom of the mountaineers continued.

At length the humanity of irreligion triumphed over the intolerance of the Church. Voltaire, Rousseau, and Diderot arose; to their efforts, and the efforts of their followers, was owing the final cessation of the long agony of the Camisards. Men who disbelieved in Christ procured for their Protestant fellow-countrymen the right of worshipping Christ in peace.

CHAPTER VI.

IF there were heroes before Agamemnon, there were also reformers before Luther. I have instanced the Waldenses as among the oldest separatists from Rome; but in all ages of that Church dissent has abounded. The Manichæans, Pelagians, and Montanists came out from her in early times. In the twelfth century the heresy of the Albigenses shook the Papacy to its foundations, and was only extirpated by means of the Norman swords which Rome called to her aid. A little later arose the minor sects of the Apostolikers and the Beghards. The locale of the first was Italy. Gerhard Segarelli, whose teachings led to this schism, was burnt at a slow fire in the year 1800. His creed seems to have greatly resembled that of the Waldenses. It was founded on the gospel in its purity, and was well worthy of commendation. The doctrines of the Beghards, on the contrary, were derived from corruptions of the Scriptures worse than any indulged in by Rome herself. They accepted the assertion of St. Paul, that those who are in Christ are no longer under the law, as a license for all imaginable crime and vice. After spreading through most of the kingdoms of Germany and committing everywhere the wildest orgies, an unsparing persecution finally exterminated them. To uncontrolled license succeeded maniacal penances. Whilst the Beghards were fiercely sinning, and the Catholic Church was as fiercely persecuting them, occurred the unique pestilence of 1848; the most awful sickness which ever devastated earth. The great agony by which Europe was convulsed gave birth to the sect of the Flagellants. They proclaimed that the Almighty was wroth with the wickedness of man, and that the Black Death was the awful token of his displeasure. Only unceasing prayer, and mortifications exceeding the mortifications of an anchorite, could induce Him to arrest the hand of the destroyer. They stripped themselves to the waist, they passed from city to city lashing themselves with cords twisted with wire. Many expired under the severity of the discipline. At length the Vatican directed all its powers against the new mania. The leaders were seized and burnt, their followers were dispersed by main force. Again, however, they re-assembled, and penetrated even into Spain and Italy, despite all the severity of the Inquisition. Scourging themselves until the blood streamed down, and chanting wildly the " Dies iræ," they created everywhere an extraordinary excitement. Princes, and even prelates, were to be found in their ranks. It was not until 1481 that the Flagellant mania ended. It had lasted one hundred and thirty-two years.

In 1374 appeared the Dancers. They outdid in wildness even the actions of the Flagellants. Half-naked, and crowned with garlands, they danced madly through the great cities of Germany and the Netherlands. They considered themselves inspired by angels; the Church reviled them as under the influence of demons. Although infinite licentiousness resulted from their own orgies, the Dancers professed extreme disgust for the corruptions of the Papacy. They cried loudly for a new Church; they plundered monasteries and slew priests. Exorcism having been tried in vain, the aid of the secular power was invoked. With much slaughter the heretical mania was, about the year 1418, finally put down.

Among the noblest precursors of the Reformation were the Lollards. Their leader, Wickliffe, was assuredly infinitely superior to Calvin and Knox, and will scarcely suffer even by comparison with Luther or Zwinglius. The imperfect accounts of his career remaining to us do not permit of any very confident statements regarding his possession of spiritual gifts. That he deemed himself a prophet sent of God to rebuke the corruptions of the Church is certain. That he raised against himself a storm yet more terrible than that which sent Savonarola to the stake, is also clear. Whether he was throughout life supported in his task by communion with spirits is unknown. It may, however, be asserted with considerable confidence that sufficient evidence remains to indicate his having been on more than one occasion delivered from imminent danger by power not of earth.

The central figure of Protestantism is undoubtedly Luther. Like a lighthouse fixed unshakably on some mighty rock, the giant Saxon towers up from the troubled sea of the sixteenth century. Against that solid form the hurricane of religious fury struck in vain ; solitary, but unconquerable, he continued to hold stoutly forth amid the tempest the light that had been given into his keeping. In himself the only potent enemy of that light was to be found. Sometimes it streamed brightly forth, lighting up with a radiance as of noonday the tossing waters around. Sometimes it seemed ready to expire. Prejudices dimmed it ; passions caused it to flicker unsteadily to and fro ; the lamp, at one time clear as a diamond, and fed with the purest oil, would a little later appear untrimmed, almost empty, and choked with murky vapours. But, in darkness or in day, Luther could not be other than great. The lighthouse, rising like a pillar of fire from the midst of the raging waves, is an object at once noble and useful. The same lighthouse left with but a feeble spark to indicate whence that blaze once issued which had directed the course of so many ships, is an object no longer serviceable, indeed, but still stately. What was a pillar of flame has become a pillar of cloud. The glory has departed, but the possibility of that glory is yet there.

Perhaps the justest comparison of Luther's character would be to a statue, magnificent indeed, but unfinished. The nobility of the features which the master's hand has carefully elaborated makes us regret the more the crudity of those parts on which the chisel seems scarcely to have been employed. We see magnificence and deformity side by side.

The Luther at one moment exalted almost to the level of Socrates, appears at another sunk to an equality with some familiar of the Inquisition. It is as though the statue I have compared him to should contain some strokes more than worthy

of Phidias, and others which would disgrace the vilest bungler
that ever hacked marble. Can we recognise the Reformer who
declared it to be against the will of the Holy Ghost to burn heretic,
in the bigot who believed that the hero Zwinglius, although he
had sealed with his blood his attachment to the Protestant faith,
was damned for all eternity, simply because he differed in a single
point from the Wittenberg idea of Scripture? Was the Luther
who "could do nothing against conscience" the Luther who,
because Erasmus claimed for himself that same liberty of conscience, cried furiously, "Erasmus of Rotterdam is the vilest
miscreant that ever disgraced the earth! Whenever I pray, I
pray for a curse upon Erasmus"?

He believed that he was justified in rejecting the Epistle of
James. In such rejection there was nothing blamable. The
gentle teachings of James accorded ill with the austerity of the
Lutheran scheme of salvation, and the great Reformer rejected
them. "I hold," said he, "that this epistle is of none authority."
As he dealt with James, so he dealt with other scriptural
writers. He admitted that it is absurd to regard the Bible as
altogether infallible. "These good and true teachers and
searchers," says he, in speaking of the prophets, "fell sometimes
upon hay and straw, sometimes on pure gold and precious
stones." He took, therefore, from the Scriptures whatever
accorded with his own belief, and denounced the rest as error, or
hastily slurred it over. The Christ he worshipped was not the
Christ of the four Gospels, but the Christ of Paul. Yet the liberty
he claimed for himself he denied to others. All who agreed with
him he welcomed with hearty geniality. His opponents he
cursed and damned with the fury of Athanasius or Doctor Slop.

He declared it blasphemy to assert that faith without works is
dead. He declared that those who do not believe Christ to be
literally present in the Eucharist, who do not receive the bread
as his body and the wine as his blood, deny Him, and bring
upon themselves the doom, "Depart, ye cursed, into everlasting
fire." He was unwilling that heretics should be burnt. He saw,
however, no objection to their being banished. He denounced

the policy of the Church of Rome in forbidding the exercise of private judgment. He raged with equal fury against those " who would speculate into God's works with their devilish whys and wherefores." He believed in the omnipotence of God, and in the possibility of communion with " just souls made perfect ; " yet he reviled every spirit that visited him as a devil. He was just when not misled by bigotry, and liberal when no prejudice impelled him to be otherwise. In short, like other men, he was " fearfully and wonderfully made "—a whirlpool of error and truth, of good and evil, in which, however, the good decidedly predominated.

What was the secret of his wonderful success ? I think it to have been that the spirits who surrounded him forced him to do their work in spite of himself. He had a warm and impressionable nature, indomitable courage, and fiery eloquence. His faults, like his virtues, were those of a high soul. He was not mean or cruel. He was simply domineering, hot tempered, and somewhat despotic and harsh. The spirits whose servant he was could not eradicate his vices ; they were forced to content themselves with turning his virtues to the best account. They kindled a flame in his breast that no persecution could quench; they thrust into his hand the standard of reform, and clothed him with the armour of faith. Thus equipped, they sent him forth to do manful battle against the corrupt domination of Rome. Throughout that long conflict they were at his side. When he fainted they inspired him; when he was surrounded by dangers they raised him up friends. No wonder that his deeds were great. No wonder that his words were, as Longfellow has described them, " half-battles for the free."

He treated these spiritual guides scurvily enough. The thoughts with which they inspired him he accepted as from God. If, however, a spirit contrived to make its presence more directly manifest, it was at once objurgated as a fiend. The devil was never absent from Luther's thoughts. As a medium he could not avoid receiving constant and striking tokens of the nearness of the spirit-world. Yet he detested those tokens. He had

directed all the rude energy of his rhetoric against the sham
miracles of the Catholic Church. He had taught that signs and
wonders were no longer permitted ; how was he to reconcile
this theory with their constant occurrence to himself ? Luther's
mode of escape was by making a scapegoat of Satan. The devil,.
he maintained, was, as a miracle-worker, more powerful than
God. Good spirits could no longer visit earth; bad ones, however, ranged up and down it at their will. By such he supposed
himself continually tormented. Whether the unearthly visitor
tempted him to evil or exhorted him to good, it was equally a
waif from the bottomless pit. On a certain Good Friday, whilst
he was in fervent prayer, there appeared to him in his chamber
a bright vision of Christ. Luther was, at the very moment of
the apparition, ecstatically dwelling, he tells us, on the inestimable
benefits of the Saviour's death. Did he not welcome the spectacle
vouchsafed him with tears of joy ? Far from it. "At first
sight," says he, "I thought it had been some celestial vision.
Presently I reflected that it must needs be an illusion and juggling
of the devil, wherefore I spoke to the vision thus: 'Avoid thee,
confounded devil!' whereon the image vanished, clearly showing
whence it came."

At Wartburg he hurled his inkstand at a demon's head, who
had visited him with the view of interrupting his translation of
the Scriptures. In the same castle some spirits disturbed in his
chamber two bags of nuts, and made noises on the stairs when
no one in the flesh could have been there. Luther vengefully set
all this down to the credit side of his account with Satan. He
tells us that whilst he was in bed his Satanic Majesty often
visited him. He would make noises as of some one walking. He
would hurl things about the room; he would strike at the
Reformer as if with a human hand. These things exactly accord
with the pranks of undeveloped spirits, as witnessed in our own
day, but they can hardly be considered in keeping with the
character of that

> " Chief,
> Who led th' embattled seraphim to war."

Yet, whilst attributing to Satan such petty practical jokes, Luther had the highest respect for the vigour of his intellect. "He is not, it is true, exactly a doctor who has taken his degrees, but, for all that, he is very learned and expert. He has not been carrying on his business these thousands of years for nothing." Again, "If the devil cannot come and strangle men with his claws, he can do so, at all events, with his pressing arguments." He relates how Satan vanquished him in an argument about the practice of celebrating mass privately. Luther had been in the habit of doing so for nearly fifteen years. One night a spirit came to him. The great Reformer at once hailed it as the Prince of Evil. An argument commenced regarding the sacrament of the Lord's Supper—a strange subject, one would think, for Satan to discuss. The spirit maintained that the wafer and wine were not really converted into the body and blood of Christ. It rebuked Luther for his foolish belief that such a change could take place; it rebuked him also for celebrating alone, and in private, a rite meant to be public, and partaken of by the whole congregation. It quoted numerous apposite passages of Scripture. Luther became convinced. He acknowledged humbly that Satan was in the right, and a sounder Christian than himself with regard to private masses. From that day he never again celebrated one. His pride was not so stubborn that he would refuse to serve God because the devil bade him. It is strange that such a mind should have been so completely the victim of a maniacal delusion regarding the omnipotence of evil. Once confronted with the question of spirit-communion, Luther's powers of reasoning deserted him. He saw nothing unlikely in Satan's seeking to do the work of God. He forgot that Christ had said, "Every tree is known by its fruits." For all spiritual phenomena he had the stereotyped verdict, "Ye are of your father, the devil."

It is, however, with regret that the mind turns from Luther to Calvin. The faults of the great Saxon were neither few nor small. He wanted courtesy, charity, and patience, and his admirers can afford to admit that he wanted them. The errors that stain his career were but those of a Titan who, after long confinement in darkness, has beaten for himself a way through the wall of his dungeon, and reels to and fro, blinded with excess of light. History, placing in the one scale his vices and mistakes, and in the other his virtues and mighty deeds, sees the former balance fly rapidly upward, and cries, "This was a man." Calvin, on the contrary, resembled an iceberg. His single virtue was consistency. He shrank from no consequence, however horrible, to which his doctrines logically led. Predestination being accepted, God becomes the author of evil. Calvin admits that He does. All sin occurs by the will of the Deity. Satan can accomplish nothing without that will. All the horrors detailed in the Old Testament were the work of God. It is absurd to pronounce Him a loving father; the human race are, with few exceptions, hated by their creator. Unborn myriads, before they have accomplished a single good or evil action, are predestined to eternal misery. Repentance for sin is useless; human righteousness is a filthy rag. The most splendid deeds of humanity are in themselves but wickedness. Unsanctified workers of good deeds merit no reward, but rather punishment. But man cannot of himself become sanctified. God has reserved Paradise for a few, who were chosen by Him before the creation of the world; all others are doomed to damnation. "There is more joy in heaven," said Christ, "over one sinner that repenteth, than over ninety-and-nine just persons that need no repentance." "Man," said Calvin, "is in his whole nature odious and abominable to God. He finds nothing in men which can incite Him to bless them. Grace delivers from the curse and wrath of God a few, but leaves the world to its destruction. I stop not to notice those fanatics who pretend that grace is offered equally to all." Could such a teacher profit earth?

He lay like an incubus on Geneva. Studying the details of his tyranny, one feels that life would have been more endurable under a Henry VIII. or a Domitian. Their cruelties reached only a few. Calvin's iron rigour pressed equally on all. His code of laws is the strangest earth ever knew; it seems sometimes inspired by Puck, sometimes by Moloch. The fantastic and the horrible are blended in a manner at once ludicrous and painful. One law was directed against sumptuousness in dress: slashed breeches were forbidden; it was made illegal to fasten nosegays with gold cord; brides were no longer to adorn themselves with gay robes and floating tresses. Wedding revelry was prohibited: not more than a single course of meat could be set on the table at a marriage-dinner, and this was to be followed by, at the most, one tart. The fashion in which hair was to be cut was prescribed. A bonfire was made of all the romances and playing-cards in the city. Sunday became the only holiday.

Every indiscretion was a criminal offence. A young girl received a severe whipping for singing to a psalm-tune in church the words of a song. A man was banished from the city for remarking, when an ass brayed, that "he sang a pretty psalm." But the worst remains behind. A law was passed condemning children who disobeyed or cursed their parents to the punishment of death. In 1568 a girl who had struck her mother was beheaded; at another time a boy, for merely threatening to strike a parent, received sentence of death. And this infernal legislation there are, even at the present day, partisans of Calvin left to praise! They find "great beauty in the earnestness with which parental authority was defended." Not so did the people of Geneva. As speedily as might be after his death they reversed the Reformer's laws. No reverence was paid to his memory; no statue has ever been erected in his honour; a plain stone with the letters I. C. marks his grave. In Geneva at the present day few names are more detested.

He had spiritual gifts. On December 19th, 1562, a vision occurred to him of the great battle between the Guisians and the Protestants then raging not far from Paris. Besides being clairvoyant he had the prophetic faculty, and predicted many events which duly came to pass. But a spiritualist can feel little desire to claim the murderer of Servetus as a useful ally. His name is the name of one whose nature was as adamant. We can hardly imagine Calvin ever to have smiled, unless it were when the news came that at length the author of the "Restitutio Christianismi" was in his power. I think of that little mount with the heap of green oak-wood, of the kindled fagots, of the long agony, lasting some say almost two hours, and I find the memory of the remorseless bigot through whom Servetus died, as provocative of indignation as one can well find the memory of a man who departed from earth some three hundred years since. Had his doctrines died with him how infinitely happier and better the world would be at the present day !

I could wish, did the limits of my task permit, to trace out the spiritual in the lives of other great Reformers. The scholarly Erasmus, the gentle Melancthon, Knox, the patriot and iconoclast, who knew neither the fear of man nor the courtesy due to woman, the meek Hamilton, the headlong Zisca, Zwinglius, the hero and the martyr, whom the utmost fury of Rome could not daunt, nor the churlish injustice of Luther render intolerant ; from the lives of all these examples of spirit-communion might be drawn. I pause a moment to do homage to the last great man. A nobler nature than that of Zwinglius never consecrated earth. Less towering than the soul of Luther, his soul was far freer from error. There are few more beautiful aspirations than that Confession of Faith in which he anticipates " the future assembly of all the saintly, the heroic, the faithful, and the virtuous," where the patriarchs of Israel shall mingle with the sages of Greece, and the upright and holy of all creeds and every era dwell for ever in the presence of their God. Honour to the truest Christian of the sixteenth century ! On the red field of Cappel died a man entitled to the reverence of every thinker who believes that the love of God is over all his children. The name of Ulrich Zwinglius may well serve for a foil to that of Calvin. As in battle his place was before the ranks of Zurich, so in liberality he was be ore all the theologians of his time. There are few divines, even in the present day, who have attained that elevated platform of thought which was the standpoint of the gallant Switzer.

In Britain the Reformation had its share of miracle. Certain instances may be found in McCrie's " Life of Knox." Among the most striking of these is the prophecy of the Scottish apostle

Wishart. Led to the stake by the order of Cardinal Beatoun, he fixed his eyes on the turret-window from which that prelate watched the tragical scene. The fire was lighted, and the powder fastened to the martyr's body blew up. Perceiving him to be still alive, the captain of the castle drew near and bade him be of good heart. Wishart answered, " This flame hath reached to my body, yet it hath not daunted my spirit ; but he who from yonder place beholdeth me with such pride shall within a few days lie in the same as ignominiously as he is now seen proudly to rest himself." A week or two later the castle was stormed by a band of Protestant conspirators, and the body of the cardinal suspended from that very window whence he had witnessed the martyrdom of Wishart.

Numerous spiritual manifestations occurred in England and Scotland during the sixteenth and seventeenth centuries. They were almost without exception attributed to the agency of the devil. The Protestantism of the two countries had adopted in their entirety Luther's ideas of the cessation of miracles from God, and the increase of miracles from Satan. Hideous laws were passed against witchcraft. The tragedies of the continent were re-enacted on a smaller scale, and for a briefer period. To the burnings and hangings of Britain and the American Colonies much of what I have written in a former chapter will apply. These Protestant persecutions essentially resembled the chief shadow of Catholic Spiritualism. On the basis of certain startling facts the wildest theories were reared. A kind of insane panic seized the nation. The various Protestant Churches, like the Catholic Church, found it politic to encourage that panic. A drivelling pedant, with whom witchcraft was as much an article of faith as the mission of Christ, and for whose folly no lie was too absurd, united the crowns of Elizabeth and Bruce. Under his patronage murder went merrily on. Christ had expelled demons by virtue of the powers which he possessed. King James determined to expel them by virtue of the tar-barrel and the stake. The result is well known. Fearful tragedies were enacted in every part of the island. To be old, frail, and attached to some domestic pet such as a cat or dog, was sufficient justification for a death warrant. Unfortunate beings who understood their situation just well enough to know that they were about to be burned alive, underwent solemn trials before the highest judicial dignitaries of the realm, and were then as solemnly conducted to execution. Students who, in Macaulay's phrase, "have the heart to go through the sickening details," will find in certain of the phenomena described at these trials a striking similarity to spiritual phenomena of the present day. There are clairvoyance, trance-speaking, the moving of heavy articles by unseen means, the levitation of human bodies, apparitions of spirit-hands and spirit-forms, raps, lights, voices, &c. With these are mingled narratives of the wildest and most incredible kind. The judicial science of the age was unable to distinguish between the one and the other, and accepted both. The custom of the present day is to carefully keep out of sight the immense weight of evidence by which certain of the occurrences were attested, and to bring prominently forward whatever is horrible or absurd. Of these latter the supply is plentiful. The senility of most of the accused, the stupid bigotry of the accusers, the prejudices of the judges, the passions of the mob, the villanies of the professed hunters for witchcraft, the detestable cruelty of the judicial murders enacted; such things furnish unequalled themes for ridicule and invective. The folly of much of the evidence may be admitted. It is also certain that some of the phenomena on which great stress was laid were attributable to what are now known as "natural causes." Yet when these and other deductions have been made there still remains a respectable residue of occurrences which a spiritualist may with confidence claim as manifestations produced by dwellers in another world.

As was natural, the clergy were the master-spirits of every cruelty perpetrated under the pretence of awarding punishment to servants of Satan. The divines of Scotland, especially, were men after Calvin's own heart. Whether Presbyterian or Episcopal, the sight of a human being dangling on the gallows or writhing at the stake was to them an exquisite delight. The next highest pleasure to the death of a witch was her torture. To bind the wretched sufferer hand and foot, and, in this condition, drag her through a mill-pond until half dead ; to thrust pins up to the head in her flesh; to whip her through their parishes at the cart's tail, these were the daily amusements of their lives. With even more reluctance than their brethren south of the Tweed did they consent to abandon them. In England the slaughter of supposed sorcerers had almost ceased by the commencement of William III.'s reign —in Scotland it was scarcely yet at its height. Nor were the black-coated tormentors beyond the Atlantic less expert in their work. One of the most frightful episodes in the history of persecution for witchcraft was that which cast a gloom over Salem in the autumn of 1692. Numbers of supposed wizards and witches were hanged. A wretched patriarch of eighty was crushed to death by means of a board loaded with heavy stones ; he lingered for two days in horrible torture before the merciful hand of death released him. And such atrocities as these Puritan divines considered deeds done to the glory of God, and complacently chronicled as worthy of imitation by succeeding ages !

A score of volumes, each larger than the present, would scarcely afford room for full treatment of the iniquities perpetrated under the name of trials for witchcraft. How Hopkins, Cotton Mather, James I., and the Westminster Sanhedrim " damned themselves to everlasting fame," how the vilest of witnesses were believed, what infamous modes of torture were resorted to, how frequently the gibbet was erected and the tar-barrel blazed,—these things it does not fall within my province to treat of. Nor can I afford to fill chapter after chapter with the instances of miraculous phenomena which have occurred in Britain since her revolt from the See of Rome. It will be sufficient that I briefly notice certain strongly attested cases, and draw attention to the Spiritual in the lives of various famous Protestants.

Few readers of Clarendon's noble history will have forgotten the account of the apparition of Buckingham's father shortly before the death of " the Wicked Duke." The spirit manifested himself to a gentleman in no way related to the Buckingham family. He desired this person to visit his son, and to inform him that, if he did not turn from his sins, his career would be cut short by a terrible fate. The selected messenger promised to act as desired, and failed to fulfil his promise. The spirit speedily returned, and upbraided him with his breach of faith. Again he consented to carry out the mission, and again broke his word. The spirit once more appeared, and spoke more angrily than before. This continued for some time ; the persecuted medium could obtain no sleep ; the menaces of the apparition became terrible. At length the object of its visitations could hold out no longer. He declared solemnly that, if some secret were made known to him, by reveal-. ing which he might conquer the ridicule that would probably greet his narrative, he was ready to obey the behest of his visitor. The spirit consented, and made a communication. The medium went next morning to Villiers House. He obtained an audience, and related the whole facts of the case to the duke. Buckingham was astounded, and confessed the secret which formed the creden- tials of the messenger to be one he had thought known only to God and himself. He exacted a promise of silence. No reform of his life followed, however, and a few months later he fell by the dagger of Felton.

Equally striking is the apparition to Doctor Donne of a double of his living wife, as related by the poet himself. This *doppel- ganger* Donne accepted for an indication of his wife's death, but he found on reaching home that his child and not his spouse was dead. There is, moreover, the famous history of Lord Tyrone's visit after death to Lady Beresford, the dame who "wore, for evermore, a covering on her wrist," rendered necessary because of the indelible marks impressed there by the grasp of the spirit. To Lord Lyttelton came, with a menacing face, the departed mother of a young girl whom he had seduced, and announced to him the day and hour of his death. His friends strove in vain to vanquish the deep melancholy which at once seized on the doomed nobleman, and at the appointed time he died. Lady Diana Rich, whilst walking in the garden of Holland House, saw an exact counterpart of herself, and passed away shortly afterwards. At Waltham in Essex a spirit announced to Sir Charles Lee's daughter her approaching death, which took place with the utmost suddenness at the hour indicated. In the reign of William III. a Catholic gentleman named Prendergast gave information to the king which led to the discovery of the Assassination Plot, and the execution of many of the conspirators, among them Sir John Friend. Years later, when Prendergast was fighting under Marlborough, Friend appeared to him, and predicted his death on a certain day. The doomed man made known what had occurred to him. The appointed day came, and a battle was fought; at its close Prendergast still lived. "What of the ghost now?" said a brother officer. "I shall die to-day, notwithstanding," replied gravely the object of the prophecy. Even as he spoke a shot was dispatched from a French battery which the order to cease firing had not reached, and Prendergast fell dead. A host of other instances might be quoted.

One of the noblest of spiritualists was Bunyan. During his whole career he was the subject of spiritual manifestations. His life was several times miraculously preserved. He heard voices; he saw visions. The world to come was to him as real as the world he lived in. At one time, indeed, it seems to have been brought so close that he became as it were one of its inhabitants. It was then that he wrote "The Pilgrim's Progress." A captive in Bedford gaol, he could explore freely the mysteries of that region where the glory of God's countenance makes eternal day. Spirits were continually at his side. In few of his subsequent writings do we trace any resemblance to the wonderful story of the "Pilgrimage of Christian." The "Holy War," perhaps, affords some traces of the genius which beams so resplendently from every page of Bunyan's masterpiece; but how faint are those traces compared with the marvellous manner and matter of that allegory which tells how Christian hasted to set forth from the City of Destruction; how, looking from the land of Beulah on the Everlasting City, he sickened with desire to taste of its glories; how his soul fainted in the black depths of the River of Death; how, to the sound of celestial music and canopied by the wings of the Shining Ones, he passed with Hopeful through the heavenly gate, and embraced in presence of the angels that Faithful whom the fiery chariot of martyrdom had borne upward from the noise and turmoil of Vanity Fair! The "Pilgrim's Progress" is the most spiritual of works. Never did another author drink in such inspiration from the invisible world. Never again was that inspiration granted in equal measure to Bunyan. He had accomplished his task. Surrendering himself to the service of his Maker, a work had been produced which can be forgotten only when all memory of the English language shall have perished from among men.

A lesser light was George Fox. "This man, the first of the Quakers, and by trade a shoemaker, was one of those," says Carlyle, "to whom under ruder form the divine idea of the universe is pleased to manifest itself, and, across all the hulls of ignorance and earthly degradation, shine forth in unspeakable awfulness, unspeakable beauty, on their souls; who therefore are rightly accounted prophets, God-possessed." Fox's struggles towards the light resembled, in the fine language of Burns, "the blind gropings of Homer's Cyclops round the walls of his cave." It is his fortune to have been always either over-praised or unjustly depreciated. Reasons equally strong may be advanced for revering him as a prophet or reviling him as a madman. Those whose attention has been directed solely to his ignorance, his eccentricities, the strange garb which he adopted, the strange actions which he persisted in, the wild vagaries of his talk, the meaningless absurdity of much that he has written, have turned from the spectacle in disgust, or pointed at him the finger of scorn. Those who have contemplated only the fervour of his religion, the warmth of his heart, the greatness of his fortitude, have claimed for him a place among the foremost of mankind. They alone judge such a man justly who, taking into consideration both the strength and the weakness of his nature, pronounce it one in which the gigantic development of certain qualities renders more striking the dwarfish proportions of others. Fox as an example of heroic fortitude and heroic sincerity, deserves our admiration and respect. Fox as a teacher, requires to be followed with ceaseless vigilance and suspicion.

His life is one long record of communion with spirits. His

visions were countless. His power of magnetic healing was great. At Twycross he healed a sick person by prayer. At Arnside he restored to a man the use of one of his arms, when it had long been impotent. At Ulverstone he was himself instantly made whole by his spirit-guardians after having been beaten almost to death by a ferocious mob. He frequently proved himself possessed of the power of prophecy. Several years before the occurrence of that great fire which consumed half London it was predicted by Fox. He warned several of his persecutors that judgments would shortly befall them, and in no case did the person so warned escape. These spiritual gifts seem to have continued in unabated vigour down to the period when, full of years, and surrounded by a circle of attached disciples, the apostle of the Quakers died peacefully in his bed.

The rappings in the parsonage of Epworth have been too often described for a detailed history of them to be necessary here. The first lengthy account of these disturbances was published by John Wesley in the *Arminian Magazine*. Had the father of the famous Methodist but thought of questioning the spirits by means of the alphabet, a great spiritual movement might have convulsed England in the reign of George I. The knockings exactly resembled those of the present day. They gave the same proofs of being governed by an intelligent power. When Mrs. Wesley desired the spirit to refrain from vexing her devotions the knocks instantly ceased. At evening prayers raps were heard everywhere in the room whilst the prayer for the king was being repeated, and the loudest rap attended the "Amen." This circumstance had evident reference to an unfulfilled vow of Mr. Wesley, sen. Here is the story in John Wesley's words. "The year before King William died my father observed that my mother did not say Amen to the prayer for the king. She said she could not, for she did not believe the Prince of Orange was king. He vowed he would never cohabit with her till she did. He then took his horse and rode away, nor did she hear anything of him for a twelvemonth. He then came back and lived with her as before, but I fear his vow was not forgotten before God."

Having frightened the daughters of Mr. Wesley the spirit was bidden by him "to cease vexing those children and come to him in his study, who was a man." It readily obeyed. He begged of it, if the spirit of his son Samuel, to give three raps. The knocking at once ceased. Strangely enough no other questions were put. When, however, any of the family stamped with the foot the exact number of noises was repeated. A gentle tapping at the bed-head of the children began at the same hour every night. At length the spirit grew weary of its fruitless efforts. Towards the end of its endeavours to communicate the raps and other noises were constant. Mr. Wesley was advised to quit the house. He steadily refused. Suddenly all disturbance ceased. "Old Jeffery," as the children named the invisible knocker, had discovered that the vicar's mind was not of a calibre to comprehend his system of spirit-telegraphy. He therefore retired in disgust.

Spiritual gifts were common to John Wesley and the other founders of Methodism—Whitefield, and Fletcher of Madeley. Wesley healed numerous sick persons by prayer and the imposition of hands. He records the instantaneous cure of a woman named Mary Special of cancer in both breasts. His last sermon was a defence and advocacy of Spiritualism. To those who, like many in our own day, cried, "Cui bono?" Wesley makes answer, "If but one account of the intercourse of men with spirits be admitted, their (the unbelievers') whole castle in the air falls to the ground. I know no reason, therefore, why we should suffer this weapon to be wrested out of our hands."

Here this chapter must close. I have passed in review various of the lights of the Reformation in Germany and England; the mighty Luther, the noble Zwinglius, Calvin, with his hateful inhumanity, the stern Knox, the fervent Wishart. I have shown that the spiritual phenomena so common in Catholic ages have occurred with equal frequency in Protestant times and lands. The simple difference is, that the one Church encourages and the other represses them. When Protestantism succeeds in casting out the demon of unbelief that has at present full possession of her various sects she will for the first time be able to receive and comprehend the teachings of Christ. The credulity which, two centuries ago, ascribed all spiritual phenomena to the devil, was bad. The materialism which at the present day denies that the dead can return is still worse. We may bear with equanimity the retirement of his Satanic Majesty into the background: Lucifer's deposition will cause few any deep concern. But a Church which denies the possibility of communion between the departed and those yet on earth simply prepares the way for the triumph of infidelity. The fruit of her doctrines, as the present state of the public mind in England and Germany amply testifies, is a widespread disbelief in a hereafter and an open denial of God.

CHAPTER VII.

"THERE is a small market-town in the Upper Lusatia called Old Seidenburg, distant from Görlitz about a mile and a half, in which lived a man whose name was Jacob, and his wife's name was Ursula. People they were of the poorest sort, yet of sober and honest behaviour. In the year 1575 they had a son whom they called Jacob. This was the divinely illuminated Jacob Behmen ; the Teutonic philosopher whom God raised up to show the ground of the mystery of nature and grace, and open the wonders of His wisdom."

Such is the enthusiastic language which the biographer of Behmen holds towards the object of his idolatry. If Jacob were "raised up to expound the mysteries of nature and grace," he succeeded but ill in his task. Far from casting light on the subject, he wrapped it in deeper gloom. Yet he was certainly a great man. He seems like a blind giant pressing eagerly towards some mark which his affliction of darkness forbids him to discover, and stumbling over every obstacle that lies in his path. His works are as it were the misty nebulæ of that to which Swedenborg afterwards gave shape and consistence. They found anciently many admirers. Charles I. praised them ; George Fox " read and commended them ; " extracts from them were discovered amongst the MSS. of Isaac Newton. The Rev. William Law, author of the "Serious Call," was a zealous disciple of Behmen. But the deformed Titan has had his day. Few are to be found in the present age willing to wander in the misty region of Jacob's spiritual experience—his signs, his teachings, and his dreams.

Sixty-four years after the death of Behmen was born a truer and a greater prophet. Emanuel Swedenborg, who saw the light in 1688, prepared the way for a revolution of the popular idea regarding the future home of man which is still being silently accomplished. He was perhaps the mightiest seer of modern times. During twenty-eight years the clearness of his spiritual vision was such that he beheld constantly the scenes and the beings of another world. He astonished mankind by describing that world as having an intimate resemblance to our own. Its inhabitants he found employed in a

> " Better business
> Than loafing around the throne."

The golden harps were invisible, and the palm-branches had retired into infinite space. For beatified idleness there was spiritual industry ; and for eternal stagnation, endless progress. Futurity was peopled as earth is peopled. There were still men and women, and these men and women retained the aspirations, the joys, the sorrows, the affections of humanity. The just were busy in the service of good, the wicked in the service of evil. The high, while teaching the low, continued themselves to soar into regions of a grandeur more and more supreme ; and the low panted upward in their footsteps. Where yesterday was Socrates, to-day stood Aristophanes. Galileo, resting for an instant on the summit to which he had just attained, might see at the foot of the mountain some one of his ancient persecutors painfully commencing the ascent. There was nothing of the selfish strife of earth. No false prophet preached the doctrine of the "survival of the fittest." Man learned at length that his destiny was to ascend, and that eternity was given him for the accomplishment of that destiny. Sin was recognised as a disease, and suffering as the remedy of that disease. Progress was light ; stagnation was darkness ; every good deed accomplished, every bad passion trampled under foot, brought the soul a degree nearer to God. Those children alone knew true happiness who did constantly the work of the Father.

Such are the teachings which have by degrees become the substance of modern thought. They continue more and more to permeate society. The revelations of modern spiritualism are at one with the doctrines of Swedenborg. The influence of the Swedish seer on the mind of man is not to be judged of by the outer and more palpable tokens of that influence. It is by such things that the vulgar judge. The material portion of the world reverence only heroes as material as themselves. Had a creature of this sort been asked a hundred years ago to decide between the relative claims to greatness of Swedenborg and Frederic II. of Prussia, with what derision would he have dismissed the pretensions of the former! Was not the name of Frederic famous throughout the civilised world? Was he not the foremost soldier of his age? Had not he resisted successfully the combined efforts of France, Austria, Russia, Saxony, and Sweden? He was dreaded and admired in every court of Europe, from that of St. Petersburg to that of Lisbon. Portraits of the potentate of Berlin were to be found in a thousand towns and cities. Statues rose in his honour. The pens of eminent writers were employed to canonise or defame him. Could any name be more secure of immortality? Could any lot be more enviable?—And Swedenborg? A poor fool who saw visions and dreamed dreams.

Yet the prophet is likely to be mentioned with reverence when the conqueror is forgotten. The work of the one is ended, that of the other has but just commenced. What does earth owe to Frederic? A series of desolating wars, as causeless as dreadful. What does his history teach us? That great qualities and great vices may be found united in a single mind; that it is possible for a tyrant also to be a hero; that a crowned robber may hold so gallantly to the booty he has snatched as to render useless the efforts of half-a-dozen of his neighbours to recover it. His example is that of successful wickedness. His efforts were directed to the hindering of progress, and the making it law among men

> " That they should take who have the power,
>   And they should keep who can."

Fortunately the confusion created by those efforts has long spent

itself. Treaders in Frederic's footsteps have arisen; even as he
himself trod in the footsteps of Alexander and Cæsar; of Henry V.
of England, and Louis XIV. of France. But of Frederic himself
there remain only the name and the example. The one has lost
its interest; the other we could well spare. Earth has recovered
from the shock of the War of the Pragmatic Sanction, and the
greater shock of the War of the Seven Years. None are left who
fought at Rosbach. Every trace of the horrible carnage enacted
there has vanished from the fields of Leuthen and Kunersdorf.
A century ago Europe had an enthralling interest in such events.
The thrones of kings, the lives of tens of thousands of their subjects, the boundaries of nations, were involved in the fate of
Frederic and of Prussia. But that interest is extinguished. The
volcano has spent its rage. We learn with equal indifference that
at Fontenoy the French were commanded by a tactician and at
Rosbach by a dunce. Even in Germany the events of the Seven
Years are in themselves no longer productive of joy or grief. No
Russian army threatens Berlin. No Austrian host is levying contributions. These things were the miseries of a far-past day.
To the Prussian of the present age they are "the shadow of a
shade."

The difference then between Frederic and Swedenborg is the
difference between a body and a soul. The one is tangible, but
temporal; the other intangible, but eternal. The warrior for a
brief space influenced matter; the seer continues eternally to influence mind. What the multitude consider the necessary insignia of
power may, indeed, be wanting in his case. No eloquent pens and
tongues have celebrated his praise. No mighty sect reverences him
as its founder. Such a reverence would have been repulsive to the
nature of Swedenborg. His teachings were for all; not for a few.
He made no attempts to collect followers. He desired no dictatorship over human minds. His mission was simply with his whole
soul and strength to proclaim the truth. Having done so he left
that truth to fight her own way, secure that "the eternal years of
God are hers." Those, then, who base their judgment of a man
solely on externals will pronounce that Swedenborg has never

greatly influenced humanity, and is now almost forgotten. Those who look deeper will perceive everywhere tokens of his power. The most eloquent divines tincture their sermons with Swedenborgianism. The greatest writers, both in poetry and prose, preach it in a different fashion. He has, as Macaulay says of Bacon, "moved the minds who have moved the world." To Swedenborg is it in great measure owing that the old unnatural heaven, the old revolting hell, have, at the present day, all but vanished into air.

The favourable testimony of an enemy is always of more weight than the favourable testimony of a friend. I select therefore from the numerous narratives respecting the proofs given by Swedenborg of his spiritual powers, that of Immanuel Kant. It is in the form of a letter to a certain Fräulein von Knobloch:—

"In order, most gracious Fräulein, to give you a few evidences of what the whole living public are witnesses of, and which the gentleman who sends them to me has carefully verified on the spot, allow me to lay before you the two following incidents :

"Madame Harteville, the widow of the Dutch envoy in Stockholm, some time after the death of her husband, received a demand from the goldsmith, Croon, for payment for a silver service which her husband had ordered from him. The widow was confidently persuaded that her husband had been much too orderly to allow this debt to remain unpaid ; but she could discover no receipt. In this trouble, and since the amount was considerable, she begged Baron Swedenborg to give her a call. After some apologies she ventured to say to him that if he had the extraordinary gift, as all men affirmed, of conversing with departed souls, she hoped that he would have the goodness to inquire of her husband how it stood with the demand for the silver service. Swedenborg made no difficulty in meeting her wishes. Three days after this the lady had a company of friends taking coffee with her ; Baron Swedenborg entered, and in his matter-of-fact way informed her that he had spoken with her husband ; that the debt had been discharged some months before his death, and that the receipt was in a certain cabinet which she would find in an upper room. The lady replied that this cabinet had been completely emptied, and amongst the whole of the papers this receipt could not be found. Swedenborg said that her husband had described to him that, if they drew forth a drawer on the left side they would see a board, which being pushed aside, they would find a concealed drawer in which was kept his secret correspondence with Holland, and there this receipt would be found. On this representation the lady betook herself, with all the company, to the upper room. The cabinet was opened; they found the secret drawer described, of which she had hitherto known nothing, and in it the required paper, to the intense amazement of all present.

"The following circumstance, however, appears to me to possess the greatest strength of evidence of all these cases, and actually takes away every conceivable issue of doubt.

"In the year 1756, as Baron Swedenborg, towards the end of the month of September, at four o'clock on a Saturday evening, landed in Gottenburg from England, Mr. William Castel invited him to his house with fifteen other persons. About six o'clock in the evening Swedenborg went out and returned shortly to the company, pale and disturbed. He said that at that moment there was a terrible conflagration raging in Stockholm, on the Südermalm, and that the fire was increasing. Gottenburg lies three hundred miles from Stockholm. He was uneasy, and frequently went out. He said that the house of one of his friends, whom he named, was already laid in ashes, and that his own house was in danger. At eight o'clock, after he had again gone out, he said joyfully, 'God be praised! .the fire is extinguished, the third door from my very house.' This information occasioned the greatest excitement in the company and throughout the whole city, and the statement was carried to the Governor the same evening. Next morning he sent for Swedenborg, and asked him about the matter. Swedenborg described exactly the conflagration; how it had begun, and the time of its continuance. As the Governor had given attention to the story, it occasioned a still greater commotion throughout the city, where many were in great concern on account of their friends and their property. On Monday evening arrived in Gottenburg a courier who had been dispatched by the merchants of Stockholm during the fire. In the letters brought by him the conflagration was described exactly as Swedenborg had stated it. On the Tuesday morning a royal courier came to the Governor with the account of the fire, of the loss it had occasioned, and of the houses which it had attacked; not in the least differing from the statement made by Swedenborg at the moment of its occurrence, for the fire had been extinguished at eight o'clock.

"Now, what can any one oppose to the credibility of these occurrences? The friend who writes these things to me has not only examined into them in Stockholm, but about two months ago in Gottenburg, where he was well known to the most distinguished families, and where he could completely inform himself from a whole city, in which the short interval from 1756 left the greater part of the eye-witnesses still living. He has at the same time given me an account of the mode in which, according to the assertion of Baron Swedenborg, his ordinary intercourse with other spirits takes place, as well as the idea which he gives of the condition of departed souls."

With feelings of admiration and affection I take my leave of the great Swedish seer. I make no attempt to canonise him as an example of perfect excellence. He had many of the usual failings of humanity. His character was disfigured by strange eccentricities. But, taking him on the whole, he was a Saul who towered head and shoulders above his generation. If any readers of this work have not yet studied the life and writings of Swedenborg, I advise them to do so without delay, secure that, when the pleasurable task is accomplished, they will confess with Thomas Carlyle " that never until then did they comprehend how great a prophet had been among mankind."

The most marked characteristic of Jung-Stilling was his intense and unquenchable faith. He had the strongest confidence in the Providence of God; the most vivid conception of the nearness of another world. His career is one of the few which from the outset to the close are delightful to contemplate. " Let this be thy greatest honour in the world," said his grandfather to him, " that thy forefathers were all men who, though they had nothing under their command out of their house, were, notwithstanding, beloved and honoured by all men." Stilling never forgot the words. He lived and died beloved and honoured by all whose love and honour were worthy to be prized.

From the humbleness of a seat on a tailor's shop-board he struggled through the various grades of merchant's clerk, schoolmaster, and family tutor, till he reached the university, which he entered with the sum of one dollar in his pocket. For years he fought against the deepest poverty. His faith was veritably tried with fire, and proved itself genuine. At times marvellous occurrences sustained it. He commenced his studies, as I have said, with a single rix-dollar for capital. For the whole course a thousand dollars were necessary. Stilling knew not where to raise the fiftieth part of the sum. Yet the anxiety which tormented him did not for an instant cause his trust in God to waver. He met an acquaintance whom he terms Leibmann. " Where," said this last, " do you get money for your studies ? " " From God," was Stilling's reply. " I," said Leibmann, " am one

of God's stewards," and handed the penniless youth thirty-three
dollars. He afterwards sent him a further remittance of three
hundred. By these and similar acts of kindness, Stilling was
enabled to struggle on until he had obtained his diploma. He
then married, and commenced practice as a physician. His
capital was five rix-dollars.

The fight was sharp. In the midst of his difficulties he contracted an intimate acquaintance with Goethe, Herder, and others
of the leaders of German thought. The first and greatest of these
became warmly attached to him. He urged him to write memoirs
of his life. Stilling consented, and, in a period of great adversity,
accomplished the task. Through the kindly offices of Goethe the
work was sold for a hundred and fifteen rix-dollars. It was the
turning-point of the author's career. The money lifted him out of
his difficulties. The book made him famous.

He was appointed Professor of Agriculture at Rittersberg. In
Elberfeld, where he had settled to practise as a physician, he owed
eight hundred dollars, and knew not how to defray the debt.
Certain of the chief merchants, however, hearing that he intended
quitting the town, made him parting presents. He counted the
sum thus obtained, and found it eight hundred dollars, neither
more nor less. [It sufficed exactly, therefore, to satisfy his creditors, and with an empty purse he left the place. A few years
later, he became famous for the cure of cataract, and at the same
time debt again pressed heavily on him. He was sent for, to
perform operations in Switzerland. One thousand six hundred
and fifty gulden were paid to him, exactly the amount that he
owed. His whole life abounds with such instances of pressing
need, and providential supply.

The most famous of his works were written under spiritual
dictation. These are "Nostalgia," and "Scenes in the Invisible
World." Of the latter we learn that "the state of mind which
Stilling experienced whilst labouring at this work is utterly
indescribable. His spirit was as if elevated into ethereal regions
a feeling of serenity and peace pervaded him, and he enjoyed a
felicity which words cannot express. When he began to work

ideas glistened past his soul, which animated him so much that he could scarcely write so rapidly as the flow of thought required. This was also the reason why the whole work took quite another form, and the composition quite another tendency, to that which he had proposed at the commencement." Of the " Nostalgia " we are told :—" There was besides another singular phenomenon. In the state between sleeping and waking, the most beautiful and as it were heavenly imagery presented itself to his inward sense. He attempted to delineate it, but found this impossible.; with the imagery there was always a feeling connected, compared with which all the joys of sense are as nothing. It was a blissful season ! "

The " Nostalgia " was received with enthusiasm. The author found that certain scenes in his work, which he had supposed to be fiction, were actual fact. A great prince wrote, demanding how he had learned the particulars of a certain secret association. Stilling could only reply that the very existence of the association was unknown to him. One day a handsome young man whom he says was the celebrated ——, but leaves his readers to guess the name, entered his apartment. This visitor saluted the author of the " Nostalgia," as his secret superior. Stilling utterly disclaimed the imputed honour. " How then," said the stranger, " did you contrive so accurately to describe the great and venerable brotherhood in the East, to point out our rendezvous in Egypt, in Mount Sinai, in the monastery of Canobin, and under the temple of Jerusalem ? " " All fiction," answered Stilling. " Pardon me," cried the other, " that cannot be ; the matter is in truth and reality as you have described it ; such a thing cannot have come by chance ! " And he retired, dissatisfied.

On the 18th of July, 1799, Stilling predicted the death of Lavater. In a letter, that day, to Antistes Hess, of Zurich, he informed him that, whilst writing, he had felt suddenly a deep impression that a violent and bloody end awaited the great Switzer. He desired that this might be communicated to him. Exactly three months later the army of Massena stormed Zurich, and Lavater was shot down at his own door. Other of Stilling's presentiments proved equally unerring. Did space permit, a number of interesting cases might be adduced from his "Pneumatology." But Zschokke, Oberlin, Madame Hauffé, and others, have yet to be noticed, and I am forced to pass on. I do so, citing that noble passage from "Scenes in the Invisible World," which contains so forcible an apology for the author's spiritual faith :—" Whether we are reckoned fools and ignoramuses, or set down as mad fanatics—it is all one. Our Lord and Master himself was pronounced such. Let us go out to Him, and bear his shame."

Zschokke was by birth a German, by adoption a Swiss. He combined the almost irreconcilable attributes of a profound thinker and an energetic man of action. Devoted, during the greater part of his life, to the public service of the Helvetian Republic, his intense patriotism yet allowed him to gratify, so far as opportunity permitted, the equally intense desire which possessed him for knowledge respecting the things of another world. He was himself gifted with a peculiar phase of mediumship. The past experiences of many with whom he conversed were presented to his mind.

"It has happened to me sometimes," says he, "on my first meeting with strangers, that, as I listened silently to their discourse, their former life, or some particular scene in that life, has passed, quite involuntarily and as it were dream-like, before me. During this time I usually feel so absorbed in contemplation of the stranger life that I no longer see clearly the face of the unknown, wherein I undesignedly look ; nor distinctly hear the voices of the speakers, which before served in some measure as a commentary to the text of their features. For a long time I held such visions as delusions of the fancy ; the more so that they showed me even the dress and motions of the actors, the rooms, furniture, and other accessories. By way of test I once, in a familiar family circle at Kirchberg, related the secret history of a seamstress who had just left the room and the house. I had never seen her before in my life. People were astonished, and laughed ; but were not to be persuaded that I did not previously know the relations of which I spoke ; for what I had uttered was the *literal* truth. On my part I was no less astonished that my dream-pictures were confirmed by the reality. I became more attentive to the subject, and when propriety admitted it, I would relate to those whose life thus passed before me the subject of my vision, that

I might thereby obtain confirmation or refutation of it. It was invariably ratified, not without consternation on their part. 'What demon inspires you? Must I again believe in possession?' exclaimed the *spiritual* Johann von Riga, when, in the first hour of our acquaintance, I related his past life to him. We speculated long on the enigma, but even his penetration could not solve it. I myself had less confidence than any one in this mental jugglery. As often as I revealed my visionary gifts to any new person I regularly expected to hear the answer, 'It was not so.' I felt a secret shudder when my auditors replied that it was true, or when their astonishment betrayed my accuracy before I asked. I will mention one example which pre-eminently astounded me. One fair day, in the City of Waldshut, I entered the Vine Inn in company with two young student foresters. We supped with a numerous company at the table d'hôte, where the guests were making very merry with the peculiarities and eccentricities of the Swiss ; with Mesmer's magnetism, Lavater's physiognomy, &c. One of my companions, whose national pride was wounded by their mockery, begged me to make some reply, particularly to a handsome young man who sat opposite to me, and who allowed himself extraordinary license. This man's former life was at that moment presented to my mind. I turned to him and asked whether he would answer me candidly if I related to him some of the most secret passages of his life ; I knowing as little of him personally as he did of me? That would be going a little further, I thought, than the physiognomy of Lavater. He promised, if I were correct in my information, to admit it frankly. I then related what my vision had shown me, and the whole company were made acquainted with the private history of the young merchant, his school years, his youthful errors, and lastly, with a fault committed in reference to the strong-box of his principal. I described to him the uninhabited room with whitened walls, where to the right of the brown door, on a table, stood a black money-box, &c. A dead silence prevailed during the whole narrative, which I alone occasionally interrupted by inquiring whether I spoke the truth? The startled young man confirmed every particular, and even, what I had scarcely expected, the last mentioned. Touched by his candour, I shook hands with him over the table and said no more."

On the 22nd of February, 1862, passed from earth Dr. Justinius Kerner. Distinguished both as a physician and a poet, he interests us yet more on account of his patient, Madame Hauffe, widely known as " the Seeress of Prevorst." Kerner's account of this extraordinary case was published in 1829, and went through three editions. Pseudo-scientists, as was natural, received it with much easy derision. Observers more worthy of the name, who had taken the trouble to inquire into the facts of the case, confirmed all that the doctor had stated. Among these last were such men as Kant, Schubert, Eschenmayer, Görres, and Werner. They, without exception, pronounced Madame Hauffé a clairvoyante of the highest order, " who lived more in the spiritual world than in the physical." Her soul was retained in its casket by the frailest of threads.

She was twenty-five when she came under the care of Kerner, and twenty-eight when she passed from earth. Even while yet a child she proved herself a medium. Her sensitiveness was excessive; she shuddered at the neighbourhood of graves, and in church could not remain below, but went up to the loft. At twenty she married, and went to live at Kurnbach, a solitary and gloomy village, lying embosomed among savage mountains. Here her ill-health and her spiritual development increased together. The physicians were bewildered with her case. Several considered her illness hypochondriacal, and her visions and prophecies wilful imposture. Her relations became prejudiced against her, and treated her with the utmost harshness. As a last resource they carried her to Weinsberg, and constituted her a patient of Kerner.

This was on November 25th, 1826. The unfortunate woman reached her new abode more dead than alive. It was imperative to give her every few minutes a spoonful of soup, to prevent her swooning away. Kerner's rebukes increased her misery; he had been prejudiced against her by the reports that had reached his ears, and considered her a compound of hysteria and cunning. He now informed her, with the utmost sternness, that her pretences of clairvoyance and magnetic slumber must at once cease. He was determined to listen to nothing which she said whilst assuming to be in such a state.

His opinion speedily altered. During two and a half years he continued to observe the manifestations which occurred to Madame Hauffé, becoming every day more convinced of their spiritual origin. Like other clairvoyants she read letters laid upon her body, which were enclosed between thick sheets of paper. She made many predictions, and the predictions were always fulfilled.

Numerous spirits rendered themselves visible to her, and were recognised from the descriptions which she gave. By means of communications from one of these visitors, a mystery was cleared up which had continued to cause unpleasantness for nearly six years. Whilst in the magnetic sleep she spoke a language unknown to any about her. She executed various remarkable drawings under spirit-influence. Revelations were made through her immeasurably beyond the scope of her intellect in its normal state. She had received but the scantiest modicum of education; yet, without ever having heard of those leaders of thought, she gave teachings mystically resembling certain abstruse theories of Pythagoras, Plato, Leibnitz, and Swedenborg. Various physical manifestations attended her; articles were thrown by invisible hands about the house in which she dwelt; furniture rose and floated in the air; she was herself levitated several times. On one occasion there appeared a figure surrounded by a bluish light, which figure was visible to all present. In the face of evidence so strong it is not surprising that Kerner, from a determined sceptic, became a firm spiritualist. All who candidly examine into the facts of the case must agree with the great German's verdict regarding his patient. " She was more than half a spirit, and belonged to a world of spirits; she belonged to a world after death, and was more than half dead. In her sleep only was she truly awake; nay, so loose was the connection between soul and body that, like Swedenborg, she often went out of the body and could contemplate it separately."

Oberlin, the great pastor of Alsace, found, on commencing his evangelical labours in Steinthal, that the people had a devout belief in the return of the departed. He was intensely grieved that his parishioners should be attached to what he regarded as a pernicious and degrading superstition. He denounced their faith from the pulpit; he reproved it in private; he set himself to reason down the chimæra. Far from succeeding, the stubborn logic of facts caused him to become himself a most earnest believer in spirit-communion. His departed wife appeared to him many times; almost daily she sat conversing with him, and, describing the conditions of life in the next world, counselled him regarding his undertakings in this. Occasionally she was visible to others of the household. These visits continued for nine years; then a spirit-message reached the good pastor, informing him that his wife had passed to a higher sphere, and could return no more. Deprived of the comfort of her presence, Oberlin found a certain solace in meditation upon the events of that long communion so suddenly brought to an end. In a simple and affecting narrative he has recorded the particulars.

I might extend this chapter to an incredible length by the introduction, from the lives of other famous men, of spiritual facts highly worthy of notice. The renowned therapeutist Gassner, the gentle and philosophic Lavater, the enlightened Eschenmayer, the learned and conscientious Schubert; Görres, in youth the fiery worshipper of freedom, in age the eloquent defender of Spiritualism; —the diligent Ennemoser, the brilliant Kant, the great Schiller, the greater Goethe,—to all these the next world was brought close, and their faith in its realities made more vivid by the veil which drapes that world being at moments partially withdrawn. In our own country, in France, in Italy, in Russia, in every land of either hemisphere, spiritualists, equally distinguished, have in all ages stood forth boldly from the common run of men, and done battle for the truth. Want of space, and no want of admiration for their valour, alone forbids me doing honour to their names. The nature of the task I have taken upon myself is opposed to a frequent descent from the general to the particular. I turn, therefore, from the dim greatness of the past, casting, as I withdraw, a look of lingering regard upon that noble company amongst whom I have been busied. From the lights and shadows which exist for us but in history, I turn to the living realities of the present.

With what pleasure does the eye of the mind rest on the great believers long departed from earth! Compared with the paths in which they trod, the pilgrimage of a spiritualist of to-day is "through pleasant meadows, and by the side of refreshing waters." How many of us, if placed in the situation of these old heroes and heroines, would cast down every weapon and flee ignominiously

from the fight! How few would have the heart to endure steadfastly to the end! Servants of God were they, for whom,
assuredly, the Master had reserved crowns of righteousness, and
to whom, as they passed into His presence, He said " Well done ! "
A nobler army of martyrs earth has seldom seen. They are
gathered from every country and era. The wise, the pious, the
gentle, the patriotic—Socrates, Polycarp, Hypatia, Savonarola—all
are there. But, purest of the pure, greatest of the great, clothed
with a celestial glory, radiant with an everlasting fame, towers up
foremost of that indomitable host the empress of womanhood, the
fear of England, the thunderbolt of France, the wonder of every
age, the reproach of her own. In that mind it is scarcely a
hyperbole to say that every virtue had met. High above even the
high teacher of Plato rises the stately form, shine the beautiful
features, of the daughter of Heaven, Jeanne d'Arc.

NOTE.—In composing the first and second parts of my work great assistance
has been afforded me by Mr. W. Howitt's valuable " History of the Supernatural."

PART III.

MODERN SPIRITUALISM.

CHAPTER I.

INTRODUCTORY.

THE chapters now opening are to myself, and I trust will prove to
my readers, the most interesting and important of the volume.
For years I have seen with pain abuse after abuse attach itself to
a cause in whose service my life has been passed, and with which
such foulnesses have nothing in common. So wonderfully have
these parasites increased and multiplied, that, like a pearl crusted
with spots of dirt, the purity and beauty of the original seem
at present almost hidden; and I cannot too strongly reiterate
my conviction, that between spiritualism and the majority of the
abuses by which it is disgraced there is just as little in common
as between a precious stone and the mud which may happen to
cling to it. Perceiving this, and guided by promptings altogether
apart from my own mind, I determined to write a work in which,
whilst the beauty and radiance of the truth were sufficiently
dwelt upon, the corruptions ever striving to darken and degrade it
were, in the interests of that truth, analyzed and exposed. An
experience exceedingly varied, and extending over a period of
five-and-twenty years, gives me, to my own mind, and will give
me to the minds of the reasoning portion of humanity, sufficient
title to be heard. Pecuniary motives in publishing this work
I have none. The desire to create a sensation is equally far from

N

influencing me. As a duty I accepted the task, and as a duty I
shall endeavour dispassionately and unshrinkingly to fulfil it. I
shall level no attacks at individuals, but will simply, by recording
facts, and making plain the philosophy of those facts, attempt
to serve the truth. That all honest and intelligent lovers of that
truth will be upon my side I am certain. That all the dupes and
tricksters who are in any way bigoted to or concerned in upholding imposture, will join in a common chorus of fury against me,
I am also conscious. Indeed, of the verity of both hypotheses I
have already been afforded convincing proof. Some time back I
briefly made known by an advertisement the work in which I was
engaged, and asked for assistance in points where I considered
that assistance might be of service. Not a single name was mentioned or even hinted at ; not an allusion made which could be
considered as directed against the fame of any individual in the
old world or the new. Generalities were all that I dealt in, and
seldom have generalities raised such a storm. I was assailed,
both openly and anonymously, with slander, lying charges, foul
personalities, venomous abuse—in short with every weapon which
the most unscrupulous partisan hatred can direct against the
object of its hostility. It was what I expected, and what I had
been forewarned of. If the attacks made on me have moved me at
moments, the support I have received from within and without,
and the consciousness of the rectitude of my intentions, have
made the effect but that of a moment. The few, but of course
unpleasant anonymous letters sent me, I pass over with contempt.
To carry such emanations to the nearest fireplace is all that an
ordinary human being can do. Of my open, and thus more
respectable enemies, I need say almost equally little. All through
my life the evil spoken of me by outsiders has been to me a
matter of extreme indifference. I am fortunate in possessing a
large circle of friends, who have in many instances known me
from my childhood. Their esteem and respect I have, and I
desire no more. Had that esteem been vulnerable to the assaults
of calumny, it would have been shaken long ere now. I believe
that there is scarcely any crime, or any mode of deception,

possible or impossible, which has not been imputed to me. Some
of these I might have accomplished unaided, but in by far the
greater number accomplices would have been imperatively necessary. The impossibility of my, under the circumstances, having
had these accomplices is a point which scandal-mongers invariably
contrive to forget. I have said that when a cowardly stab is
dealt me in the dark I bear it quietly ; having confidence in the
good sense of my friends, and caring nothing for what my enemies
may think, or profess to think. I speak this simply with reference
to my moral character. There I belong to myself, and conscious
of their baselessness, can look with forgiving contempt on " the
small whispers of the paltry few." It is far otherwise when my
character as a medium is impugned. In this I am the exponent
of a cause counting its adherents by millions in both the old world
and the new. As the servant of a power outside of, and uncomprehended by myself, I am compelled to protect this phase of my character from misconception and misrepresentation. Where, through
the malignancy of enemies, libels tending to throw suspicion on
particular manifestations occurring through me have been circulated,
I have uniformly, if able to trace those libels to their source,
succeeded in proving them groundless. If in the case of honest
inquirers doubt has arisen, I have always found my best remedy
to be perfect passivity. Again and again the particular manifestation called in question would be repeated through me, and repeated
under conditions utterly precluding the idea of trickery. I may
add that I like, and have always liked, to meet with an intelligent
and honest sceptic. The questions asked by such a one are, as a
rule, pertinent and natural. His reluctance to accept untested
phenomena is only the natural reluctance which all beings gifted
with reason feel to commit themselves to a blind faith in the
unknown, and readily vanishes when that unknown becomes the
known and proved. I have never myself found the spirit-world
" up in arms," when confronted with a doubter of this class.
Can there by any possibility be a more illogical cry than that
vociferated everywhere at the present day ? The same folly
appears and re-appears under a hundred different shapes. " Make

no attempt," cries one, "to bring over sceptics." "The spirits desire no converts," adds a second. "Let us shut out all but the enthusiastic and easily duped from our *séances*," proposes a third. Such are the insane utterances which at present grieve and disgust sensible spiritualists, and which lead directly up to the frauds it is my aim to denounce and expose. I am confident of reckoning on my side all whose eyes are fairly opened to the imminence of the evils which menace our cause. The best friends of spiritualism are inimical to its present aspect. Men of science who have investigated or would desire to investigate the subject, are repelled by the attitude which certain calling themselves spiritualists assume, and by the seething mass of folly and imposture which every attempt at examination discloses. This condition of things has long been to me a wonder and a grief. After much consideration, I determined on the present work. Before commencing it, I apprised various friends of my intention, and requested their counsel and opinions. Those opinions were in the majority of instances favourable. I was pleased to find that a wide-spread conviction existed, both of the necessity of such a protest as this volume constitutes, and of my fitness for the task of uttering it. To give the whole, or even the greater part, of the letters which have encouraged me is impossible ; and I content myself with returning thanks to their writers. But there are certain prominent spiritualists, old and much valued friends of mine, and names of weight in the movement, whose expressions of opinion I desire, and have obtained permission to quote. Let me submit first to the reader the sentiments of my friends, Mr. and Mrs. S. C. Hall. The former writes to me (under date 11th January, 1876) :—

"MY DEAR DANIEL.

"I rejoice to know that you have been called upon to do this work : I believe it is an inspired call ; that you are the only person who could do it, and that you will be aided by holy, good, and pure Christian spirits and angels sent direct by God. I shall pray fervently for help to you in your holy work.

"Spiritualism now is in a sad state of disorder, and is producing frightfully evil work. It may be—I trust and believe it will be—released and relieved from the burden of filth that weighs it down, and, I repeat, nobody living in this life can do the work so effectually as you can.

"You will pray—you have prayed—for the guidance of God and our Lord Christ, and the direct help of beatified angels. You will have all these, I am very sure.

"M. and I had much talk over this matter last night, when your letter came ; and she bids me say, with her affectionate regards, that she takes exactly the same view as I do—and with me prays that God will be your guide. We are fully sure He will be.

"The excuse for trickery I now find to be that evil or deceptive spirits 'come in,' and do the tricks—for which the medium is really not responsible ; that in a normal state he or she would be incapable of fraud ; that the spirits do the cheating independently of them.

"But surely such spirits, such *séances*, such persons, are to be avoided ; each and all shunned, in private or in public circles. It is the pitch that cannot be touched without defilement.

"Ever your friend,

"S. C. HALL."

"It is clear to us, my dear Daniel," writes Mrs. Hall, "that God has spared you for the express purpose of proving pure spiritualism to be the handmaid of Christianity :—that is what I always believed it to be."

The following lines are from the pen of that eloquent defender of true spiritualism, Mr. William Howitt :—

"This, my dear Mr. Home, is what I said so much disgusted me with the spiritualists. The petty cliques, the low aims, the spites and factions of spiritualists; the lying mediums and lying spirits who speak through them, confirm everything that the outsiders say of spiritualism being from the devil. The materialists, Carpenter, G. H. Lewes, the *Times*, are always writing against spiritualism, but they produce no effect. The thing lives in spite of them ; but, if anything can kill it, it will be the follies and contemptible meannesses of the spiritualists themselves."

"I have been informed by two or three people," Dr. Sexton tells me (June 6th, 1876), "that you have given up the idea of publishing your new book. Is that so ? I hope not. The need for such a work increases day by day : in fact, if something be not done—and speedily—to put an end to the outrageous trickery that passes current under the guise of spiritualism, the whole thing will be ruined. The worst part of it is that mediums who have been caught cheating are still tolerated in the movement, and defended by men whose sole business ought to be to drive them out of our ranks. I have to suffer terribly for the course I take. What with my denunciation of the tricksters, and my advocacy of Christianity, I am avoided and shunned by great numbers, and denounced as a traitor to the cause. Still I shall go on doing what I believe to be right, and leave the issue to God."

In a previous letter he says :—

"It is really heart-breaking that a noble cause should be thus dragged in the mud. If you saw the letters that I receive on the subject from good, pious, Christian men, you would grieve more than you do, and I know that you feel it keenly as it is."

It has been again and again repeated to me that I should find no other medium in favour of my work. Let me submit a couple of extracts which would seem to disprove this assertion. In a letter dated February 17th, 1876, Mrs. K. Fox-Jencken thus expresses her sympathy with the objects I have in view:—

"MY DEAR MR. HOME,—

"I was very happy to hear from you, and to learn that you were writing such an important book. I am truly glad, and I think it will be one of the most valuable works ever written. Anything that I can do to aid you in bringing it forth I will do with all my heart. No one has dared to do this except yourself; I was myself contemplating it but thought I would wait. Some good spirit must have admonished you to do it.

"Yours,

"K. F. JENCKEN."

"I know," writes Mrs. M. Sunderland Cooper to me, "that you are doing a work which is right and just, and I think every honest and truthful medium will give you a helping hand. And this I propose to do. I gave the first public *séance* for spiritual manifestations in New England. I was then a mere child. My father edited and published the first spiritual paper ever published in the world—Dr. Laroy Sunderland; you have no doubt heard of him. But the pioneers of spiritualism are pushed on one side, and Indian gibberish, and dark *séancism* ('Punch and Judy shows,' as you call them) are all the rage now. And the mediums who have these dark circles, no matter how many times they are exposed by investigators for the truth, are allowed to go on, and upheld by some of the spiritual papers of the day."

With these quotations I may rest content. There are various persons styling themselves "mediums" whose approbation I should be very sorry to have for any work of mine, but whose opposition I consider a striking testimony to its value.

To return to pleasanter themes. Only a fortnight back there reached me, from an esteemed co-worker in the cause of truth, the accompanying expression of opinion :—

"*Sept.* 1st, 1876.

" MY RESPECTED FRIEND,—

"Your most unexpected, but, I must assure you, most welcome letter, came two weeks ago, but found me suffering from fever, from which I have only so far recovered as to-day for the first time to be able to sit at my desk. Had it been otherwise I should have written by return mail a Godspeed to the great and needed enterprise in which you are engaged. A book like that you propose is needed, and no one can prepare it better than you. We here are in a strange state of transition ; and it seems to me the larger the camel offered by the mediums the better for the credulous mass of swallowers. The demand for marvels is insatiate—so great that, like H——, a class propose to shut their eyes to make them greater. Spiritualism will run a brief career to ruin if this tide is not at once stayed. It is a great science. It rests on *facts*, well observed and recorded, and the mass of loose observations which passes for such is of little account. In my connection as reviewer with the press, I am amazed at the mass of rubbish borne on this great tide.

" Most fraternally yours,

" HUDSON TUTTLE."

Such are samples of the communications which have from time to time cheered me whilst I laboured on the present work. Every friendly opinion of my task, however, has not been so favourable. Of the dissuasive counsels tendered me, some have evidently proceeded from a misconception of my aims. Thus my friend, Mr. William Crookes, writes to me :—

"*Jan.* 21st, 1876.

"I am doubtful whether such a book as you propose to publish will do any real good. You know mediums have the reputation of being very jealous one of another, and consequently, any accusations which may be brought by one against another, however well supported they may be by facts, are explained away in this manner. And even when two partners quarrel, and one makes a clean breast of it, or when one medium makes a confession of fraud, and explains how it is done, very

few thorough-going spiritualists will believe them, but will rather call in
the agency of bad spirits, trance, &c.

"Another thing you must bear in mind—you, or I, or any other
tolerably clear-headed observer may be perfectly sure that cheating is
being perpetrated by some professed medium ; we may even have had a
full confession by the medium that the whole thing is a fraud ; yet it
may be so difficult as to amount practically to an impossibility to bring
this fraud home to the impostor in so clear a manner as would compen-
sate one for the vexation and trouble which would thereby be caused."

I have no intention of making charges against particular persons.
I simply design to put the array of facts which I have collected in
so clear and strong a light that the reasoning portion of the world
may find it easy to draw conclusions from the said facts. From
the unreasoning portion of humanity it is of course quite natural
that such outbursts as the following should proceed. Be it
remarked that the writer is of mature years, and claims the title of
" a leading American spiritualist."

"*March 10th,* 1876.

"ASTONISHMENT ! SURPRISE ! MARVEL ! Have the heavens fallen
upon you, Mr. Home, and crushed out your humanity ? . . . . Have you
forgotten the golden rule of Confucius : 'Do unto others,' &c. ? Have
Christ's teachings, 'Love one another,' &c., been in vain ? Do you
believe in one of the unvarying laws of God—compensation ?

"You may be 'taking the bull by the horns,' but you are certainly
entering the field, as it were, of the deadly rattlesnake, that warns you,
and does not strike without a warning. Your road before you is a
' broad one,' but it leads to destruction ; for, as sure as there is a God, as
sure as justice, sooner or later, hounds out malice and evil, so sure you
will be called to account for your slanders—and I write advisedly.

"I cannot think of a more ungracious, ill-repaying task than that of
exposing the faults of others. 'I will repay,' says the Lord, and can
you not trust to Him ? Every 'exposure,' *however true and well-sustained
it may be,* will only be a thorn—a sharp, a cruel thorn—in your future
path. Your alliance with the Russian nobility, your high social position
in England, will not shield you. You will fall like LUCIFER, and, if not
with a bullet through your head,* I believe it will be with shame and
sorrow in your heart. You will go down to your grave mourned by few
but despised by many ; whereas you have it in your power—no, you *had*
it, to make the world rejoice that you had lived. . . . . You will doubt-

* Did Lucifer fall "with a bullet through his head ?" If so, we need
hardly be surprised at Shakspeare's assurance that those who fall, fall like
Lucifer, "never to rise again."

less say that you only promulgate the *truth.* Is the *truth* even to be spoken at all times? *What is truth to-day may not be so to-morrow.* A man or a woman may be immoral this year, and as pure as an angel the next. The thief upon the cross was forgiven at the last moment. 'None of these condemn thee, neither do I," was the beautiful expression of Him who *loved* so much, and said, ' Let him who is without sin throw the first stone.' *Conversions* at our many ' revivals' mean that the person was a sinner, and has now become good ; and while you might have said of some of these converted ones, ' You are a vile wretch, a drunkard, a slanderer' (meaning ' you were '), you would have done a great wrong and spoken falsely, whereas a little while before it might have been the truth.

"But really what have *we* to do with the faults of others? When Christ turned to the back-biters what did he say? ' Pluck the beam," &c. ; and this implied more : ' Mind your own business, and let your brother alone ;' and if you had done this, Mr. Home, you would have withheld a stinging shaft that will return to you, a bitter draught you will sooner or later be obliged (or your memory will) to accept. . . . . Now, Mr. Home, ... I cannot but ask God to forgive you, for ' you know not what you do.' The *interior* ' light' of which Christ spoke, I am morally certain you do not possess, and I beg of you, with all the earnestness I can command, with much admiration of the good you have done as a wonderful medium, to seek that light. Moses, Plato, Jesus, Apollonius, Plotinus, Pythagoras, Porphyrius ; and in more modern times, Bacon, Flood, Cagliostro, the Fakirs of India, had this light, and the Fakirs have it now. It is God's divine truth ; the absolute wisdom and perfect intelligence of the Buddhists.

" . . . . I pray for your health and happiness.

" G. D——."

Such is, with the exception of a few omitted sentences, a *fac-simile* of this incomparable production. Since the writer's large charity leads him so benevolently to pray for me, I am benevolent enough in return to abstain from giving his name. To comment on his letter is, of course, almost impossible. I cannot refrain, however, from lingering a moment over that astonishing list of " possessors of the interior light." Omitting the name of Christ from such a comparison, may we not expect to hear soon that " Socrates, Solomon, Isaiah, Jeremiah, and Nebuchadnezzar in ancient times ; and Sir Isaac Newton, Dr. Mesmer, Joe Smith, and Messrs. Maskelyne and Cooke in more modern days, were prophets of God, and Maskelyne and Cooke are his prophets now " ?

Unsatisfied with inflicting on me such a letter as the foregoing, the writer is hard-hearted enough to add a postscript of two closely written pages. Here are a few extracts which excellently illustrate the character of their author :—

" You say you are a great invalid. A person told me that he knew a man still paralyzed, who came by his misfortune in this wise. One day he had been abusing unmercifully a child left to his care by a deceased brother ; and, as the man, or brute, passed out of the room, the deceased brother met him in the hall (so he says) and with a mighty blow felled him to the earth. He arose paralyzed, and still sits thus in his chair. ' Whom the gods wish to destroy,' &c. *God will not*, our *good loving God*, will not help you to publish your book. . . . .

" Now, Mr. Home, as a brother spiritualist, as one who wishes you well, as one who will pray for your liberation from these un-Christ-like diabolical spirits, as one who is much your senior in years, take my advice and *abandon* the idea and the practice of *exposing others*, and you will thank me, and thank God, and the *loving, forgiving* Jesus, for being led to do it. You see already how you are accused publicly of being now 'a tool of the Jesuits ;' and hosts will believe it, and hate you for it.

" God enlighten you is the prayer of

" Yours,

"G. D——."

Strange that a man should reduce himself to the writing of letters such as this ? Let us blush once more for human nature, and pass on. To be angry with the effusion is impossible, for it seems to me sunk even beneath the level of contempt.

I might quote other letters of the kind; but, after such a jewel as the foregoing, they would pall. I content myself, therefore, with remarking that the intellectual capacity of all these correspondents appears to be of about the same calibre, and that the said calibre is not extensive.

The moral status of such people is as little satisfactory as their mental capacity. Like Sheridan's Sir Benjamin, they have a pretty turn for slander. If no falsehoods are to be had second-hand, they set themselves to coin a few. They even have the audacity to print these fabrications. Towards the close of 1876 there appeared in an American newspaper, the *Cincinnati Com-*

mercial, an attack upon myself, purporting to be furnished by its English correspondent, a Unitarian preacher. Whether the well-known authors whose names this obscure journalist makes use of are in any way responsible for the assertions attributed to them I am unable to say authoritatively; but I should decidedly fancy that they are not. In any case, I deny the said assertions *in toto*. None of the adventures fabricated for the injury of my reputation ever occurred, whether at Florence or elsewhere; and I can only regret that the correspondent of a journal of any standing (to which class I imagine the *Commercial* to belong) should descend to the ungentlemanly behaviour of giving circulation to stories that he must surely know to be without authority or foundation. His animosity against spiritualism is no doubt great, but I can hardly be expected to admit that as an excuse.

He does not stand alone. One person writes to me that the well-known fact of the hand of Napoleon I. having been seen, during a *séance* at the Tuileries, to take up a pen and inscribe his name, is an invention of mine. He adds that he placed himself in communication with the late Emperor of the French, who denied the occurrence of the manifestation in question. Possibly this person's business connections may have brought him into communication with some one in the Emperor's culinary department. I do not doubt the possibility of such a correspondence as this last; but that his Majesty should have condescended to gratify the personal dislike of the individual in question towards me by telling a falsehood I both doubt and disbelieve. My correspondent forgets that I published the account of the phenomenon in question many years before the death of Napoleon III. Had no such manifestation occurred, the assertion would not long have remained uncontradicted.

A would-be controller of both spirits and spiritualism writes me a threatening letter from America. After piling slander upon slander and falsehood on falsehood, he crowns the edifice with the promise of publishing " a complete history of the Lyon case." Does he wish to spare me trouble? I have published half the evidence in the second volume of " Incidents in My Life," and I intend that the remainder, together with the judgment of V.-C. Giffard, shall appear in the third.

For there are many false opinions afloat regarding this same case. Thus, a London magistrate, when favouring the world with *his* ideas of law and justice in the case of Dr. Slade, must perforce introduce me in the doubly incorrect character of the injuring party in the suit and a "professional medium." I never was a professional medium. Against men and women who are I have nothing to say, provided that they be but honest. For myself, however, I have all through life felt an invincible repugnance to making merchandise of the gift bestowed on me. Large sums of money have been offered me for but a single *séance*, and they have been invariably refused. I make no boast of the fact; but it gives me, I think, a title to utter such a protest against the abuses of spiritualism as these chapters constitute.

And now I proceed to my task. If I am wrong, I err only through the sincere desire of doing good. My whole being is bound up in the cause as an exponent of which I was early set apart, and to advance whose mighty truths I have laboured for a quarter of a century past. An injury done to that cause, I feel like a wrong inflicted on myself. I utter my protest, then, against the follies and knaveries which at present disgrace it; and I utter that protest as a species of alarum which, I hope, may rouse all true spiritualists to action and unity. Spiritualism can well be compared to a noble corn-field. The wide plain is before us. As we sow thereon, so shall we reap. Lovers of the truth will desire that the harvest should consist solely of that truth. There are among us, however, not the one enemy of the scriptural wheat-field, but a thousand enemies, whose delight it is to be ever scattering the tares of falsehood. We, as the husbandmen, have a perfect right to uproot these. "Ill weeds grow apace," and, if left to flourish unchecked, speedily sap the life from the delicate corn. They come to a rank maturity, and flaunt everywhere their gaudily coloured flowers. Children—or those credulous and enthusiastic spiritualists whose one desire is some new marvel more incredible than the last, and who may fitly be compared to children—are attracted by the worthless plants, and, trampling down the wheat with contempt, hasten to secure the showy toys. It is ours to convince them of their error; and, while seeking to convince, destroy the causes of that error. When the last weed has been extirpated, and the golden harvest of Truth smiles in its full glory, we may point with pride to the cheering sight before us, and cry, " See that for which we have striven!"

NOTE.—Among the readers of these pages will doubtless be many who have known me at various periods of my career, and who may preserve the recollection of interesting incidents which have escaped my memory. I shall consider it a personal favour if such will kindly furnish me with any details of these bygone manifestations, &c., addressed to the care of W. Crookes, Esq., F.R S., 20, Mornington Road, N.W., London, England.

CHAPTER II.

DELUSIONS.

ONE of the most delicate yet momentous portions of my work is that with which I deal in this and the following chapter. It is hard to know how best to treat of those who, themselves deluded, delude others. Such culprits against progress need not be dishonest. In many instances a latent and perhaps unsuspected insanity lurks at the bottom of the whole; in others, overweening pride, or love of rule, forms the motive power of the wild rush on to ruin. But to analyze the subtly mingled causes of the disastrous effects which have from time to time brought misery to many and astonishment to all, would be beyond the scope of a work like this. These wrecks lie scattered through the histories of all polities and religions. They are the tombstones which point out the graves where lie buried the errors of the past. We must expect to find such in spiritualism. Let us, then, turn our attention to them, not in curiosity, not in contemptuous scorn, but with a desire to shape from these landmarks of ruin, beacons which may warn the future from such dangerous ground.

In every instance where a dictatorship is sought to be established in spiritual matters, it behoves lovers of the truth to join in resistance to an attempt so inimical to the dearest interests of that truth. The weaker portion of mankind have ever been but too ready to kneel in worship before such gods of clay, and the one course that their stronger brethren can take is, to demonstrate the hideousness and impotence of the idol. Had a method of searching scrutiny and prompt denunciation of unfounded claims been instituted by the undeceived portion of those to whom such claims were submitted, many movements, mistakenly termed religious, might have been checked at the outset. There are men—and women not less often than men—who hold it gross injustice that they should not have been born to mitres or crowns. In all who have striven to found sects or communities, and establish themselves as the high-priests of such, this characteristic has been dominant, conjoined usually with a certain enthusiasm, which aids in attracting minds weaker, though perhaps yet more enthusiastic, than their own. Such always render blind submission to the energy which has fascinated them, and become the blindest adorers of the pseudo-prophet or prophetess. I recall an instance in which a young man of good position, possessed of high literary gifts, and, in his earlier years, of sound judgment, was submitted to an ordeal sufficient to have utterly overwhelmed any ordinary organization. He emerged from it with his intellectual power almost unscathed, but the injury which a reason once eminently masculine had undergone was sufficiently evinced. He became the humble and unquestioning adherent of one among the pseudo-religious charlatans referred to.

It is not to be doubted that these "God-inspired" beings are at times sincere in their wild visions and impracticable theories. So are those sincere, who, being yet more advanced in their idiosyncrasies, and having them less under control, are entitled "dangerous madmen," and restrained in asylums. Yet the insanity partially swayed by reason of the one is, in reality, much more dangerous than the raging madness, into which no suspicion of reason enters, of the other. Bedlam makes no proselytes; nor, if the whole of the tenants of asylums were let loose in a body, could they do more than appal, disgust, and perhaps injure bodily, those of mankind who encountered them. But all history teems with the mischief which minds, less disordered than these, but still disordered, and accompanied with an energetic will and a restless thirst for domination, can do to natures weaker than their own. I might produce instances from every century of the Christian era, but a reference to the nineteenth will be sufficient for my purpose. Joanna Southcote and Joe Smith, to select two instances out of many, lived and worked harm in the century yet unfinished. Of all beliefs spiritualism is the one where such as choose to assume to themselves a prophetic character may most readily expect to find adherents. We are granted proofs of the continued existence of the loved and lost ones who have been released from the fetters of earth, and it is not unnatural that those through whom such proof is granted should be looked upon as gifted with some quality of soul superior to the endowments of their fellow-men. This is a sad and most fatal error. We who are mediums have in no way natures stronger than the natures of others. It is, on the contrary, unquestionable, that the supersensitiveness of our organization causes us to be but the more easily influenced and led astray. Every teaching obtained through a medium should be tried by the most searching tests, and rejected or accepted as it bears the refining fires of common sense and reason. A spirit, on manifesting, may simply describe himself as John Smith, or may assure me that he is Socrates. Naturally I regard the humbler name with the less suspicion. It is, to my experience, a more probable thing that he should be an ordinary Englishman than a great Greek. Besides, as John Smith he may, without making pretension to superior wisdom, give to Mary Smith, his mother, overwhelming proofs of identity. Here the outside world can have no pretext for interference. Should he, however, arrogate to himself the position of a teacher, others than Mary Smith must be allowed to decide respecting the validity of his claims. All fortunate enough to be convinced of the great truth that death is rather an awakening than a sleep, are interested in deciding whether spirits or mediums who teach that evil is good and folly wisdom; that man is destined to undergo transformations as numerous as those of the harlequin in a pantomime, and, returning continually to the stage of earthly life, play more parts there than Shakspeare ever dreamed of; or that doing evil that good may come is acceptable in the sight of God; or that beings in either world who appear by their actions and doctrines children of darkness are in reality angels of light;

shall be permitted with impunity to poison the minds of those weak enough to listen and admire.

I know that not in our own cause solely is evil to be found. Crimes and vices of a hue often far darker than anything which has disgraced spiritualism are to be met disgracing religious denominations everywhere throughout the world, for the same rules which apply to mediums apply to the exponents of all beliefs having reference to a life to come. What fatal teachings a mass of priests, pastors, rabbis, or whatsoever these shepherds of souls choose to be termed, have inculcated in all countries and centuries, the religious strifes by which the world has at different times been convulsed sufficiently prove. To the depths of infamy in which ministers of every creed have plunged themselves, annals stained with inconceivable crimes bear witness. It is pointed out by our enemies that among spiritualists excessive disunion exists, and that men professing a common faith in the possibility of communion with spirits, regard each other, in many cases, with the deadliest hate. It is, alas, but too true! and deeply do I regret it. But what of the adherents of every orthodox faith? Has not the saying, "See how these Christians love one another," a saying which was in its origin so beautiful and so true, been, for at least a thousand years, a mockery and a by-word? Did Dominic and De Montfort preach to heretics with aught but fire and sword? Was it not the legate Arnold, to whom, when a town of thirty thousand inhabitants, part heretic part Catholic, had been taken by storm, came the captains of the Catholic host for instructions? The task of selecting from the Albigenses the sheep of the Roman fold might have perplexed Solomon. With a blasphemy unmatched in history, Arnold cut the Gordian knot. "Kill them," said the holy man, "kill them all—the Lord can choose his own."

Did not Torquemada, again, burn, in an inquisitoriate of less than the tenth part of a century, above five thousand unhappy wretches, and torture and imprison ten times the number whom he slew? Did not a pontiff of the Catholic Church decree a solemn thanksgiving because some sixty thousand heretics had

been massacred in France? Did not Cranmer burn Joan
Bouchier? Did not Calvin burn Servetus? Did not Elizabeth
hang, draw, and quarter every Catholic priest who fell into her
hands? Have not Catholics persecuted Protestants, Calvinists
persecuted Lutherans, Puritans persecuted Papists, with a fury
utterly antagonistic to the teachings of Christ? And, finally, is
it not altogether certain that there exist bigots in every Church
who, did the greater enlightenment of their brethren permit,
would plant the stake in the market-places of the present day?

None can regret more than myself the evils which degrade that
spiritual movement whose welfare I have so much at heart.
But what of the clergy of to-day? Are they not as liable as
mediums to betray the sacred trusts confided to them? The
movement known as "modern spiritualism" sprang into prominence
a little more than a quarter of a century since. During that
quarter of a century numerous wickednesses have unquestionably
been committed by men and women really or professedly mediums. And what of clergymen within the same period? Have
not murder and every imaginable crime been committed over and
over again within the last twenty-five years by the shepherds
of orthodox folds? Have they not, in but too many instances,
forgotten the sacredness of the work to which they are devoted,
and brought ruin and infamy into once happy homes? Is not
their immorality a proverb in many countries? Have they not,
by the greed of gold and the lust of power, been tempted to
commit deeds recorded in characters of everlasting blackness? Is
it not their mission to preach peace, and have they not often by
every means in their power incited to the shedding of blood?
Within the past fifteen years I have known clergymen nail the
flag of declared war to their steeples, and, in sermons delivered
within walls dedicated to the worship of a loving God, prompt
his children to mutual slaughter. I have known clergymen also,
who were faithful servants of Christ, good men and true, who
worked earnestly below to fit themselves and others for the life
to come. It is not as an attack on the Churches that I have
written the paragraphs to be found above; I simply desire to

point the old moral that to err is human, and, as a certain
analogy exists between the position of the clergy and that of
mediums, I have selected the clergy for the purposes of comparison. Similar temptations try both classes. Both are liable
to seek to become masters where, in fitness, they should serve.
The same duties are incumbent on the men who sway the minds
of congregations that crowd to hear them expound the Divine
word, and on the medium who has, in the order of nature, been
set apart as a chosen instrument through whose peculiar organization is permitted the refutation of the fallacy that the things
to come are "unheard, unfelt, and unseen," and through whom
the realities of the next world are brought close to those who
have not yet experienced the change called death, that, inspired
to higher and holier actions, the "places" may be honourable
ones which, according to their merits, shall be prepared for them
there.

"In my Father's house are many mansions," said Christ;
"I go to prepare a place for you." Christians of all denominations are too apt to lose sight of this great fundamental truth.
A most perfect explanation and reconciliation of the supposed
discrepancies of spiritual teachings is contained in the above
heavenly and inspired words. That they were inspired, none
save the peculiar class of fanatics who deny a hereafter can
refuse to believe. Recall the circumstances under which they
were spoken. The darkest hour in the life of Him "who had
not where to lay his head" was at hand. The great crime of
the Hebrews approached its consummation; already upon the
Messiah fell the shadow of the cross. Yet, when earth yielded
no ray of love or hope, Christ rejoiced because of his nearness to
the Father's house; and, rejoicing, thought of the "many
mansions" and the "places" there to be prepared. If all men
be made alike at death what need of "many mansions," and why
seek to "prepare a place?" Were the dogma correct, that from
earth the "elect" depart to a uniform assembling point, "before
the throne of God," there, arrayed in the same white robes and
wearing the same golden crowns, to wave palm-branches in

concert through a wearisome eternity, and that the "reprobated" as uniformly depart into a darkness lurid with unquenchable fire, the meaning of the Messiah's words would be lost. That they were not without meaning—and a mighty one—the spiritual revelations of this age have made amply manifest. We find in the world of the future a diversity of conditions endless as in our own. Everywhere good and evil are in ceaseless activity, everywhere humanity is sinking farther from or advancing nearer to its God. But the prospect, considered as a whole, is cheering. There is reaction here and there. The great progress, however, goes steadily on. Wisdom and virtue continue to expand, and with the passing of each year or period of years the cry of the majority of spirits is the triumphal one, "Nearer, O God, to Thee!" Thus, in eternity as on earth, the watchword of humanity continues to be "Excelsior."

For the love of the Father is, like Himself, omnipresent. "All discord," as a great poet wisely tells us, "is harmony not understood." The jarring notes which so many of us produce from the instrument termed Life, it is the province of God to blend into accordance. The children who, whilst on earth, have misconceived his attributes, are certain of enlightenment hereafter. He waits only until they seek Him in humility to be instructed. Man must learn before he can teach, and human philosophy becomes ridiculous when it assumes to be an "intellectual all in all." To such wisdom perverted to foolishness did Christ allude when He said, "Thou hast hidden these things from the wise and prudent, and hast revealed them unto babes." Judæa was filled with men, who, too proud to obey God, thought themselves fitted to command their fellows. Doubtless places calculated to afford the lessons they so much needed were prepared for them in a future world.

Spiritualists have had among them many such erring brethren. Discontented with equality, these pretenders aspired to lead. The majority were stopped at the outset of their career. The ridicule directed against them, or the common sense of those whom they sought to dupe, proved insurmountable obstacles. Others, however, succeeded in pushing their struggles for domination far enough to cause more or less of harm. They drew together followers, and formed sects. Utterly incompetent for the task they had taken upon themselves, these would-be builders invariably found their exertions lead to ruin. The flimsy absurdities with which they disfigured our cause did more to injure it than the fiercest attacks of enemies from without. Their conduct and "revelations" were the grief of all sincere spiritualists and the laughing-stocks of the sceptical world.

Two prominent prophets of this class arose in the year 1850. The names they condescended to be known by whilst on earth were Scott and Harris : both rejoiced in the title of "Reverend." Mr. Scott had long been a shining light among the New York Baptists, and Mr. Harris had held forth from a Universalist pulpit. Their secession to spiritualism appears to have taken place about the same time, and the events I shall now narrate led to an intimate acquaintance between the two converts.

In the town of Auburn, N.Y., a circle known as the "Apostolic" had been formed. The medium secured was a Mrs. Benedict, and the attendant spirits belonged to the most select class. A chief rule of the association forbade the receipt of communications from any born out of Judæa ; or after the first year of the Christian era. The beings whose presence was desiderated appeared highly to appreciate this resolve. St. John and the prophet Daniel became the directors of the favoured circle. Communications, whose utter lack of meaning was set off by bad grammar and worse orthography, speedily showered down on happy Auburn. Nevertheless, matters prospered not ; a heartless world refused to waste attention on the Apostolic Circle, behaved it never so strangely. In this emergency a fresh champion was sought, and found. By advice of "John" and "Daniel" the Auburn spiritualists summoned the Rev. J. D. Scott to put his hand to the plough.

He came, and lent himself with enthusiasm to the work. "St. Paul" was speedily added to the other guides of Mrs. Benedict ; and improvements of grammar and orthography displayed themselves in the messages received. One of these messages fell into the hands of the Rev. T. L. Harris. The idea of being put in communication with such an apostle as Paul greatly excited him ; and Scott and Mrs. Benedict were sent for. By the aid of these spiritual sponsors Mr. Harris became "remodelled." On their return to Auburn he went with them as the "oracle" of that Hebrew of the Hebrews who experienced such a mighty spiritual manifestation on his way to Damascus. Scott claimed to be the mouthpiece of St. John.

A periodical was at once started under the title of *Disclosures from the Interior*. The two editors, Harris and Scott, contented themselves at first with being known as "chosen vessels." Soon presumption, and the unlimited folly of their dupes, tempted them a step farther. They claimed to visit the celestial regions in trance. Whatever they spoke, wrote, or thought, was the inspiration of a chosen band of apostles and prophets directed by "the Lord Himself."

The outcry grew strong in Auburn. Sensible spiritualists were disgusted, and withdrew from all communion with the two ex-Reverends and their flock. The extravagances of Scott and Harris, however, only waxed the wilder. Threats of mobbing were made by the rougher among the unbelievers. The position of the "chosen vessels" became unsafe. Under these circumstances an exodus was resolved upon. The spirits entered warmly into the plan, and full instructions were received from them. Mountain Cove, Fayette County, Virginia, was to be the new resting-place of that ark which unworthy Auburn had cast forth. No less a person than Isaiah would guide the little band of brothers to the chosen spot; which, it appeared, was the prophet's favourite spiritual residence. All property was to be in common. The golden day of "liberty, fraternity, and equality," had at length arrived.

About one hundred persons accompanied Mr. Scott to Mountain Cove ; Harris for the present held aloof. His brother "vessel" speedily soared to a height of blasphemy such as few human beings have attained before or since. Prophets and apostles were despised as human and created. Nothing would content the reverend gentleman but the Creator Himself. In his own words he "came even unto the counsels of the Most High." Full authority was delegated to him in all matters "social, religious, and financial; temporal or eternal." On the 2nd December, 1851, he called together the faithful and informed them that, in the fashion of Moses, he had conversed "face to face with God!" Such were his words, and the ineffable idiots whom he had gathered together heard them with credulous awe.

Scott now appointed himself "medium absolute." Nothing but pure truth, he gave his followers to understand, could or would henceforth be received through him. Whoever dared to express a doubt of that truth must be cast forth as an unworthy heretic.

Notwithstanding these claims dissensions arose. A charge of licentiousness was preferred against the "man of God." He investigated it himself, and promptly decided the accused to be innocent. Still the unpleasantness continued. Money ran short. The faithful, whatever their disagreements in other matters, were unanimous in declining work. Several families left the place. A plantation which had been purchased was returned to its former owner, as the payments on it could not be met. It was necessary that Scott should have a new vision. "I must go," said he, "to New York, and seek there minds for the carrying-on of the Lord's work."

Arrived in New York he resumed his old connection with Harris. The confederates succeeded in bringing over several persons of property to the enterprise. The Mountain Cove estate was repurchased. In May, 1852, the Rev. T. L. Harris proceeded there, accompanied by his family and his dupes. A fresh gleam of worldly prosperity shone on "the Holy Mountain —the New Jerusalem," as the partakers of its joys enthusiastically termed it. The arrogance of the reunited prophets and the credulity of the faithful were stretched to the utmost. It was proclaimed that God had chosen Scott and Harris "as his mediums, through whom He might communicate with man on earth." Their minds were to become blended into spiritual unity. The utterances proceeding from their lips would "instruct and comfort the people of the Lord." Neither of the prophets could lie ; and besides being infallible they were supreme ;—the only children of the Truth. All other persons claiming to be mediums received their inspiration from the devil, and ranked among his servants.

I find the following sentences given as a specimen of the revelations with which the faithful were "instructed and comforted." They are from an address spoken in the "interior condition" by Scott :—

"I read, written in letters of fire, 'Dost thou believe ? and what dost thou believe ? Who, thinkest thou, called thee here ? Who inspireth ? Not an angel, for he is led ; not a seraph, for he is controlled ; not created existence, for that is inspired. Who, then, thinkest thou, called thee to the mountain ? Who but God inspireth ?' . . . . I am that I am inquireth of thee ; and prepare to answer thou Me. None other than God, thy Redeemer, calleth thee. None other than He who hath the keys of Death and Hell addresseth you through one of your members.'"

Even this was mild compared with what followed. Harris declared Mountain Cove to be the gate of Heaven. The redemption of man could only be accomplished there. Whoever opposed "the two perfect prophets" was to be driven from the holy place. For such outcasts there remained no longer any hope of salvation. Not even himself or Scott could again open "the gate of Heaven" to them.

The house wherein the two prophets dwelt Harris pronounced "*the veritable house of God.*" It was necessary that an estate should be added to it. Accordingly, the seers indulged in yet another vision. The Lord desired a certain piece of land to be leased to Him as his heritage. A meeting of the faithful was called. Harris and Scott pointed out that as they, and they alone, were the "chosen vessels of God," the lease must be drawn in their names. The request was too reasonable for refusal, and the worthy stewards commenced forthwith to administer the estate they had acquired in so spiritual a manner.

The crowning stroke of impiety was at hand.

Persecutions had been directed against all rebels from the domination of the "perfect mediums." Endless discord convulsed the little community. As the "New Jerusalem" seemed ready to fall to pieces, an assumption was resolved on whose boldness should awe even the most mutinous. Some time in the autumn of 1852, therefore, Harris and Scott revealed themselves to their amazed followers as the two witnesses spoken of in the eleventh chapter of Revelations. They claimed the whole of the super-mundane gifts assigned to these witnesses by St. John. Power to send fire from their mouths, and with it consume their enemies; power to shut heaven so that it rained not; power to turn the waters of earth to blood, and to smite men with plagues: all these weapons were at the command of the ex-Universalist and the ex-Baptist. They did not, indeed, design to use them except at the last extremity. If the dwellers on the "holy mountain" would but turn again into the way of righteousness, all might yet be well. "*O Lord*," said Harris, in one of his prayerful rebukes to the chosen hundred, "*Thou knowest we do not wish to destroy man with fire from our mouths!*"

Blasphemy could hardly go farther. Several listeners were disgusted, and withdrew from the brotherhood. The majority, however, accorded full credence to the claims of the reverend "witnesses." The state of mind of these believers is a thing to be contemplated with wonder and awe.

But a dissolution was inevitable. Even fanaticism has its tender points. Though there were dwellers in the "New Jerusalem" for whose utter and abject credulity no impiety was too impious and no folly too foolish, a test of faith was now insisted on which even these could not support. The Rev. Mr. Scott made an onslaught on the pockets of the faithful. "Spirits," he justly remarked, "operate from the interior; but man in clay demandeth external benefit." He called on his followers, therefore, to yield up to him the whole of their possessions, pecuniary or otherwise. "Come!" cried he, "with thy substance; give it to the Lord." The gift, of course, was to be made to heaven as manifested in its servant, Mr. Scott. How many responded to the appeal the history of the movement saith not. Mountain Cove, however, lost at once all vestiges of fraternity. The New Jerusalem became a Pandemonium. Quarrel succeeded to quarrel, and departure to departure. Various charges were made against the two prophets of the community. At length, when of the Virginian Israel scarcely any but the leaders remained, those leaders recognised the necessity of causing their light to shine elsewhere. They struck tents accordingly, and departed. Of the wealth of the faithful scarcely a farthing remained. Such was the end of one of the darkest follies of modern spiritualism. ·

Had a sufficient degree of opposition been organized against this movement at its outset, it could never have worked such extensive harm. Even after the settlement at Mountain Cove, the steady and unfaltering resistance of the more sensible brethren to the dictatorial claims of Scott and Harris might have done much. But such brethren were few, and they contented themselves with quitting the place in disgust. The attempts at mutiny were desultory and ill sustained, and their only effect was to incite the reverend "witnesses" to some of the most blasphemous antics that ever made spirits or spiritualists blush.

With the career of Mr. J. L. Scott I have henceforth no concern. The name of his fellow-prophet, however, continued, even after the dispersion of the Mountain Cove flock, to be intimately linked with spiritualism, both in America and England. For a few years his mediumship was at once brilliant and useful. He published in rapid succession a series of fine poems—"A Lyric of the Golden Age," "An Epic of the Starry Heavens," "The Morning Land," &c. The spirits who inspired these productions he asserted to be Byron, Shelley, Coleridge, and others of the great departed. Unequal and, in places, slightly turgid, the compositions given by Mr. Harris to the world bore the impress of high spiritual inspiration and masterly poetic power.

But so commendable a course could not long be persisted in by the restless "prophet." He cast away the pen, and, thrusting himself into that field of action for which he was so ill qualified, commenced a career of the wildest apostasy and excess.

On his return to New York from the deserted paradise of Mountain Cove he had, for a short while, figured as a lecturer. In this capacity he poured forth floods of virulent abuse against Christ and the Christian Gospel. None who listened to those attacks can have forgotten their vehemence. I was myself present on one occasion and, rising in utter disgust, left the building. "They were too strong," says Mr. C. Partridge, "even for those whom Mr. Harris now denounces as rejecting the divine authority of Scripture." For, in no long time, this human weathercock again veered round. He was determined, at any cost, to have a church, and to be to that church a dictator and a prophet. His first attempt was made with those New York spiritualists who had been edified by his diatribes against the Bible. They could not, however, be tempted. Ready to engage him as a speaker, they declined to find a master in him. One such experiment as Mountain Cove was sufficient.

Disappointed in this quarter, Mr. Harris changed his tactics. From the coarse assailant of Christianity he transformed himself once more into its devoted champion. From an ardent spiritualist he became an equally ardent denouncer of spiritualism. He first preached to a small congregation in New York. This little gathering was known as "The Sacred Family." Whilst acting as its father the prophet sent forth another epic to the world. He very reasonably styled this new production, "The Song of Satan." It contained an elaborate exposition of the devil-theory regarding spiritual manifestations. The Byron, Coleridge, &c., by whom Mr. Harris had formerly been controlled, were merely fiends masquerading in the guise of those great poets. From their snares he was now free. A select cohort of angels had come down to take charge of the "Sacred Family" and its leader. All other spirits manifesting anywhere on earth were waifs from the bottomless pit.

Soon the prophet grew weary of his New York flock. He

determined to travel, and fixed on England as the country to be now illuminated. Calling the "Sacred Family" together, he informed them that he had become developed above their comprehension. The Lord had instructed him to proceed to Europe, and disseminate there the supernal wisdom which burdened his mind. He made choice of a successor "fitted for the New York plane of teaching," and set off.

Arrived in London, it speedily appeared that the "supernal wisdom" with which English spiritualists were to be favoured was comprised in a series of rancorous attacks upon their brethren in America, which attacks were usually of the most baseless nature. Having succeeded in creating much ill-feeling through these libels, Mr. Harris considered his mission satisfactorily disposed of, and, despite his being developed above American comprehension, condescended to favour the States once more with his presence. A second "Sacred Family" was inaugurated, and in its, doubtless, happy bosom the perfect medium of the Virginian New Jerusalem still remains. His converts and "spiritual children," I may remark, contain among them persons whom one would have thought little likely to bow to the yoke of an unstable and brain-sick enthusiast. No extravagance, however, of his later attempt at sect-founding has as yet approached the madnesses in which Mr. Harris indulged at Mountain Cove.

Almost contemporary with this American insanity, a movement was carried on in the city of Geneva, the freaks of whose founder equalled the blasphemies of Harris and Scott; whilst the credulity of the dupes even surpassed the confidingness of the Mountain Cove disciples. The little table through which "St. Paul" gave directions for the founding of the Virginian "New Jerusalem," was the prototype of a table, equally small, and venerated still more highly by certain dwellers in the staid city of Calvin.

Towards the close of 1853 persons could be found everywhere throughout the world who took great interest in the "turning and tipping of tables." Professor Faraday's verdict was delivered about this period. As regards spiritualism in its entirety, that verdict was an essentially foolish one, for on no better grounds than the data furnished by a few hasty observations, Faraday considered himself competent to condemn the whole subject. I am convinced, however, that as regards the particular instances of phenomena which came under his scrutiny, his theory was just. The more I have seen of the persons known as "tipping mediums," the more unable I have been to trace the movements of the table and the messages communicated through those movements to any other source than the so-called mediums themselves. Yet in at least one-half of the cases observed by me, the persons concerned were innocent of all wish or effort to deceive. They simply laboured under undue excitement of the nervous system, and every attempt to dispel their hallucinations failed.

I knew once an old lady who, before dining, invariably seated herself at small table, and commenced to tip it. The table was supposed to stand as representative for the spirit of her deceased husband. When the tipping was fairly started, interrogatories began.

"Dear Charles, may I eat fish to-day?"

The table would execute affirmative motions.

"Thank you, dear Charles, I thought I might, for I felt a strong desire to have fish for dinner."

At times the response was in the negative. Then came something like the following:—

"Ah! I thought so, Charles! I felt one of my chills coming on, and fish is bad for me when I have my chills."

I never knew an instance when the answer was not in full unison with her own wishes. This delusion extended itself to every action of her life, and I had to proceed with great caution in attempting to convince her that the "dear Charles" of the table was simply a fantasy due to unconscious muscular exertion and an excited brain.

I recall another case. In 1855, I was one day dining with Lord H——. A well-known baronet was at table. Spiritualism became the subject of conversation, and Sir R—— inquired whether I could obtain manifestations at will. I told him, as is the truth, that I could not.   He laughed, and remarked, "I am a better medium than you then ; for I can tip the tables at pleasure." I replied that I had not the slightest doubt of his ability to do so, and continued, " Perhaps you will show us this talent after dinner." No sooner had we reached the drawing-room than he selected the species of small table known as a " what-not." He seated himself, and the tipping commenced.   Nothing could have been more evident than that he accomplished it himself.   " Perhaps, Sir R——," I said, "you will allow me to place a sheet of paper between your hand and the table ? "   He gave · permission, and I spread out the sheet, so that his hands would rest on it. The table no longer tipped, but the paper moved very visibly. It was afterwards reported to me—I hope, incorrectly—that Sir R—— had said, " Oh ! Home was jealous of my power as a medium."

Were it necessary, I could subjoin to these two instances hundreds equally striking.   In none was the motive power traceable to spirits.   Regarding " writing mediums," the same thing may be said in ninety cases of every hundred.   In the early stages of my own career I was a writing medium.   Little by little, I began to reason respecting the messages given through me.   I found them strongly tinged with my own bias of thought ; and I at once ceased seeking for such communications.   Since then I have only written medially when my hand has moved altogether automatically, and my attention was so completely diverted that I could not catch the faintest inkling of what was written.

I should not, it is true, be warranted in asserting even such tippings as those of Harris and Scott's " St. Paul " to be the results of deliberate imposture ; but I am perfectly satisfied that they constituted a monstrous delusion, in which disembodied spirits had not the slightest share.   St. Paul as little controlled the Mountain Cove leaders as did Tom Jones.   The same absence of all spiritual tokens is discernible in the wildly blasphemous attempt at spiritual dictatorship which I am now about to describe.

The method of obtaining communications was through a very

small table. The medium laid his hands on the said table, and it tipped out messages by means of the alphabet. *There is not a single instance of the table having been levitated, or of a movement when no person was in contact with it.*

In the American folly, Harris and Scott never went beyond St. Paul, as a servant for tipping purposes. Their higher flights of blasphemy they reserved for their inspirational moments. Our Genevan enthusiasts took a bolder stand. They solemnly consecrated their table, and proclaimed that it was tipped by the Messiah himself. They set a chair apart at their meetings, which chair was supposed to be invisibly filled by Christ. Nay, they ventured even farther than this. On one occasion God the Father was introduced as communicating a miserable species of homily, pilfered from various portions of Scripture. The messages, whether pronounced to emanate from Raphael, from Gabriel, or from the persons of the Trinity, were received with credulous ecstasy, preserved, arranged, and published in volume shape. I have copies of two of these precious productions. One bears the following title-page :—

"POST TENEBRAS LUX.

ROME, GENÈVE,

ET

L'ÉGLISE DE CHRIST.

DICTÉ AU MOYEN D'UNE TABLE PAR LE FILS DE DIEU,
LE SAUVEUR DU MONDE,
SEUL MÉDIATEUR ENTRE DIEU ET LES HOMMES.
1856."

I do not print the names of the persons concerned in this movement, but they are at the service of any desirous of privately investigating the case. These unfortunates have abandoned their delusion. They are reduced from positions of comfort and even of wealth to a condition bordering in instances on absolute want. To-day, October 5th, 1876, I had an interview with the deepest sufferer of them all. At the age of seventy-two she is still young in patience and hope. As she narrated to me her losses and trials the peaceful smile that lit her face was the very gleam one might suppose to irradiate the countenance of some martyr, while, with his last accents, he breathed forgiveness to his enemies. From the notes I took whilst listening to her, I, with the help of a retentive memory, proceed to lay bare this item of Genevese history in almost my informant's own words.

"It is a sad story, sir. Perhaps it would be well to seek to forget it, but, as you truly say, it may serve to warn others. God grant that it should!

"I am unable to give you the exact date, but some time in 1853 a strange piece of news reached us. We heard that, at the house of a Mr. X——, some little girls had become developed as writing mediums, and that Mr. X—— himself had great power over a table, through which messages were given. He was a teacher of music, and a good and truly pious man. (Oh! he was honest, as we all were.) Well, out of curiosity I went to see these things, and, finding that the *séances* began with prayer, and that all the messages given were pure and good, I came home, and asked my husband to investigate the matter. How many times since then has he said, 'It was you who first led me into it.' These words were not said complainingly, for what right have any of us to complain? We all thought we were doing God's work, and even now, sir, I can only say that, if it were a delusion, I still believe God will pity us, for our object was to glorify Him. My husband was a man of great intelligence, and in proof of it I need only say that he had been Professor of Mathematics in the college here. At the time alluded to, however, he no longer taught. By a number of fortunate speculations he had acquired a large fortune, and we were living in ease and luxury. (I see you are looking round my poor little room, sir; but it must have been the will of God, and that consoles me.) Mr. X—— said his table was moved by our Saviour; but now, in looking back, I wonder how we could have been foolish enough to credit such a thing. We were told by 'the table'" (the words she used were "the Saviour," but this constant repetition of a holy name is so repulsive that, for the remainder of the narrative, I substitute " the table,") " that we must take Mr. X——, his father, mother, &c., to reside in our house, and share with them the fortune it had pleased God to give us. I said to my husband, ' Let us give them a large sum of ready money instead, and ask them to live elsewhere; for their tastes are not mine, and I could not be happy with them.' My husband answered, ' The life of the One we worship was a life of self-abnegation, and we must in all things copy Him. Overcome at once these worldly prejudices, and your sacrifice will prove your willingness to obey the Master.' Of course I consented, and seven additions were made to our household. Then began a life of utter recklessness as regards money. ' The table' ordered us to purchase another carriage and four new horses. We had nine servants in the house. Not only that, but ' the table' ordered us to build a steamboat. Very expensive it was. Painters and decorators were set to work on the house in which we lived; and, however rich and beautiful our furniture might be, ' the table' made us replace it with newer and still more costly articles. (All this, sir, was to be done that our mansion might be worthy to receive the One whom we foolishly believed came to it.) We were told, too, by ' the table' that it was necessary everything should be made as ostentatious as possible to attract the notice of the outside world. We did as we were ordered. We kept open house. The results were what might have been expected. People came, and made a pretence of being convinced. Young men and women visited us, and ' the table' ordered them to be married. When they consented, the necessary outfits were furnished at our expense. Not only that, sir, but as often as these couples had children, the children were sent to us to be brought up, and I well remember that at one time we had eleven infants in the house. Mr. X——, too, married, and his family went on increasing itself. At last, no less than thirty of us regularly sat down at table together. This continued for three or four years, until one day we discovered that our means were nearly all gone. ' The table' told us to go to Paris, and ' He' would provide for us there. We went, and my husband was bidden to speculate on the Bourse. He did so, and lost. Still we had faith. As there were now but few in the family, we contrived to live on, Heaven only knows how. I have been for days together without other food than a crust of dry bread and a glass of water. I must not forget to tell you, sir, that whilst in Geneva we had been bidden to administer the sacrament of the Lord's Supper, and that there were sometimes from three to four hundred communicants at table. A monk from Argovie, too, left the convent of which he was Superior, and renounced the Catholic religion to join us. You see, sir, we were not alone in our blindness.

"Even during our trials in Paris our faith held firm. My husband often said that 'the table' had sent us there, and that he would not return to Geneva without 'his' permission. At last we asked for that permission, and were told we might return. Ah! it was then that we fully realised our position. We were poor, and those who had profited by our fortune whilst it lasted were the first to turn their backs upon us. I do wrong, though, sir, to tell you this, for it betokens a restless and complaining spirit, and I have no right to murmur.

"I had almost forgotten to relate that, amongst other wild fancies, 'the table' bade us buy a manufactory in France. We did so, and the undertaking proved a total failure. The place was sold for ten thousand francs, not a tenth of what it had cost us.

"You are looking at that large engraving, and wonder, no doubt, how it comes to have a place in my humble room. Well, sir, during the height of our folly, Mr. X—— was inspired with artistic ideas, but, strange to say, could not give expression to them. A professional painter was engaged, therefore, and X—— described to him his visions. That large engraving is taken from the picture which represented X——'s idea of the Crucifixion. It is at the moment when our Lord says, 'I thirst.' The original painting was sold at auction by our creditors, with our house, and whatever else remained to us. No, sir, we have never seen Mr. X—— from that day. He married my niece whilst we were all living together, and had four children by her. She was called by

God, and X—— has married again, and, I hear, never alludes to
the past. Yes, he has been in Geneva, but he did not come to see
us. Why should he? he is poor like us. I will tell you one
little thing which has happened within the past three or four
months." (The incident not being at all to the credit of X——, I
refrain from giving it. The character of the narrator is well
displayed by the self-rebuking manner in which her narrative
terminated.) "Indeed I am wicked, sir, to have told you such a
thing as this. God forgive me! I ought to have been silent
about it. Please, *please* forget that I told it. I am a sinful old
woman, and I bow my head in all humility to ask heaven's pardon
for speaking such harsh words. Even in his wanderings, my
husband" (*the unfortunate man is insane*) "never makes allusion
to the past. Oh! I am perfectly convinced, sir, that it was not
our connection with this affair which deprived him of reason. He
began to work with his head very young, and mathematics fatigue
the brain so. It is very, very hard not to have him with me, but
he is at times beyond my control. Still I wish I could be allowed
to have him here, and care for him.

"It is a sad story, as you say, but we were all striving to obey
the dictates of what we thought to be a high and holy power. I
assure you some of the messages were very beautiful, quite
superior to what Mr. X—— could have given. Well, the day of
life will soon terminate for us, and then we shall read the riddle.
Speaking of those messages, I fear, sir, that even when we
believed ourselves most humble, there was a strong tinge of
vanity in our thoughts, for we all, of course, believed ourselves
the chosen of the Lord. I remember that often, on seeing a
funeral move past me, with its gloomy hearse and trappings of
sorrow, I have said to myself exultingly, 'Ah! how happy it is
that we shall have no such ordeal to endure;' for 'the table' had
told us that, as the chosen of the Lord, we should none of us see
death, but be translated bodily to 'his' Father's home. Remember,
sir, that neither Mr. X—— nor any others of those concerned
made, or sought to make, money out of the affair. We were
all of us honest in our convictions. We bear our crosses cheer-

fully, therefore I cannot but think that, although we may have erred, the Lord will repay us, since we erred out of love for Him."

I left that little room with a heavy heart. What an incomprehensible thing is human nature! A man seats himself before a table a foot or so in diameter, and tips out blasphemies to the laborious calling of the alphabet. This, only *this*, is sufficient to cast people, pious, intelligent, honest, of high social position and large fortunes, into a delirious ecstasy of credulity, from which they awake only to utter ruin! Nay, they hardly awake from it even then. We see them in the above narrative still hoping against hope that their faith may have had some foundation tending to warrant it; still blind to the character of the man through whom they have been despoiled of their all. That man seems to me one of the strange beings, half fanatic, half impostor, who abound in all ages of the world, and who, whilst deluding others, fall more and more into the habit of deluding themselves, till they may end by becoming fanatics more fervent than those who originally were their dupes. Certainly there was nothing in the proceedings of this person to warrant our supposing him possessed of much intelligence, or any capacity for weaving deeply meditated schemes. His blasphemies were of the rankest kind and his mode of operations was baldly simple.

I have just obtained some further light as to the origin of the " messages." A hard-shell Calvinist, pastor of a Genevan church, was amongst the deluded worshippers of the little table. With this old man (he is now eighty-four) I, very recently, had an interview.

"You are most welcome," said he, " to any information I can give; but I have little to tell. I took the matter up because the messages given were in perfect accord with Scripture; and I at last dropped it, because some ideas were communicated which did not harmonize with the Bible and my belief. I gained nothing by it. On the contrary, I had, at the outset of my connection with the affair, a good income, and I returned to Geneva from that Paris journey with only two hundred francs in the world. I certainly consider that the matter, and the peculiarly Biblical formation of the messages, were superior to what Mr. X—— could have given. The communications more resembled my ideas than his. My hands were usually on the table too. Do I not now think it blasphemy? Certainly not. Why should not such things be? The Bible has bidden us expect a second coming of Christ. He came to a manger before; why not to a table now? It was all very strange; and it is nonsense to talk about the messages proceeding from the mind of some one present. Why, there was not even a medium there! I am not a medium. Mr. X—— is not a medium. No! he had not an excitable nature."

The memory of the old gentleman must have played him false. I have questioned persons who knew X—— from childhood, and their testimony is uniformly the same. "A most impulsive nature, with very kind instincts, but self-deluded. He brought his friends to ruin, and himself shared their fate. His vanity was flattered, and would brook no demur. He, or his table, invariably became angry when any one rejected or desired to calmly investigate his monstrous pretensions."

The preface to the volume of "messages" confirms strongly the truth of the above description. It is supposed to be dictated by the angel Gabriel, and contains the following :—" And whosoever laughs in his heart " (at the contents of the book) " is a blasphemer, and must not remain with us."

In the volume itself Christ is introduced as uttering the following threats :—" Look at my cross ; but let him who mocks it take care of himself. We are not on Calvary here. . . . . You would like to see miracles! Miracles were only done, and will only be done, for believers. When I was on earth men asked me to do miracles, and I replied, ' Generation of vipers, begone to your father, and *he* will make miracles for you. He is waiting for you in the everlasting flames which consume him and his angels.' Sinner! I did not come here to-night to ask your belief in the phenomenon you have before your eyes." (Wonderful phenomenon truly! A man, seated at a small table, with his hands placed upon it, tips it monotonously towards himself. A child ten months old might have done the same, and a theologically-inclined boy of ten years, who had mastered the Bible as interpreted by Calvin, could with ease have constructed the " messages ").

Is there not a certain analogy in the above to the dark *séances* and puppet-shows of the present day ? The honest sceptic who wishes to investigate is deridingly informed : " You want to see miracles, do you ? Miracles are done with us only for the true believers." Had such a course been pursued at the outset of the movement, would spiritualism to-day have counted twenty adherents in any country of the old world or the new ? But I must return to my old pastor.

" Mr. X——," he informed me, " was a musician, and very enthusiastic. I do not term that excitable. I think we were all calm when we sat around the table. As I have said, the messages were, at first, holy, heavenly, and perfectly in accordance with my views of the Bible. What caused me to retire was that I found the table afterwards become rather uncertain on various points. To this day, however, I am convinced that those beautiful communications could not have proceeded from the mind of Mr. X——. The affair remains a deep mystery to me."

The chief mystery it presents is the blindness of the dupes concerned to the most palpable facts. The old pastor, Mr. B——, was a thorough Biblical scholar of the school of Calvin. He made it his custom to open every *séance* with prayer. Besides this, he generally kept up a running fire of theology all through the proceedings. These scraps of Calvinism the " medium " X—— had only to treasure up, and, reproducing them through the table, behold the messages ! No wonder that those messages agreed so completely with the Scriptural views of the old pastor. No wonder he was flattered to find that heaven and he were so completely at one on the questions of election, predestination, and so forth. The whole thing is simply a reproduction of the case of Allan Kardec, with the exception that Kardec's interpreters wrote down his ideas instead of spelling them out by means of a table. The delusion was honest, but, for all that, it must be pronounced a delusion. Be it remarked that in the Genevan episode not only was the personal vanity of all concerned flattered, but also their national pride, and their religious sympathies and antipathies. Geneva was to be the chosen city of the Lord, and Rome tottered on the verge of destruction. I find in the volume of which I have spoken messages describing the two as follows :—

"Rome. Behold the lamp of the demon !"

"Geneva. The Eternal hath chosen it, from whence to reveal Himself to the whole of mankind as a God, jealous and forgiving. God in his goodness lighted in Geneva a torch of Truth and Life. God gave Geneva as a retreat for the Bible. The Eternal required a new Bethlehem. He chose Geneva. And yet the new Bethlehem, though glorious, can only offer the Little Child a *table* for shelter. You laugh, reader. Yes, you are so highly placed that you can disdain Me. Is it not truly vulgar that the Son of God should speak through a simple table ?"

Such is a fair sample of the incomparable homilies which were considered so far beyond the capacity of Mr. X——. The second of the works in my possession might also well be credited to a lunatic asylum. It has the following title page :—

"RÉVÉLATIONS DIVINE ET MYSTÉRIEUSE,

OU

COMMUNICATIONS ENTRE LE CIEL ET LA TERRE

Par le moyen d'une table.

Genève, 1855."

Various of the communications are too unpleasant to quote. In one place the angel Gabriel manifests, and informs the adorers of the table that God the Father and God the Son are about to speak through it. Then follows a dialogue between the Divine Persons so heralded.

This can never be termed spiritualism. Just as soon might the ravings of those lunatics who declare the moon to come down every night and whip them, be deemed doctrines inherent to our cause. As I study this incident of religious monomania, I discern more and more clearly that the only spirits concerned in this and kindred follies are the twin-demons of Vanity and Pride. It is so with Kardecian dreams and fallacies. The votaries of those doctrines are, almost without exception, to be found in the working

and *bourgeois* classes. They console themselves for their humble
position and contracted minds by the reflection that they have been
before, and may be again, powerful potentates, or men of mark in
the realms of action and thought.

Perhaps the strangest shadow which ever darkened spiritualism
was that cast upon it by the utterly absurd incident known as
" the new motive power."   In this extraordinary display of human
folly four persons were chiefly concerned.   These were the Rev.
John M. Spear, medium and Universalist minister; his friend, Mr.
Hewitt, editor of the *New Era*; Mrs. A. E. N——, of Boston, and
her husband, Mr. N——.   If we except Mr. Hewitt, whose chief
failings seem to have been gushingness and credulity, the mind of
each of the above persons was marked by extraordinary idiosyncrasies.

John M. Spear's enthusiasm was of the philosophical sort.   He
" lived by faith ; and trusted for direction and financial resources
to the invisible world."   His mind was occupied with confused
ideas regarding the possibility of interblending matter and spirit.
The result was extraordinary.   To these ideas did the " holy motor
machine " owe its birth.

The mother of " The Thing," as Mr. Hewitt reverentially termed
it in the columns of the *Era*, was Mrs. N——.   John M. Spear
constructed the machine, and this lady engaged to endow it with
perpetual motion.   Spirits, she declared, had informed her that
they "would make of her a second Mary, and she should become
a distinguished mother in Israel."   Although two children had
already been born of her in an ordinary manner, she believed herself destined to bring a third into the world, which should owe its
existence to no earthly father.   This " spirit-babe " was to be the
motive power of John M. Spear's machine.

Mrs. N—— became pregnant.   Mr. Spear toiled industriously
at the frame which was to contain the " power," and in due course
finished his task.   The machine was carried to High Rock, in Lynn,
Mass., a place made celebrated in American spiritual annals by
more than one ridiculous, and at least one tragical event.   The
language of the *New Era* became glowing.   It was announced

that an "association of Electrizers" in the spirit-spheres were about to reveal to mankind a "new motive power, God's last, best gift to man." The "Thing" once born, would "revolutionize the world."

At length the hour drew nigh. Mrs. N—— went down to High Rock. John M. Spear, the machine, and various attendants from earth and the spirit-world, awaited her there. In presence of this devoted band the mystical delivery of the wondrous babe took place; in other words, "the power was imparted to the machine." It moved slightly. John M. Spear shouted for joy. The editor of the *New Era* hastened back to his office, and indited an article, from which the following are extracts :—

"We are prepared to announce to the world :—

"First, That spirits have revealed a wholly new motive power, to take the place of all other motive powers.

"Second, That this revelation has been embodied in a model machine, by human co-operation with the powers above.

"Third, That results are, thus far, satisfactory to its warmest friends.

"THE THING MOVES.

"We have the birth of a new science, a new philosophy, and a new life. The time of deliverance has come at last, and, henceforth, the career of humanity is upward and onward—a mighty, a noble, a god-like career. All the revelations of spiritualism heretofore; all the control of spirits over mortals, and the instruction and discipline they have given us, have only paved the way, as it were, for the advent of a great practical movement, such as the world little dreams of; though it has long deeply yearned for it, and agonised, and groaned away its life because it did not come sooner. And this new motive power is to lead the way in the great speedily coming salvation. It is to be the physical saviour of the race. The history of its inception, its various stages of progress, and its completion, will show the world a most beautiful and significant analogy to the advent of Jesus as the spiritual saviour of the race. . . . Hence we most confidently assert that the advent of the science of all sciences, the philosophy of all philosophies, and the art of all arts, has now fairly commenced. The child is born; not long hence he will go alone. Then he will dispute with the doctors in the temples of science, and then—— ! ! "

Breath failed the editor, and other fanatics took up the cry. The machine was hailed as the "New Creation," the "Philosopher's Stone," the "Act of all Acts," the "Greatest Revelation of the Age." John M. Spear sat for a moment in the seventh heaven, and Mrs. N—— already felt the halo of a Madonna encircling her brow.

Alas for the "wonderful infant!" Alas for the folly of its devotees, and the money and faith they had so uselessly thrown away! The main mechanism of "The Thing" remained, as it had ever been, inert. The motion perceived at the moment of birth was confined to a few balls suspended by wires. These oscillations, as a Massachusetts spiritualist plaintively remarked, could scarcely be considered sufficient to constitute a "physical saviour." Common sense spiritualism declined to recognise the "Advent."

Several prominent spiritualists, amongst whom was Andrew Jackson Davis, visited High Rock, and inspected the machine. They agreed as to its utter uselessness. The general opinion, however, was that its construction had certainly been directed by spirits ; and that John M. Spear and the other parties to the affair deserved pity rather than the blame now liberally showered upon them. With this verdict I coincide, and can endorse the following expressions of Mrs. Hardinge :—" That Mr. Spear honestly believed in a spiritual origin for the various ' missions ' he undertook, and the remarkable part he played, none who have ever come into personal relations with him can question. The unwavering fidelity with which he adhered to his purposes, and the patience with which he endured reproach and odium for their execution, would attest his sincerity, were other evidence wanting." It must ever be regretted that an excellent heart should have been so often and so far led astray by the perversities of the head with which it was connected.

" Let the machine," one spiritualist wrote, " stand at High Rock as a lasting evidence of human credulity." I appreciate his feelings and echo his words. How appropriately, had the machine been left there, might the " Punch and Judy " cabinets of the present day, and the insignia of the Theosophical Society, be collected together at the same place. But it was not to be. The worshippers of the " holy infant " trusted that a change of scene would develop the power they still supposed to be latent within it. "The machine," says Mr. Spear, "was moved to Randolph, New York, that it might have the advantage of that lofty electrical position." Such advantage it did not long enjoy. Ribald paragraphs respecting the transaction had gone the round of the press. The mystifying and revolting story of a perpetual motive power born of a woman furnished space for endless invective and satire. The comments of the journals stimulated the public to fury. A large and disorderly crowd entered at night the structure which had been raised as a temporary cradle for Mr. Spear's "physical saviour." They tore the machine in pieces, trampled the shreds under foot, and scattered them to the winds. From the threats uttered, it seems that a similar fate was reserved for the constructors of the "Thing," could the furious mob have seized them. Such was the ignominious end of the metal Frankenstein destined to revolutionize the American world. The frame lay in atoms. The mysterious "motive power" was relegated to an obscurity more perplexing than ever. No new pæans gladdened the subscribers to the *Era*, and John M. Spear turned sadly to less glowing schemes. A fond hope, however, remained to him that time would yet behold the realisation of his cherished idea. "Thank God," he wrote, "the principles which have been presented, and the philosophy which has been communicated, are beyond the reach of the mob, and cannot be harmed by the slanders of the pulpit or the misrepresentations of the press." And, consoling himself with the line :—

"Truth crushed to earth shall rise again,"

the servant of the "Associated Electrizers" departed from the spot where was extinguished the "Greatest Revelation of the Age."

So rose, progressed, and fell, three of the wildest follies which have disgraced modern spiritualism. Other insanities of the kind have since occurred. There were in America the Kiantone movement, the "Sacred Order of Unionists," the Cincinnati "Patriarchs," and, worst of all, the "Harmonial Society." Mrs. E. Hardinge describes this last as "one of the most extraordinary evidences of human folly, credulity, impudent assumption, and blasphemous pretension that the records of any movement can show."

The "Society" did not directly originate through spiritualism. On the contrary, it was simply a parasitical excrescence foisted upon that movement by interested persons. As in the case of Mountain Cove the leading spirit was an ex-Reverend. A certain T. E. Spencer, formerly pastor of a Methodist flock, planned, and, with the aid of his wife, carried out this infamous affair. A settlement styled "Harmony Springs" was formed in Benton County, Arkansas. All applications for membership Mr. Spencer submitted to his "controlling angels." These displayed a worldliness of mind hardly to be expected from such elevated beings. Rich dupes were eagerly welcomed into the Harmonial paradise; but its gates remained inexorably closed on the poor. Once admitted, the neophyte found his wealth melt with wonderful rapidity. The Spencers, like Dives, clothed themselves in fine linen, and fared sumptuously every day. Their followers were enforced to content themselves with an extremely meagre vegetarian diet; the inducement to do so being the hope of earthly immortality. For the doctrines of the "Harmonial Society" were extremely curious. Many spirits, Mr. Spencer taught, perished with the body. Others languished for a short time after the separation, and then expired. Only human beings who followed the Spencerian system could arrive at immortality, which immortality should be earthly. And an indispensable condition of the system was that its promulgator should have full control of the property of his dupes.

In a year or two the bubble burst. Dark rumours issued from Harmony Springs. It appeared certain that, whether immortal or not, Spencer and his followers, male and female, were extremely immoral. Dissension, too, was rife among the community. For a time Mrs. Spencer quieted recusants by diatribes on the annihilation which awaited them should they persist in their mutinous conduct. "Death," she remarked, "is the prying into things that are of the world, and acquisitiveness, and keeping anything to yourselves, and looking into things too much for your knowledge, and inquiring into things that the angels only hint at, and questioning what the angels say or do, and doubting much, *and fixing up separate dishes for yourselves!*"

Despite this sublime philosophy matters continued to grow worse. Several members determined to take legal measures for the recovery of their cash. On learning *this* the Spencers gathered together what was left of the spoil, and fled. They were pursued, arrested, tried, and sentenced to imprisonment. Of the large sums that had been embarked in the "Harmonial Society," scarcely a dollar remained.

In this, as in all other enterprises of the kind, ridicule, disappointment, and ruin, were the portion of the dupes. Nor can one compassionate them very highly. They appeared to have taken leave of common sense, and to be utterly destitute of reason. No claim was too absurd for credence. The extraordinary spiritual pretensions of the self-constituted prophets who domineered over them were accepted without the slightest examination. That two ex-reverends could be the witnesses foretold by John, that a machine might be endowed with life, that earthly immortality was attainable by immoral practices and spare diet, the faithful religiously believed. Nor, reviewing the long record of human credulity, need we be surprised. Two very opposite errors exist, into which, according to their bias, mankind are liable to fall. On one side we have the bigoted sceptic who disbelieves, in face of the plainest evidence, that spirits can communicate with man. The father of such an one ridiculed the notion of an electric telegraph ; his grandfather laughed at Watt and Stephenson, and wrote in the *Quarterly Review*, when railway travelling was first proposed, "Twenty miles an hour ! As well trust one's self to be fired off from a Congreve mortar." Others of his ancestors imprisoned Solomon de Caus in a madhouse, and all but broke the heart of Columbus. As a contrast to this species of mental deformity we have the bigoted enthusiast, who accepts the wildest dreams without examination, and feels insulted should any one speak of proof. Such enthusiasts adored Joanna Southcote as a prophetess ; and such put faith in all the lies of Titus Oates. During the Middle Ages they searched for the philosopher's stone; and persecuted old dames who rode on broomsticks, and kept familiar demons in the shape of cats. In Mandeville's time they sent ambassadors to Prester John. In the era of Procopius they knew Britain to be an island inhabited only by the invisible spirits of the dead. At present one class of such persons put faith in Papal Infallibility, and another, under the name of " Re-incarnationists," vamp up the worn-out follies of Brahminical India, and seek to reconstruct the exploded theories of Pythagoras.

CHAPTER III.

DELUSIONS (continued).

I CLASS Kardecism amongst the delusions of the world, and I have excellent reasons for the course I take. I knew well the founder, or rather the reviver, of this phase of paganism. His entire honesty of purpose I do not for a moment doubt. He was perfectly convinced that he had dug from the grave of Pythagoras a light which should illumine the world. This intensity of conviction mastered not only himself but others. His earnestness was projected on the minds of the sensitive magnetic subjects whom he termed his mediums. The thoughts thus forced into their brains, their hands committed to paper, and Kardec received his own doctrines as messages from the spirit-world. Had these teachings really emanated from the great minds which were professedly their authors, would they have taken the shape they did? How came Iamblichus to be such a master of good modern French? Through what cause had Pythagoras so completely forgotten his native Greek? If, too, these communications were really the work of disembodied spirits, by what right does "Par Allan Kardec" appear on the title page of every volume? And then the teachings promulgated. Are they truths? If so, let us have some *fact* in support of these truths; the wild dreams of believers and the revelations of clairvoyants will not suffice. I am well known to be a clairvoyant, and have the right and the power to speak with confidence regarding this particular phase of psychology. All students of the question are aware that two forms of clairvoyance exist; the one entitled "natural," the other induced by magnetism. I have never yet met with a case of magnetic clairvoyance where the subject did not reflect directly or indirectly the ideas of the magnetiser. This is most strikingly illustrated in the instance of Allan Kardec. . Under the influence of his energetic will his clairvoyants were so many writing machines that gave his ideas as he desired to have them. If at times the doctrines promulgated were not exactly in accordance with his wishes, he corrected them to meet those wishes. It is, or ought to be, well known that Allan Kardec *was not himself a medium*. He simply magnetized or psychologized minds frailer and more sensitive than his own. I can testify to the fact that, before I knew, or could by any possibility have known, of his passing from earth, I received, in presence of the Earl of Dunraven, then Viscount Adare, a message, saying : "I regret to have taught the *spirite* doctrine. Allan Kardec." ("Je regrette d'avoir enseigné la doctrine spirite. Allan Kardec.") By comparison of the minute of this occurrence with the minute of his passing away, the interval between the two was found so short as utterly to preclude the idea that even a telegram could have reached me regarding his departure from earth. As, moreover, his decease was preceded by no illness, the possibility of that decease had never been for a moment present to my mind. I could not, on receiving it, at first credit the above message. It was *not*, I may remark, received during a *séance*, but suddenly interrupted a conversation beween Lord Adare and myself.

The subjoined most remarkable communication was dictated through M. Morin, whom in earth-life Allan Kardec considered one of his best mediums, and relied on greatly. To say the least it is reasonable, and bears the impress of truth.

"All. Kardec.

"M. Morin, médium, somnambule parlant,

"Communicant chez M. Caussin, Rue St. Denis, 345,

· du 6me novemb., 1869.

"All. Kardec parlant par la bouche de Morin.
　　　　Sa confession posthume.

"Dans les dernières années j'ai travaillé avec soin à éloigner toutes les intelligences, tous les hommes entourés de l'estime public et qui, travaillant à la science spirite, eussent pu accaparer pour eux une partie des bénéfices que je voulais pour moi seul.

"Cependant, plusieurs, d'entre eux, placés très haut dans les sciences et les lettres, se seraient contents en se dévouant au spiritisme de briller au second rang, mais dans mon effroi d'être éclipsé, je préférai toujours rester seul à la tête du mouvement spirite ; en être à la fois la tête qui pense et le bras qui agit.

"Oui, je l'avoue, c'est ma faute si le spiritisme n'a jusqu'à ce jour compté dans ses rangs aucun de ces champions princes de la parole ou de la pensée ; chez moi l'homme avait dompté l'esprit."

Sur l'avenir du spiritisme, tel qu'il l'avait conçu, et sur les conséquences actuelles :

"De mon vivant, le spiritisme, tel que je le concevais, me paraissait ce que l'homme pourrait rêver de plus grand, de plus vaste ; ma raison s'égarait.

"Maintenant que, débarrassé de l'enveloppe matérielle, je regarde l'immensité des mondes, je me demande comment j'ai pu me draper dans mon manteau de demi-dieu, me croire un deuxième Sauveur de l'humanité. Orgueil insensé que je déplore amèrement.

"Je vois le spiritisme tel que je l'avais conçu, si petit, si restreint, si éloigné, dans ses parties mêmes les moins imparfaites, des perfections qu'il doit atteindre.

"Considérant les résultats produits par la propagation des idées spirites, que vois-je à présent ?

"Le spiritisme trainé dans les bas-fonds du ridicule, représenté par d'infimes personnalités que j'ai trop élevées moi-même.

"En voulant produire le bien j'ai motivé beaucoup d'aberration qui enfante le mal.

"Au point de vue de la philosophie, peu de résultat. Pour quelques intelligences combien d'ignorants !

"Au point de vue religieux, que de superstitieux sortis d'une superstition pour tomber dans une autre !

"Conséquences de mon égoïsme.

"Si je n'avais pas écarté les intelligences transcendentales le spiritnalisme ne serait pas exclusivement representé dans la majorité des adhérens par des adepts pris au sein des classes laborieux, les seules chez lesquelles mon éloquence et mon savoir ont pu avoir accès.

"ALLAN KARDEC."

I append a translation of the above :—

"All. Kardec.

"M. Morin, inspirational medium.

"Communication given at the house of M. Caussin,
Rue St. Denis, 345, Nov. 6th, 1869.

"Allan Kardec speaking through M. Morin.

His posthumous confession.

"During the last few years of my life, I sought with care to keep in the background all men of intelligence who merited public esteem,

who were investigators of the science of *spiritisme*, and might have taken
for themselves a share of the benefit which I wished for myself alone.

"Nevertheless, many of these, occupying high positions in literature
and science, would have been perfectly satisfied, in devoting themselves
to *spiritisme*, to have shone in the second rank ; but, in my fear of being
eclipsed, I preferred to remain alone at the head of the movement, to be
at once the thinking brain and the arm of action.

"Yes, I acknowledge it to be my fault if *spiritisme* to the present day has
numbered in its ranks none of those champions—princes of language or of
thought ; with me the man (or my humanity) overcame my intelligence."

In speaking of the future of *spiritisme*, as he had understood it,
and of the actual position :

"Whilst I lived *spiritisme*, as I had conceived it, seemed to me all that
mankind could imagine of grandest and most vast ; my reason was bewildered.

"Now that, free from the material envelope, I look on the immensity
of the different worlds, I ask how I could have clothed myself in the
mantle, as it were, of a demi-god ; believing myself to be a second
Saviour of humanity. Monstrous pride which I bitterly regret.

"I now see *spiritisme*, such as I had imagined it, so small, so contracted, so far from (even in the least imperfect of its teachings) the perfections it ought to attain.

"Taking into consideration the results produced by the propagation of
the ideas *spirits*, what do I now see ?

"*Spiritisme* dragged to the lowest depth of ridicule, and represented
only by puny personalities, which I had striven too much to elevate.

"In seeking to do good I have incited much aberration productive
only of evil.

"So far as the philosophy is concerned how small the results ! For
the few intelligences it has reached, how many are unaware of its
existence !

"From a religious point of view we find the superstitious leaving one
superstition only to fall into another.

"Consequences of my egotism.

"Had I not kept in the shade all superior intelligences, *spiritisme*
would not be represented, as it is to the majority of its adherents, by
adepts taken from amongst the working classes, the only one where my
eloquence and my learning could gain access.

"ALLAN KARDEC."

Such is the message submitted to us through the instrumentality
of M. Morin, and claimed to be from his former hierophant. I
pass now to an examination of the philosophy, if philosophy it
deserves to be termed, unfolded in " Le Livre des Esprits."

"*Q.*—What foundation is there for the doctrine of re-incarnation?

"*A.*—The justice of God and revelation.

"*Q.*—What is the aim of re-incarnation ?

"*A.*—Expiation ; progressive improvement of mankind. Without this aim, where would be its justice ? "—*The Spirits' Book.*

Justice and Expiation are thus the key-notes of that fantasia with which Allan Kardec would have bewildered the brain of man. His scheme of creation is a plagiary from the severer schools of Christianity ; but a plagiary which omits their central figure, Christ. For the Messiah he substitutes an endless dream of change. He discards the theory of Pythagoras, so far as it relates to man's entrance into the bodies of animals ; but he discards this only to accept and refine upon other parts of the Pythagorean system. Like most theologians he finds in the Deity more of anger than of love. His Father is the Father of Calvin and of Knox. These, however, teach that God's wrath is pacified by the sacrifice of his Son. Kardec informs us that God pacifies his wrath by confusing the identity of his creatures. The order which reigns in the material universe finds no counterpart in spiritual things. The quiet harmony with which system wheels round system serves only to mock the confusion prevalent among the souls for whom those systems were created. It would seem that the happiness of just men made perfect is, in the Kardecian heaven, coincident on their having at last found out " who they may possibly be." The Biblical assurance that " there is no rest for the wicked," acquires a new and startling significance from the views put forward under the title of Re-incarnation. Unhappy spirits, we learn, spend a considerable portion of eternity in finding out how much " worse confounded " their confusion may become. Their constant dread is that, in forgetting the incidents of their earthly lives, they may have also forgotten the lessons of those lives, and so be sent back to learn them more perfectly. The incarnations, it seems, which spirits undergo " are always very numerous." Yet the soul " never loses its individuality." Fairly stated, the Kardecian argument would appear to be that a soul must lose its individuality in order to find it.

There is no limit to the monstrous perplexities which continued incarnations involve. It is, according to Kardec, part of the justice of God that a grandmother may be her own granddaughter. The Nero of the first century becomes the Madame Guyon of the eighteenth. "The soul of a bad man can become the soul of a good man. If he have repented, his new incarnation is the reward of his efforts at amendment." On the question being put, " Can a spirit who has animated the body of a man, animate that of a woman in a new existence, and *vice versâ ?* " the reply was, " *Yes.*"

From such propositions as these an almost infinite succession of revolting corollaries may be deduced. Some among these corollaries are of a nature which I dare hardly do more than indicate. We might, for instance, meet with such a case as the following :—Two persons marry. Children having been born to them, the parents in due course pass from earth. They are once more incarnated. In this existence, however, the man has become the woman, and the woman the man. Should they again marry, how are we to read the riddle of their relationship, and the relationship of their children ?

 The doctrine of re-incarnation, in fact, destroys all relationship. It takes away whatever binds society together. It crushes the holiest feelings of our nature. What is left to us when all that we love has lost its identity ? The re-incarnationist delibe-rately cuts himself off from the hope of being once more rejoiced by—

> "The touch of a vanished hand
> And the sound of a voice that is still."

The hand has vanished from us to the clasp of somebody else, and the voice, though it may not be still, has forgotten us for ever. The same fate awaits ourselves. We, too, must pass away and forget. We, too, must spend eternity in a sort of bewildered wonder as to what will next be our lot. We are more unhappy than the old Biblical heroes who had "no abiding place on earth." They looked for an eternal dwelling-place hereafter, and crowns which should never fade away. But we, if Kardec and Kardec's "spirits" prophesy aright, possess no continuing city either on earth or in heaven. We are doomed to a ceaseless and unhappy wandering. Innocent of the crime of Cain, we share his punishment. And we are no longer men and women. We have no longer wife, husband, mother, father, sister, brother, son, or daughter. Such words have lost their meaning. Indeed, we are not even masters of our own souls. The world of the re-incarnationist is simply a stage from which puppets dance on and off as the showman pulls the strings. With each change of scene the puppets are taken to pieces and thrown into a promiscuous heap, from which new dolls are constructed as casually as the shifting figures of the kaleidoscope. Yet Kardec asserts that this doctrine is "at once eminently consolatory and strictly conformable with the most rigorous justice," and thousands of enthusiasts endorse his assertion.

It is evident, however, that even the warmest of these disciples accept the new faith with sweeping reservations. Human nature revolts from re-incarnation in its Kardecian entirety. For the logical outcome of the system is an annihilation as complete as that anticipated by the hardest Materialist, and far more painful. In a few thousand years there would remain nothing of a world conducted under re-incarnationist conditions, save an insanity of confusion. The children would have become undistinguishable from the fathers. The only thing remaining in life would be a frantic endeavour to grasp some tangible idea. Naturally, even fanaticism shrinks from this. Re-incarnationists, therefore, far from surveying their creed in its full scope, grasp only at portions which may be moulded to suit the wishes they have in view. Treated in this manner, Kardecism becomes a truly plastic faith. Even the maternal heart can find comfort in re-incarnation by resolutely refusing to note the direction of the great wave, and attending only to minor eddies. Thus we hear of a French lady, whose only daughter dies while still quite a child. Another is born to her. The second girl receives the same name as the first. Surprised by the coincidence, friends naturally question the mother as to the reasons that may exist for such a re-naming.

She explains that there is nothing of re-naming in the matter; the second daughter is simply the first given back to her by God. She tells how one day, whilst she held the baby on her knee, it suddenly spoke, and said : " Mamma, do you not know who I am ? " Startled by such an occurrence, she could scarcely find breath to reply, " No, my child." " I am your little *Mimi*," was the answer, " and I have come back to you. Look at me, dear mamma, and you will see that I am really your Mimi." And the mother looked, and saw that the features of the child were assuredly those of her lost daughter. Such are the fond dreams for which, even in re-incarnation, the heart of a mother will find scope.

There is a touching something in the above incident. What, however, save bewilderment, can be extracted from the narrative I now give ? It appears here, as it appeared in the *Spiritualist* of September 18th, 1874 :—

" As *The Spiritualist*, Vol. V., No. 8, page 85, contains Miss Kisling-bury's very judicious remarks about the two contending theories in spiritualism, allow me, in my turn, to communicate to you a fact, which seems strongly to corroborate my belief in re-incarnation, and which happened to me in the summer of 1869.

" A very distinguished French writing medium, Madame C——, had come to spend some weeks at my house, at N—— W——, and we had asked our leading spirits whether it was possible or not to evoke, during the sleep of the body, the spirit of a person now alive ? Soon after there fell from the ceiling, on the table where Madame C—— was writing under spiritual control, a small oval bronze medal, quite tarnished, with some dry yellow earth sticking to it, bearing on one side the likeness of Christ, on the other one that of the Virgin Mary, and seeming, by its style, to belong to the sixteenth century. We were then told that this medal had been buried a long time ago, with a person who had constantly worn it, and who had died a violent death— that this person was now re-incarnated in Germany—that an object which had belonged to her formerly was necessary to establish between her and us a fluidical connection, which might enable her to come and appeal to us for assistance against a sort of painful obsession under which she was labouring—that her name began with an A—and that we were to call her ' *In memory of the town of Dreux.*'

" Accordingly, on the following and some other evenings we set to work, Madame C—— (whom I had mesmerised to sleep for better control) holding the pencil : and presently the spirit wrote, in small, hasty writing :—' I am here.'

" ' *Quest.*—How is it that you are already asleep ?' (It was only ten o'clock.)

" ' *Ans.*—I am in bed, ill of fever.'

" ' *Quest.*—Can you tell us your present name ?'

" ' *Ans.*—Not yet. When I wore the medal I was in France ; in the reign of Louis XIV. I was killed by a man who was carrying off a lady from the monastery where I was a nun.'

" ' *Quest.*—Why did he kill you ?'

" ' *Ans.*—He did so unintentionally. I had just returned from Dreux, where I had been sent on an errand by our Abbess. I overtook them unawares, and threatened to scream ; he then struck me on the head with the pommel of his sword, in order to stun me into silence, and killed me.'

" ' *Quest.*—How did he manage to enter the convent ?'

" ' *Ans.*—By bribing the man who kept our doors, and who feigned to be asleep while they were stealing his keys. When he saw that I was dead he was frightened. He and his servant bore me off and buried me in the first place they found fit. There are now houses built all over it, but my grave exists, still unknown, in a garden.'

" ' *Quest.*—What place was it ?'

" ' *Ans.*—The Pré-aux-Clercs, Paris.'

" ' *Quest.*—Was the man who killed you a nobleman ?'

" ' *Ans.*—Yes. He belonged to the *Lesdiguières.*'

" ' *Quest.*—Who was the nun he carried off ?'

" ' *Ans.*—A novice of a noble family. He had led her already to a coach, which was to carry her off in another direction than the one he intended to take ; they were to meet again later. So she knew nothing about my death. They fled to foreign countries. She died soon after.'

" ' *Quest.*—What did your spirit do when it left your body ?'

" ' *Ans.*—I hastened straight to our Abbess, but she was terribly frightened when she saw me, thinking it was a nightmare. I then roamed about the chapel, always thinking myself alive still. I only understood that I was dead when those who were burying me said a prayer before covering my body with earth. A great trouble overcame me then, and I felt it a hard task to pardon them. I have great difficulty in obeying your call, because as soon as I am asleep, I am usually forced to return to Dreux and to haunt the church under my former aspect, as I used to do before my present incarnation. It is a terrible subjection, a constant hindrance to my progress, as it paralyzes all my efforts to come into contact with the good spirits who guide and comfort those who are in the flesh and asleep. Emile ! You must help me to free myself.'

" After some words of advice and encouragement, and my promise to help her, we continued :—

" ' *Quest.*—In which street at Paris was your monastery situated ? '

" ' *Ans.*—Rue de l'Abbaye.'

" ' *Quest.*—Under the patronage of which saint ? '

" ' *Ans.*—Of St. Bruno ; the congregation of the Ladies of the Passion.'

" ' *Quest.*—Does the monastery still exist ? '

" ' *Ans.*—Destroyed ; plundered during the revolution.'

" ' *Quest.*—Is there anything now remaining of it ? '

" ' *Ans.*—A wall.'

"[Having, after this, written to Paris for information, the friend to whom we wrote informed us that, after many long searches, he had indeed found out, incrusted between houses, an old wall, which once, as was said, belonged to a lady's monastery.]

" ' *Quest.*—Have you, in your present incarnation, any recollection of the one gone by ? '

" ' *Ans.*—I have a sort of apprehension, as if I were to die of a violent death—an injury to the head. It makes me very nervous at times ! I see now that it is only a reflex of the past. I also dream of phantoms in monastic gowns, and of murderers rushing at them ; also of a spectre in an ancient dress, who grins at me.'

" ' *Quest.*—Do you live far off ? '

" ' *Ans.*—In Germany.'

" ' *Quest.*—Is your name a German one ? '

" ' *Ans.*—Yes. Those questions hurt me ! '

" ' *Quest.*—Do I know you ? '

" ' *Ans.*—To be sure you do ! '

" ' *Quest.*—Where do you live ? '

" The medium then begins to trace with great difficulty :—F . . . Fu . . . I exclaim, under sudden inspiration, *Fulda !* and at the same moment Madame C—— gives a shriek and a violent start, nearly upsetting her chair. She says she felt a commotion, as of a strong electric discharge. I understand at once that the controlling spirit is that of my cousin, the Countess *Amelie of* Y. . . who lives in Fulda (a small town about five hours' journey away by the railway), where she occupies a high charge in a Protestant Chapter of noble ladies.

" ' *Quest. (after a long pause.)*—Why did you give the medium such a shock ? '

" ' *Ans.*—I did not want you to know yet.'

" ' *Quest.*—Did your body awake ? '

" ' *Ans.*—No ; but I was startled.'

"While we were still (Madame C—— and I) debating whether it were really my cousin or not, the medium's hand unconsciously wrote down a name which cut short all my doubts, as it referred to a secret known only to the Countess of Y—— and myself.

"'*Quest.*—How am I to ascertain your identity, and make sure that you are not a frivolous spirit, mocking us ?'

"'*Ans.*—When you meet me, before long, ask whether I have any dreams, in which it seems to me as if I were killed ? I shall say no, and add, that I dream sometimes of a priest murdered by ruffians. You may also show me the medal : I shall feel then as if I had known it before.'

"With this communication we closed our evocations of Amelie, which had taken us several evenings.

"A few months later I met my cousin at my sister's country seat. Amelie, as was her wont, began joking with me about my faith in spiritualism, declaring that it was all delusion and deception. I bore her merry attacks merrily, defending, however, my theories about dreams, reminiscences, spirit messages, and so on, till I came to ask, as in a joke, whether she, for example, never dreamt that she was being murdered ? She answered 'No,' adding, after a slight pause, that, in fact, she had sometimes a disagreeable dream, always the same—a sort of nightmare—which made her nervous and uncomfortable for the whole day after. On my insisting upon receiving the particulars, she said at last, that she dreamt of a Catholic priest in sacerdotal dress, flying from a burning church, with armed men at his heels, who wanted to kill him. After changing the conversation, I took the medal out of my pocket and showed it to her, feigning to have bought it at an antiquary's. She handled it about for some moments, and then began to examine it so long and so closely that I, at last, asked her 'What was the matter ?' whereupon she answered that 'she could not understand how that object seemed as familiar as if she had possessed or seen it formerly, although she could not, for the world, recollect under what circumstances !'

"I now told her all about our evocations ; and she, being very much struck by my narrative, requested to be shown the medial writing. This writing, I had thought, was not like her own. I had known hers only by her letters, in German, written with pen and ink, while the former, traced by a French medium, was written in French. When she saw it she exclaimed that it was positively *her* writing, when she used a pencil instead of a pen ; and forthwith she wrote some words which I dictated, and which proved to be exactly like the original.

"She got into a great fright at the thought of her soul haunting an old church, and I advised her, in order to paralyze the attraction, to pray every evening for help to her guardian angel, and to say three times aloud, before going to bed, '*I will not go !*'

"Since she has done this, I was informed by my leading spirits that she has entirely succeeded in ridding herself of the aforesaid subjection.

"This, my dear sir, is my personal experience of a fact, interesting enough I think, to find a space in your columns ; and I would be thankful for every explanation of it, given in the non-reincarnationist sense, in favour of the French proverb which says, *Du choc des opinions jaillit la vérité.*"

There is nothing in the above which can be construed as a proof of re-incarnation. The whole may be explained by the theory that the Countess of Y—— and Madame C—— being sensitives, the same spirit had contrived to impress the same ideas on the brain of each; with greater clearness in the case of the latter lady. I do not advance this supposition as the true one. I advance it, however, as at once more plausible and more reasonable than the theory which attributes such dim reminiscences to a transmigration of souls. The hypothesis I have offered covers the facts of the case at least as well. It is less far-fetched. It accords better with proved phenomena. To speak of such is useless, indeed, in the present instance. Re-incarnation remains, and always must remain, a theory whose very nature renders it incapable of proof.

Putting aside the revolting confusion to which it logically leads, how illogical are the delusions into which it betrays its votaries! It is evidently impossible that the particular qualities of mind which, nineteen centuries ago, were put together to constitute Julius Cæsar, can be reproduced through more than one man or woman at a time, even in this age of wonders. And, although a lady may be firmly convinced that, in a former incarnation, she was the consort of an emperor or king, it becomes perplexing when one encounters half-a-dozen other persons equally enthusiastic, and equally certain of their identity with the said empress or queen. The souls of famous men and women would appear to cut up into more fragments than the wood of the true cross. As I remarked once in a published letter of mine :—"I have had the pleasure of meeting at least twelve Marie Antoinettes, six or seven Marys of Scotland, a whole host of ¦Louis and other kings, about twenty Great Alexanders, but never a plain 'John Smith.' I would indeed like to cage the latter curiosity."

M. Kardec's mesmerised mediums tell us that spirits never degenerate. "Can a man," it was asked, "descend in his new existence to a lower point than that which he has already reached?" The reply came promptly, "As regards his social position, yes, *but not as regards his degree of progress as a spirit.*" The Alexanders and Cæsars with whom we are inundated have thus advanced to a higher degree of intelligence than when they scattered the hosts of Darius, or drove Pompey from the Pharsalian plain. Why then, in the name of all that is mystifying, do they accomplish so little? Where were these heroes in the day of their country's agony, when French eagles looked down only on disaster, and a German army lay outside the walls of Paris? From all the Hannibals, the Scipios, the Charlemagnes, the Turennes, the Condés, whom France possesses, could not one warlike patriot have come forward as her saviour? Either want of patriotism is a Kardecian virtue, or greatness of mind has place among "the impurities which spirits must strip themselves of."

Perhaps, indeed, the soul becomes bewildered with its multiplicity of existences. Thus, we can well conceive that if, after having figured on earth's stage as Nero, Constantine, Mahomet, Charlemagne, Friar Bacon, &c., a spirit should be incarnated as Pierre Dubois, he may find even three-score years and ten, if he be allowed so much, insufficient to determine whether he shall set fire to Paris and fiddle whilst it is burning; transfer the metropolis of France from the banks of the Seine to the shores of the Gulf of Lyons, or the Bay of Biscay; collect Catholics, Voltairians, Protestants and Positivists under the banner of a new religion; or invent some material of murder which shall be to gunpowder as gunpowder was to the spears and axes of the fourteenth century. Is it surprising if, confused by the entrance of so much genius into one small mind, the unfortunate mixture of great men spends his—or I might more appropriately say *their* time, in perplexedly trying to determine to what he had best turn his powers? And before he has settled whether there is more of the Mahomet or the Friar Bacon in him, death knocks, and the world finds that it has profited by this particular re-incarnationist as little as it profits by the philosophy of re-incarnation in general.

What miserable times must the poor nondescripts have in the

spirit-world! Imagine two collections of existences meeting, and perplexedly iterating to each other :— .

> " Perhaps, my friend, I'm you !
> Perhaps, my friend, you are me !
> Perhaps, we both are somebody else !
> And 'tis puzzling, you'll agree."

In this very dilemma lies the essence and the drawback of the Kardecian philosophy. But the spirits may console themselves with memories and anticipations of their greatness, past and future. For, as I have remarked, it is very, very seldom that the ordinary run of human minds are re-incarnated. Your heroes and geniuses seem to reserve to themselves " the right of re-admission to earth." How lamentable it is that their last state here should be so worthless in comparison with their first! But, no doubt, it consoles the frivolous lounger of Parisian *salons* to assume that he was at a far back day Condé or Molière, and that, as "spirits cannot degenerate," he must now, although he appears a dunce, be raised above the mental platform on which he stood as victor of Rocroy or author of " Le Misantrope."

What becomes of ordinary souls ? Shakspere and Sophocles must be very weary of the many parts they have to play ; but the curtain never rises for the entrance of plain John Smith. He dies, and earth knows him no more. No doubt he is one of the spirits M. Kardec tells us of, " who at their origin have only an instinctive existence, and have scarcely any consciousness of themselves or their acts ; it is only little by little that their intelligence is developed." But where does that intelligence become developed ? The spirit cannot, surely, depart from earth a plain member of the Smith family, to return in a year or two a full-blown Alexander ! Has Dame Nature, then, some far-off planetary workshop, where the raw material of a hundred butchers or bakers is kneaded into one conqueror or inventor ? Or can the mass of humanity be composed of insignificant, jog-trot creatures ; content to be born in an ordinary manner, to live an ordinary life, to possess the ordinary hope of immortality, and to depart from earth with the vulgar expectation of finding " a place prepared for them," according to their merits ? I sincerely trust that this last supposition is the correct one. If it be, we unfortunates whom the re-incarnationist pities as suckled in the outworn creed that no individual can possess more than one soul, need hardly envy our kaleidoscopic brethren. We need not lament that we are not as Cicero-Napoleon-Jones; or if a touch of longing thrill us when contemplating his greatness, we may stifle it by reflecting that, however obscure our identity may be, that identity is peaceful and unperplexed. We are safe, moreover, from such nightmare visions as that which caused a feminine re-incarnationist to describe to the world the monstrous intertwinements of two complicated souls. These souls pass a confused series of existences in various planets. They change from sex to sex. After a series of perplexities, always absurd, and often disgusting, the soul which happens at that precise moment to be the woman is summoned to earth. In her previous existences she has sometimes been married to her fellow Tiresias, but, oftener, has dispensed with the Hymeneal knot. However, she contrives to forget her much-incarnated lover, and weds with an ordinary mortal. A child is born. Confusion madder than the maddest intricacy of an insane brain ensues. The discarded lover, watching his opportunity of revenge, has appeared on earth in the form of the said child. Through the carelessness of a nurse, however, he is killed whilst still young. His mother-wife is reported to have married again, very recently, and to remain at present in an agreeable state of doubt as to whether she have not literally wedded her grandmother.

Such is re-incarnationist literature. There is much more of this kind of thing than is sketched above. There are works infinitely madder and more disgusting than anything I have quoted. There are others distinguished chiefly by the perverted ingenuity they display. A second feminine disciple of Kardec has elaborated a theory of emanations. Disincarnated beings who wait their turn of material life are made up, we learn, of numerous souls, fitting one within another like the ivory balls of China. Should one of this strange race of beings wish to communicate with mankind, he throws forth a soul, which throws forth another, which continues the emanating process until earth is reached. Then these curious links hand up and down the electric chain they have formed their own communications and those of the human beings with whom they are in sympathy. The task finished, they uncoil, and creep once more the one within the other.

These theories find accepters. The more absurd and contradictory they appear to ordinary minds, the more do they delight enthusiasts. Nor need this be wondered at. Contradictions crop up everywhere in the revelations of Kardec himself, and whosoever accepts those revelations evidently has a vigorous capacity of credulity. How puzzling must spiritualists who are not "Spiritists" consider such doctrines as the following :—

"*Q.*—Do spirits employ any time in transporting themselves through space ?

"*A.*—Yes, but their motion is as rapid as that of thought.

"*Q.*—Is not thought the movement of the soul itself, a transportation of the soul to the object thought of by it ?

"*A.*—Wherever the thought is there the soul is, since it is the soul that thinks. Thought is an attribute.

"*Q.*—Is the spirit, properly so called, without a covering ; or is it, as some declare, surrounded by a substance of some kind ?

"*A.*—The spirit is enveloped in a substance which would appear to you as mere vapour, but which, nevertheless, appears very gross to us, though it is sufficiently [vaporous to allow the spirit to float in the atmosphere and transport himself through space at pleasure."

If "wherever the thought is, there the soul is," how can these spirits inform us that spirits travel ? Travel implies time, and thought is instantaneous. Perhaps, indeed, they would answer that the duration of a journey is equivalent to the time occupied in the formation of a thought regarding that journey. A spirit wishes to traverse a distance of some millions of miles, and, presto ! it is accomplished. The wish and the deed were one.

But, if so, why say that "the motion of spirits is as rapid as that of thought ?" According to the teachers whose utterances are supposed to be given to the world by Kardec, that motion *is* thought. If a spirit can but form an idea of any sphere, the said spirit finds itself instantly there. Distance matters nothing.

Distance *is* nothing, for to thought distance is inappreciable. To select an earthly and therefore familiar illustration, it is the same thing as regards time occupied whether a man in London thinks of Brighton or of Queensland. He forms a thought of the province fifteen thousand miles away just as rapidly as of the town from which he is only fifty miles distant. Thought, then, knows nothing of time or space.

But matter does, and the Kardecian spirits are clothed in matter. " It would appear to you mere vapour, but it, neverthe-less, appears very gross to us." What then enables it to race as swiftly as thought? Even vapour must take an appreciable time to traverse a given distance, and that time increases with the increase of the distance to be traversed. But to thought the dis-tance of the farthest star is as inappreciable as that of the nearest planet. Evidently, then, these Kardecian teachings are incon-gruous. The dilemma they present is the following one. If in the next world spirits are still enveloped in matter, they cannot travel with the rapidity of thought. If they travel with the rapidity of thought they cannot be enveloped in matter. One or other of these statements must necessarily be false.

I pretend not to decide which. Neither can I pretend to decide why Kardec's mesmerised clairvoyants and writers have advanced such doctrines as the following:—" All spirits are created equal, not knowing whence they come, for their free-will must have its fling. They progress more or less rapidly in intelligence as in morality. The state of the soul at its first incarnation is a state analogous to that of infancy. In proportion as spirits advance they understand what has retarded their progress. A spirit may remain stationary, but he never deteriorates."

Is the Greece of to-day more intelligent than the Greece of Homer and Socrates? Is the France of our century more moral than the France of fifteen centuries back? He will be a bold man who answers Yes. And if not, can the change be called progress? Even a Kardecist will scarcely claim it as such. Why then, if whole nations of spirits may deteriorate in particular respects, are we told that spirits *never* deteriorate?

The mistake arises evidently from the mistaken view its author took of the civilisation of to-day. He saw that the world, as a whole, has progressed. What he did not see was the true source of that progress. He accounts for it by supposing that spirits return to earth in a more enlightened state with each successive incarnation. Reasonable men will account for it by pointing out that it is the tendency of truths to accumulate ; that the heritage of knowledge we leave to our children is greater than that we inherit from our fathers ; in other words, that mankind progress in proportion as they laugh at the teachings of Kardec and follow those of Bacon.

The assertion that all spirits are created equal is certainly a convenient one when taken in connection with other parts of the re-incarnative theory. Homer, Socrates, Shakspeare, Galileo, Newton, and their fellow monarchs of mind, were, of course, simply incarnated beings who had reached their twentieth or thirtieth incarnation. The drunkard of the present age is no doubt a returned drinker of the days of the Cæsars. The missionary who preaches to Hindoos or South Sea Islanders in the nineteenth century probably preached to Ephesian or Corinthian Pagans in the first. The different qualities and powers which the minds of men exhibit are thus dismissed as being nothing more than different stages of development, induced by the few or many incarnations which the exhibitors have passed through.

And here be it noted that M. Kardec's mediums assert the moral qualities of the parent to have no effect on the moral qualities of the child.

" *Q.* Parents often transmit physical resemblance to their children ; do they also transmit to them moral resemblance ?

" *A.* No ; because they have different souls or spirits."

So the experience of centuries is as nothing ! The millions of instances in which proof has been given that virtues and vices can be transmitted ; that drunkenness in the parent induces drunkenness in the child ; that fear experienced by the pregnant mother will impress timidity and nervousness on the mind of her infant ; that particular talents may descend from father to son ; that particular forms of insanity can be inherited : these, and countless other evidences of moral resemblance are calmly set aside by the Kardecian "Nay." I fear few who have made any study of mental pathology will be inclined to bow to the doctrine that physical resemblance is all a parent can transmit.

Of the many other contradictions which re-incarnation presents, I have space to notice but few. It is admitted, for example, in the "Spirits' Book" that "incarnated spirits lose the remembrance of the past." Yet, in another part of the same volume we find the following dogma :—

"Q.—Is the spirit of a child who dies in infancy as advanced as that of an adult ?

"A.—He is sometimes much more so ; for he may previously have lived longer, and acquired more experience, especially if he be a spirit who has already made considerable progress."

Such doctrines really require little more than to be stated. They refute themselves. If the incarnated spirit loses the remembrance of the past, of what value is the experience of former lives? They are as if they had never been. How absurd then to tell us that the child who dies in infancy may be more advanced than an adult, because he may previously have lived longer and acquired more experience. The contradiction involved is of the plainest nature. Put succinctly, it is as follows :—"This child is wiser than you, because he knows something that he has forgotten !"

"Q.—Do the beings whom we call angels, archangels, and seraphim form a special category, of a nature different from that of other spirits ?

"A.—No ; they are spirits who have purified themselves from all imperfection, have reached the highest degree of the scale of progress, and united in themselves all species of perfection."

What is left to God when his children "reach the highest degree of the scale of progress and unite in themselves all species of perfection ?" The created become equal to the Creator. Yet the authors of this doctrine tell us also that—"Spirits are the work of God, just as a machine is the work of the mechanician who made it ; the machine is the man's work, but it is not the man." And since when has the work of the mechanician been estimated

as highly as the maker ?   Since when has it been the custom of
man's work to progress to an equality with man himself ?   Yet we
are given to understand that man, here compared to a machine,
can uplift himself to an equality with his maker, God !

It will be new to many that re-incarnation is the resurrection
of the body which Scripture speaks of. "English spiritualists,"
remarks a distinguished re-incarnationist, "do not believe in
re-incarnation, *the resurrection of the flesh, as it is termed in the
Bible.*" And M. Kardec supports by a most astonishing argument
his opinion as to "the doctrine of the plurality of existences"
being "the anchor of safety which God in his mercy has provided
for mankind." "The words of Jesus Himself are explicit as to
the truth of this last assertion ; for we read in the third chapter
of the Gospel according to St. John that Jesus, replying to
Nicodemus, thus expressed Himself :—' Verily, verily, I say unto
thee, Except a man be born again he cannot see the kingdom of
God.' And when Nicodemus inquired, ' How can a man be born
when he is old ?   Can he enter again into his mother's womb, and
be born a second time ? ' Jesus replied, ' Except a man be born
of water and of the spirit, he cannot enter the kingdom of God.
That which is born of the flesh is flesh, and that which is born of
the spirit is spirit.   Marvel not that I said unto thee, Ye must be
born again.' "   And the above texts are gravely advanced as
Scriptural supports to the theory of a " plurality of existences ! "
Truly, that theory rests on adamantine foundations !

We say to the re-incarnationist, " Give us proof—a single proof
even, if it be decisive and well-attested, that the dogmas you
advance are facts." He meets us with such evidence as the
following :—

"When first I saw Katie, a very extraordinary and spontaneous sympathy drew us all at once to each other. I asked my leading spirits about
its cause, and they told me that some hundred years ago we had intimately met in Turkey, where she was a slave named *Sulmé*, who died
young, of a violent death. . . . In the letter mentioned just now, I tried,
without stating anything more positive, to rouse her remembrance, in
begging her earnestly to look into her past existence, and to try to
recollect *me*, in a country far away (of which I described the principal

features), asking her, at the same time, whether the name of Sulmé did not wake any echo in her mind. Here is the answer I got from her, through M. de —— :—

" 'My dear friend, I would wish very much to see you before I go. Can you come to me? I cannot remember anything about a former existence, but fancy I· have known you before. Try to recollect if we have met. The name you mentioned seems familiar to me ; why cannot I remember?' "

I have known a man who was convinced that, at some misty period before that eventful one when

> " Came forth the elect, the Ascidian,
> From the mixture of sea and of slime,"

he had slept in the bosom of the earth as the mineral, Sulphur. To this unfortunate circumstance, and the having been subsequently incarnated as a tiger, he attributed the fiery temperament he possessed. And I have known another man who remembered having been of old a piece of steel. Perhaps I may place with these the laundry-woman who once spoke to me regarding "the faint recollection she had of having been a queen."

Does re-incarnation offer us nothing save these less than trifles in support of its gigantic assumptions, and speculations as revolting as daring? Absolutely nothing. The whole system is, indeed, but a vision, and, like all visions, the fabrics which constitute it are of the most baseless sort. I may confidently affirm that there never was an incident advanced as testimony in favour of that system which would not more easily and naturally bear an explanation other than the explanation sought to be placed on it.

The doctrine carries within itself the seeds of inevitable decay. It may, by its startling nature, captivate weak or enthusiastic minds, even as a modification of the same teachings captivated men in the far-back day of Pythagoras ; but brought to the test of reason it appears miserably wanting. True philosophy launches its fiat against dogmas which, in the very spirit of mediæval theology, require men to accord faith to them, but render no reason why such faith should be accorded. Upon the active life and the guided thought of the nineteenth century, re-incarnation.

intrudes itself as the fossilized skeleton of some schoolman who swore by Aquinas, and disputed according to the rules of Aristotle, might intrude upon a party of scientists busily working by means of the light which Bacon afforded. In its dead hand it carries a scroll proclaiming, "My mission is twofold. I take the place of Christ, and I confound the identity of man." And when the new doctrine has been expounded, and the startled listener inquires, "What proof do you offer me of all this? How can I discover whether I have lived before on earth or not? *Why does the incarnated spirit lose the remembrance of his past?*" the spectre turns over the leaves of the "Spirits' Book," and points to the page where is stereotyped the old, old formula, old as the dogma it was first invented to support, old as Superstition herself;— "Man cannot and may not know everything; God in his wisdom has so ordained."

It is the dreary belief of re-incarnationists that spirits who have not completed their appointed number of "expiations," wander hither and thither during the years or ages which intervene between each incarnation, wondering, with a sort of vacuous perplexity, what will happen next. There have arisen, however, certain mighty inquirers who, by turning the antiquated telescopes of Paracelsus and the Rosicrucians on these unhappy beings, have made marvellous discoveries, and arrived at marvellous conclusions. It was, indeed, the wildest of poor M. Kardec's many delusions to suppose that these shadows had before dwelt on earth. "They are the emanations of matter thrown off in the efforts of Mother Nature to produce her noblest offspring—the sentient human being. They have neither souls nor consciences, and are thus devoid of moral restraint." Let an awe-struck world listen to these solemn revealings of America's chief Occultist, and "in reverent silence bow."

Having "neither souls nor consciences," it is somewhat puzzling to imagine what elementaries can consist of. Had they been very material substances one or more of the species would have assuredly been caged at the numerous *séances* which, we learn, they attend. Are they too small for the microscope to reach?

Are the atoms of which they consist too refined and too loosely-hung together for the grasp of mortal eye or hand ? Are these weird creatures illustrations of Tyndall's molecular theory, or of the doctrine of spontaneous generation ? I know not; but this I know, that, like the genie of the Arabian Nights, whom a fisherman outwitted, their beginning and end is smoke.

" They second every crazy scheme propounded to them." This I consider a libel on the species. They have not yet given any sign of seconding the crazy scheme of a society enthusiastically constituted to hunt down and (*literally*) bottle one of these wondrous little imps. The said learned body, it appears, was " organized in the city of New York, October 30th, 1875, and the inaugural address of the president of the society delivered at Mott Memorial Hall, in the city of New York, November 17, 1875." Never did a more astounding flourish of trumpets sound in the form of an inaugural address. The learned and worthy president displayed the second officer of the society as a phenomenon, before whom Kepler would fade into nothingness and even Galileo and Newton grow dim !

" Without claiming to be a theurgist, a mesmerist, or a spiritualist, our vice-president promises, by simple chemical appliances, to exhibit to us, *as he has to others before*, the races of beings which, invisible to our eyes, people the elements. Think for a moment of this astounding claim ! Fancy the consequences of the practical demonstration of its truth, for which Mr. Felt is now preparing the requisite apparatus ! What will the church say of a whole world of beings within her territory, but without her jurisdiction ? What will the academy say of this crushing proof of an unseen universe given by the most unimaginative of its sciences ? What will the positivists say, who have been prating of the impossibility of there being any entity which cannot be weighed in scales, filtered through funnels, tested with litmus, or carved with a scalpel ? What will the spiritualists say, when through the column of saturated vapour flit the dreadful shapes of beings whom, in their blindness, they have in a thousand cases revered and babbled to as the returning shades of their relatives and friends ? Alas ! poor spiritualists—editors and correspondents—who have made themselves jocund over my impudence and apostasy ! Alas ! sleek scientists, overswollen with the wind of popular applause ! The day of reckoning is close at hand, and the name of the Theosophical Society will, if Mr. Felt's experiments result favourably, hold its place in history as that of the body which first exhibited the ' Elementary

Spirits' in this nineteenth century of conceit and infidelity, even if it be
never mentioned for any other reason ! "

Never mentioned for any other reason !   The Theosophical
Society need entertain no dread of oblivion.   It is destined to
occupy a niche in history between the Lagadan College of Swift
and the philosopher who planned to extract gold from sunbeams.
" Think of our astounding claims ! " cries the president.   The
world has thought them over for above a year now, and still they
are—claims.   The high-priest swings his censer and prays
anguishedly to Adon-Ai ; the vice-president and his chemical
appliances are there ; the saturated vapour ascends, and the whole
array of Theosophists kneel around ; but the " elementaries ? "—
" The dreadful shapes " flit as yet only through the high-priest's
brain.   Distorted and eerie shapes they indeed are.   Vainly does
Mr. F—— " prepare the requisite apparatus."   The " races which
people the elements " refuse to people his laboratory ; and the
world grows impatient, and the Theosophists are in the position of
the priests of Baal.   They have called on the elementaries " from
morning even until noon, saying, Hear us ! but there was no
voice, neither any that answered."   The spiritualists whom they
have contemned are converted into so many Elijahs, who " mock
them, saying, Cry aloud, for are they not your servants ? either
they are talking, or pursuing, or on a journey ; or they sleep and
must be awaked."   Will not the society carry out the parallel to
the bitter end ?   We shall hear of them, perhaps, dancing wildly
in front of their Memorial Hall, or building altars in some New York
park, and hacking themselves with knives and lancets.   Alas for
that day of anticipated triumph, when the president, clad with a
robe of Tyrian dye, should have taken his stand at the head of
Broadway, crushing the " editors and correspondents" who had
made themselves merry over his pretensions, by the exhibition of a
stoppered phial, neatly labelled " spirits," and tenanted by that
" shadow of a shade," an elementary !

The most perplexing thing of all is, that the said elementaries
have been previously caught and commented on.   " Our vice-
president promises to exhibit them to us, *as he has to others* before."

And when did this previous exhibition take place? In what corner of the earth were the unhappy "emanations" hunted down? What occultist or occultists enjoyed the privilege of "babbling over" the "dreadful shapes?" Did they test them with litmus, or carve them cunningly with scalpels, or filter them through funnels, or weigh them with scales? Possibly the elementaries were disgusted with the shabby treatment they received, and decline a second visit. In that case it is not to be wondered at if the "columns of saturated vapour," like the smoke of Baal's altar, ascend uselessly to heaven; and that, though high-priest and vice-president pray and prophesy with due fervour from morning even until the time of the evening sacrifice, there should be "neither voice, nor any to answer, nor any that regarded." The "emanations of matter" may have no souls, but they are altogether too smart for the Theosophical Society.

And the society appears to have discovered this; and, since the vice-president's promises are saturated vapour and nothing more, his chief has ordered, regardless of expense, the best thing in the way of magicians that Africa can furnish. A "newly-affiliated member" has been dispatched to those haunts of sorcerers, Tunis and Egypt. The little fiasco of the chemical apparatus and the "dreadful shapes" is ignored. The high-priest's rhodomontades are as wordily-grandiloquent as ever. "One of these African sorcerers will, for a small fee, show you images of the dead, and enable you to converse with them in audible voice. They will walk, self-levitated, in mid-air; climb poles which rest upon nothing, until they positively go out of sight" (the poles, or the conjurers?), "and dismember themselves even to decapitation without injury. . . . You" (the newly-affiliated member) "have the opportunity to introduce to western scientists, under the patronage, restrictions, and guarantees of a scientific (?) society, those proofs of occult powers, for lack of which they have been drifting into materialism and infidelity."

"The Theosophical Society," remarks the New York *World*,* "engages itself to pay for bringing the fiend over. That seems to us unnecessary.

* August 4, 1876.

Let him levitate, and hitch Mr. S—— on behind. Let them appear together hovering over New York from the eastern sky, a true sign in the heavens, a new constellation of the Gemini, whereat the multitude shall flop confounded, and confess a new faith, while the Theosophical Society, assembled on Pier No. 1, hold the president forcibly down from joining them aloft. No true philosophy can, at this day, be kept selfishly secret. Old Socrates killed this esoteric business. It will be the square thing to let the fiend float in sight of the whole people, and his time ought to be taken at both ends. We don't often get a fiend pure and simple. Let us not entreat this one so shabbily that no more will come to us."

And when will the first fiend arrive? No doubt the day after the circle has been squared, and the philosopher's stone discovered.

The single outcome of occultism is brag. The tree which Mr. Felt planted and African magicians are to water may be pretty, but it bears only an enormous crop of empty promises. Words— idle words, are the stock in trade of the society, from the president down to the youngest member. The literature of the movement, if such unproductive folly deserve to be termed a movement, is equally idle and equally empty. It consists so far of a volume termed "Art Magic." This book is made up partly of descriptions of travel, partly of stories respecting Oriental jugglers and dervishes, and partly of rubbish dug from the forgotten works of Cornelius Agrippa and his mediæval compeers. The only spirit I have yet heard of as evoked by a perusal of "Art Magic" is the spirit of credulity.

A faith that promises everything and accomplishes nothing is unlikely to have much influence on the future of the world. We may look with pitying indifference, therefore, on these English-speaking fetichists who stand frantically inviting us to—

> "Come and worship Mumbo Jumbo
> In the mountains of the moon."

CHAPTER IV.

MANIA.

SINCE mental disease has been made the subject of careful study, the difficulty of determining where the responsibility for an action ceases has vastly increased. We reason, with reference to the characters of others, by induction ; assuming from the knowledge we possess of certain of its qualities what the mind as a whole may be. But in the most logically conducted process the absence of necessary data may lead to a false conclusion, and in inquiries conducted with regard to the human mind we are peculiarly liable to go astray. No subject of inquiry has so fascinated philosophers as that of pure metaphysics, and none has ever proved so value-less. It is, in the language of Bacon, a tree with a magnificent display of leaves, but never producing fruit. The outcome of inquiries purely metaphysical, if unsupported by revelations from another world, has in all ages been endless bewilderment and strife. The inquiries conducted into the deeper subtleties of insanity seem, at the present day, to have plunged physicians into a bewilderment almost equally profound. The soul is too fear-fully and wonderfully made for the dissection of even its morbid peculiarities by merely human hands. If a case be strongly marked, indeed, doctors seldom disagree. It is easy to decide that a man who requires to be restrained by force from doing meaningless injury to his fellow creatures or himself is irrespon-sible for what he does. The indications here are too decisive for a doubt. It is when a multitude of facts and symptoms jostle each other—some apparently irresistibly proving that reason still retains her throne ; others as clearly demonstrating her overthrow—that medical men give deplorable proofs of their inability to decide whether or not they are dealing with a mind diseased.

There exist, and have existed since the creation of our species, minds in which some brilliant quality increases constantly in stature and splendour, while the rest of the faculties remain stunted or commonplace. There are other minds in which, from the first, some taint of unsoundness has place, that, constantly enlarging, usurps at last the place of reason as an adviser, and permeates every action of life. It is with regard to beings so unhappily constituted as these last that human philosophy is most frequently at fault. By every test that can be applied the person so afflicted is sane. His or her life is, to all seeming, the ordinary life of humanity. No magistrate would reject the testimony of those of whom I speak ; they are competent to marry, to inherit estates, to carry on businesses, to transact all the affairs of the every-day life of the world. Even their nearest and dearest may see in them little or nothing that is peculiar. Yet the poison is there, working 'unseen beneath the surface, and influencing every action of existence. When, at length, the crisis of the malady has arrived, some fearful action startles those around, and a thousand tongues and pens begin busily and unavailingly to discuss the mental condition of the doer of the deed. That deed is, in most cases of such malady of the soul, a self-inflicted death.

I am not aware that in England, or on the Continent of Europe, any instances of suicide have been plainly traceable to spiritualism. Even in America the number of victims has not been large. But the subject is a dangerous one for those mentally afflicted. The spot which I have alluded to as tainting certain minds is in many instances a species of false enthusiasm which, with the lapse of years, becomes but the less regulated and the more excitable and unreflecting. In the case of communion with another world the perils to such a class of minds are peculiarly great. By their fervid imaginations that world is depicted in the brightest of hues. In every one of the countless trials and miseries which beset our earthly life they fly for refuge to the thought of the happiness to be found in another sphere. Thus the longing for the imagined joys of immortality, and the temptation to seek by suicide to attain

them, become, by continual growth, irresistible. It may happen
that, in process of time, the gloom of some really great affliction,
some trial hard to be endured, darkens the present path of these
longers for a future life. At once a mournful end invests with
tragic interest the name of the man or woman whom such a
sorrow has befallen. No spiritual interference is necessary. Of
the suicides by professed spiritualists which have been recorded,
there is not one in which the theory that death was brought about
by the evil suggestions of disembodied beings can be supported by
a fragment of anything deserving the name of evidence. I do not
say that such tempting may not have taken place. There may be
debased beings in the world of spirits who are watchful for the
opportunity of doing evil, and who, having acquired influence over
the minds of those yet on earth, will use it for the purpose of
leading astray. By such it is possible that the more impressionable of the victims to a disgust of life, who have been found in the
spiritualist ranks, may have suffered themselves, knowingly or
unknowingly, to be guided. The hypothesis is, I have admitted,
a possible one. But I do not think it, in general, at all probable ; nor, with regard to the various cases I might lay before the
reader,* would the testimony be found to bear it out. Delirious
broodings, exaggerated in a particular direction at the expense of
all other attributes, until the balance of the mind had been overthrown, and the sufferer was, for every action committed under
the influence of that delirium, practically irresponsible, were the
tempters that hurried these victims to their sad and untimely
graves. That bringing near of another world, which to so many
has been the source of consolation unspeakably divine, was with
them the innocent means of intensifying to a more terrible pitch
the original disease of their minds. In the wild hope of thereby
at once participating in the joys of the next world they rebelliously
abandoned this present one, and passing into futurity by a road
the most terrible of all to travel, have left their histories as
melancholy examples of the mischief that ensues when a mind,
weak but enthusiastic, unresistingly abandons itself to one insane
and absorbing idea.

* They are omitted, on account of their tragic nature.

CHAPTER V.

THERE are works purporting to be contributions to the literature of spiritualism which reflect much discredit on the writers who produced them. The one thing kept throughout in view is effect. Superficially glanced over, these compositions appear valuable. Critically examined, they prove worthless. The impression left by a book of this class on the mind of a careless reader is usually attained by the most unworthy means. Theories are palmed off as facts. Trifles favourable to the ends which the author has in view are magnified into mountains of evidence. Inconvenient truths are suppressed. Where suppression is impossible, the distortion of the truth is resorted to. The writer appears to consider him or herself engaged in the construction of an edifice in which a certain effect has, by fair means or foul, to be obtained. If the materials proper for the task seem opposed to the desired result, they are at once rejected, however sound. In their place the first rubbish forthcoming, provided that it be but showy, is pressed into the builder's service. Legends which, however attractive, bear too often in themselves the marks of their falsehood and unsubstantiality, fill the gaps caused by the casting aside of unpleasant facts. When completed, the work exactly resembles the makeshift buildings seen on the stage. Viewed at a little distance, and in a proper light, the thing is charming. But approach it more closely, and examine it by the clearness of noon: we are disenchanted at once, and for ever. What was at first sight a fairy palace, is now a miserable composition of daubed canvas and pasteboard. A single blow would suffice to lay the whole structure in ruins. So with the flimsy productions I treat of. They are, in general, exceedingly taking, when beheld by the false glare of credulity. But expose them to the sober daylight of reason, the paltry tawdriness of the decorations, and the weakness which those decorations were intended to hide, become at once apparent. Before the first assault of a competent critic the unstable fabric goes down, and utter is the ruin thereof.

The book which furnishes the subject of my present chapter may fairly take rank as one of the worst compositions of this bad class. Let me, before entering on its examination, guard myself against a supposition some readers may entertain, that I am representing such writings as peculiar to spiritualism. They are to be met with everywhere, and infest all departments of literature. In some their influence is in the highest degree pernicious—in others, comparatively harmless. At times, indeed, they are allowable. No one, for example, expects strict consistency and unswerving accuracy of statement in a novelist or a poet. It surprises us little to meet with exaggeration in the leader-writing of sensational newspapers. But in works that claim to be works of science, in records that are put forth as records of facts, we are surely entitled to demand strictness in examining evidence, caution in putting forward or endorsing statements, a careful separation of the true from the false, and the proved from the merely probable, a judicial impartiality in coming to decisions; in short, common-sense, candour, and honesty of purpose. Not one of these attributes, I regret to say, can be considered as attaching to the work before me. Had the author of "People from the Other World" put forward that volume as a romance, one might have been content with remarking that it was sometimes dull and sometimes absurd, and would have been a better book if the writer had taken more pains. But it is gravely advanced as a truthful and dispassionate narrative of certain observations of recondite phenomena, made with scientific care, and published in the interests of the world at large. It is dedicated to two English scientific men. The title-page bears the words of Bacon: "We have set it down as a law to ourselves to examine things to the bottom, and not to receive upon credit, or reject upon improbabilities, until there hath passed a due examination."

In " People from the Other World " the author has observed one, and but one, of the laws here laid down by the prince of philosophers. He certainly cannot be accused of " rejecting upon improbabilities." On the contrary, his depth of credulity is absolutely fathomless. This, however, is not the condition of mind which Bacon desiderated, nor is it, I submit, one proper to scientific investigation. For the rest, the placing of such a motto on the title-page of such a book is one of the most laughable displays of folly with which I am acquainted. " I have set it down as a law to myself to examine things to the bottom." How modest this assumption on the part of a man who tells us (p. 842, " People from the Other World ") that the manifestations, as a record of which he constructed his book, " were not happening under test-conditions, and hence would not satisfy the judicial mind ;" who confesses (p. 847) that " Chittenden was no place for him to try philosophical experiments ;" and who sums up by hoping (p. 409) that his readers " will bear him out in the statement that all his efforts have been to interest American scientists in the phenomena to such an extent that they would commence real investigations, in comparison to which these made by himself are but child's play." What, in view of such an avowal as the last, is the value of his investigation, or pseudo-investigation ? On p. 414 of his work he is kind enough to answer the question. The narratives that he gives are sufficient " to arouse the greatest wonder." Could less be said of the histories of Munchausen, or the equally veritable tales of the Thousand and One Nights ? Is it not too much that a man should trumpet himself forth as a devotee of science who, in reality, and by his own confession, is merely seeking to act as showman to a couple of persons whose claims to mediumship he does nothing either to prove or to negative ?

" I do not receive upon credit," says he. " There must pass a due examination." Such is the assertion made in taking the motto of Bacon as one suited to his own circumstances. He reiterates that assertion with even greater distinctness in the pages of his book. " We should take nothing for granted, and respect no man's judgment who does. We should demand from the spiritualist as broad a basis of facts for our belief as we do from Huxley before receiving his theory, or from Tyndall, if he would have us accept any of the dogmas propounded in his Belfast address. A philosophy that shrinks from crucial tests I want none of. No real investigator takes things on faith. We should flout at and cease debate with the spiritualist who assumes to set his creed above all other creeds as too sacred to be tried and tested by every appliance of reason and science. The individual preferences or fears of mediums are nothing to us, for we are in quest of the truth, and would seek it even at the bottom of a well. We should weigh the mediums and their phenomena in the balances, and reject whatsoever appears false." I agree most cordially with every word. The doctrines here repeated are doctrines which, during my whole career, I have never ceased inculcating. But what do we find in " People from the Other World " when we turn from theory to fact ; from the author's magnificent sentiments to his pitiful practice ? Joseph Surface's life and language were not more contradictory. One-third of the volume is devoted to stories received at second-hand, of whose truth or falsehood the writer knows nothing, and which are, therefore, utterly worthless as evidence. Internally they are equally valueless. They come exactly under the definition of "old women's tales." With just such narratives may Mrs. Sairey Gamp have enlivened over the tea-table the sullen moods of Mrs. Betsey Prig. The " investigator," indeed, to whose taste for authorship we owe " People from the Other World " would appear to have a great deal of the Gamp about him. All through his book he continues to direct rapturous apostrophes to a certain " science," conspicuous by her absence from his writings. I cannot venture to remark, as the vehement and ungrammatical Mrs. Prig remarked of Mrs. Harris, that " I don't believe there's no such person." Of this, however, I am certain, that, though the said science undoubtedly exists, the writer with whom I am dealing knows nothing at all about her.

Had his mind been of the scientific cast he would never have filled paragraph upon paragraph with records of phenomena, only to remark naïvely that, after all, these records are of no value. I may instance the story given on page 234. Not satisfied with narrating this affair, he accompanies his account with a *fac-simile* of the truly "wretched Latin and bad English" obtained under such suspicious circumstances. The excuse offered is that it "is probably the first thing of the kind which has appeared in a newspaper." I am not aware whether the New York dailies for whom these sensational narratives were in the first instance constructed had before inflicted on their readers illustrations of such doubtful interest. Certainly, however, it is "the first thing of the kind" which has adorned the pages of any work professedly devoted to philosophical investigation. And as he has acted here, so does this writer act all through. Facing page 148 will be found what is styled "the picture of a young girl, with her head and shoulders emerging from a sort of fog or steamy vapour." I turn to the accompanying letter-press for an explanation. There I find it recorded that this engraving is a copy "of one of Mumler's so-called 'spirit photographs.'" (The inverted commas are our author's). "*I have no confidence in this picture,*" he continues, "*or, in fact, in any emanating from the same source, as directly or indirectly of spiritual origin.*" Why then cause it to be engraved, and engraved in a volume which has not the slightest reference to the genuine or fraudulent nature of alleged spirit-photographs? The author seems to anticipate that such a question may be asked. He seeks, therefore, to guard against it by a maudlin dissertation on the Holmeses, Dr. Child, the Hon. Robert Dale Owen, a Chittenden spirit who, "losing power, sank into the floor up to her waist," and "certain communications" sent him from various persons, "attesting to the fact of their seeing materialized spirit-forms dissolve." It is difficult for a plain man to extract the few grains of meaning concealed in this bushel of rigmarole. Put in the clearest form, however, the drift of these paragraphs and others of a kindred nature evidently is,—"I, who now address the public, have very little to offer that is worth the offering. It is convenient that I should swell my volume to a certain size. This

I accomplish by inserting a number of worthless stories picked up at second or third-hand from various people. Don't think, however, that I am weak enough to believe in these stories. The reader may do so, if he or she please; but I myself have not the slightest faith in them." And this is a scientific investigator! This is the man who takes mottoes from Bacon, and dedicates his worthless speculations to Mr. Crookes! The dullest school-boy would blush to contradict himself thus. The most abject dunce that Satire ever pilloried would be ashamed of the company of such a philosopher. That any human being should have the folly to construct such a work is strange enough. That, after having constructed it, he should consider it a work of philosophical research, and under that designation send it forth into the world, is enough, in the words of a great essayist, "to make us ashamed of our species."

As a composition it is almost below criticism. As a display of reasoning it is altogether beneath contempt. This last proposition I shall have occasion presently to substantiate. For the present I confine myself to a few words regarding the literary demerits of the volume before me, and to a brief exposition of the motives which have led me to attempt the examination of this most worthless and most dishonest book.

It would be waste of space to discuss at any length its endless literary shortcomings. The supply of such sentences as the following is almost inexhaustible. "Poor Mrs. Eddy's *misfortunes* followed her even into the grave, as she one day told the children *it* would." "He hired three or four of the children out to one showman, who took them to nearly all the principal cities of the United States, and to another who took them to London." Grammatically considered, this sentence leaves us in an agreeable state of doubt as to whether one showman took the children to another, or one city of the United States took the children to London. What the writer probably meant was, that the father of the Eddys, after receiving back his olive branches from the first showman, hired them out to a second.

"I am quite aware of the fact that, as a scientific experiment,

s

the procuring of the second set of names has no value ; for no one was present when *it* was written, or can affirm *it* was not by the medium himself, so I let that pass. But what shall be said of the cards written in the light-circle before twenty people, which bear so marked a resemblance to *them ?* " To what does the word " them " apply ? After careful consideration, the only meaning I can arrive at in the sentence last given is, that the cards bore a marked resemblance to the twenty people ! This is evidently not what the writer intended to convey, but his mind seems too contracted to have much grasp of language. But enough of so tiresome a task. I have selected these charming specimens of composition from pages which I had marked for other purposes. To wade through the whole volume in search of its thousand absurdities of grammar, &c., would be more than human nature is capable of bearing.

" Why devote space, then, to the dissection of so worthless a performance ? " the reader will ask. I grant that, intrinsically, this volume has no value whatever,—that it is ten times more meaningless than the gospel of Mormon, or the speculations of Joanna Southcote. But things which are in themselves valueless often deserve attention on account of the harm they work. Weeds grow faster than the corn into which they intrude themselves, and require, therefore, to be rooted up, or they spoil the harvest. This book is emphatically a weed, and one of the worst, perhaps the very worst, of its species. Other productions of the kind infest spiritual literature ; but there are few which display such an utter lack of principle ; such a happy audacity in assertion, or so complete a disregard of facts. A certain cleverness in distorting occurrences to whatever form the peculiar genius of the writer considers desirable, renders the work dangerous. This capacity for making what is more than half a fabrication resemble the truth is invariably inherent in certain dispositions.

When I had succeeded in struggling through " People from the Other World " my first feeling was one of mingled amusement and pity. The lackadaisical sentimentality of the style—the maudlin feebleness of the reflections, made me set down the writer as a good, easy blue-stocking of fifty, who was concealing her identity under a masculine *nom de plume*. Very foolish she seemed to me, intensely gushing, still more credulous, and totally unfit for the position she had thrust herself into. I have since, however, discovered, and can assure my readers, that the author in question is really of the sterner sex. Besides the title of a man, he arrogates to himself that of a philosopher. How he could be guilty of such a production as "People from the Other World" is, therefore, the deepest of mysteries. He has written three letters to me since the appearance of his book, which letters I hope will be published *in extenso* in the forthcoming volume of "Incidents in My Life." Self-respect prevented me from answering the last of these communications. To adopt to this writer the language he hurls at others, he "sheds a magnetism as disagreeable as dirty water, or the perfume of the *Fetis Americanus*."

Yet he has his ludicrous side. Could we but put out of view the more unpleasant attributes of such a mind, much amusement might be derived from its ridiculous qualities. His self-conceit is ineffable. His dearest pleasure is to pose himself in some impressive attitude. Now he is the adorer and benefactor of mediums. Now he is the lofty denouncer of "calumnious behaviour reserved for blackguards *and* mediums." (The italics are his own). At one time he is putting on his paper armour, and taking pen in hand, to do battle for the Eddys against the world. A little later we find him, according to his own confession, "waiting patiently for a grand exposure" of the same Eddys. Now he is the humble admirer of spiritualism and science; and, clinging to the coat-tails of distinguished spiritualists and scientists, pathetically implores these people to lift him into notice. Now he starts forth before the public as a sort of Pagan wet-nurse, ready to suckle grown up infants in "heathen fantasies outworn." Again, he is the smart investigator whom "the conductors of two of the great New York Dailies would not have engaged to investigate and describe the phenomena at the Eddy homestead, had they supposed him either of unsound mind, credulous, partial, dishonest, or incompetent." Now he *is* a spiritualist; now he is *not* a spiritualist. In short,

his changes are Protean. Through all, however, he seems troubled
with an uneasy consciousness of absurdity. If he be a Bottom, he
at least suspects himself to possess an ass's head. For a moment
the particular attitude he is taking appears to him the perfection of
grace. Presently doubts arise, and he begs earnestly the opinion
of bystanders as to his position and get-up. The next instant we
behold him dismounted from his late pedestal, and in full career
towards some new hobby-horse.

It is probable that nine-tenths of my readers are but very imperfectly acquainted, or not acquainted at all, with the Chittenden
career of this literary phenomenon. That career is not one
spiritualists may be proud of. I shall seek, therefore, in
sketching the circumstances under which "People from the Other
World" was written, to accomplish my task with the utmost
brevity.

The author of the work in question was, he tells us, sent to the
Eddy ghost-court in his capacity of newspaper paragraphist. The
appointment was lucrative, and its holder in no hurry to terminate
it. This idea has struck others besides myself. "Both Mrs. ——
and I," writes an American friend of mine, who was present at
Chittenden during this pseudo-investigator's "investigations,"
"are convinced now that there was a *determined* resolve in his
mind to see and hear nothing that lessened the chances of his
lucrative position there."

He possesses a fervid imagination, and brilliant powers of invention. There are few who can see farther through a stone wall.
This imagination is as powerful a talisman as any mentioned in the
"Arabian Nights." The "glamour" of mediæval magic was as
nothing in comparison. Not only, under its influence, do night-
gowns, scarfs, and smoking-caps figure as "magnificent costumes,"
but incidents are described which never occurred, and portraits are
given without the faces supposed to be copied in those portraits
having ever been seen. And here come under notice the irremediable blemishes of the book ; those which, above all, demonstrate
how unblushing is the assurance of its author.

"The light has been very dim," says he, on page 168, "and I

have not been able to recognise the features of a single face."
On the next page I find,—" What go to constitute a likeness are
a number of lines about the eyes, nose, and mouth, as thin as a
knife-blade's edge; the expression of eye, shape of features, colour,
and hair—these, in such a light as this, are indistinguishable."
The paragraph immediately following tells us that the light is so
poor, " one cannot, with untrained eye, distinguish accurately
between forms varying as much as six inches in height." Similar
avowals occur all through the book. Strong as they may appear,
the testimony of unprejudiced observers is still stronger. The
light at Chittenden was a libel on the term " darkness visible."
What, in view of such a fact, can be the value of the engravings of
" materialised " forms, &c., with which the volume is profusely
decorated ? Not one has the slightest pretension to be considered
a portrait. They are, without exception, fancy sketches evolved
from the inner consciousness of the artist. It is thus romances
are illustrated. It is *not* thus that men truly scientific illustrate
their works. But, putting this aside, *what was the value of the
numerous recognitions of departed relatives and friends which we are
solemnly assured occurred ?* Does not every candid reasoner
answer, as I answer, that they were valueless ? Even had these
so-called recognitions been honestly described, they would serve
only to prove the insane enthusiasm of persons able to conjure up
departed relatives in figures whose features they could not discern,
and whose voices they did not hear. But the descriptions, as I am
now about to show, are *not* honest.

On page 271, we learn how there appeared " an Arab, an old
friend of a lady well known in magazine literature as ' Aunt Sue.'"
Our author's description of the said Arab is glowing. " He was
of short stature, slight and wiry build, and his very salaam to the
lady, when recognised, was in marked contrast with the con-
strained bows of the Indians, and the more or less ungraceful
salutations of the whites. *His name is Yusef.* He was dressed
in a white tunic, gathered at the waist by a sash, and the skirt
ornamented with three equi-distant bands of red, of the same
width. On his head was the national fez, and in his sash was

thrust a weapon of some kind which I could not see distinctly. A number of questions propounded to him were answered by respectful bows, and his parting obeisance was of that deferential, but, at the same time, self-respecting character, that is peculiar to the people of the Orient."

Why answer questions by respectful bows ? Either this taciturn Eastern had forgotten his native tongue in another world, or had forgotten to materialise organs of speech when returning to this. But now for a "plain, unvarnished" account of what really occurred. It is furnished by the very "Aunt Sue" to whom the visit and salaams of this obsequious spirit were directed. Here is what this lady writes me :—

" May 15th, 1876.

"MY DEAR DAN,

    "You shall have my experience with pleasure. Mrs. C. and I read" (our author's) " glowing description of ghosts and things in the vicinity of, and at the Eddy homestead ; and we said, ' Let's go : it is among the lovely hills of Vermont, and we will have a good time any way.' And we went. We were introduced to the Eddy brothers, and shown to our room. You don't want to hear about the peculiarities of the *ménage* there. Suffice it to say we went prepared to accept a gridiron for a bed, and a stove pipe for a pillow, if necessary, and to take all creature discomforts philosophically ; and we took them.

    "The evening came, and we all sat about—after tea—in the sitting-room (so-called because there were chairs in it, and mostly nothing else), awaiting the announcement that the Hall—the large room up-stairs over the dining-room—was ready for us. Up we went, and sat on the benches prepared for us. All on the front row joined hands ' to make a magnetic chain,' though where the magnetic current went at either end, I don't know. The man with the violin played vigorously. The light, back of us all, was turned so low that it was impossible to distinguish features two feet from us. When the curtain over the door of the cabinet was lifted, and a ' form' appeared, the violin was hushed ; the ' form' was mum, until the front bench, beginning with No. 1, commenced to ask the stereotyped question ' For me ?'—' For me ?' until the form bowed. ' Oh ! for me ?' said No. 1, 2, 3, 5, 7, as the case might be. ' Is it father ?'—no response. ' Is it uncle ?'—still silent. ' Is it Charlie Myrtle ?'—the form bows. ' Why, Charlie, I'm so glad to see you !' Then it is reported that ' Charlie Myrtle' was distinctly recognised, and that is about all there was of it. What *I* specially noticed was, that the shawls and scarfs ' materialised' by ' Honto,' a light one and a dark one, were always of exactly the same length ; the light one about three yards long, and the dark one about two yards. 'The magnificent costumes' seemed to be composed of a loose, white wrapper (nightgown?); dark calico tunic, some scarfs and Indian caps (smoking ones?), which different combinations made quite a variety of costumes ; but I would defy any one to describe them minutely by the dim light in which they always appeared. One evening the 'For me ?'s' had been negatively answered, until it came to my turn. I asked 'For me ?' and the figure bowed. 'Is it Ruloffe ?' I inquired. The figure slowly nodded assent. At the close of the *séance*" (our author) " asked me concerning 'Ruloffe.' I informed him that I had been told, mediumistically, that one of my 'spirit-guides' was an Arabian called 'Ruloffe.' He remarked that 'Ruloffe' was not an Arabian name, and 'Yusef' would be more appropriate. I replied, smiling, that one name would answer my purpose as well as another ; so it was 'Graphic'—ally announced that 'Aunt Sue' had had an interview with one 'Yusef.' And that is the true and veritable history of that little episode. I certainly shall never recognise Mr. 'Ruloffe' or 'Yusef' if I meet him on the thither shore, if the light should be as dim there as it was at Chittenden.

" AUNT SUE."

In view of such a misfortune the author of " People from the Other World " kindly supplies a no doubt correct portrait of " *Yusef* " in his work ; which portrait may serve as a guide to my friend " Aunt Sue," when she encounters her spirit-visitor of Chittenden on the " thither shore."

How much credit such revelations do to the ingenuity of that philosopher whom " two of the great New York dailies " successively engaged as special correspondent to the Chittenden spirit-court ! Certainly he is by no means " incompetent " as a sensational journalist. As an investigator, however, he must be pronounced " credulous, partial," and, above all, incorrect. I would beg him, therefore, to " spare himself the trouble, and the public the annoyance," of inflicting upon a much enduring world any further volume of such unattested absurdities as " People from the Other World " mainly consists of.

There was present with " Aunt Sue " at Chittenden a friend of that lady—Mrs. C——. She has kindly furnished me with notes of the " materialisations " witnessed during her stay, and the following are extracts. Mrs. C—— speaks for " Aunt Sue " and herself.

" We could *detect* no fraud, as all *real* opportunity for investigation had been dexterously cut off—notwithstanding the clumsy expedients resorted to by" (the author of "People from the Other World") "as 'tests ;' but that we were in the presence of real spirits we never for once believed. The only persons allowed to take a seat upon the platform were a Mr. Pritchard and a Mrs. Cleveland ; dear old gullible souls who could be readily psychologized into believing that they were eating a piece of the moon in shape of ' green cheese.' These both touched and conversed with the *substantial* shadows which stepped cautiously from the door of the cabinet, as if making sure that some investigator were not ready to spring upon them ; and occasionally went through the shuffling manœuvres characterised by (our author) as *dancing !* while no one of the audience-circle was permitted to advance near enough to distinguish their features. in the distressingly subdued light of the solitary lamp, acting its part in the fraud upon a distant table.

" Every evening Mr. P—— had a visit from his aged mother—attired in a *robe de nuit*,—*she,* understand, was thus attired, not *he.* Every evening. Mr. P—— saluted her with a ' Good evening, mother !' and she replied, in a husky whisper, ' Good evening, my son !' Every evening she added, ' I am glad to see you, my son !' and then asked, ' Why didn't Mary come ?' Every evening she was blandly assured that Mary was not in health, and could not be there ; but still the question was renewed, and then the aged spirit shuffled back, and disappeared through the door of the cabinet. I asked this gentleman if he recognised his mother beyond all peradventure in this spirit. He admitted that he did *not* see much likeness as he *remembered* her ; but he had not seen her for the two or three years before her death, and ' no doubt she had altered.'

" Mr.—— " (our author) " would brook no antagonism in conversation to the methods of the media ; nor even lend an ear to the suggestion of any doubts of their honesty."

So unphilosophically did this pseudo-philosopher strut his hour on the Chittenden stage ! The spectacle must have been at once trying and amusing to the ordinary men and women present. Some of the antics they witnessed would have drawn a smile from the Wandering Jew. Others might have ruffled the temper of Job. How our investigator assumed the chief direction of what he appropriately styles the " performances ; " how he courted the wonder of the public with such programmes as " The Spinning Ghost ! " " Mystery of Mysteries ! " " The Malicious Barber ! " " The Smoking Squaw ! " " Wonderful Feats ! " " Whence comes the Power ? " " Four Hundred Spirits ! " &c. ; how he " went for " intrusive sceptics ; how he acted as the trumpeter-forth of prophecies which were never fulfilled; how he accepted any story which anybody present chose to relate to him, so that it did but go to confirm the spiritual origin of the manifestations; how he bought scales with which to weigh the spirits (this being certainly a new mode of trying them); how, when he was refused permission to use the scales himself, that "dear old soul," Mr. Pritchard called off the weights for him; and how, notwithstanding all this, he "has excluded from his case every individual phenomenon that can be explained upon the hypothesis of trickery," are not all these things written in his "Other World" chronicles? Behold him there, "standing" (in a Napoleonic attitude) "upon his story of phenomena observed, with the confidence of one whose house is built upon a sure foundation."

I have now to notice the brilliant displays of reasoning with which this "investigator" has favoured the world, both in his book and subsequently to its publication. The reader will confess that seldom before have human minds been astonished with such utterances. For most of these absurdities I can find no place whatever in the whole system of logic. Every new "explanation" contradicts one previously tendered. Such conflicting sophisms were surely never resorted to before or since, unless by a mono-maniac or a Theosophist.

"Nor will it escape the notice of the intelligent," I find, in the preface to "People from the Other World," "that the Philadelphia tests go far towards corroborating the Chittenden experiences, for, if "materialisation" can occur in one place, it may in many, and hence the supposition that real ghosts were seen at the Eddy house is made to appear only half as improbable. The cheerful alacrity shown by the Holmeses to submit themselves to crucial test conditions makes the behaviour of the Eddy boys appear in a correspondingly unfavourable light. It was alleged as an excuse at Chittenden, that the author's magnetism was so positive and repellent to the spirits as to prevent their bearing his near approach, whereas the fact appears to be that they can allow him to handle them, to gaze into their faces from a distance of six inches, and otherwise to come to closest quarters, without causing them the slightest inconvenience." If these words mean anything, they mean this :—" The Holmeses allowed certain tests. The Eddys might have allowed those tests, and ought to have allowed them. Therefore, as the Holmeses are mediums, the Eddys are mediums also." Truly, an owl of any standing would be ashamed of coming to such conclusions.

I might extract many such gems from the work before me. Will my readers believe that on p. 168 of "People from the Other World" the author laments that it was impossible for him to make his experiments at Chittenden under test conditions, and that he afterwards coolly heads p. 218, "Another Test?" What, moreover, are we to think of the investigator who, after placing in capitals over p. 307 "Abundant Tests," and entitling Chapter XXIII. "Tests continued," tells us, on p. 342, "The things I saw were not happening under test conditions." And, as he has behaved in the volume itself, so did he behave after its publication. Chapter XV. of his book is an account of what, he tells us, were "Philosophical Tests." Yet in a letter published January 1st, 1876, in the columns of the *Banner of Light,* he confesses his belief in the Eddy spirits to be "the result of intuition, not of absolute demonstration," * and demands piteously, "What tests did I have that would be deemed conclusive to a scientific association ?" And are not "philosophical tests" deemed conclusive by the scientific associations of either Europe or America ? If the tests science employs are not philosophical what are they ? Surely never before did any being capable of using a pen so completely stultify himself. When such contradictory nonsense is brought forward as "a sure foundation" on which this writer may rest his claims to be considered "an investigator in the interests of science," what can we do but treat the assumption with mingled derision and contempt ?

Since the appearance of "People from the Other World" its author has favoured our own planet with displays of absurdity that reveal still more vividly the utter absence from his mind of all

---

* "No *real* investigator takes things on faith."—*People from the Other World,* p. 170.

reasoning power. I had stated in a letter of mine that one of his friends was in a certain European city in the year 1858. He rejoined, with the fierce triumph of one who completely demolishes a calumny, that " he could tell me " the person in question was somewhere else in the years 1859 and 1860. Such is invariably his style of argument !

He thinks nothing whatever of contradicting himself point-blank. On p. 418 of " People from the Other World " he asks, " What does the reader say when I tell him that, on the evening of September 28th, I saw the spirit of a woman who was murdered on the night of Sunday, August 27th, 1865, at Williston, Vt. ? " The reader will no doubt say that, if this writer saw the spirit, he saw it. Not at all ! In letters published since the appearance of his book, he has burst upon the world in the attitude of a great discoverer. The discovery he has perfected is that the spirits who produce the physical phenomena at *séances* are none of them human. They are sylphs, gnomes, elementaries, and have never lived on earth. " It is these beings," he wrote to me, " who produce the phenomena of physical mediums." But " materialisa-tion " is a physical phenomenon. Therefore, according to the rules of logic, the spirit that materialised on the evening of September 28th, 1874, had never lived on earth. Never having lived on earth it could not have been the soul of a woman murdered there, and whilst the above-quoted passage remains uncontradicted in the book before me the author is deliberately endorsing what he now knows to be incorrect.

Mark, too, what graceful compliments this nineteenth-century reviver of Paganism pays to spiritualists ! Physical phenomena are not the productions of departed human beings. All the " exhibi-tions of tender pathos," therefore, at Chittenden, the " sobs, wails, and outbursts," the " reunion of those parted by death," the " mothers weeping with joy at the sight of their beloved ones," were simply sad mistakes, the results of mischievous frauds enacted by beings altogether alien to humanity, and who contrived to deceive certain fathers, mothers, sons, daughters, &c., by masquerading in the shapes of their departed relatives ! But the author of " People from the Other World " is not satisfied with exhibiting himself as the abettor of so shameless and wicked a deed. He remembers that there are other spiritual phenomena besides those classed as " physical." He writes, therefore, a letter to the New York *Tribune*. * In this he informs the world that nine-tenths of *all genuine spirit-manifestations whatever* owe their origin to beings which "are not spirits of men or women from the earth, but something quite different, and something that does not inhabit our future world." Surely then, that poor tithe of phenomena remaining to us must be produced by human spirits of a high order! Surely, if so few of her children return to earth, those few must be earth's dearest and best! By no means. " The wise, the pure, the just, the heroic souls, who have passed on before us into the silent land," continues the author of " People from the Other World," in his letter to the *Tribune*, " cannot, and do not, come back!!"

Let me, in the name of the spiritualists of all times and countries, thank this calumniator. What! the beloved ones who have given us such glorious tokens of their presence were none of them "wise, pure, just or heroic souls?" The few spirits really human which attend at *séances* are then the vilest of the vile, the refuse of our species? If a departed friend give such convincing proofs of identity that even the philosopher I am dealing with cannot claim this particular spirit as an " elementary," he or she must necessarily have been on earth a drunkard, a libertine, a murderer, or in some way stained with shocking vice or crime! And the author of this shameless libel on the spirit-friends so dear to us has the pleasing audacity to reproach me in print with what I " seem likely to say about mediums!" This, too, when it was impossible that he could have the faintest inkling of what I intended to say. To turn his own words against him, " is not the worst " truth *I* ever uttered regarding deceitful or pretended mediums (for with all honest brethren I am in perfect harmony), incomparably milder than the mildest accusation which this self-elected critic has fulminated against our spirit-guardians in his published diatribes? And the crowning wonder of all is that he loves the spirits whom

* About the end of September or beginning of October, 1875.

he slanders! In one of his letters to me he describes spiritualism as a cause to which I merely profess to be devoted, but to which he really is devoted, heart and soul.

For he is a spiritualist of the most ardent type. " If to have long acknowledged that phenomena occur in the presence of mediums which are not the effects of legerdemain," says he, " *and to admit that they rooted fast and strong my faith in God, and my soul's immortality,* makes me ‾a spiritualist, then I have been one for many years." As my friend, Mr. Roberts,. of Burlington, N.J., well remarks, in his caustic criticism of the *Tribune* letter, these sentiments, if honestly spoken, show their author to be a spiritualist in the only sense to which that term is applicable. In another of his letters this staunch spiritualist explains why he published an account of the manifestations at Chittenden. He " wanted to do this much for a cause that had been dear to him for more than twenty years." Moreover, " every cent paid him as copyright for his book has been donated by him to help that cause, in such ways as seemed most judicious." Surely we believers in the return of the departed have here a brother! The value of that brother may be small, but he is undoubtedly a spiritualist.

So thought the New York *World,* and classed him accordingly. At once our author was up in arms. Will it be believed that, in the very letter to the *Tribune* from which the sentence beginning, " If to have long acknowledged "—is quoted, he writes, " The *World,* reviewing my book, calls me a spiritualist, and so have other papers, *whereas nothing could be more opposed to the truth!* " What are we to think of such inconsistency? Can it be a reasoning being who, in one and the same letter, says, " It is altogether false that I am a spiritualist," and, a little further on, " I beg pardon, I am undoubtedly one ? "

I have in my possession a letter from him, dated March 1st, 1876. Enraged by certain utterances of mine (which, I may remark, parenthetically, in no way concerned him), he casts about in this communication for a crushing reproach, and finds it. " Such behaviour," he tells me, " is reserved for blackguards—*and mediums.*" Yet we find him, March 8th (only a week later)

writing to the *Banner of Light,* "I am the friend of mediums "
(*and blackguards, of course*). "No man will go farther, or sacrifice
more of time, of labour, or of money, to protect them from iconoclasts." All this for a class of people whom he esteems disgraces
to humanity!

In fact, on his own showing, it is impossible that he can consider
mediums as otherwise than utterly and irredeemably bad. Here
is the definition he gives of such persons :—"They are slaves.
While under control their own will is set aside, and their actions,
their speech, and their very consciousness, are directed by that of
another." And to whom are we slaves? "To spirits," says our
author, "of whom nine-tenths are lying 'elementaries,' whose
dearest delight is to deceive mankind; the remainder consisting of
the very dregs of the human race." If such are the masters, what
must the servants be? Good does not serve evil. This "friend
of mediums" confesses as much. "It is," says he, in the *Spiritualist* of January 28th, 1876, "a direful calamity to yield to
physical mediumship to the extent of perfect passivity. It is the
same as saying to give one's self over as the helpless slave of the
elementaries." There is certainly no small share of absurdity in
all this. Mediums are first defined as, of necessity, slaves, and
then reproached for being slaves. But, to return to our main
inquiry, what use do the "elementaries" make of their victims?
Our philosopher informs us: they teach mediums, it seems, "to
lie, cheat, and indulge in immoral practices." Such conduct is, of
course, quite natural in such beings. And, if nine-tenths of the
spirits act thus, we may be sure that the other tenth, having no
"wise, pure, just, or heroic souls" among them, will not be behind
hand in wickedness. Yet of people who "lie, cheat, and indulge
in immoral practices," this writer declares himself the friend!
Were it not that his estimate of mediums is just as false as his
estimate of the spirits who control them, a homely proverb, which
I need not particularize, would here be in point. I remember,
however, though I do not quote it, a passage written by Leigh
Hunt regarding one of Wycherley's heroes.

I may turn from this part of my subject. If our Pagan friend is to be credited, the spirits "whom he loves" are nine-tenths enemies to humanity, and the other tenth disgraces to humanity. If *he* is to be credited, the mediums of whom, in his own language, he is "the friend, the warm and *appreciative* friend," are slaves to these spirits, and learn from them to lie, cheat, &c. As malignantly and wrongfully as he has judged myself in particular, does he judge all spirits and all mediums. Yet he has the exquisite impudence to write to the *Banner of Light* regarding me :— "The worst thing I" (our author) "ever said against mediums is incomparably less harmful to them than the best this self-elected purist and purger seems likely to put in his book." Cool, certainly, after addressing a whole class in much such words as Christ's to the Pharisees, "Ye are of your father, the Devil."

Our author acts at present in the capacity of president to the very peculiar body known as the "Theosophical Society." * As such he has recently given one more proof of his utter disregard for consistency. The society has dispatched a member to Africa in quest of a magician. The president writes to impress this member with the importance of his mission. "You have the opportunity," he remarks magniloquently, "to introduce to western scientists those proofs of occult powers for lack of which they have been drifting into materialism and infidelity." This is equivalent to a confession that no one at present affiliated to the Theosophical Society can afford to a scientist "proofs of occult powers." Yet, in "People from the Other World" the author writes of a fellow theosophist : "Instead of being controlled by spirits to do their will, it is she who seems to control them to do her bidding. Whatever may be the secret by which this power has been attained I cannot say, but that she possesses it I have had too many proofs to permit me to doubt the fact." He afterwards found this assertion too sweeping. His third letter to me contains the following words :—"I certainly did assert that ——, instead of being controlled by spirits, controls them. This I now find to be true only in part. I failed to discriminate as to the spirits over whom occultists have control. I should have said that no one can

* See Chapter ii., on "Delusions."

dominate real *human* spirits, but only the elementaries." If this fellow theosophist can "dominate elementaries" what need of a wizard from Tunis or Egypt to "dominate" them? If such "wonders occur in her presence," why is not every scientist in America by this time a convert? Evidently facts and statements do not agree.

Indeed, what the president diplomatically terms his "blunders" are, on this subject, piteous. I subjoin a few of his statements respecting the fellow theosophist alluded to :—"This lady is one of the most remarkable mediums in the world;" "She is no medium;" "She *was* a medium until the age of twenty-five;" "She conquered her mediumship;" "She controls spirits to do her bidding;" "She never pretended to control human spirits;" "She is an adept in occultism;" "She never claims to possess occult powers." What is an amazed reader to think of all this? I quite accept our author's remark that on his head must fall the weight of these contradictions. "They are expressions," he wrote to me, "for which I alone am responsible."

By his own confession he knew, when he published the above statements, that certain of them were untrue. "I called her, in writing my book, 'one of the most remarkable mediums in the world,'" he says of this sister in occultism. "At that very time she denied the possession of mediumship, but, thinking I knew better, I assumed to classify her, without her consent, as I did." No doubt he is also entirely responsible for the following assertion regarding the same person, which assertion occurs in his first letter to me : "It was her *spirit-controls*" (underlined by him) "who made her do the crazy things she did." Will the president enter the plea here, "Another *blunder* of mine?" It is, to say the least, curious that he should talk of the spirit-controls of a person who, he tells us, controls the spirits.

On page 855 of his book he "doubts if any circle ever witnessed a more astounding spiritual feat than that he is about to relate." Then follows a sensational account of a buckle brought by alleged spirit-power from a Russian grave. Much has since been said and printed about this occurrence. The matter is not worthy of any extended notice; but I desire to state that I still maintain the impossibility of any such manifestation having occurred. The said buckle formed part of a Russian decoration. "This," says the narrator, "with all other medals and crosses, must have been buried with the body, as is the universal custom." In Russia decorations are never buried with the dead. Until very recently, they were, without exception, returned to the government.

Not feeling very strong on this point, our author summoned to his aid another theosophist, the Baron de Palm, whom the Society a few months later were called on to gratify with pagan funeral rites. This person wrote a letter which the president caused to be published. Baron de Palm confesses that on the demise of the wearer of any order the insignia are returned to the sovereign by whom they were conferred. "But," he continues, "almost invariably the recipient has duplicate and triplicate sets of his decorations. The triplicate set is buried with the body." I have little acquaintance with the customs of the Baron's country, Bavaria, and do not feel called on to speak authoritatively of what is unknown to me. It would have been well had others imitated this carefulness. In making public Baron de Palm's letter, the author of "People from the Other World" proved strikingly how unfamiliar Russian customs are (as the Baron has it) "to a class of people whom we call snobs." Nowhere in the Czar's dominions can duplicate and triplicate sets of decorations be found. The wearer has invariably but a single set. This suffices alike for "common wear, select occasions, and *grand tenue*," since Russian holders of insignia are usually able to afford the expense of servants by whom their decorations may be kept in order.

On page 452 of "People from the Other World" the author talks of "M. Aksakow, the eminent St. Petersburg publisher, former tutor to the Czarowitch." M. Aksakow is not, and never was, a publisher, and never was tutor to the Czarowitch.

And now for a brief summing-up. In this writer's own judicial language, "Let us see how far we have gotten on our way towards the truth."

It will be perceived that his "investigations" (so-called) at

T

Chittenden were utterly worthless. He carried them on, for the most part, in darkness so great that the features of a face could not be distinguished at the distance of even two feet. He was not permitted to approach within five times that distance of the " spirit-forms." Except a Mr. Pritchard and a Mrs. Cleveland, none of the sitters ever mounted the platform while the "forms" were there. On these two " dear old gullible souls" our philosophical theosophist mainly depended for his " facts." He saw very little himself. He verified nothing whatever of the little that he did see. With the aid of hearsay and exaggeration he has succeeded in producing a romance—not very clever, indeed,—but which reflects more credit on his ingenuity than his candour. To style it an account of scientific observations made in the interests of the truth was the acme of absurdity. Given the same conditions as at Chittenden, a writer equally unscrupulous could produce a still more startling narrative from the feats of those very clever conjurors Maskelyne and Cooke, or from the feats of any other chiefs of the juggling fraternity. It is not in darkness like the darkness of the Eddy homestead that the facts which are the true stays of Spiritualism require to be groped for. Nor, though the author of " People from the Other World " becomes owlish enough when exposed to the clear light of truth, does he seem to have that bird's capacity for seeing when all light is wanting. On the contrary, the greater the darkness outside, the more ludicrous is the confusion of his mind. The most palpable snares are fatal to our poor philosopher.

I offer no theory as to the origin of the manifestations which he has recorded. In spite of jealously-preserved darkness and utter want of tests the Eddys may be mediums. The conditions are suspicious ; but no reasonable man will base a verdict on suspicion alone. The work before me counts as simply nothing. It presents not a single proved fact either for or against the " materialisations " of the Vermont homestead. How worthless the author of " People from the Other World" knew that book to be, one can sufficiently estimate from the fact that, not long after its publication, he wrote to the New York *Sun* (Nov. 30th, 1875) respecting

" the grand exposure of the Eddy spiritual manifestations which he, in common with the whole public, had been patiently waiting for."

NOTE.—There is to be found in "People from the Other World" a misstatement regarding myself which, as being a personal matter, may, I consider, be more appropriately dealt with in the forthcoming volume of "Incidents in My Life."

CHAPTER VI.

SCEPTICS AND TESTS.

CERTAIN spiritualists have, of late, astonished the world by informing it that the best method of proving the facts of spiritualism is
to debar all possibility of proof. No tests are to be imposed at
séances. No light is to be allowed ; admittance is to be accorded
only to persons whose credulity is unmistakable, and whose enthusiasm has been put past all doubt. It is from this happy class that
the champions of suspicious phenomena, and more than suspected
media come forth.

"I was pleased to learn," remarks one Quixote, "that the sensitive
Mrs. —— has decided not to admit any person to her *séances* whose name
has not been previously handed in, submitted to her controlling band,
and approved of by them. Faith that spirits return is now so widely
held, that public approbation will be given to any refined, delicate, and
sensitive mediums, whom a breath of suspicion or a disparaging word will
agitate, agonise, and temporarily unfit for spirit control, if they bar out
from access to themselves the suspicious, hypercritical, rude, and ill-man-
nered, and husband their peace and forces for use in the presence of none
but those devoid of hostility to spirit-advent and mediumship."

The best commentary on the above is that the sensitive
Mrs. —— has since been detected in unmistakable imposture.

"It was really refreshing," writes another of the genus enthusiast, variety
gushing, "to read in last week's *Banner* the two communications from
Professor —— and Mrs. ——. With the aid of such able defenders, I
hope the long and sorely persecuted materializing mediums will soon
feel themselves able to dispense at *séances* not only with all *testing
scientific* enemies, but with what are still more cavilling, scientific and
would-be *scientific* friends. Let all such be debarred the privilege of
joining in spirit-circles, until they become humble enough in their minds

to be willing to receive spiritual truth in crumbs apportioned by the guardian spirits of the mediums to their respective needs and capacities to swallow and digest."

Anyone desirous of doing the utmost harm possible to our cause need only write or collect a score or two of such effusions as these, and submit them to the world as principles adopted by spiritualists. The perniciousness of the doctrine is palpable to every mind whose share of sense is of the size of a mustard-seed. Spiritualism is so utterly at variance with many popular ideas, that a hundred various schools of belief which agree in nothing else agree in directing their antagonism against it. Its adherents, therefore, must build with adamant. The New Testament parable of the two houses is here applicable. Those who accept nothing as proof which leaves the tiniest loophole for the entrance of doubt; who try all mediums and all spirits by the strictest tests; who refuse to be carried away by enthusiasm or swayed by partisanship; whose search is for the truth, and nothing but the truth; these are the spiritualists of whom the spirit-world is proud. The spiritualism to whose advancement their efforts are devoted is, indeed, a "house built upon a rock."

. There exist, however, other spiritualists, whose ideal would seem to be the house built upon the sand. They tell us that it is their design to advance the cause of Truth; yet their lives are devoted to inflicting injury on that truth. No material is too flimsily unreliable for builders of this class. Out of dark *séances*, and foolish reports of the same, and unreliable phenomena, and unlimited enthusiasm, they contrive to construct their house. So that the effect of the whole is glaring, it matters little how shaky the component parts may be; there is enough of the mortar of credulity to hold all together. Sensible persons turn from the sight with shame and disgust, and strive to convince of their error the enthusiasts to whom that sight is owing. Such efforts, however well-intended, are usually vain. More obstinate than their Scriptural compeer, the spiritualists of whom I treat are not to be convinced of their folly even when the flood has swept away the flimsy erection on which they have wasted time and pains. They industriously proceed to rear another edifice of the same kind, and, pointing to it, ask triumphantly what harm has been done.

Some, indeed, have contrived to improve even on the above process. Their house may be destroyed, but, to save the labour of rearing a new one, they quietly assure mankind that the old building is still there. By these expressions I mean that, when the theory of such an enthusiast is demolished, or his pet-medium convicted on the plainest evidence of fraud, he will find you, in half the time which it occupied Puck to put a girdle round the earth, "explanations" of the behaviour of the medium, and "reasons" tending to prove that, although his theory be demolished, it is still sound. And these are the persons who "would dispense at *séances* with scientific enemies, and still more cavilling scientific friends!" That is to say, instead of leaving imposture to enter, if at all, like a thief in the night, they would fling wide every door for its admission.

The most cowardly thing in the system of such philosophers is the method by which they "explain" imposture. I call such "explanations" cowardly because they have the un-Saxon-like quality of attacking those who cannot defend themselves. In order to whitewash some Ethiopian of a medium they blacken the spirit-world. There is proof that imposture was committed; there is no evidence that any but incarnated men and women were concerned in it; yet spirits are accused as the criminals; are tried without being present, and condemned, though not a shadow of testimony is advanced against them. The stupidity of such conduct equals its wickedness.

Our opponents have not been slow to recognise the weakness and the folly of these theories. "Are lies told in the circle?" remarks one attacker of spiritualism. "Bad spirits! Does the 'materialized' form bear too striking a resemblance to the 'passive?' Bad spirits! Is the bull's eye turned on too quickly, revealing the medium off his seat, and endeavouring to escape from his bonds? Bad spirits! Is the sensitive being favoured by the 'starry hosts" a drunkard? Bad spirits, undoubtedly! So it is all through. Blind faith is the only royal road: proof you cannot have."

Happily it is by no means thus all through spiritualism. The most prominent workers for the cause resolutely refuse to accept blind faith as the only " royal road." The weighty and judicious article I proceed to give is from the eloquent pen of Hudson Tuttle, and well expresses the views entertained on the subject by every thinking spiritualist :—

"HIGH-PRIESTHOOD OF MEDIUMS.

"The *Banner* of February 26th, 1876, contains an article from T. R. H—— which is fraught with the most mischievous tendencies. What makes the matter still worse is the fact that Mr. —— has boldly spoken what a large class of spiritualists really think, but fail to articulate. It has been repeated that spiritual phenomena were for the express purpose of convincing the sceptic. To convince, they must be given under test conditions, such as do not violate the laws of their manifestations ; yet in the face of all science, Mr. —— says :—

"'I hope that the day is not far distant when mediums, as a general rule, will acquire strength and independence sufficient to enable them to deny altogether having their divine powers tested in any way whatever.'

"This is the first intimation we have had that mediums had special *Divine power*, too holy and sacred to be gainsaid ! What does this lead us to ? To medium-worship ? Is there to be a class set apart like the Levites of old time, who are to set themselves above the rules governing others, and are we to accept whatever they please to call spiritual without question ? Why, an infallible Pope is a pigmy to such a colossus, which would bestride the judgment, bandage the eyes of reason, and make its votaries Punch and Judy figures to dance as the medium pulled the wire ! If this be the end of spiritualism, to receive its greatest strength from ' untested,' ' untrammeled' mediums, its career is short, and it runs swift to ruin.

"We venture to assert that the strictly test conditions imposed by Prof. Crookes, and his accuracy of observation, have done more to impress the learned world with the claims of spiritualism than the haphazard observations and laudating letters of any number of common observers. Every spiritualist in the world points with just pride to his splendid investigations. Who quotes the wonder-tale of any one who has sat in a dark circle, when the ' conditions' were those of fraud, and no safeguard imposed to prevent deception ?

"No amount of such evidence that can or may ever be produced has a feather's weight with the sceptic. Yet it is claimed that for the benefit of the sceptic the manifestations are given to the world.

"I have studied the laws of spiritual phenomena somewhat, and no one will accuse me of seeking the injury of the cause to which I have given the best hours of my life, nor of knowingly endeavouring to institute conditions contrary to the spirit-force. Because I love spiritualism, is why I would strip it of all this falsehood, and cleanse its skirts of the stain of deception.

"Prof. Crookes placed a wire cage over the musical instruments, and tunes were played upon them, by which it is proved that the spirit-force can act through such wire cages. Why not place a wire cage over the instruments, in all cases sealed to the table, and then there could be no dispute if they were played upon ? Or in case of the medium disappearing, place such a cage over her, or over the paraffin in the 'mould' experiment ? Why must there be always some weak place left to excite the scepticism of those whom it is desirable to convince ? Why is the honest investigator who proposes such absolute test conditions at once hailed as a Judas ?

"When mediums will not comply with conditions that I know by my own experience, and the recorded experience of others, are not detrimental to the manifestations, I have no desire to confer further with them.

"Why the honest medium should rebel against such 'test conditions' I confess I do not understand. Certainly nothing can be of more value to them or the cause than thorough investigation, and the placing of every observation on absolute grounds. Because a medium has been tested once does not prove the genuineness of any other manifestation received under less stringent conditions.

"Science is the classification of accurately observed facts. Spiritualism claims to rank as a department of science, and the task of spiritualists for the present and future is to make good its claims. This can be accomplished only by making the conditions of every manifestation as strictly test as possible. After those have been established, of course others not under test conditions have a significance and value, depending, however, not on themselves, but on those of like character which have been established.

"In opposition to this course of slowly winning our certain way by patient, honest investigation, Mr. ——, as champion of a mediumship which scorns to be trammeled and tested, arrogates a 'divine' sanctity, which at once places the whole subject beyond investigation, and leaves the investigator outside bound hand and foot, privileged only to open his mouth and receive what is given by the 'spirits.'

"The constant exposures of the tricks of mediums throw obloquy and reproach on all, for when one is exposed it is thought others may be. The evil has become great, and every spiritualist should feel it his duty, while defending the true and honest, to expose imposture. The genuine medium should court rather than shun test conditions, and refuse to hold séances under any other. Then there would be an end to fraud, and the manifestations would have value in the records of science.

"Let no spiritualist believing with Mr. H—— accuse 'men of science' of refusing to investigate. He advises mediums to 'deny altogether having their divine power tested,' and how can any one investigate ? If we accept that, we merit the scorn of all thinking men, and will be swift in receiving it."

Side by side with the above protest must the following excellent utterances of the Boston *Spiritual Scientist* be placed :—

"HOW QUESTIONABLE MEDIUMSHIP IS SUPPORTED.

" In a recent article relating to ' Materialization' T. H——, a ' veteran' spiritualist, as none of our readers can doubt, embraces the opportunity to continue his practice of manufacturing sentiment in favour of ' conditions' that will admit of trickery on the part of the medium, either in a normal state or as the unconscious instrument of spirit-power. He says that the ' conductor of the circle on the spirit side' (?) was willing that professional sceptics should examine all the surroundings of the circle-room and cabinet provided some truthful spiritualist was with them at the time ; and further, that he would permit them to be present at the *séances* if they would occupy positions outside of the circle, apart from the wire, and permit themselves, after being searched, to be securely tied, hands and feet, and placed in a strong wire cage with a rope or small chain put tightly about their necks and fastened to an iron ring in the wall.

" Mr. H—— may have written the above in an attempt to be funny : if so, the old saying that ' many a true word is spoken in jest' is quite applicable : for it certainly expresses the attitude of ' questionable mediums' and their ' veteran' supporters toward a class of spiritualists who, standing between the public and those who *would* be representative mediums, labour to separate the true from the false and endeavour to discover what portion of the manifestations can be accepted as having a spiritual origin. They would also experiment to know more of the laws governing the phenomena of Spiritualism. These are intelligent investigators ; but Mr. H—— and other ' veteran' supporters of questionable mediumship, are pleased to term them ' professional sceptics.'

" The individuals who possess this ' questionable mediumship' are usually wanting in the mental development that would enable them to appreciate the vast importance of the principles of the spiritual philosophy. They cling to spiritualism for the ' loaves and fishes'—the dollars and cents that it contributes to their pockets—and they are shrewd enough to discern what conditions are conducive to best results in this direction. First, it is necessary to secure the attendance of a few ' veteran' spiritualists ; credulous wonder-seekers, who can write a fair descriptive article of what they *think* they see. The more credulous these ' veterans' are, the more they are in demand and the more wonderful are the manifestations that they witness. They are given front seats in all circles, FREE, and from this time forth are the particular favourites of the materialized spirits ; who greet them with fond caresses, permit them to cut locks of hair from their heads, examine drapery, and do other things to the end of the catalogue of wonders that have been chronicled in the columns of papers ever open to such trash. These 'veterans' form a body-guard around these mediums, and defend them from charges of fraud, and deny any person the right to test their 'divine powers.'

"The arrogant assumptions of both mediums and 'veterans' are supported by another class of 'representative' spiritualists who are in some way dependent upon spiritualism and the favour of its adherents for an easy living. These are obliged to sail with the tide ; if they would win popularity they must be in advance when the public feeling is to be moulded in any particular case. The cheapest stock for an investment of ideas in case of an *extempore* speech is to give out a weak sentiment of charity for the 'world's saviours,' the 'persecuted media,' &c. *ad nauseam.*

"The opinions of the 'veterans' and the speeches of the 'representatives' find their way into print because they are best suited to the interests of those who might publish a journal 'for money—not for spiritualism.' Should the people be taught to think for themselves the wonderful stories would lose their interest, and spiritualists would donate that money to spiritualism which is now given in support of shams.

"See then what spiritualism is struggling against. See why many true spiritualists are prevented from identifying themselves with a cause they truly love. They wish to serve the bread of life, to teach the truth of truths, to preach, that all may hear, the joyful tidings of a future existence and communion between the two states proven ; but their efforts are impeded by those who would control spiritualism for their own selfish advancement ; opinions contrary to their expressed views are denounced ; investigation is discountenanced. 'Believe everything,' they say, 'and you are accepted as one of us. Reject anything, and we and the rest of the 'veterans' will class you as a 'professional sceptic.'"*

* I am classed, not only as a "professional sceptic," but as "jealous of all mediums." The latter accusation is hurled at me wherever I attempt to utter a word of warning. Only a few months ago Mr. Benjamin Coleman, in writing to the *Spiritualist,* said:—"The opposition which the Davenport brothers met with in this country a few years ago was stimulated by the bitter hostility of a rival medium who refused to witness their exhibition, but loudly condemned them as impostors."

Should Mr. Coleman have the intention of styling me a "rival" of the Davenports, I must beg to repudiate the proffered honour. I believe the whole statement to be simply a wild assertion on the part of the writer. If he *did* point it at me, I can correct his bad memory by assuring him that the Davenports gave their last "exhibition" April 8, 1865, and that I arrived from America (where I had been during the whole period of the Davenports' stay in England) towards the end of May, 1865.

Surely the nadir of folly is reached at last! It seems scarcely credible that any human being professing to be in possession of his senses should gravely enunciate such a proposition as the one regarding "professional sceptics," commented upon in the above article. So Professor Huxley is to be searched by some "truthful spiritualist," should he attend a *séance*, and Dr. Carpenter can only be permitted to attempt the verification of his "unconscious cerebration" theory under the uncomfortable conditions consequent on being "tied securely hand and foot, and placed in a strong wire cage, with a rope or small chain put tightly about his neck, and fastened to an iron ring in the wall!" The mind must be thoroughly reason-proof which considers spiritualism benefited by absurdity such as this.

A somewhat more enlightened view of the subject is contained in one of the leading articles of the *Spiritualist* for June 28rd, 1876. The soundest portions of the teachings advanced are as follows :—" Experience has proved that, so far as physical manifestations at *séances* are concerned, it is necessary to obtain them under very strict test conditions whenever it is intended to publish the facts. . . . The facts of materialization are of too much importance to rest upon doubtful evidence so far as publication is concerned ; hence experienced spiritualists in this country will never commit themselves to publicly recognising as genuine any full-form manifestations which may be witnessed on the premises of the medium, in which an ordinary room is used as a cabinet."

So far good ; but the reasons which the writer submits as chiefly leading him to advocate stringent tests are, in my opinion, unsound :—" The spirits who produce materialization manifestations are, for the most part, tricky. Unprogressed spirits will sometimes fight their way in, and, by means of spirit-hands and arms, impose upon the best friends of the mediums, at one end of a room, by producing that which is not what they state it to be, and all the time the medium may be in a dead trance at the other end of the apartment. It is also a strange fact that, if a physical medium resolve to play tricks, there are spirits who will help him."

Is it a fact? It may be; but where are the proofs? The "Jedbro justice" dealt out to spirits by behaviour such as this out-Jedwoods even Jedwood. Accusation and condemnation press hard upon each other; but the evidence which should support them is never forthcoming. It is only within the last few years that these "tricky materialization spirits" have been heard of. Fifteen or twenty years back, when a trickster was detected in the act of simulating spiritual phenomena he accepted his fate resignedly; and bore in submissive silence the consequences attendant on his villany. Why need he have done so? If the frauds of late brought to light be mainly referable to the influence of bad spirits, is it not more than probable that the frauds which disfigure the earlier history of the spiritual movement are also referable to such influence? And can we believe that, if the fraudulent mediums of those earlier days had been simply unconscious instruments in the hands of evil beings, they would not have discovered and proclaimed so exonerating a fact? Or are we to suppose that they were conscious of innocence, but sacrificed their own reputations to shield the reputations of their guardians? Either theory is absurd. The simple realities of the case are that, fifteen and twenty years ago, imposture either had not discovered this method of cloaking itself, or did not suppose that there were spiritualists foolish enough to accept such libels on the spirit-world.

We hear much of "Fathers of English Spiritualism." If the paternity be genuine, I must needs be the grandfather, for they are, almost without exception, my converts; and thus, in a symbolical sense, my children. I must confess that I stand in the position of many parents; being heartily ashamed of some of my offspring. With me, their father, they were thorough in their investigations, and based conviction only on absolute certainty. Now, they have cast caution aside, and seem to experience an insane pleasure in being duped. Should I try to convince them of their folly they turn on me in fury; and, if unable to injure me otherwise, degrade themselves by inventing and circulating monstrous falsehoods, which they trust will damage my moral character. Truly, I am an unfortunate father. Happily, however, this class of my children is in a decided minority; and of the majority I may well be proud. These last, and not their self-assertive brethren, were the real founders of our cause. While pseudo-"Fathers of spiritualism" blew the trumpet of their own praise, others worked. Some of those workers have retired with sorrow and disgust from the wilderness of puppet-shows at present miscalled spiritualism. Others are rejoicing in the change which has freed them from the cares of earth. Amongst these last, let me name with affectionate remembrance my friend, Mr. William Cox, of Jermyn Street. Years before modern spiritualism had birth, he was, by thought and act, a spiritualist. Thus, when the subject arose into prominence, it came to him as a familiar, rather than a novel guest. His house was a home for mediums arriving from every country, and he the best of hosts; a man incapable of an unworthy action; the very soul of truth. At the time of the Sir David Brewster falsehood he first took up the cudgels in my defence. We owe a grateful tribute to men of his stamp, and his name should not be forgotten. But I must turn from this pleasant theme.

The first "discovery" made in the interests of mediums was, that "colouring matter might be transmitted from the materialized hand or form to the medium." Various committees had hit upon the plan of secretly placing paint on the instruments used at dark *séances.* The said instruments having been actively swung and sounded, stains of paint would be found on the "medium's" hands. For a time spiritualists no less than sceptics were content to denounce such persons as impostors. At length some veteran dupe delighted his fellow-enthusiasts with the ingenious "explanation" above mentioned. It was the first thing of the kind, and obtained a rapturous reception. Such success naturally excited emulation. There arose a race of spiritualists whose lives were devoted to the upholding of the extraordinary theory that because when fraud was committed, the mediums concerned appeared to be the guilty parties, they must needs be innocent; and because the spirits appeared to be innocent, *they* were assuredly guilty. And now these "explanations" fall upon us "thick as autumn leaves in Vallombrosa." Here is a sample of the class; extracted from the columns of the *Banner of Light;* (was not such a title given in jest to such a paper?)

"The use of a medium's physical organs in the performance of what is assumed to be a spirit-manifestation, though it may engender suspicions of fraud, does not of itself prove the medium fraudulent, nor does it exclude admission that some spirit produces the witnessed result. 'Come now, and let us reason together,' and do it logically.

"It is a general habit to regard all sane men and women as being actual authors of, and, therefore, responsible for whatever their tongues utter or their hands perform, and this habit is so prevalent and so active that the wisdom and justice of its promptings are usually conceded without question or consideration. What this habit exacts may be generally just toward those who are non-mediumistic, or relatively so; may be just toward all whose physical organs are never controlled by other will-power than that of their legitimate owners. But the latter class does not embrace all mortals, and consequently there may be persons whom public habit condemns unjustifiably.

"Whether a medium's hands are used in distributing flowers about a room, in procuring rag-babies, in obtaining paraffin moulds, and other acts which engender suspicions of fraud and falsehood (though made a primal question by the world's habit), has really but little, if any, pertinency in the case of a genuine and well-unfolded medium. If the limbs of one who is meanwhile entranced to absolute unconsciousness be used by a spirit, the work performed by using them is just as much that of a controlling spirit as the same would be if he performed it without the use of those limbs, and the medium's denial of any participation in or knowledge of what his limbs have been seen performing, may be made in all sincerity, honesty, and truthfulness, because the fact that the body was subject to the will of an outside intelligence involves a presumption that the owner of the body was not in condition to operate through it nor to know what was done through it."

There is just one flaw in the above delicious morsel of logic. The foundation on which this superstructure of argument has been reared with so much care is, in reality, no foundation at all. The weakness of the proposition with which our author starts is such that an attack directed against it sends the whole theory instantly to the ground.

That proposition is contained in the sentence:—"The use of a medium's physical organs," &c. The arguer knows the weakness of his position, and attempts to mask it in the following manner:—

" Whether a medium's hands are used in distributing flowers about
a room, in procuring rag-babies, in obtaining paraffin moulds . . .
has really but little, if any, pertinency." Indeed! Suppose
even that the point were conceded of mediums being sometimes
" entranced to absolute unconsciousness " whilst acts of fraud are
committed, our enthusiast is no nearer than before to the points he
seeks to establish. Ample evidence remains to convict the mediums
of conscious imposture. Whence come the flowers, the rag-babies,
the paraffin moulds, the masks, the shawls, &c., which constitute
the paraphernalia of fraud ? Evidently and undeniably from the
places where they have been concealed by the pretended medium,
previous to the commencement of the *séance*. Was the impostor,
at the time of concealment, in a state of " absolutely unconscious
existence ? " When, before a sitting, a woman laughs and talks
with her intended dupes; having paraffin moulds, or shawls and
veils for " materialization " concealed about her person ; when a
man carries newspapers in his pocket to eke out a " spirit-dress ; "
and has one thin fabric concealed in his neck-tie, and another
arranged to appear the lining of some article of dress, is all this
the work of spirits ? The impostor is not in a trance. He does
not even pretend to be in a trance. Yet, should a careful search
be instituted at that moment, the destined apparatus of fraud is
discovered hidden about the person of the " medium," or in the
cabinet where he intends to " manifest." These discoveries have
occurred. They will, I suppose, occur again. What, in face of
such damning testimony, becomes of the " bad spirit " hypothesis?
Its place is with last year's snow. And yet, should fraud be discovered at the close of a *séance*, instead of just before the commencement, spirits, and not mediums, are to be held responsible
for introducing the shawls, masks, or rag-babies seized ! Verily,
the brains of some spiritualists are fearfully and wonderfully made.

Since the charges against the other world break down so utterly,
and " evidence there is none," certain persons seek to introduce to
us imaginary spirits confessing imaginary sins. Thus we have
(always in the *Banner of Light*) the following puerile nonsense
saddled on a " controlling spirit ":—

" Friends, in the lessons of to-day may you learn many of the laws of
spirit-control. While you are looking with distrust on those who are
giving physical manifestations, and are endeavouring to pick everything
to pieces lest you should not get the truth, the whole truth, and nothing
but the truth, we bid you, as we have once before bade (*sic*) you, be careful
what you do. We warn those who, with the hammer calling itself truth,
are pounding to pieces the very souls of our mediums in different parts
of the country. We say to them, Step lightly, walk carefully. . . . I
know this—that many times mediums are moved like automatons in
their circle. Even those who may be used for bringing flowers, or for
other manifestations, often move their arms or muscles in obedience to
our world. . . . Hence there has been the cry of 'humbug.' Mediums
have been called humbugs when they were really truthful to themselves,
and could not tell why it was so. We have once before called your attention to this subject, and we would again impress it upon your minds to
be cautious, to look well before you wound by the deadly shaft of slander
the good name of those who are trying to do all they can for the spirit-
world."

One is driven to the conclusion that, if the above really proceeded from a spirit, that spirit was the Rev. Mr. Chadband
returned to cry out once more, " My friends, what is Terewth ? "
But I know of nothing which should lead us to attribute such folly
to the spirit-world. The whole communication has a mundane, an
excessively·mundane air.

The same may be said of almost all the messages received in the
Banner of Light circle-room. Ninety-nine out of every hundred
spirits have the same peculiarity of speech. "I went out of the
the world," is the stereotyped remark, " on such and such a
morning or afternoon." I may add that I knew intimately two of
the persons whose spirits have been represented as communicating.
Nothing could be more unlike their styles of thinking and express-
ing themselves than the " messages " attributed to them.

The position taken by an enthusiast who gives vent to the cry
of "Bad Spirits!" is that of an accuser. He makes certain
charges against the men and women who have departed this life.
Now, it is a fundamental maxim of every impartial legal code that
the *onus probandi* should rest with the prosecution. It is not
sufficient that the accused should be unable to make his innocence
manifest. His accusers must demonstrate his guilt.

But the philosophers with whom I am dealing totally reverse this process. Nay! they do more than reverse it. Not only do they condemn those against whom no evidence is brought; but they acquit persons of whose guilt the evidence is conclusive. In every exposure which has been "explained" by some libel on the spirit-world the evidence against the inculpated medium has been such as would have ensured his or her conviction ten times over in the most impartial court of justice. Specimens of that evidence will be found in my chapters on "Trickery and its exposure." Yet these enthusiasts coolly put all such testimony aside. They would rather believe the purest dwellers in the spirit-world guilty of wicked and meaningless fraud, than admit that the lowest wretch who ever advanced pretensions to the possession of medial powers will act the hypocrite, when a hundred circumstances combine to make it to his interest to lie and cheat. And so our "loved and lost" only come down from the Beautiful City, and through the Golden Gates, to "speak lies in hypocrisy," and revel in the meanest sin! It is difficult to think calmly of such a doctrine, or to speak with patience of its professors. If, as David said, all men be liars, let us at least have the consolation that those are less prone to the vice in question who have passed from the temptations of earth. My own very varied and extended experience has always gone to prove such the case.

A peculiarly-illogical folly of "vindicators of persecuted mediums" remains to be noticed. The circumstances which lead up to it are usually as follows: Some "persecuted" being has been detected in plain and unmistakable fraud. Perhaps it was in the "paraffin mould" business—perhaps in the "materializing" line of life. The detectors of the fraud, having their senses about them, and feeling naturally indignant at the imposition sought to be practised, testify publicly to what they have seen. Should the medium, or pretended medium, concerned be of any note, indignant enthusiasts rush from all quarters to the spot. A *séance* is instantly convened; all but the faithful are excluded. Some mild test is imposed to give a certain colour to the report that "manifestations were obtained under the severest test-conditions imaginable." The evening passes merrily; the results are magnificent. Perhaps a half-dozen of "materialized forms" appear; perhaps the carpet is littered with paraffin moulds. The sitters are jubilant. The persecuted and interesting medium is uplifted to the seventh heaven, and receives the adoratory congratulations of all present. The editor of some "leading spiritual paper" rushes to his office, and prints in big type a brief and brilliant pæan like the following :—

"Yes! —— was completely vindicated last night.". How vindicated, in the name of common sense? Even if, on the evening in question, the manifestations were genuine, by what strange process of reasoning can this be considered to invalidate the fact that fraud was detected and exposed at a previous *séance*? Yet such is precisely the manner in which nine "vindications" out of ten are accomplished.

We see then two classes of spiritualists. On one side is the searcher for truth, on the other the whitewasher of falsehood. The first says to the sceptic, "Examine, test, and then, if the evidence be sufficient, believe." The second says, "Believe, and when you have given sufficiently enthusiastic proofs of your credulity you may be permitted to examine a little, though never to test." The first says, "These phenomena should be observed under scientific conditions." The second tells us, "I hope the day is not far distant when mediums will deny having their divine powers tested in any way whatever." With which class is the victory to remain? In which host are the worthiest warriors ranked?

The first says, "I know that humanity is liable to err. Irrefutable evidence compels me to admit both that there are pretenders to mediumship who possess no medial gifts whatever; and that men and women exist who, being truly mediums, will yet stoop, when manifestations are not forthcoming, to lie and to defraud. I believe, too, that in another world we grow better and not worse. Therefore, it seems to me improbable that the goodness of God should permit spirits to return to us whose sole intent is to work evil. If this be so, prove it; I see no evidence that spirits plan and carry out the deceptions often practised at *séances*; but I see ample testimony that human beings are guilty of such frauds. I prefer, therefore, to condemn this world rather than the next."

The second tells us, "Your friends who return to you from beyond the grave are, almost without exception, liars and cheats. Their dearest delight is to deceive spiritualists, and inflict injury on mediums. Whenever, therefore, imposture is discovered at a *séance*, blame the spirits. They make masks and exhibit them. They dress up rag-babies; they fill the pockets of the medium with flowers; they introduce paraffin moulds; they will simulate materialized forms with shawls and veils, and afterwards hide the shawls and veils carefully away; they will tie newspapers around the legs of a medium, or cover him with 'spirit-drapery,' or decorate him with false whiskers and a turban. What proof have we of all this? Oh, none! but it is a subject which requires faith rather than proof. Be assured that you had better believe all acts of imposture spirit-manifestations. Unless you do so much weakening of the foundations of spiritualism will be effected."

As one or other of these doctrines prevails so will be the future of spiritualism. If we wish the name to become a by-word and a mockery, and the cause a rank field of corruption, let us hold our *séances* only in the deepest darkness, and drive far off all enquiry and every species of test. If we wish that our belief should conquer, and its truth be made manifest, let us court examination, and do all things in the light. Where there is secrecy there will be suspicion. To have no concealments is the one effectual method of defeating fraud.

CHAPTER VII.

In dealing with spiritualism it is the custom of a certain class of minds to break loose from all restraint. "Reason being weak," and enthusiasm strong, the very thought of communion with the dwellers in another world appears to intoxicate these unfortunates almost to madness. Their vagaries are often scarcely distinguishable from those beheld in madhouses, or at the wilder kind of revival meetings. The disease manifests itself in a variety of ways. Some of the men and women attacked by it pin themselves to a particular delusion, with a fanatical tenacity which nothing can affect. Others flit tirelessly from mania to mania. One or more of the class will invariably be found at every "materialization" séance where the light is too poor to distinguish features. Should two of this kind of Greek meet, the "tug of war" is never far off. When the first indistinct form appears both are ready to recognise a relative in it. With equal vehemence do they

> "Swear from out the press
> They know him perfectly, and one can swear
> He is his father, upon which another
> Is sure he is his mother's sister's brother."

If we are to believe the conjurors, Maskelyne and Cooke, such visitors are frequent at the Egyptian Hall. "The 'materialized spirit' there," they tell us, "is often addressed in an imploring tone by some of the faithful amongst the audience, with 'John! John! speak to your old friend, John!'"

It is always at dark séances that this form of folly blossoms in the highest perfection. The "phenomena" witnessed at such gatherings are, in but too many instances, the laughing-stocks of sceptics, and the shame of every sensible spiritualist. Satirical verse has been directed at them. Our opponents remind us that—

> " Shakspeare's spirit visits earth, to tell
> How he and Washington are very well;
> And Lindley Murray, from the body free,
> Can't make his verbs and nominatives agree."

The reproach is mild. Spiritual journals have again and again published communications whose absurdity is simply sublime. These follies are usually of the same type. A great spirit has, for no conceivable reason, earthly or heavenly, descended from his high home to perform strange antics before a little circle of spiritualists. And how wofully these spirits have deteriorated! How wonderfully they are clad! The favourite costume of Oliver Cromwell when " materializing " himself consists, we learn, of a " white muslin skull-cap, black velvet suit, and yellow top-boots."

His shoemakers, however, understand their business but badly, since in giving, by particular desire, " the stamp that dissolved an English Parliament," Oliver altogether disarranged his ill-fitting " tops," and was forced to stoop and adjust them. Then the spirit shuffled with awkward dignity round the table, and after solemnly kissing the whole of the sitters, male and female, bore back his skull-cap and yellow boots to the summer-land.

Italy would seem to surpass both England and America in the number and quality of the " people from another world" who visit it. In " Notes of a Séance held at Naples " we find that, " Of the spirits who manifested three were in the flesh, and amongst the disincarnated the most noteworthy were Margherita Pusterla, Dionysius of Syracuse, Genseric, Cleopatra, Richard Cœur de Lion, *Aladdin*, Belcadel, Guerrazzi, Manin, and Vico." After these came " Abraham, Melchisedec, Jacob, Moses, David, Sennacherib, Elisha, Joachim, Judith, Jael, Samuel, Daniel, Mary Magdalene, St. Paul, St. Peter, and St. John." Even this concourse did not suffice. "The Biblical spirits," we are told, "came one after another, before the Nazarene. St. John immediately preceded him, telling us that he came to purify us before receiving the Great Master." Comment is as unnecessary as impossible.

America, it appears, rejoices in a spiritualist terming himself "the prophet and servant of God." This valuable exponent of our cause lately drew together in Philadelphia other enthusiasts as crazy as himself, and styled the astonishing assembly "A National Convention." His own part in the said convention was a truly benevolent one. Before the reformers whom he had gathered he drew from his pocket a frightened pigeon, and, tossing it up to the roof, proclaimed that the era of universal brotherhood had at last arrived, and that, in token thereof, he let loose the dove of peace.

Many years ago I had an experience with this man, which, I think, deserves to be placed on record. I was at the time very young, not being above eighteen, and was staying with friends in Hartford, Conn. One day, whilst the younger members of the family and myself were together, the servant brought word that "a strange-looking man had called, asking to see Mr. Home." I sent back a message to the effect that I was unable to come, and that one of my friends would see him, and learn his business with me. Presently I changed my mind, and went myself. In the drawing-room I found a visitor whose singular appearance somewhat surprised me. He was standing with his eyes tightly closed, and a generally-cataleptic air pervading him. However, I had not much time to study his looks. At the sound of my footsteps he moved slightly, and, without opening his eyes, ejaculated :—

"I don't want you; I have come for Daniel Home!" and motioned me away with his hand.

I regarded him quietly for a moment, and then asked, "What is your business with Daniel Home?"

"I can't tell you; let him come himself."

"Unless you tell me, he will know nothing about it; let me hear what you want."

*" I am the spirit of his mother, speaking through this medium.
I have come to tell Daniel that he must travel through the country
with this brother in the cause, and make a charge of twenty-five cents
for admission to his séances. Unless you let me speak with Daniel,
the medium will shake the dust of the house from his feet, and my son
will come to ruin."*

The disgust and anger I experienced were such that I did not
trust myself to reply. I silently left the room, and begged my
friends to get the fellow out. He was sent from the house; and
probably remains to this day in ignorance that, whilst he supposed
himself addressing some one of the family whose guest I was, his
pretended message was really delivered to the person whom it most
concerned.

A few years later I met him again. Hearing, whilst in New
York, that he was giving *séances* in Fourth Avenue, I determined
to return his Hartford call. I found him seated before a small
table, not much above a foot across; which table he caused to
tip, and in this manner "spirit-messages" were given. I withheld
my name, and he was thus left without the faintest conception as
to the identity of his visitor. He received me graciously, and
enquired whether I should like to ask the spirits if I were a
medium. I signified that I should. The farce commenced.

" Will this brother be a rapping medium ? "

The table tipped once. " No, dear brother, you will not be a
rapping medium."

" Will he be a writing medium ? "

The table gave two tips. This, as all spiritualists know, is considered to signify " doubtful." " Perhaps, dear brother, you will
be a writing medium."

" But," said I, " the table always tips *towards* you. Will not
the spirits tip it in an opposite direction ? "

" Oh, certainly they will ! " He commenced trying to tip as
desired. As his hands were laid flat on the table, and had no purchase, they naturally slid along the top without effecting anything.
He looked towards me.

" If you will put your foot against the leg of the table nearest you " (and, of course, farthest from the medium), " the spirits, my dear brother, will tip as you wish."

The coolness of the request amused me. I did as desired. My foot afforded the requisite fulcrum, and the table began to tip towards me in the liveliest manner possible. Such were my experiences with the " prophet and servant of God " who addressed the " Philadelphian Convention " of July, 1876.

The wildest imaginings of the Catholic children, who beheld " the Virgin washing her feet in a brook," have been more than paralleled amongst spiritualists. Some years ago our cause rejoiced in a " medium " of twelve years old, who was assuredly a highly-favoured boy. Angels of the most select class guarded him. The chief of the band was no less a personage than the Virgin. Herself and coadjutors possessed, it was declared, an insatiate appetite for plum-pudding and dried fruits. I have myself heard the uncle of the lad in question relate, with the gravest conviction, how at their *séances* spirit-voices would suddenly speak from out the darkness, telling the sitters, " Here we are ! The Virgin Mary's coming, get out the sherry wine, and the raisins."

It would seem, indeed, that materialized spirits are rapidly developing a taste for the good things of earth. They commenced by timid sips from glasses of water. Next we hear of an angel band who had advanced so far as to " mix glasses of very nice gin and water," and who, " for several years, always had a Christmas party, at which they used to slice up, and hand round the plum-pudding to the sitters." Nor did they, it seems, forget " to partake sufficiently themselves of the good things provided." The habits of these strange beings were convivial. Champagne formed an invariable element of their Christmas feasts, and they would " carefully unwire corks, and extract them by means of the screw." This feat, we are told, acquired additional interest from being performed in total darkness. In fact, all for which the sitters could vouch was, that dinner, dessert, and wine had been duly honoured. Spirits, they were assured, had borne their part in the consumption ; they believed it, and were happy.

Not always, however, is the spiritual presence left so entirely to faith. Materialization has become too solid a process to be affected by daylight, or the human eye. Thus it was that two or three enthusiasts who had gathered together in a North of England town, were treated to "phenomena," which one of the party described * in frantic terms as—

"A MOST ASTOUNDING AND PERFECT SEANCE.

"Materialization Extraordinary in Good Daylight. The Spirit Partakes of a Substantial Repast of Well-Buttered Tea-Cakes, Tea, Milk and Sugar; with His Guests Specially Invited. He (The Spirit) Also Bountifully Extending Said Good Things to All the Sitters (Eleven in Number); Whose Names are Hereunto Attached in Solemn Attestation of the Truth of the Following Record."

After this display of capitals the chronicler proceeds to remark that he "shall offer no excuse or apology to Mr. Editor for writing and forwarding the report which follows." This, of course, is in consideration of its value. It would be difficult, indeed, to over-estimate the impression which such reports make on sceptical minds, and the immense success they have in bringing over sensible men to our cause. From the one in question I glean the following particulars respecting "this most lengthy and momentous *séance*, which extended over the long period of three hours and twenty minutes."

Speaking from the cabinet, the spirit instructed the sitters to prepare tea whilst he "materialized." All were immediately at work. "Soon the table was set near the centre opening of the curtains, with chair for our celestial host and visitor to sit on; and soon the table was adorned with table-cloth, teacups and saucers, sugar and milk vessels with contents, a fine lot of well-buttered tea-cakes, warm and ready for use, a large Britannia-metal teapot, with fragrant contents, *and spoons withal to sweeten the same.*" Strange beverage! which required to be sweetened with spoons in place of the sugar humanity ordinarily uses.

* *Medium,* August 18th, 1876.

Singing, it appears, followed. "In the fluidic element of its delightful cadence, the curtains seemed to open, as if by silent magic, and there stood our celestial brother, 'John King,' dressed for the occasion. Instantly all was silence. The spirit bowed a reception, and the solemn yet joyous greeting burst forth from every heart and lip. The spirit took his chair and, adjusting it, sat down, and soon began to be talkative as well as the company at table, and invited them to begin, not forgetting to set the example. Of course, we were all guilty (more or less) of bad manners, in watching our host, to see how he partook of these substantial and earthly things. And, when we had all finished one cupful, with due complement of tea-cake, our friend the spirit seized the teapot in the usual way, and poured out to each a second cup, inviting all to proceed; then, handing round the plate of cake, which, as a matter of course, we all seemed eagerly to accept of, he did not forget himself; and then he extended the cake and the tea to all in the room, by special notice. Whilst engaged with our second cup, my right-hand friend, Mr. P—— queried, and said, 'John, do you de-materialize your tea and cake as you take it, or are you completely and fully materialized?' To which he answered, 'I am fully materialized.' Then it was observed, 'It will be dissipated when the form is de-materialized.' When the tea-party had ended, the table was soon cleared away, the spirit remaining materialized all the while. . . . When the table had been taken away, the door was still wide open. On enquiry, the spirit said he could stand the light, and he walked about in it, and said, 'Give us more light. Men say they want more light now-a-days. Let us have more light, Mr. P——.' And Mr. P—— gave all the light that could stream into the room by the door and the hall-window; and the spirit walked about in triumph." The giving more light was certainly commendable, but there would appear to have been something of darkness in the mind of the genius who penned the foregoing account. His final impression of the *séance* was that it constituted a "pentecostal and glorious communion, in which he had been bathed with heavenly simplicity and love during the long period of three hours and twenty minutes." Exhausted by this outburst of eloquence, he hastes to conclude the report which he had "undertaken to give on behalf of the invisible and the visible brotherhood of immortal beings." "Thus," he perorates, "thus ended the most remarkable and momentous *séance* ever witnessed by any one present at the same . . . a season of truth and reality never to be forgotten so long as mortal life continues."

This writer has at least one brother spiritualist as gifted as himself.

"*O tempora, O mores, mutantur !*" cries the second enthusiast. "A few years ago the hour of seven on Sunday evening would have found me either with surplice on shoulder, or seated, with due solemnity, in the old church pew. Now I find myself, by polite invitation, seated in the drawing-room of Mrs. ——. Here, in this vestry, we await the arrival of our officiating priest. No priestly robes wears he, no cowl, no shaven head . . . Service-time arrived, without the tolling of a bell, we repair by twos, like unsurpliced choristers, to the dining-room. That is to be our church for the evening. Our only visible altar, the table, around which we sit, not kneel . . . . A pause. Our host and hostess rise, withdraw to the side, and return with flowers of chastest white. With these they make their first offering of the evening to Mrs. ——, as priestess of the new communion. Not with thanks from mortal lips alone were they received . . . . Our little congregation waited on the spirit-world for directions. They came. We sang . . . The lights are lowered. . . . . Be patient. Medium, go into that corner recess called a cabinet." (O, shades of Punch and Judy !)

"We sit awhile gazing at the curtain. A face appears. It is a lovely face, all aglow with life and beauty. An angelic smile is upon the lip ; the eye is alight with sweetest tenderness ; the whole expression is one of universal love. Upon the forehead is a star of glistening jewels. The diamond, ruby, sapphire, chrysolite, and oriental pearl sparkle and blend, and blend and sparkle in symbolic harmony."

Truly, it was an unkind cut on the part of the spirit to "dematerialize" that star. The "glistening jewels" would, doubtless, have been an acceptable present to the circle, and especially to the writer of the sentimentality above quoted, who has given evidence on other occasions of the interest he takes in precious stones. But by what name are we to hail the wearer of the star ? Our enthusiast proceeds glowingly to enlighten us. "The form retires

and reappears many times, each time growing in brightness and
beauty. The hand is waved in graceful salutation. The well-
shaped arm is projected, with its pendant drapery. The finger is
placed upon the jewelled star on the forehead. And there before
us is the form of Mary, Queen of Scots ! " Certainly, this revelation surprised me. I have had the honour of speaking face to face
with some six or seven Marys of Scotland. Each of them, although
reincarnated in a less exalted condition of life, retained a distinct
recollection of the days when she feasted with her courtiers in
Holyrood, or listened yieldingly to the suit of Bothwell. These
" sad, discrowned queens " were of all ages and appearances, and
the only thing difficult to discern amongst them was the slightest
trace of anything queenly. Besides these substantial Mary Stuarts
there are any number of Marys yet in spirit-land, whose presence
has been manifested at a thousand different circles. Surely,
however, we have at last hit upon the consort of Darnley. The
reporter of the *séance* in question exhausts a whole vocabulary of
amazed negatives in raptures regarding the " spirit's " charms.
" No wonder that such beauty led captive the hearts of men. No
wonder that a Bothwell could intrigue to possess himself of such a
form. No wonder that a Norfolk paved his own way to the
scaffold to call her wife. No wonder that an ugly English queen
should be jealous of such a Scotch sister. No wonder that history
played out so tragical a drama in the person of one from whose
every feature such gleams of other than human beauty shone forth.
There she was ; the Mary Stuart of what precise date I know not,
but some time before A.D. 1587, back again among us in material
form, after nearly three centuries of spirit life ! Visibly back
again ! Nay, more ; audibly so. She speaks to us. From those
lips come words ; few, it is true, but sounding to us across the
ages as :—' I, Marie Stuart, whose head was laid upon the block,
and whose blood was lapped by a dog, am not dead, but alive
for ever.' Is it possible ? Can this be a real spirit form ? "
Strange doubt to intrude on such a mind ! " Watch that aperture in the curtain," continues our interlocutor, authoritatively.
" The invisible spirit clothes itself with a visible form before our

very eyes. We trace its growth—watch yet longer." In the attitude of " watching yet longer " I leave the reporter in question. A second Truthful James, he stands exclaiming :—

> " Do I sleep ?—do I dream ?
> Do I wonder and doubt ?
> Are things what they seem ?
> Or are visions about ? "

Such spiritualists and such incidents do harm chiefly by their folly. There are, however, absurdities, purporting to be the work of spirits, which appear to every sensible human being at once degrading and mischievous. They would be ludicrous were they not so disgusting. Of late they have fallen on spiritualism in a plentiful shower. I select a few which appear to me the worst.

Towards the end of 1875 a man was executed in England for a cold and cowardly murder. The execution had hardly taken place before a medium announced the coming of the estimable being in question to control her. This, however, was not enough. It seemed good that a worthy and venerable name, respected by spiritualists as that of an early and courageous supporter of our cause, should be dragged into contact with the name of the homicide. Accordingly a self-styled Judge Edmonds was introduced as his sponsor in the spirit-world. The following edifying extract from a " spiritual " journal describes the results of the first " control " :—

" I was receiving a communication from a spirit-friend, through Mrs. ——, when the utterance of the medium was impeded and her face assumed the fixed appearance of a corpse. Her companion was much alarmed, but knowing that she was in good hands I waited the result with interest. Soon the medium's hands were used to manipulate her neck and chest, and she gasped convulsively for breath. At a signal I approached the medium, and also made some passes over the region of the neck and throat. The spirit now indicated, in reply to questions, that he had met with a violent termination to physical life, and further indicated that he was '————.' The animation now somewhat returned to the medium's face, and looking upwards the spirit said that he beheld his mother, but at such a distance from him that there was no communication between them. He complained of the intense cold and darkness of his situation. I spoke to him encouragingly, and the influence which he derived from our sphere somewhat subdued his despair and reconciled him to existence. He relinquished control with thanks for what had been done for him.

"'Judge Edmonds' now spoke in a hearty, friendly manner, stating that he had brought the spirit there, knowing that his effort to aid him would be seconded, and thanking me for the assistance I had rendered. He said '———' was an intelligent and mediumistic spirit, and would in time become very useful in the work of human progress. His personal condition was not due to grossness, but to moral influences, from which he would rapidly emerge after that interview. . . . ."

"The conversation was at last rather abruptly terminated, as the ·'Judge' stated he had exhausted so much power in bringing '———' that he had none left whereby to enable him to express his views, but he promised further intercourse on a more suitable occasion."

Whether the further intercourse did or did not take place I have not been able to discover. Some months later, however, a lengthy communication was published which purported to have been received from the same assassin. Looking at the various facts of the case, I think I am justified in calling it one of the most revolting things ever seen in print.

Our murderer commences by remarking that when the drop fell he "seemed to rise above the fog and smoke of London into some brighter and purer atmosphere." He goes on to tell us that many things have become plain to him which were dim and obscure before. "I would endeavour, for the instruction and benefit of my fellow-countrymen,"· says he, "to make known my mature conclusions and convictions as to the murder, and my own execution for it."

The first conclusion he arrives at is that he committed the deed in question. "I confess the murder. I confess that, driven to the last extreme of difficulty by the importunities of the poor girl, I was led to shoot her. This I confess—and it is with the deepest sorrow that I confess it."

Scarcely has he said this before it appears to him too sweeping. The world may be led to entertain the absurd idea that he repents. Repent, indeed! of such a trifle as deliberately taking the life of a fellow-creature. The spirit energetically hastens to prevent the notion, or dissipate it if it be already formed. "My sorrow is, in another than the ordinary sense, 'the sorrow that maketh not ashamed,' for I am educated enough, and have thought enough to see clearly that, granting the previous chain of inevitable events, *I could not have done otherwise; that I was and am, as all men are, the victim of imperious, invincible law, working on for ever towards pitiless and unseen ends.* But, though I am at one with the philosophers and deep, hard thinkers of modern times, so far—though I am relieved by this strong assurance of the imperishable necessity of things from the tumult of wild reasonless remorse which assails the thoughtless and the vulgar—though I now, speaking in a larger, clearer atmosphere than that of the Old Bailey, and before judges other than poor pompous Cockburn, and eyes other than those of the leering, jeering, heartless and brainless spectators of my trial—withdraw, to some extent, that last confused and partial confession, wrung from me by bitter mental and physical agony, and the well-meant prayers and entreaties of the chaplain and my friends, while, on the other hand, confessing my complete guilt (as the term goes) in reference to the murder, more fully than I did therein—though I feel and do all this keenly and unwaveringly, I am, notwithstanding, placed at last (as all men will one day be placed) on a platform of lucid thought sufficiently high to enable me to experience *the most heartfelt sorrow for my sad offence,* while at the same time possessing *the pure calm of an absolute certainty that that crime, in the essential nature of things, could never have been avoided, and that I was but an instrument in the rigid hands of undeviating fate.*"

One hardly knows how to deal with such mischievous nonsense. What could lead this orator to talk of "deep, hard thinkers?" There is little trace of deep thought in the tangled web of foolishness displayed above. He tells us that he was "the victim of imperious law, an instrument in the iron hands of undeviating fate." Then he expresses "the most heartfelt sorrow for his sad offence." What should lead an instrument to express sorrow? Does the gun express sorrow to its employer for the number it kills? However, his sorrow "is the sorrow that maketh not ashamed." This is equivalent to telling us, "I feel no remorse for the crime I committed." Nor does he. "I am relieved by this strong assurance of the imperishable necessity of things from the tumult of wild, reasonless remorse which assails the vulgar." It seems strange that this contradictory, illogical materialism should have been admitted to the pages of a spiritual journal.

What did he think of in the hour immediately preceding death ? Was there any dim horror of meeting his victim haunting him ? Listen ! "I thought of" (the murdered woman) "too, but not with such marked sadness, as I expected to meet her soon, and go through many comforting explanations." Are we really requested to believe that at such a time such a man could have a thought like this ?

This strange being read the various London newspapers containing accounts of his execution ! "By-the-bye, it was stated in one paper that when I approached the scaffold my hair was seen to be carefully combed. This is true." And, further on, he remarks concerning "the two swift glances which the reporters told you I took towards the spectators."

It is not surprising that he should be thoroughly dissatisfied with his fate. "Capital punishment was, in my case, and is in nearly all modern cases, a profoundly barbarous and pernicious blunder. . . . . I rejoice to think that my case will be looked back upon in history as one of the crucial cases which helped materially to disclose to the nation the utter folly of the whole thing, and so for ever to put an end to it." Would to heaven one could for ever put an end to pseudo-spirit-communications such as this !

The above assassin does not stand alone in his theories and teachings. John Wilkes Booth is reported to have manifested to a certain American circle. The remorse that besets him can be sufficiently judged of from his communication. "I, and Lincoln," he remarked, "often have a cosy chat up here. We agree that it was just as well I shot him. You see, it was set down in the order of things for me to do it, and I don't see why I should be blamed for accomplishing my destiny. The world was all the better for it."

The world is not much the better for such communications as these. Were they generally accepted among spiritualists, spiritualism would be the greatest curse which could befall mankind. They are by no means, however, to be regarded as doctrines germane to our cause. Only a few crack-brained and perverse-minded enthusiasts promulgate such nauseous folly, and only a few vicious and silly listeners are attracted by it. The wickedness of the belief equals its stupidity. Picture a world from which all sense of moral responsibility has been withdrawn, and in which all crime is dismissed with the one remark, "Destiny." Such fatalism resembles that of the wild enthusiast who maintains that "once in Christ" he can sin no more. Indeed, it goes further. Maniacal Christians assert only that for the elect crime is impossible. The fanatics I am dealing with dismiss crime altogether from their idea of the universe. A man, they teach, is no more blamable for alternating good with evil than the night is blamable for succeeding the day. Humanity is simply a machine, and free-will a delusion. Contemplating such a scheme of creation as this, one is driven to remark that—

> " If it be true indeed,
> The vicious have a comfortable creed."

It is one, at least, which few ordinary men and women will envy any person the possession of. I protest, however, with my whole heart, against the saddling of such earthly trash on spirits.

A less revolting absurdity, but one equally baseless, is that which puts forward mediums as a race of inferior saviours to whom heavily-laden spirits may come, and find relief. One of these gifted beings describes in the *Spiritualist*, June 5th, 1874, "a singular experience with a spirit calling himself an Egyptian :"—

" He looked," she tells us, " a tall, dark spirit, wearing robes, his eyes glittering, his countenance sullenly serious ; except when he indulged in mocking laughter, which he frequently did. I had much mental, or perhaps I might say voiceless, conversation with him, in which the attitude I bore towards him was one of considerate regard and pity. I spoke to him reasoningly, even affectionately. No doubt my feelings were inspired. I will not dwell upon the different arguments I used, inspired by my guides, to induce him to change his manner of life, and seek to rise. But I felt after a time he was moved. He relented, drew nearer to me, and seemed to regard me with a deep interest. He seemed to search me, and at length a humbled, grateful, softened feeling appeared to be creeping over him, which he sullenly refused to yield to entirely. I knew it was the loving sphere of my dear guides, as well as the feelings they gave me towards him, which were gradually influencing him.

. . . . . "My whole soul from the first had been filled with an earnest, pitying desire to help him. Just at this moment, as if carried beyond himself, he wrote energetically, 'Dear, dear woman, I thank you much—I love you !'

"I shrank at this, but continued :—

" '*I am glad you love me, Thoth ; it will do you good. But I want you to love my guide.*'

" ' I do love your guide.'

" ' *Do you know him ? do you see him ?* '

" ' I do know him ; I see him.'

" ' *He will help you, Thoth, if you wish to rise out of your present state, and will try to do so.*'

" ' I will try.'

" ' I am glad, Thoth. You give me great happiness. I am sure you see that I am most anxious for your good.' "

Hereon the spirit proceeds to inform the medium that he intends making a confession.

"I have been in this world," he tells her, "upwards of three thousand years of your time. I have not progressed, because I was of a dark nature by choice. I loved evil. . . . . I am a stubborn one. It is not easy to change a nature that for three thousand years has grown wrong."

Yet the " dear, dear woman " accomplishes that change in about the space of three days !

"*I repent,*" writes the spirit. " You know not what it is to wring these words from me. I mean it ; it is beginning ! A hell will I endure, if needful. At last the spark has been fired. The voice of love, which I have resisted all these ages, at last I have heeded. I am to become an angel then ! And you have touched me in the right place. *You are Thoth's saviour !* "

There are persons who accept all this, but who cannot accept a belief in Christ. They denounce the claims of the Gospel. It does not, however, appear startling to them that a few minutes of such conversation as is given above should dissipate the darkness of three thousand years. The cheering belief of spiritualists is that the ministering spirits of light are eternally busied in urging to better things their suffering and erring brethren. Yet thirty centuries, and all the hosts of Heaven had made no impression on Thoth. And this medium subdued him with an hour's talk! Surely she would be invaluable as a visitress to those penal establishments whose unfortunate inmates sit fast bound in wickedness and iron. If a sinner of three thousand years' standing can be cured by her in so short a time, she would assuredly make sharp work of pickpockets of ten years' experience, or burglars of twenty.

The communications attributed to spirits are, the reader will perceive, sometimes ludicrous in their absurdity, sometimes revolting. A few "messages," however, contain teachings whose soundness is past question. Of this class is the "Essay on Wisdom," which tells us that "Wisdom is what is wise. Wisdom is not folly, and folly is not wisdom. Wisdom is not selfishness, and selfishness is not wisdom. Wisdom is not evil, and evil is not wisdom. All is not wisdom; all is not folly." The caution with which this inspired being philosophises is particularly commendable.

Some are more daring in their utterances. Thus we have a spirit who unlooses you the Gordian knot of planetary life; "familiar as his (earthly) garter." His chosen medium gives the benefit of this scientifically-minded being's experiences in a small pamphlet of inestimable value. On Jupiter, it seems, glass is the one necessity of a comfortable existence. The dead are cased in glass, and placed as ornaments in the houses of the living. The said houses are themselves constructed of glass (stones being, presumably, never thrown in the planet). "Lemena," the spirit tells us, is the name by which these rows of Crystal Palaces are known. We hear also of a mysterious kind of sacrament which, about once in seven years, is rolled through the glass cities on a glass car.

x 2

The dwellers in these cities, and partakers of the said sacrament, are from seven to eight feet high. As household pets they have a useful race of parrots, which vary in height from two to three feet. A visitor to any of the glass houses of Jupiter invariably finds " a parrot sitting behind the door, *knitting night-caps.*"

These interesting discoveries have been paralleled by other mediums and other spirits. There is a " sphere " where the elevated portion of the inhabitants feast monotonously on pork and beans. What the " vulgar herd " are enforced to content themselves with, our informant saith not. Another spirit dictates particulars respecting life in a certain planet—Mercury, if my memory serves me rightly. The production best adapted to the soil and climate of that world is, it appears, the rice-plant. It is no longer, however, a " plant." Favourable influences, and agricultural skill, have united to render it, like Wordsworth's philosopher, " a self-sufficient all-in-all." It grows, we are told, to a height exceeding that of an English oak. The *Mercurial* being who desires to enjoy in perfection *otium cum dignitate* must invest, when young, in a rice-swamp. He selects a particular individual among the gigantic stalks which have become his property. Then, like the Jack of beanstalk fame, he proceeds to exercise his climbing capabilities. Arrived at the gigantic and cauliflower-like head of the plant, he contrives to burrow out an abode for himself. There, after the fashion of a rat in a Cheshire cheese, he remains till food is exhausted, and his house seems ready to fall about his ears. His last rice-pudding duly honoured, he decides on making tracks for " fresh stalks and dinners new.". Surely it is to a Hindoo spirit that we owe this remarkable dream.

These " spirit-teachings " are not always content with being simply absurd or astonishing. A fervid re-incarnationist, and devoted disciple of Allan Kardec, has given to the world a volume (" Le Flambeau du Spiritisme ") whose blasphemous folly is hardly to be matched by any publication in any language. There is not a page of the work but must excite the heartiest disgust in the mind of any ordinary person. Yet to read it without laughter is impossible. The lisping French in which it is written seems that of a child six years old. The " spirit-authors," however, are represented as being no less personages than the twelve Apostles of Christianity. We are gravely assured that at various periods they dictated this incomparable production to the person who has caused a few copies to be published. The subject is the life of Christ. The mixture of ribaldry, insanity, and absurdity is almost incredible. One of the Apostles favours us with particulars regarding the every-day doings of the Twelve. " We always took a small boy with us to clean our shoes. The Master liked us all to look well, and he was very particular that our shoes should be nicely blacked." The ordinary attire of Christ consisted of a flowing robe, and " bright blue boots." On one occasion He was reviled as an impostor. The incident is thus described :— " How can you call me an impostor ? " said the Master, turning round. " Don't you see my curly yellow hair, and my nice blue boots ? Would I have such things, do you think, if I were an impostor ? "

An apostle gives various " facts " respecting a journey to Jerusalem. " We were very poor, and we sold little pamphlets of the life and doings of Jesus to bring us in money. We made great haste to get to Jerusalem, for fear that the newspapers should get hold of our coming, and announce it." Lest my readers should doubt their eyes, I hasten to assure them that this is an exact translation of the passage in question.

Arrived in Jerusalem, matters become even worse. The eleven other apostles are discontented that Judas should carry the bag, " as he was always a very loose sort of character." " The Master," after a supper, " joins in a round dance with his Apostles and Mary Magdalene." Various incidents follow which I dare not even hint at, and then comes the trial before Pilate. It was a very cold day. The Apostles, we are told, remonstrated with the governor for leaving Christ to sit on the stone of the pavement, and, bringing in rushes, strewed them there. Then, turning to Pilate, they hoped he would not take offence at what had been done. Let our " spirit-author " relate the sequel :—" Oh, that's all right," said the governor; "I have no objection to that. But, mind you," he continued, turning to Christ, *"none of your miracles here." ! !*

And this book was published to advance the doctrine of re-incarnation! It must be confessed, indeed, that every re-incarnationist possessing a spark of sense expressed disgust on its appearance. For there are parts which it is simply impossible to quote. Such a tissue of folly and blasphemy was surely woven from the brain of a madman. And there are *three hundred pages* of the nauseous stuff.

Other works almost equally astounding have proceeded from the pens of re-incarnationists. I do not, however, design to notice them here. Let me direct the reader's attention to a pleasanter theme—the nobleness of the mission which a particular spirit is sent on earth to fulfil. His appearance is quite in keeping with the grandeur of his task, and the purity of his mind. A mediumistic beholder thus describes him :—

"A radiant figure stood in our midst directly in front of me ; . . . . his face more beautiful than I had ever seen it, with a spirit delicacy and beauty unsurpassable ; the regular features wearing an expression of God-like majesty, the eyes shining like stars, and the flesh almost transparently luminous. But, brighter than all, shone the cross, formed of long rays of light, brilliant as the sun ; behind which John's figure, clothed in radiant white, seemed almost to disappear and be lost ; although shining brightly itself, it appeared as if it would be refined away into the very brightness of life, and yet the noble face, with the long black hair and beard, and beaming eyes, was intensely vivid. The sight was ravishing, and filled me with such delight that it was some little time before I could be brought down to the more ordinary stage of writing, under control, the following explanation given by John King of the Cross of Light in A.'s picture :—

"'It means the purity of my mission. I bear a cross in coming to earth, because I endure a good deal for you all, and my cross is pure and white, because my work is pure and good ; and I bear my cross upon my face, as it were, because it is a Divine mission, in which I find my glory—the glory of an angel. Therefore the cross is luminous. I love my work for its good and use, and upon the cross's arms I lightly rest my upraised hands to indicate that love. It is no burthen upon my shoulders, but, borne before me, becomes the insignia, or badge of my office in the spirit world, and is my support, consolation, joy, and uplifter; for by it my soul makes its progress into higher states of purity through the love of that humanity for which I work, to aid in uplifting mortal man to a knowledge of spirit life.'"

Sublime !

> " How pure in heart, and sound in head,
> With what divine affections bold,
> Must be the man whose thoughts must hold
> An hour's communion with *such* dead !"

This devoted missionary desires to be known to man by the humble *alias* of " John King." On earth he was evil and famous. Now, it is at once his duty and his pleasure to do good to his fellow-men. He is the reprover of the sinful, and the comforter of the sad. His is a divine mission, and in it he finds his glory, " the glory of an angel."

Imagine the sanctity of the atmosphere which surrounds this spirit. Imagine the reverent awe with which all present listen to the words of wisdom that he communicates. Imagine his

> " Voiceless prayer,
> Soft rebukes, in blessings ended,
> Breathing from his lips of air."

And then imagine him throwing a sofa-cushion at the head of a sceptic. Imagine him looking beamingly on, whilst his subordinate, " Peter," pulls the noses of those present in the circle, and beats people about the head with pasteboard tubes. Imagine him rubbing a paper tube over an inquirer's cranium, and remarking, " This is hair-brushing by machinery." Imagine him, whilst in " materialized " form, presiding over a tea-party of enthusiastic old women, " seizing the tea-pot in the usual way, and pouring out to each a second cup."

Such is the " Divine mission in which he finds his glory." He enlivens it occasionally by a little of what some spiritualists consider (Heaven save the mark !) " facetiousness." " I'll tell you what," he remarked to one gentleman, " you ought to find spiritualism a jolly thing. I'm jolly enough. Look here now! I'll sing you a song of my own composition :—

> " I wish I had a bird
> I would stick it on a spit " (and so on *ad nauseam*).

" Have you not," he asked on another occasion, " have you not seen the swift-running tide, Bending with violence the firm gutter-side ? " Over which question, no doubt, the recipient ruminated perplexedly.

" Regular baths, and a bottle of Guinness's stout every day after dinner," John considers efficacious in bringing about a fit tone of mind for inquiring into spiritualism. His own ideas on the subject are not always so lofty as when he " loved his work for its good and use," and found it his "support, consolation, joy, and uplifter." " Look here, H——," he remarked on one occasion, " I've been put to do this work of convincing mortals for a certain number of years, to work out my own salvation, and, as I have to do it, I think it's as well to make myself jolly over it." " He then," says Mr. H——, " began to whistle in a devil-may-care kind of way." Such is the fashion in which John King " makes his progress to higher states of purity."

I have already called attention to the select nature of the spirit-band which favours Italy with its presence. The " bright, particular star" of that band has, however, departed from an ungrateful earth. Our planet is no longer illuminated with the glory of the Archangel Gabriel. Once Naples was his chosen mundane residence, but he has been forced to shake the dust of that city from his celestial shoes. The events which led to the departure of so distinguished a visitor were, some years back, narrated by the London *Echo*, as follows :—

" A M. Valente, of Naples, has just been condemned by the Correctional Court of that city to six months' imprisonment for 'spiritistic' swindling. This Valente, formerly an officer in the service of his Bourbonic Majesty, was, says a Naples correspondent, the spiritual medium of a small but select gathering. Valente, when in his state of ecstatic coma, was favoured by visits from no less a person than the Archangel Gabriel, a dignitary whose celestial functions do not, it seems, afford him the means of making both ends meet, for the burden of his song was still that he wanted money, and the money was always forthcoming, and delivered to Valente for transmission to the Archangel, or to be applied as he might direct. In this way Valente became by degrees the cashier of the society, and, incredible as it may appear, its richest, softest, and most fervent adept, one Agillo Braga, suffered himself to be stripped by degrees of all his worldly possessions, being, however, duly rewarded for his self-denial by the receipt of an archangelic diploma, conferring upon him the dignity of Nuntius or Grand Master of the little community. Valente had the keys of the money-chest, and when poor Braga wanted a pocket-comb or twopence to replenish his snuff-box, he had to prefer his request in writing for presentation to the Archangel. But, while in the heyday of his prosperity, our Valente fell a victim to the passion that rules the court, the cottage, and the camp. In an evil hour for him a widow lady, one Geronimo Merici, in age somewhere upon the confines of gorgeous summer and mellow autumn, was admitted among the members of the society. She was a widow of recent date, and all her thoughts were set upon one object, to be put in communication with the spirit of her departed lord. The Archangel was willing to arrange the matter upon the payment of certain stipulated fees, and at last, thanks to the liberality of the widow and to the intercession of Valente, it was settled that the visitor from the spirit world should appear on a certain night in the lady's chamber, borrowing for the nonce the terrestrial semblance of Valente himself. Enthralled Valente, in this thou reckonedst without thy host! The widow hesitated, suspected, and finally declined to receive her visitor except in a purely ghostly and immaterial shape. Valente, finding her inflexible on this point, dropped upon his knees, confessed his imposture and the intensity of his passion, and offered his hand and his 'rich booty' to the charming widow, on condition of her helping him to make a clean sweep of what remained in the pockets of the spiritist community. Another and a worse mistake. The lady betrayed him to Braga, who after a severe internal struggle opened his feeble mind to conviction, and applied for a legal remedy. The trial, which occupied some days, was full of amusing incidents. The Court, in consideration of the temptation afforded to the swindler by the colossal stupidity of his dupes, took a lenient view of the case, and sent Valente to prison for six months with the addition of a fine of 51 francs."

Colossal as the stupidity of these dupes appears, we can almost equal it in England. If we have not archangels demanding money for themselves, we have inferior spirits begging jewels for their mediums. Italian spiritualists fully recognise the importance of the fact. "Where were you," an enthusiast dating from the very city where "Gabriel" dwelt, asks his opponent, "when, in the twenty-seventh year of Modern Spiritualism, in the City of London, there took place one of the most memorable *séances* since the beginning of our era?" The only memorable points about the affair in question are the false doctrines and the strange demands saddled on the spirit said to have manifested. As to the *séance* itself, it simply ranks with many hundred other assumed "materializations." There were no tests, and infinite credulity and enthusiasm.

Numerous appearances of the supposed spirit had previously occurred. This, however, was to be his final visit. About a fortnight before he had announced himself as the recipient of a call to a higher sphere. "Just the night previous we had had his most perfect embodiment, when he had appeared to us with a 'John King' lamp fully lighting up his face; moving about the room with life-like activity and ease, and conversing with us with all the freedom of one in the body, like ourselves. . . . To hear that we were never again to have such a pleasure was like another death, and fell upon our hearts desolately, like an ice-cold freezing rain, killing the tender buds of our newly-awakened hopes."

A special *séance* was arranged in order that this very material form "might bid a final adieu to his brother." The meeting came off.

"The spirit," we are told,* "materialized with unusual power and strength. He brought with him his lamp, and remained with us in continued conversation for the space of an hour, if not more. His voice was stronger than ever before, and he spoke in the most solemn and impressive manner regarding certain things he wished his brother to do for him. Kneeling before us upon one knee, with one hand held by each of us, as we leaned over to draw as near to his face as possible, after earnestly enjoining upon his brother the accomplishment of a certain duty which he wished him to undertake, he made a most startling disclosure to us.

"'I have to inform you,' he said, 'that my last life on earth was a re-incarnation. In a former existence I was a Persian prince, and lived upon this earth some hundreds of years before Christ. In that life I was possessed of a quantity of beautiful and valuable jewels. Strange to say, I have become aware of the existence of some of those jewels in this

* *Medium,* August 13th, 1875.

very city of London. They are diamonds of the purest water and bril-
liancy, and, moreover, they are charmed stones, and would therefore be
of inestimable value to their possessor. I wish you, my dear brother, to
become the purchaser of those stones. They are for sale in a shop in this
city. I know exactly where they are, and the price—a price much
beneath their value. They are five diamonds set in a hoop ring. I can
give you the name of the man, the name of the street, and the price.
But you must lose no time, for there is a person after them, and if you
do not purchase them by eleven o'clock to-morrow you will lose them.'
He then gave us the most circumstantial directions as to the situation
of the shop, the name of the jeweller, the exact position of the ring
in the window, even going so far as to tell me what omnibus I was to
take to bring me to the spot, that his brother might have my aid in
finding the ring." (Well-informed "spirit!") " 'Be sure,' he continued,
' that you say nothing to the man as to the value of those stones—a
value beyond all earthly price, indeed, for they have been endowed with
rare virtues of a spiritual kind. This ring, my dear brother, I wish
you to present to our medium, as a testimonial of my gratitude to him
for his services in enabling me to materialize for you. It has given me
a very great pleasure to return in this way and confer with you again.
You cannot estimate as we spirits can all that a medium gives up for
these materializations, and I feel I cannot thank him enough for giving
so unselfishly his life and strength to our service. Therefore I wish him
to have the ring. It will be a talisman to protect him; it will increase
his power as a medium, and with that ring he can never want for a
friend; indeed, he will bear a species of charmed life. I wish you also
to make a formal public presentation to him of that ring.' . . . Much
more was said. Our adieux, tender and affecting, as to one we were
never to see again (except clairvoyantly), were made, and again and
again were his solemn injunctions repeated. We were only permitted
to kiss his hands, his head he would not allow us to touch, and our dear
brother, rising to a standing position, slowly retired from us, repeating
in solemn tones 'Farewell! Farewell!'"

Whatever disclosures the " spirit " may have made, there is one
little point on which the earth-dwellers concerned in this affair are
jealously reticent, viz., *the address of the jeweller from whom the ring
was bought.* I maintain, as I have all along maintained, that, could
this be procured, the " flashing gems," far from having existed in
their present form for over two thousand years, would turn out
to have been cut in Amsterdam. I have asked for the said address,
and it has been refused to me. I can see nothing to alter, there-

fore, in the following letter. It first appeared in the *Medium* of August 20th, 1875 :—

"MY DEAR MR. BURNS,

"Ill as I am, and unfit for letter-writing, it is my duty to make a protest against such a statement as the one by C—— W——, contained in the *Medium* of August 13th. As a spiritualist, it is a duty to say that I have never, in the whole course of my experience, met with a spirit teaching the old doctrine of Pythagoras, lately re-advocated by Allan Kardec, who, more than twenty years ago, tried to convert me to his way of thinking (I say this advisedly, for he told me it was 'by a careful study of the Pythagorean philosophy that he had been induced to believe as he did'). This absurd statement first teaches re-incarnation and then makes a present of precious stones (the which, I will wager, can be traced to having been cut in Amsterdam). If spirits, after being twice incarnated, have still nothing better to do than to give 'the exact position of the ring in the window,' and 'the omnibus' one is to take, then God help us, for it is a fearful absurdity, to say the least of it. Mrs. —— is a most decided sensitive, and I can well account for her seeing the imagined dual presence. Let her be in a clairvoyant state away from the influences at that time surrounding her, and she will then explain the whole affair. We must use the reason God has endowed us with, and such statements are only calculated to do great harm to the cause we advocate. It is almost as bad as one case in my knowledge, where the person very solemnly declares that a spirit visits her frequently, and she gives details so disgusting that they are unfit to be heard. All this is the effect of a poor diseased brain. Spiritualism has its great and glorious uses, but this side of the question shows its abuses to the very fullest extent, and it behoves us to lift up a warning cry. I know nothing of Mr. ——, but if I were in his place I would sooner wear a serpent's poisoned fang than a ring given under such circumstances.—Yours,

"D. D. HOME."

["It is well known," adds the Editor of the *Medium*, "that Mr. Home has received from various crowned heads, as well as persons of note, most valuable presents of jewels, but they were never given or suggested by spirit-intercourse. This was the ground taken by Mrs. Lyon, but she *signally failed to prove it,* as all the Chancery records can testify."]

The ring was presented ; the presumed spirit glowingly " explained " the whole business in the following speech :—

"Friends ! In this work of repeated materializations of my spirit-form, which I have just completed—because, being called to a higher plane of existence, I shall never more clothe my spirit in temporary flesh at your circles—I was commissioned by a band of higher spirits. . . . One of the fields of progress opened to me was working for the good of mankind at your circles. We always raise ourselves when we try to raise others. I have to reveal to you, my friends, that I, the spirit who has (*sic*) so frequently materialized here in London, was a re-incarnation upon this planet. In my. former existence I was a Prince of Persia ; my name was *Hafiz Hemishpha*, and I was a descendant of *Kai Kaoos*, called *Cyaxares I.* by the Greeks, of the *Kaianian* dynasty, some six hundred or seven hundred years before Christ. I was not aware of this previous existence when first I entered the spirit-world after my last re-incarnation, but by degrees I entered into the knowledge that I had doubtless lived before. Within the last few days of your time, since, indeed, I received my call to ascend from the earth-sphere, I have lived through an eternity, and entered upon an eternity's stores of knowledge, principally by the aid of a wondrously wise Jewish spirit, or, more properly speaking, angel, who has revealed to me, and awakened within me, the recollection of former states of existence. They are mostly undeserving of being dwelt upon here ; the principal one, and the one before the last, having been that of a Persian Prince. Rising from that life to a state of great happiness in the spirit-world, the desire for re-incarnation was not awakened within me for a long period. At length my soul felt its necessities ; the planet had advanced to a state of higher civilisation. I required new experiences of mortal life, new conquests over self and the grossness of matter. This also is too vast a subject to dwell upon this evening. Who can read the secrets of a man's life ? who can judge of the unfoldments of a soul, and its necessities ? Only God, and that soul itself. I descended to earth again, and was born of American parents. What I gained by that existence I know somewhat, but not yet all, for the soul of man is wonderful, and himself is revealed to himself in the slow progress of eternities. This revelation is a part of the work I was deputed to perform by the higher spirits, of whom I have spoken.

*　　*　　*　　*　　*　　*

"And now, friends, I can never more materialize. It is not permitted to those who have left the earth-sphere and risen higher, unless by a particular dispensation for purposes of usefulness to mankind. Indeed it is too painful a process for the more etherealized inhabitants of our world to resume those garments of heaviness, as I have so frequently done. And now I will say, Farewell ! My blessings upon you all ! "

Was ever " spirit-communication " more painfully ridiculous ? As taught by *Hafiz Hemishpha*, alias ———, alias ———, the doctrine of re-incarnation defines the next world to be a place where souls deteriorate. Some twenty-five hundred years ago

Hafiz rose from earth "to a state of great happiness in the spirit-world." After a long period of blissful idleness he became awakened to the embarrassments of his position. Earth had got ahead of heaven. The life which we "incarnated" beings sometimes find so weary and so trying is, it seems, contemplated by the "pilgrims of eternity" with envy and reverence. To "satisfy the necessities of the soul,"—to make "new conquests over self," poor humanity must, perforce, skip backwards and forwards between this sphere and the next; like the harlequin of a pantomime through his trap-doors. Certainly, this is a cheerful creed. Not only are we to lose all trace of identity, but all prospect of happiness. What is the use of any longer singing that—

> "We are going on a journey
> To a bright and better land?"

The "better land" is, we find, a savage desert, from which souls come back to civilise themselves; much as an Asiatic might journey to England for the instruction his native land could not afford him. The angel-spirits who guard us are lower in the scale of humanity than those whom they guard. Such are the chimæras to which this shadow, with the string of aliases, would have us bow.

I need not linger over the subordinate absurdities of his speech. Any little slips are atoned for by the fine concluding outburst :— "What I gained by that existence I know somewhat, but not yet all, for the soul of man is wonderful, and himself is revealed to himself in the slow progress of eternities." Certainly, this is at once lucid and sublime ; the spirit meant, no doubt, that it takes "eternities" (whatever they may be) for a man to find out how many other persons he has been. As I entertain no hope of ever making such a discovery myself, I quite agree with him that, in the majority of cases, the "progress" of such a revelation will probably be slow.

The whole thing has a most unpleasant look. Is this bad example of enticing enthusiastic believers to bestow presents of much value on mediums the only example which "Hafiz" can set?

Is the absurd doctrine of the spirit-world being a place where everybody progresses backward the only doctrine he can teach? If so, it is indeed well that he has retired for ever from among us, and can "shuffle on the garments of heaviness," in the way of "materialization," no more. Pity though that he, or his Jewish friend, cannot " clothe the spirit in temporary flesh " just once, in order to tell us *the name of the jeweller from whom the ring was bought,* and settle for ever the question as to Amsterdam.

There are rank harvests of absurdities which I have not space to notice. They crop up with the suddenness of the prophet's gourd, flourish for an hour, and as rapidly decay. It would be, however, an utter misnomer to term these wretched follies and wickednesses spiritual. They are no more part of our movement than the polype is part of the body to which it clings. Insanity sometimes snatches at spiritualism as a theatre whereon to display its antics. Needy sharpers turn their attention to it as a thing out of which money may be made. It is such lamentable occurrences that make the cause unpopular. The sacredness attaching to a communion with the departed renders even the thought of the follies and vices with which it is sought to sully that communion infinitely maddening. How painful then is it for reasoning men and women that day after day absurdity should succeed absurdity, and fraud, fraud! " Still they come." The climax of stupidity which disgusts us one week, is next week set off by its natural anti-climax of wickedness. Where there is so much of brainless enthusiasm, there are certain to be persons ready to prey on that enthusiasm. The damaging absurdities treated of in this chapter lead smoothly up to the still more damaging exposures treated of in the next. Thus spiritualism is placed between two fires. On the one side she is assailed by false friends, on the other by a hostile world. I have no fears regarding the result; but the circumstances of the battle are hard.

What, for instance, can be done with such spiritualists as a Frenchman of rank, and advanced in years, whom I will style Count Z——. During the winter of 1875 I heard that he had been boasting much of a wonderful medium just discovered by him, and that he was holding *séances* with the said " medium "—a gentleman of position and good family ; but who, to my certain knowledge, even then professed atheistical doctrines. It seemed to me, therefore, that this mediumship must be pretended. I said so ; and a dozen parrot-voices at once took up the old cry, *Home is jealous!* In fact, so much had I to endure regarding my jealousy, that I determined to obtain convincing proof of the true nature of the mediumship in question. Meeting Count Z——'s " medium " in the south of France, I interrogated this gentleman on the subject, and obtained from him a certificate, of which the following is a literal translation :—

"9th May, 1876.

" In response to the desire of Mr. Home, I declare by the present document that I have never assumed to myself the power of mediumship. On the contrary, I have always, in those private gatherings where people *amuse themselves* with spiritualism, and where it was sought to make me pass for a medium, denied being one ; and have pointed out that, as I am a materialist and atheist, it is impossible for me to believe in the doctrine of spiritualism.

"FREDERIC S——."

I sincerely wish the writer of the foregoing a speedy deliverance from that atheism on which he at present appears to pride himself. Certainly, however, the " spiritualism ! " in which he became mixed up was unlikely to conduce to his conversion to a belief in immortality. His own account of it ran as follows :—

" I told Count Z—— that the whole of the ' manifestations ' he witnessed in my presence resulted from trickery ; that I was not a medium, and had no belief in the thing. ' Yes, yes,' he replied, ' I am sure you are quite honest in thinking you do these things yourself ; but I know better. It is not you, it is the dear spirits, and you are the most wonderful medium in the world.'

" When all this began in Paris, I and some ladies who stayed in the same hotel, often went into fits of laughter over the Count's credulity. Whilst sitting together, one of us would slily pat his head, or pinch his knee. ' Dear, dear spirits,' he used then to remark, ' please do that again.' Often, too, the person nearest the fireplace would watch for an opportunity of giving the sheet-iron screen a kick. Always, when this occurred, the Count would cry out in an exultant voice, ' The dear spirits are imitating thunder.'

" Not only have I told him that these things were done by ourselves
for amusement, but I explained to him how they were done. ' Those
flowers,' I would say, ' which were found on the table last evening
I took from my pocket and placed there.' Still the only reply was, ' Yes,
yes, you think so, but I know better—it was the dear spirits, and you
are the most wonderful medium in the world.' Nothing could convince
him otherwise."

Yet Count Z——, and such as he, are considered *supporters* of
our cause !

Let me with a few words dismiss the people and the actions that
remain to be noticed under the present heading. There are
" spirits " who, after having been " reduced to the necessity of self-
release " from earth, return there to make such communications
on behalf of " materializing mediums " as the following :—

" Far be it from me to keep silence, while the belittled and
belittling croakers are doing their best to disgrace and ruin a band
of as true and noble workers as the age may boast of—and all for
the reason that their sphere of faith, sight and action, is quite
above and beyond the reach of microscopic eyes. Do these penny-
a-liner journalists, and all the obscene birds for whom they cater,
know, or think, what they are about ? I believe not. If they
did, they would see themselves murderers of the most malignant
type. They foul the finest character, and then, with long faces
and solemn drawl, pronounce it carrion ; and they taint with their
own foul breath the purest air." After this the spirit remarks that
" were his voice clothed with thunder, and his pen armed with
lightning, he would make all these skin-deep exposers shiver in
their shoes." Manner and matter continue equally beneath contempt through the whole communication. I dismiss it, therefore,
and proceed. What I have given may serve as a specimen of the
trash which the most degraded of spirits must blush to find
attributed to them.

England, and still more, America, have numbers of such adver-
tisements as " Madame ——, Clairvoyant on business, love,
marriage, &c. ; " " Professor ——, Astrologer, may be consulted
daily, on the events of life ; " " Madame ——, magnetic treatment,

love powder, one dollar." These setters of traps for the foolish can in no sense be considered spiritualists. The only spiritualists blamable in the matter are the one or two editors who admit such announcements to their columns.

I have already shown what perplexing "people from the other world" are occasionally reported as presenting themselves at *séances*. One or two other examples deserve to be touched upon. The following extract introduces and explains itself :—

"A monthly has appeared in Boston—a novelty in the periodical world, for it professes to be edited by a disembodied essence. Nor are the spirits content with the spiritual direction, for with an eye to the loaves and fishes, one of the number acts as business manager; though the visible person, the amanuensis and publisher, is a physician. There are angels of darkness as well as angels of light, and in the *Voice* a strict impartiality is preserved, for one of the first angels who has come upon the stage is James Fisk, jun., and now we learn the secret of that speculator's life. He describes himself as having been, when in the flesh, the unconscious medium of a band of reckless spirits who manipulated him as a skilful pianist handles the keys of his instrument, and he could no more help doing what he did than could the instrument discoursing the music of the operator. The editor in chief has that spiritual penetration into the weakness of humanity which tells him that if he would interest the public he has to give voice to the bad spirits rather than to the good. People want to know what the rascal did and why he did it; and Fisk, jun., was a good subject to commence with."

Possibly those beings were members of the above band, who, at a particular *séance*, caused the instruments to play by "spirit-power" their favourite tunes; the said tunes being "Durang's Hornpipe," "Yankee Doodle," and "The Devil's Dream." We hear, too, of a spirit whose "ordinary manifestations are working a sewing-machine, and playing upon a mouth-organ." Another celestial visitor "wrote a letter, directed the envelope, put a stamp on it, and mailed it in the iron-box at the street corner." But such stories are numberless.

They have as little of the spiritual in them as have the wild dances in which "mediums" (generally females) indulge under the influence of imaginary Indian controls. Like these, they are the products of over-heated and morbid minds. I believe that of the many and glaring absurdities upon which I have commented in this chapter, not a twentieth are attributable to spirits. It is not to drink tea and play on the fiddle, to give blasphemously-ludicrous communications regarding Christ and His Apostles, to strut about in skull-caps and yellow boots, to beat people over the head with paper tubes, to throw cushions at sceptics, to hold up murderers as respectable objects, to tell people by what omnibuses to travel, or to describe the next world as a place where humanity deteriorates, that departed spirits return to earth. Their mission is great—their opportunities are limited. What time have they then to waste in idiotisms, of which a school-boy would feel ashamed? Let us refer such to their proper sources; some to insanity, some to knavery—many to this world, few to the next. Let us recognise the height and the holiness of phenomena which show how

> " The beloved, the true-hearted,
> Revisit earth once more."

Let us put from our path all which savours of folly or of fraud, and press, steadfastly and undeviatingly, towards the truth. It is full time that the errors I have been treating of should " die among their worshippers."

CHAPTER VIII.

TRICKERY AND ITS EXPOSURE.

"THE most severe blows that spiritualism has sustained have been those aimed by unprincipled and avaricious mediums, who, when the manifestations failed to come as freely as the circumstances required, practised imposition to supply the deficiency." So wrote Mrs. Hardinge, in her "History of American Spiritualism," and every year fresh evidence testifies to the truth of her assertion. Wherever the facts of spiritualism have penetrated lying imitations of those facts may be found. The producers of such imitations are of both sexes, and every age. They may be divided into three classes. The first is made up of persons who, while really possessing medial gifts, will, when much tempted, resort to fraud. The second section consists also of mediums; but of mediums who, being utterly unprincipled, rather prefer to cheat than not, and who will, therefore, lie and deceive even when no encouragement exists to do so. It is with such that the most frequent and damaging exposures occur. They are seldom expert conjurors. The difference between the false and the genuine phenomena witnessed in their presence is too glaring to escape the notice of any person not blinded by folly and credulity. Soon, therefore, some decisive exposure crushes the faith of all but the insanely enthusiastic, and Othello, in the shape of the untrustworthy medium, finds his occupation for the present gone. It is true that he almost invariably resumes it when the storm caused by his rascality has blown over; but meanwhile our cause has received another wound, and the broad and easy way of fraudulent mediumship has been once more demonstrated to lead to destruction.

In the third class I place those charlatans who, though destitute of any real claim to the title of medium, find it profitable to impose themselves as such upon credulous spiritualists, and to imitate the phenomena by methods of more or less dexterity. This species of impostor usually varies the monotony of his frauds by showing how those frauds were accomplished, and, after disgracing the spiritualists who have received him as an exponent of truth, disgraces the unbelievers who receive him as an exposer —not of spiritualism, but of his own villainy.

The first class alone affords any very tangible hope of reformation. Mediums who have been led by temptation into ill-doing are, in general, capable of repentance and amendment. It is true that even these persons well deserve both rebuke and punishment; but their guilt is not so glaring as that of the swindler who habitually mixes genuine mediumship with fraud, or as that of the still more degraded creature who makes a lying pretence to gifts of which he possesses not the slightest share. Against these last it behoves every honest searcher for the Truth to be up in arms, and to strike with no hesitating blows.

For the evil has assumed gigantic proportions. Dishonesty, and its natural ally, darkness, are arrayed against honesty and light. It is with pleasure that I see signs of an organized attempt to abate the nuisance. Certain enlightened spiritualists, and a few (alas! a very few) select mediums who, in the consciousness of their honesty, can afford to encounter fearlessly investigation and the sun, are banding themselves against those "children of the night" who affect carefully-darkened rooms, and *séances* from which all opportunity for enquiry is excluded. To aid in this noble work of putting down imposture and destroying abuses my present volume is written. The battle in which I and other honest men are engaged will no doubt be hard. Experience has organized trickery to a high pitch, and the dupes are many. Let lovers of the truth, then, do their best to cast light upon the dark places with which spiritualism is cursed. I have acquired from various sources information regarding the fashion in which certain impositions are accomplished, and I proceed now to detail the *modus operandi* of such fraudulent manifestations. Once awakened to these cheats, investigators may with ease guard against their being practised.

The form of fraud at present most in vogue is the simulation of a spirit form or forms. To be successful such simulation usually requires the aid of a room so ill-lighted as practically not to be lighted at all, a "cabinet" into which the medium withdraws from the view of the sitters, and various other "conditions" of the sort. When the rules of such *séances* are broken, awkward discoveries occur. Sometimes the light is turned up suddenly, and the medium revealed in his or her "spirit-dress." Sometimes the "spirit-form" is grasped, and found to be none other than the medium. But should all go well, the credulous are often highly gratified. Figures appear, clad in flowing and parti-coloured robes. The display of drapery seems most extensive. Yet when the medium is searched at the conclusion of the *séance* no trace of this drapery can be found. Whence has it vanished? The believers present reply that "the spirits have de-materialized it." The sceptics probably examine the cabinet, and are astonished that they find nothing. Perhaps the evidence I have to offer may throw a little light on the concealments sometimes practised. Let me commence with the narrative of an unimpeachable witness, my friend Serjeant Cox :—

"DEAR HOME,

"I am satisfied that a large amount of fraud has been and still is practised. Some of it is, doubtless, deliberately planned and executed. But some is, I think, done while the medium is in a state of somnambulism, and therefore unconscious. As all familiar with the phenomena of somnambulism are aware, the patient acts to perfection any part suggested to his mind, but wholly without self-perception at the time, or memory afterwards. But such an explanation serves only to acquit the medium of deliberate imposture ; it does not affect the fact that the apparent manifestation is not genuine.

"The great field for fraud has been offered by the production and presentation of alleged spirit-forms. All the conditions imposed are as if carefully designed to favour fraud if contemplated, and even to tempt to imposture. The curtain is guarded at either end by some friend. The light is so dim that the features cannot be distinctly seen. A white veil thrown over the body from head to foot is put on and off in a moment, and gives the necessary aspect of spirituality. A white band round head and chin at once conceals the hair, and disguises the face. A considerable interval precedes the appearance—just such as would be necessary for the preparations. A like interval succeeds the retirement of the form before the cabinet is permitted to be opened for inspection. This just enables the ordinary dress to be restored. While the preparation is going on behind the curtain the company are always vehemently exhorted to sing. This would conveniently conceal any sounds of motion in the act of preparation. The spectators are made to promise not to peep behind the curtain, and not to grasp the form. They are solemnly told that if they were to seize the spirit they would kill the medium. This is an obvious contrivance to deter the onlookers from doing anything that might cause detection. It is not true. Several spirits have been grasped, and no medium has died of it ; although in each case the supposed spirit was found to be the medium. That the detected medium was somewhat disturbed in health after such a public detection and exposure is not at all surprising. Every one of the five* mediums who have been actually seized in the act of personating a spirit is now alive and well. There need be no fear for the consequences in putting them to the proof.

" But I have learned how the trick is done. I have seen the description of it given by a medium to another medium who desired instruction. The letter was in her own handwriting, and the whole style of it showed it to be genuine.

" She informs her friend that she comes to the *séance* prepared with a dress that is easily taken off with a little practice. She says it may be done in two or three minutes. She wears two shifts (probably for warmth). She brings a muslin veil of thin material (she gives its name, which I forget). It is carried *in her drawers !* It can be compressed into a small space, although when spread it covers the whole person. A pocket-handkerchief pinned round the head keeps back the hair. She states that she takes off all her clothes except the two shifts, and is covered by the veil. The gown is spread carefully upon the sofa over the pillows. In this array she comes out. She makes very merry with the spiritualists whom she thus gulls, and her language about them is anything but complimentary.

" This explains the whole business. The question so often asked before was—where the robe could be carried ? It could not be contained in the bosom or in a sleeve. Nobody seems to have thought of the drawers.

" But it will be asked how we can explain the fact that some persons

---

* Since this was written by Serjeant Cox the numbers have greatly increased. I doubt if there remain now five " materializing mediums " who have *not* been seized in the act of personating a spirit-form.

have been permitted to go behind the curtain when the form was before it, and have asserted that they saw or felt the medium. I am sorry to say the confession to which I have referred states without reserve that these persons knew that it was a trick, and lent themselves to it. I am, of course, reluctant to adopt such a formidable conclusion, although the so-called 'confession' was a confidential communication from one medium to another medium who had asked to be instructed how the trick was done. I prefer to adopt the more charitable conclusion that they were imposed upon, and it is easy to find how this was likely to be. The same suspicious precautions against detection were always adopted. The favoured visitor was an assured friend ; one who, if detecting trickery, would shrink from proclaiming the cheat. But one was permitted to enter. A light was not allowed. There was nothing but the 'darkness visible' of the lowered gas rays struggling through the curtain. I have noted that no one of them ever was permitted to see the face of the medium. It was always 'wrapped in a shawl.' The hands felt a dress, and imagination did the rest. The revealer of the secret above referred to says that, when she took off her gown to put on the white veil, she spread it upon the sofa or chair with pillows or something under it, and this is what they felt and took for her body !

" The lesson to be learned from all this is, that no phenomena should be accepted as genuine that are not produced under strict test conditions. Investigators should be satisfied with no evidence short of the very best that the circumstances will permit. Why accept the doubtful testimony of one person groping in the dark when the question can be decided beyond dispute once and for ever by the simple process of drawing back the curtain while the alleged spirit is outside, and showing the medium inside to the eyes of all present ? Where absolute tests are refused upon any pretence whatever, and where the conditions imposed are just such as are calculated to prevent detection if trickery is designed, we are bound to look with the utmost suspicion upon all that is done, and, indeed, we should refuse to take part in any such unsatisfactory experiment.

" In the investigations in which you so kindly assisted me there was nothing of this precaution and mystery. You sat with me anywhere, at any time ; in my garden, and in my house ; by day and by night ; but always, with one memorable exception, in full light. You objected to no tests ; on the contrary you invited them. I was permitted the full use of all my senses. The experiments were made in every form ingenuity could devise, and you were as desirous to learn the truth and the meaning of it as I was. You sat alone with me, and things were done which, if four confederates had been present, their united efforts could not have accomplished. Sometimes there were phenomena, sometimes there were none. When they occurred they were often such as no human hand could have produced without the machinery of the Egyptian Hall. But these were in my own drawing-room, and library, and garden, where no mechanism was possible. In this manner it was that I arrived at the conviction—opposed to all my prejudices and pre-conceptions—that there are forces about us of some kind, having both power and intelligence, but imperceptible to our senses, except under some imperfectly-known conditions. I did not, and with subsequent extended inquiry I cannot now arrive at the conclusion you have come to, that these invisible agents are spirits of the dead. On the contrary, the more I see of their operations the more I am satisfied that they are *not* such. The solution that most presses upon my mind is that this earth is inhabited by another race of beings, imperceptible to us in normal conditions, probably our inferiors in intelligence, by whom what we witness is done. If it be not this the agent is the spirit of the medium more or less separated from the body. But whosoever that agent may be, the medium through which it is enabled to manifest its presence, and to operate upon molecular matter is the Psychic (that is to say, the soul) force of the assembled sitters. But now that the pheno-mena themselves, or some of them, have received general acceptation as facts in nature, it may be hoped that many observant minds will investi-gate them with a view to learn their precise nature and extent, as produced under absolute tests. Then we shall be in a position to inquire what they are, whence they come, and to what they point.

" It is a great misfortune to the cause of truth that your state of health prevents you from contributing to this great work. But I hope still that your recovery may enable you to do something more to promote honest investigation into the greatest and the grandest mystery that could engage the human mind.

" Yours most truly,

" EDWARD WM. COX.

" *March 8th*, 1876."

The narrative above given bears a peculiar value from the circumstances attending the confession of imposture to which it refers. The exposure meets even the conditions demanded by those enthusiasts who would rather libel a hundred spirits than believe one medium guilty of trickery. " The only conclusive proof that a medium has perpetrated fraud," a philosopher of this class writes, " is proof that the physical organs of the medium acted in obedience to his or her own will and purposes at the time when the seemingly fraudulent acts were performed." This proof the " medium " in question herself affords.

But there are numerous other methods by which impostors of this class may successfully conceal the materials necessary for the deceptions they contemplate. To expose those methods the *Religio-Philosophical Journal* some months back printed an article which the *Spiritual Scientist* promptly copied. The course of these serials was in honourable contrast to that uniformly pursued in such cases by the least creditable of American spiritual publications—the miscalled *Banner of Light.*

" All the material for bogus mediums to imitate spirit manifestations can be so concealed about the person," the *Religio-Philosophical Journal* points out, " that the most rigid search may fail to find it. A common silk neck-tie tied around the neck under a paper collar, will conceal a gauze-like texture, white silk handkerchief, &c., sufficient to produce your sister, mother, or daughter, as the case may be. The expert, too, can conceal them in the lining of his pants, vest, and coat, with threads so arranged as to deceive the eye, and in a moment's time they can be taken out and replaced. Those who have never investigated this matter would be astonished at the small space required for the articles necessary to materialize a first-class spirit.

" Tissue paper also acts an important part in bogus materialization, it being used on the head and various parts of the body to complete the dress. It can be concealed in the lining of the vest, coat, or pants, and you may search for it but will not discover it easily. It is an easy matter to deceive three out of five who attend these bogus circles. . . . . Some people like to be humbugged ; they take pleasure in it, as those did who attended G——'s circles in New York."

Such are the means by which pretended materializations are accomplished. The ordinary mode, it will be perceived, is to conceal the " spirit-dress " about the person. This, however, is not invariably done. A notorious trickster, whose exposure and punishment occupied some time back the attention of the spiritual press, was accustomed to operate in a different, but equally elaborate manner. On entering the *séance*-room his first request would be to see the " cabinet." " Cabinets " usually contain a chair or a couch. The " medium," after a glance round, seated himself on one or the other, and commenced a desultory conversation. Presently he rose, with some such remark as "It's growing late ; we had better begin the *séance*. First," he would add, " let me retire with some of you and be searched." The retirement and the search duly took place. Nothing could be found. The medium re-entered the recess, and the circle was arranged. Presently the curtains parted, and a much-draped form appeared. Was it possible that all this could be accomplished by imposture? After various of these exhibitions had taken place, the question received an answer in the affirmative. That conversation in the cabinet had a deeper significance than might at first have been supposed. Whilst the impostor's tongue was busy his hands were by no means idle. The light talk he started was merely intended to afford him time for concealing somewhere about the couch or chair on which he sat a tight little parcel containing his "spiritual trappings." This accomplished, he was, of course, perfectly ready to be searched. The most rigid investigation of his dress was vain. Shawl, veil, &c., all of the lightest and thinnest fabric, awaited him in the cabinet.

The number of such swindlers is astonishing. The harm they do our cause is incalculable. As the *Spiritual Scientist* well remarks, in its leading article of March 16th, 1876 :—

"It would be interesting information if any one could tell us of the number of darkened parlours on back streets that are the scenes of frequent *séances* for spirit-materializations. A description of the 'wonders' that are here witnessed would be highly interesting to credulous people, but a careful investigator would ask more particularly concerning the conditions under which these manifestations are obtained. A few words tell the story. They are patterned one after the other—the original being the one that has been the longest in the business. The individual who would attend these shows is obliged to make a personal application ; he is met at the door by a strong specimen of the *genus homo* who informs the humble applicant that his petition will be referred to John King. (John King is the familiar name for the manager on the spiritual (?) side of the show.) The answer of John King will be given to the applicant if he will call at some future day ; and, it may be said, the success or failure of his attempt to enter the charmed circle will depend greatly on his personal appearance, and the number of ladies that are to be present on any evening he may wish to gain admittance. These shrewd managers have found that the best conditions are obtained when the ladies are in a large majority, and the number of men present does not exceed one to every two friends of the operator or medium. If an applicant should gain admittance he is assigned to a seat in the back part of the room ; the front seats are reserved for the tried friends of the spirits. The sitters in the front row hold in their hands, and are held by, a stout wire bent in the form of a horseshoe ; at either end sits a friend of the medium. The medium enters ; she may be a small, slender, middle-aged lady, or one that is fat, fair, and forty. She takes her seat in one corner of the room or behind a pair of folding doors in a dark ante-room, or in an alcove furnished with doors opening into closets. Any of these are favourite conditions ; and a correct type of several of the apartments of 'materializing mediums' in this city. A curtain now conceals the medium from view. Someone starts a discordant noise which is called singing ; and the manifestations commence. The standard stock in trade consists of the materialized forms of an old woman and a sailor ; these you will find at nearly all the *séances.* In addition each medium has an attendant 'materialization,' whose office corresponds to that of the *genus homo* in the circle—he keeps things in order.

"The above is no exaggeration ; it is a faithful representation of the majority of the so-called materializing *séances* in Boston. Woe to the man or woman who ventures to suggest other conditions ; he or she is sent to Coventry immediately, and is ever afterwards looked upon as a suspected person whose presence endangers the success of the enterprise. There are enough patrons from among the weak and credulous phenomenalists—people who will recognise in the materialized old lady the shade of their grandmother. Better make a few dollars and be safe, than endeavour to make a few more by admitting sensible people who will readily discover the imposture.

"It is a reflection upon spiritualists that test mediums who are always able to give some message, token of love or valuable information from the dwellers-in-the-spirit, should be neglected for a darkened room where forms that may be inflated masks, or something else, flit in an uncertain light at intervals for about an hour and then vanish, leaving the minds of the audience in a state of unpleasant uncertainty. It is no wonder that spiritualism languishes, and that its adherents are unable to support a single course of lectures in Boston. The causes are apparent." *

An article like the above is at once honourable to the writer, and cheering reading for all lovers of the truth. It contrasts well with the shameless and foolish manner in which other spiritual papers (so-called) have sometimes attempted to explain away the most glaring fraud.

"Light" was the dying cry of Goethe. "Light" should be the

---

* Every true spiritualist owes a debt of gratitude to E. Gerry Brown, editor of the *Spiritual Scientist* (18, Exchange Street, Boston), for an honest and manly stand against the impostures of the day. Unlike spiritual editors (so-called) who "run their papers for money," he has preferred to run his excellently conducted journal in the interests of pure spiritualism. May the success he has deserved crown his efforts.

demand of every spiritualist; it is the single test necessary, and it is a test which can and must be given. By no other means are scientific enquirers to be convinced. Where there is darkness there, is the possibility of imposture, and the certainty of suspicion. In the light no loop-hole remains at which either doubt or deception can creep in. The sceptic has opportunity for the use of all his senses. Should he refrain from applying the fullest tests, the responsibility is with himself.

In October, 1875, I wrote as follows to my friend, Dr. Sexton : "I implore you to advocate the suppression of dark *séances*. Every form of phenomena ever occurring through me at the few dark *séances* has been repeated over and over again in the light, and I now deeply regret ever having had other than light *séances*. What we used to term darkness consisted in extinguishing the lights in the room, and then we used to open the. curtains, or, in very many instances, have the fire lit (which, if burning, was never extinguished), when we could with perfect ease distinguish the outline form of every one in the room."

Of another class are the dark *séances* at present held. Sometimes the pitchiest blackness prevails ; instruments rattle discordantly ; voices bellow through paste-board speaking-trumpets. Persons in various parts of the circle are touched or patted by supposed spirit-hands. Nothing is offered that can in the slightest degree be considered as approaching a test ; the imposture is often of the baldest and grossest character ; yet the " medium " is congratulated on the success of the *séance*, and credulous fools are happy. Perhaps the sitting is for " materialized " forms or faces ; in such case the proceedings are regulated according to the character of the persons present. Should these be unknown, or regarded as possessing a fair share of common sense, nothing goes well. The circle is described as " inharmonious." The cabinet is jealously guarded. A distressingly tiny ray of light having been introduced " materialization " takes place. All that the persons present can perceive is something white ; shape or features there are none. Such is a faithful portraiture of perhaps the majority of sittings for " spirit forms."

If, however, the audience consist of known and enthusiastic dupes, conditions are at once pronounced favourable. A larger share of light is admitted; the form appears, and moves about among the believers present. Their credulity rapidly mounts to fever-heat. Patched and darned shawls are discovered to be "robes of delicate texture and surpassing gorgeousness." A kerchief twisted round the head becomes an unmistakable turban; false whiskers and Indian ink produce "a manly and noble face;" rouge and pearl-powder, in conjunction with a skilfully-arranged head-dress, are sufficient to send the credulous into raptures over "the vision of surpassing loveliness" presented. The familiarity of the spiritual visitors is charming; they have been known to seat themselves at the tea-table, and make a hearty meal, "enquiring jocularly whether the muffins were well buttered." They have mixed stiff glasses of grog for the sitters, and, not satisfied with mixing, have themselves partaken of them. In such little re-unions tests are never employed or mentioned. Not a dupe present but would rather perish than take a suspicious peep into the cabinet whilst the "materialized form" is out, and moving about the room. Not a hand among the party but would rather be cut off at the wrist than grasp, in detective fashion, the said form. The spirit is in every respect at home, and may walk in and out of the cabinet as he or she lists.

The darkness of the *séance* is thus proportioned to the sense of the sitters. Where scepticism is rife the most jealous precautions are adopted lest that scepticism should behold too much. To meet this condition of things various supposed tests have been devised. If they be of an inconvenient nature, the impostor, whom they are intended to unmask, usually declines them. If, on the other hand, they appear such as may be eluded by jugglery or confederacy, they are at once adopted. The most common method is to fasten the medium by some means; often painful, and, almost without exception, imperfect. Such tyings are simply useless. There is no binding submitted to by mediums to which professional con-jurors have not also been submitted. The feats accomplished by Maskelyne and Cooke in the way of releasing themselves from

ropes, &c., have been such as to drive certain credulous spiritualists
to a most audaciously foolish expedient. These persons had again
and again put forth jubilant utterances respecting the rapidity with
which pet mediums of theirs were released by " the spirits " from
their bonds. Maskelyne and his partner proceeded to yield to a
tying at least equally severe; they released themselves with even
greater rapidity. Some enthusiast, jealous for the reputation of
his favourite medium, lighted on what was considered a happy
idea. The amazed jugglers were gravely congratulated on the
excellence of their physical mediumship; denial availed nothing.
In spite of all they could say, print, or prove, rabid credulity continues to rejoice over them as " the best of living mediums for the
production of strong physical manifestations." Surely spiritualism
must have fallen very low, when a couple of professed conjurors
are hailed by spiritualists themselves as its best exponents.

I need not dwell long on the point which at present occupies
me. Almost every sensible person knows how easy it is for hands
of a particular shape to release themselves from even the most
complicated fastenings. The trick is seen every day in the street.
The larger the wrist, and the narrower and slenderer the hand and
fingers, the better suited are they for this particular form of jugglery. Other aids are also forthcoming; at times the tying may
be done by a confederate. In this case the fastenings are so
arranged that, whilst apparently tight, they become at once
relaxed on a particular drawing-together of the body, and may be
slipped off with the utmost celerity. Uneasy workings of the
hands and arms are often employed to derange the operation of
fastening, and may succeed to a greater or less extent. In fact
the tyer and the person whom he binds are placed in a position
somewhat analogous to that of armoured ships and heavy
ordnance. Whatever thickness of plating the Admiralty may
adopt, a gun is presently devised to pierce it. However cunning
the knots employed, jugglery speedily contrives some mode of
overcoming them.

Handcuffs have often been advocated; they are as useless as
other forms of binding. Keys may be carried in the mouth, and

cuffs opened. When, however, the hands are of the shape I have indicated they slip from such fastenings as readily as from ropes. The following extract details the result of a test of this kind. I take it from the columns of the *Religio-Philosophical Journal* :—

"After this Mrs. —— went back into the cabinet, and closed the door; in a minute the door was opened, and we found an iron ring upon her arm (all done by spirits, without removing the cuffs, of course). At this point one of our party asked to take the handcuffs; the request was granted. A stripe of black paint was made inside each cuff (entirely unknown to the medium), and they were carefully replaced on her wrists, so that the paint was not seen by her; then the door was closed, and she proceeded to put the ring on again. When the door was opened all were able to see paint on the medium's hand, from the wrist to the ends of her fingers. This closed our investigation and the performance; all were well taken aback by the discoveries made."

Exposures, indeed, occur with great frequency. One of the most decisive was reported in the L—— *Daily Courier* of Christmas Day, 1875. After describing the "manifestations" witnessed at previous *séances* the journal thus narrates how matters went on the evening of the catastrophe :—

"Several gentlemen had formed a very strong opinion as to the utter imposture of the whole thing. There was but one chance remaining, and that not availing the spiritualists would have achieved a great result. However, the fates were in other directions, and the spirits themselves must have played against the spirit-conjurors. The eager circle gathered together for a final manifestation. The stock-broker was there, hoping, probably, to get some augury that would help in his speculations; the master-carterish individual was also present, drinking in the wonders with great relish; there, likewise, was the dapper young gentleman who had come in his gymnasium dress, labouring, it is believed, under the delusion that the gigantic spirit was that of a noted ex-pugilist named King, with whom he was eager to have a 'set-to.'"

Near the cabinet sat "a strange man in spectacles." The

occurrences of the evening were varied: " Poor Old Joe," and the " John Brown chorus," brought forth " a baby-spirit, believed by the sceptical to be nothing more than a newspaper sheet." Shortly afterwards a trifling discord marred the harmony of the circle. " Some one having tampered with the gas, manifestations were interrupted for a time, but harmony was restored, and the baby-spirit came again." The end, however, approached. " A tube of paper was handed out, presumably by a spirit, and then came the form of 'John King;' first, as if tentatively selecting his position, and eventually appearing full at the aperture in the curtains. This was the critical moment; the strange man in spectacles bounded like a panther towards the cabinet, and made a grab at the spirit. The white drapery, or whatever it might be, was seen to shrivel up, as if vanishing away. 'Gracious heavens! could it be a spirit after all ?' was the question that overwhelmed for a moment the minds of the spectators. But, at the same instant, the brawny person, already described as a master-carter, sprang from his seat, and seized the medium on the left-hand side; so that the hapless impostor was thus caught in a vice. A howl of terror escaped his lips, and, as the gas was being turned on, another conspirator against the spirits made a dash at the cabinet and brought the whole arrangement to the floor. The medium was handed out, and disclosed a most ludicrous make-up. About two yards of tarlatan was arranged round his head turban-wise, and covered him in front down to the thighs. On each leg was tied loose a newspaper—both copies of the *Daily Courier*—and these served as the spirit's pantaloons; in the full blaze of the gaslight they reminded one of the top-boots of a brigand in a melo-drama. When dragged into the light the terrified medium was still clutching one end of the strip of tarlatan, doubtless thinking his spirit-dress would be some protection to him against the violence of the sceptics."

It would appear that the irate meeting resorted to personal chastisement of the impostor. Such punishment was regretable, as being wasted on a decided unworthy object. Indeed, the harm done to the few persons directly concerned was trifling compared

with the harm done to a great cause. In all cases like the foregoing the press pounces on the exposure with journalistic alacrity.
The newspaper happy enough to get the first grasp at the facts of
the case, draws up a strong account, interspersed with sneering
comments on the folly of people who are " dupes to spiritualism."
This account is bandied about from one organ of public opinion to
another. Persons who were on the threshold of being persuaded
to investigate read the narrative, and draw back. The incredulity of sceptics is immensely strengthened. Meanwhile the
enthusiasm of the more rabid among spiritualists becomes roused,
and it is ten to one that some such rush into print with blatant
" explanations " of imposture so palpable as to disgust all reasoning adherents to the cause. The fraudulent medium may not have
a word to offer in his own behalf, but misguided admirers will
assuredly utter a thousand.

I have remarked upon the readiness with which journals outside
the movement call attention to flaws in the fabric of spiritualism,
and the length at which they dilate on the said flaws. It would
be well had the press honesty enough to be equally unreserved
regarding the long array of tested facts which are the pillars of
our cause, and which spiritualists can render as reasons for their
belief. Perhaps it is the reluctance of adverse newspapers to
publish evidence in our favour that makes various spiritual
journals so slow to insert exposures of imposture. A narrative
has been sent me, with the names of seven witnesses appended,
which was refused publication by one of the journals in question.
Yet the trickery it refers to was of the most shameless sort, and
detection thorough and convincing. I quote from the letter in
question the description of the catastrophe :—

"We sat as usual at eight o'clock, commencing with a hymn from
the "Spiritual Lyre." 'James Lombard' was the first presentation,
who, after calling several of the sitters some very objectionable names,
retired to make way for the manifestation of John King. When this
gentleman was announced, he beckoned the sitters one by one, and
touched their hands and faces. My friend, Miss ——, having previously resolved on her course of action, requested to be touched on the
hand, and was touched accordingly. She then asked the spirit (?) to

be allowed to shake hands. The request was granted ; but she was told not to come too near, or she would melt him. She grasped the offered hand tightly, and lifted the curtain : the light (which at all the materialization *séances* was allowed to burn dimly) was immediately turned up, and Mr. R—— stood discovered, with one hand held by Miss ——, the other engaged in taking from his head and face a pair of false whiskers *à la* John King, and some white muslin which had served as a head-dress. Not even being entranced, he entreated the persons present not to expose him. . . . . When counselled by us to give over his nefarious practices, he replied that he should do no such thing. ' Did we think he was going to work while a living could be got so easily by this means ?' "

The above impostor, although he "had no intention of working" while a living could be obtained by trickery, appears no longer to find dishonesty a paying policy. The cheats he resorted to were so clumsy, and their exposure was so frequent, as to disgust even the most credulous of enthusiasts. It deserves to be remarked that he was the companion and pupil of the "medium" whose newspaper trappings and tarlatan turban were dragged into the light at L——.

More than one "materializing medium," indeed, has learned the tricks of his trade from the same personator of John King. Thus an ambitious teacher of—let us say—drawing, who advertised in a spiritual journal that he would give art-lessons in return for "development," was taken in hand by the person in question. The process appears to have been at once simple and easy. Eight days after its commencement the teacher of drawing burst forth on the world a full-blown " medium for materialization." His paraphernalia of " Punch and Judy box," darkened room, &c., were as excellently devised to prevent investigation as the most thorough-going enthusiast could desire. His guardian angels were numerous and select. Queens and princes, Jews and Persians, spirits a thousand years older than the advent of Christ, and others whose incarnation adorned our own century, group themselves gracefully around him. There is, however, just one perplexing peculiarity in the brilliant band. The medium has a slight defect in his speech, and every individual of the substantial " shoal of shades " who throng to his cabinet labours under identically the same defect. Strange! to say the least.

If such be the pupil, what of the master? He must be a decidedly highly favoured mortal who, from the superabundance of his spiritual gifts, can create a "fully-powered medium" in a space so short as eight days. Yet the reputation borne by this talented developer is, to put it mildly, unenviable. He appears to have been once on the point of making an engagement with a music-hall proprietor, under whose auspices he might expose, not spiritualism, but the gross frauds by which he had imposed on a portion of the adherents to that cause. It is certain that in the presence of various spiritualists he avowed the "phenomena" witnessed through him to have been the results of trickery, and it is certain, too, that he gave mock *séances* with the object of injuring one who had been most kind to him, and who is well known as an honest man, but whose mediumship this impostor wished to make appear of the same fraudulent type as his own. It is certain, finally, that the editor of a spiritual paper wrote and printed an article declaring the estimable being in question to be "according to his own confession a professional cheat, and quite willing to make a living by receiving money under false pretences." What is the value of "mediumship" developed at a source so foul? The aspirant after spiritual gifts who takes as hierophant a "professional cheat," need hardly be surprised if spiritualists acquainted with the character of the master look suspiciously on the disciple. That master has assuredly done his little utmost to injure the truth.

Perhaps he consoles himself for the more than tainting of his name by the reflection that he is but "one of a goodly company." The hardest trial which those who truly deserve the name of spiritualists are called on to endure is the constant outcome of accessions to the already long list of detected tricksters. Even as I pen these lines journals reach me with tidings of three additional "materializing" exposures; one in England, the others in the United States. All are connected with "cabinet manifestations," and all involve the personation of materialized forms by the medium. Of the first American imbroglio the *New York Times* opines as follows (August 23rd, 1876) :—

"It is pleasant to note that Mr. C——, of Rochester, has finally had the good sense to begin the task of investigating the materializing business in the only rational manner. Mrs. M——, a medium of extraordinary powers, undertook to exhibit a company of select and first-class ghosts to a Rochester audience a few nights since. Mrs. M—— was assisted by Mr. M——, who acted as master of ceremonies and introduced the ghosts with brief and complimentary biographical sketches. The medium was tied with the usual ropes in the usual cabinet, and the audience sang hymns, in accordance with Mr. M——'s request, doubtless in order to prevent the ghosts from cherishing any longing to permanently return to a world where people who can't sing are always ready to try to sing. After the spirit of Daniel Webster had thrust his head out of the window of the cabinet, and made the astonishing revelation that there was 'a Mr. Smith' in the audience, and that he rather thought he had met a Mr. Smith while in the body, the ghost of 'Sarah' walked out upon the platform, clad in white, materialized to the apparent extent of a hundred and fifty pounds. This was the moment for which Mr. C—— had waited. He leaped on the platform and seized Sarah in his arms. The ghost, regarding this as a liberty, shrieked loudly ; Mr. M—— caught up a chair and knocked the investigator down, and Sarah, escaping into the cabinet, was seen no more.

"There was, of course, a tremendous uproar. Mr. M—— loudly proposed to destroy Mr. C—— on the spot, as a villain who had laid his hand on a female ghost in other than a spirit of kindness. Mr. C—— argued that his destruction was unnecessary and undesirable ; and the audience was divided in opinion as to whether C—— or M—— was the person who stood in need of immediate destruction. The presence of mind of Daniel Webster happily restored order. That eminent ghost yelled out of the cabinet window that the medium would die if the audience 'didn't everlastingly sing something,' and some sympathetic spiritualist suddenly striking up that pathetic hymn beginning 'Tramp, tramp, tramp,' the audience joined in, and Mr. M—— postponed his bloody resolution.

"With the singing of the hymn the exhibition ended. Mrs. M—— was found in the cabinet still tightly bound, and with her face covered with blood, which, as Mr. M—— explained, was in some vague way the result of Sarah's hasty 'de-materialization' of herself. At any rate, no wound could be found upon her person, and though Mr. M——, with great liberality, offered to put a bullet through Mr. C——, or to provide him with an additional and obviously superfluous head, he finally decided that his first duty was to wash Mrs. M——, and to send Daniel Webster to inquire whether Sarah had sustained any serious injury."

The final scene of this eventful history I find to be "the preferring of charges against the husband of the pretended medium, his conviction, and sentence to a fine of twenty-five dollars, or three months in the county gaol."

The second materializer had much of method in his "mediumship." The town favoured with his presence was Rochester, N.Y., and his career, though short, seems to have been decidedly brilliant. Nemesis, in the shape of sceptical investigators, pursued him, however, and, at length, when ingenuity availed no longer, the affidavit of the entrapped "medium" made clear to whoever cared to read it the mystery of his shows. I extract the chief points of the document in question :—

"The first séance I held after it became known to the Rochester people that I was a medium," our penitent illusionist writes, "a gentleman from Chicago recognised his daughter Lizzie in me after I had covered my small moustache with a piece of flesh-coloured cloth, and reduced the size of my face with a shawl I had purposely hung up in the back of the cabinet. From this sitting my fame commenced to spread."

He procured a confederate. A secret closet was arranged in 'which this person could be hidden on séance occasions, and from which he came forth in the character of any spirit whose "materialization" the two worthies considered desirable. The entrance to this closet being undiscoverable, confederacy appeared impossible; and as the "medium" submitted to the severest tests, every "form" which glided into view of the audience was, to use his own words, "a staggerer for doubters."

In the day-time both spirit and medium rehearsed for the evening's performance. "My accomplice used false hair, wigs, beards, &c., and put flour on his hands to give a ghostly appearance. For baby faces we had a piece of black velveteen, with a small round hole cut out. This, placed over the face, gave the appearance of the tiny features of a babe."

The "medium," it would seem, sometimes did a little in the spirit way himself. "I had my accomplice paint me a couple of faces, the one a man's, the other that of a woman. I then proposed to have two apertures in the cabinet, one on each of the doors, which was done. On the night in question I entered the cabinet, and the singing and music commenced. I straightened out a piece of wire, attached one of the faces to it, rolled the mask up, poked it through the screen, and then unrolled it by turning the wire. I also had a piece of thick, dark, worsted cloth which I used as a beard for myself. . . . . So on this night two faces appeared at once, and almost threw the meeting into ecstasies."

Being at another time hard pressed (whether for time or disguises I don't know), the " spirit " merely held his coat-tails up to his chin, to form a pair of whiskers as he peered through the aperture. A presence of mind that, which, as Lord Dundreary (whose ghost was doubtless being presented) would say, "few impothtaws cwould imitwate."

But this genius no longer adorns the scene of his triumphs. "J——," says the *Spiritual Scientist*, "has left the city of Rochester, for obvious reasons." With a regret that the talents this pretended medium evidently possessed should have been wasted in such unworthy deceptions let us also pass on.

I had intended to describe at least one additional instance of detected fraud. In view of the present position of " materialization," however, this chapter is already sufficiently long. One can hardly take up a newspaper, whether English or American, without lighting on the history of some new exposure. I therefore confine myself to the notice of a point on which much misconception prevails.

Nothing can be more unjust than the often-repeated assertion that spiritualists, however honest, are, on discovering imposture, invariably disposed to hush it up; their reason being the harm which such histories, when made public, inflict on the cause. It is an indubitable fact that, of the many exposures of fraudulent materializing mediums recorded, the most noteworthy have been accomplished or aided by prominent spiritualists. I may point as an example to the case of Henry Gordon of New York. Let me add, however, that Gordon was assuredly, when I knew him, a genuine medium. Becoming surrounded by various of the enthusiastic *gobemouches* who care nothing for scientific investigation, but who insist on sensational phenomena, he was led to attempt the fraudulent practices which ended so fatally for him.

His exposers were spiritualists. So were the exposers of a medium* whose malpractices came to light in that very building where, a few weeks later, the gas, on being turned up, revealed the too thoroughly materialized John King of the tarlatan turban and newspaper wraps. A noticeable feature in the case is its resemblance to that of Henry Gordon. To my knowledge the person chiefly concerned was, in past years, possessed of genuine medial powers. The same class of enthusiasts who encircled Gordon came round this medium also, and, by their folly and voracious appetite for marvels, tempted him to ruin. He commenced to hold dark *séances;* allied himself to the ranks of rope-tiers and "cabinet mediums," and—behold the end!

Nothing is more astonishing to reasoning spiritualists than the gross imposture by which the credulous portion of their brethren are often deluded. Thus, we may read of a medium "still in the trance, walking about, and exhibiting the materialized spirit by the light of a candle held in his hand; calling up each one of the company in his turn, and subsequently, under the same control, and in a good light, seemingly picking up from the carpet a length of pink tarlatan, which visibly grew in his hands; materializing and de-materializing it in the open room as he advanced and receded before us; waving, twisting, and wreathing" (what a wealth of incomplete participles), "waving, twisting, and wreathing it as if in sport, and finally causing it to disappear in the air before our very eyes." And an American paper once described how "Mrs. —— asked the spirit whether she could disappear before the visitors as she had done on former occasions. To this interrogatory she made the same reply as she had to the other, and, surprising to relate, gradually faded away into thin air before us until not a vestige of her was to be seen."

* Since the above was written, at least three additional instances of discovered fraud have been put on record, where the discoverers were spiritualists.

Surprising indeed ! But to relate the simplicity of the means by which these wonderful results are attained will possibly be found more surprising still. The disappearance of the "spirit-form" is usually accomplished as follows :—

Behind the cabinet curtains stands the concealed form of the pretended medium. In his hand he has a length of some gossamer-like fabric, arranged to simulate a robe, and gathered at the top into something like the shape of a head, or surmounted by a mask. This puppet-like construction he cautiously advances through the opening of the cabinet until it is in view of the sitters. Let any reader attempt the process, and the completeness of the deception will amaze him. With lights down, the sitters at some distance from the cabinet, and expectation wrought to the highest pitch, this unsubstantial doll will have the closest resemblance to a human form. Should any very enthusiastic spiritualists be present, the spectator need not be surprised if two or three at once recognise a relative, and declare the form to be a materialized visitor from another world in spite of all the evidence to the contrary that can be offered them.

But we will suppose the fraudulent medium we were treating of keeps the "form" in sight for some little time. The company, at first sated by the marvel of its presence, find an appetite for new wonders growing on them. "Can the dear spirit," it is asked, "de-materialize before us?" The dim light is just sufficient to dimly reveal the dear spirit nodding assent. The figure commences to dwindle and fade. The drapery seems to dissipate into thin air. The head sinks down until it rests upon the ground. And then credulous old women tell us of "spirits who, losing power, sank into the floor up to the waist," or remark that "the head remained some time after the rest of the form was de-materialized." Let us see how such de-materialization is accomplished.

When the impostor has caused his puppet to nod assent to the request that it may fade away in sight of the company, he com-mences cautiously to draw towards him the lower extremity of the "spirit-robe," and at the same time lowers the upper part of the form towards the floor. His own person, it must be remembered, is wholly concealed. The figure dwindles and dwindles, and the awed company see it by degrees growing "beautifully less." At length the whole of the robe is within the cabinet. The mask, or gathered part which simulates the head, rests on the ground close to the entrance. These masks, be it observed, are constructed to inflate or shrink together, as may become necessary. Should one be employed, therefore, the "medium" has only to cause it to collapse. Should the cranium supplied to the "materialized form" consist of some gauzy fabric gathered into a bunch, he simply allows it to spread out on the floor, and then dexterously draws it towards him. In either case the deception is complete. The head appears to have suddenly crumbled into nothing. The audience are enthusiastic with delight and amazement.

"But," it will be remarked, "we read often of the materialized form and the medium appearing together; and appearing where no secret ingress to the cabinet could exist, and confederacy was an impossible thing. Is not such a *séance*, however suspicious the cabinet and other surroundings may be held, a triumphant proof of the reality of materialization? Can these occurrences be explained on the theory of fraud?"

Easily enough. The medium (so-called) is perhaps seated within the cabinet. The dummy which does duty as a materialized form he holds upright by his side; or may even thrust it forward to a position outside the curtains. And such puppets any impostor can, with slight practice, cause to bow, dance, and walk a step or two, in an exceedingly lifelike manner. Even should the performance be clumsy it matters little, unless some sceptical spiritualist or investigator have place among watchers. *Gobemouches* swallow whatever is offered to them, and strain neither at camels nor at gnats. I have myself sat as spectator at a *séance* where the faces displayed were simply so many masks presented before an aperture. I called the attention of a credulous spiritualist beside me to the empty and eyeless sockets. His reply came promptly, and with a certain triumph:—"The dear spirits have not had time to materialize the eyes." Is it surprising that cheats should be found to practise on folly like this?

To return to our materializing medium and his "forms." There are still at least two methods by which "spirit" and mortal may be made to appear at the same moment. The first trick is sufficiently exposed by the letter of Serjeant Cox. In the instance yet to be described the medium stands somewhat apart from the angel visitor. Both forms bow, advance, recede; go, in short, through the usual pantomime. A curtain, however, is between the two, and this conceals the outstretched arm by which the impostor is enabling his puppet to play its part in the deception. Such are the duplicated figures which adorn the materializing stage.

And the "tests" which are to prevent these deceptions! Truly fraudulent mediums must be astonished by the simplicity of the preventatives sometimes applied. Thus, in the case of a female, we are often informed that her dress was nailed to the floor. The usual very material forms appear. When the *séance* is announced to be at an end, the sitters enter the cabinet. Its occupant is found calmly seated in her chair. The dress is fastened as it was fastened at the commencement of the *séance*. Everybody feels secure. Should a report be issued, it concludes by stating that "whatever may be thought of the forms seen, they were not personations by the medium." Yet it is next to certain that they were. The occupant of the cabinet has simply unfastened her dress at the waist, and stepped out from it. Then the curtain rises on the usual John or Katie King.

Of ropes, handcuffs, &c., I have already given my opinion. To release himself from such bonds is part of the stock-in-trade of every third-rate conjuror.

Noise, however, is often caused during the process, and if heard might excite suspicion. The audience are therefore requested to sing. The worse the voices of those present, the more readily and loudly they comply. "Yes, we will gather at the river," makes night hideous, and effectually precludes the possibility of detection. Whilst the rest of the apartment is thus filled with a gush of most excruciating harmony, the cabinet becomes for the nonce a dressing-room. Possibly the medium is a woman. The doleful sounds without may strike on her ears, but the fair being heeds them not.

Like Jezebel she is tiring her head. A pocket-handkerchief or a simple strip of muslin bound round the face alters it so as to render recognition almost impossible in the dim light which is religiously preserved. Let the reader put this to the test. Pin together the window-curtains, and step behind them; pass around the face such a band as I have mentioned, and take care that the hair is concealed by it. A little cosmetic or rouge may be employed to heighten the effect. Now turn up the eyes in approved " dying-duck " fashion, and expose the face to those outside. The change from its ordinary expression will be startling. Half-darkness is, of course, desirable; but impostors arrayed in the manner described, have been known to expose themselves even to a strong light without detection.*

If the " spirit-form " displayed be masculine, some hair on the face is, of course, desirable ; and whiskers and moustaches may be cunningly concealed. One person confessed to me that he had carried them fastened in the hollow under his arm. So with the other paraphernalia of " materialization." The exceedingly fine india-rubber masks employed when it is desired to exhibit a variety of faces, females may hide in the gathers of their dress, or even in their hair. Indeed, should the audience be sufficiently enthusiastic, and countenances only on the programme, those countenances may be furnished by so simple a means as a few engravings. Though the likeness held up to the cabinet-aperture be that of a Wellington, one excited beholder will recognise in it his much-loved grandmother, and another dispute the claim by pronouncing it the face of her equally venerated aunt. I have witnessed these sad exhibitions, and know, therefore, of what I speak.

The duty performed in this and the succeeding chapter is not an agreeable one. Like all duties, however, it is necessary that it should be accomplished, and accomplished thoroughly. I have put my hand to the plough, and do not intend to turn back. I know well what awaits me. All who are interested in the upholding of such practices as I here seek to expose will join in a common howl of fury. Punch-puppets of " John Kings " will be made to

---

* Deformed hands and feet are sometimes given to " spirit-forms " by the simple process of bending back a few fingers or toes.

squeak out indignant anathemas from the depths of their jealously-guarded boxes. The mouths of *gobemouches* will open more widely than ever to emit reproaches on my conduct ; and shocked upholders of the " divine rights of mediums " will lift their hands in astonished horror. Let the storm exhaust itself. The consciousness of right is with me, and, as a medium and an honest man, I insist on being heard.

I say, then, that to the credulous enthusiasts whom I denounce do we owe the wave of imposture which at present threatens almost to obliterate the landmarks of spiritualism. I say that I will visit the kitchen of any such, and, should the scullery-maid be one degree removed from helpless idiocy, will teach her in a single hour to go through the usual repertory of dark *séance* tricks undetected by her masters. If I, however, afterwards inform those masters that the whole thing is imposture, the doors of that house will be immediately and for ever closed upon the utterer of such a calumny. The scullery-maid will be put forward by one party as an additional proof that "Home is jealous of mediums," and by the Occultists and Kardecists as conclusive testimony of my having been "bought over by the Jesuit party in the Church of Rome to injure spiritualism." I defy any one acquainted with the libels circulated respecting me in the past to pronounce the above picture overdrawn.

Let it not be thought that I pronounce what is known as spirit-materialization impossible. I firmly believe such a phenomenon to have occurred through the mediumship of others, and I know it to have occurred through my own. Through me, indeed, the first phases of this species of manifestation were witnessed. I allude to the years 1852, '53, and '54. Perhaps I may qualify this statement by saying that it is possible forms had been seen previously in the presence of the Fox girls ; but I am not aware that such was the case. *In every instance when these phenomena have occurred through my own mediumship no preparations were made, and I, as medium, was seated among the other persons present.* At the house of my friend, Mr. S. C. Hall, the first materialization which can be construed as involving the use of a curtain occurred. The figure was distinctly seen to appear above the curtain in question. Speedily curtains were the rage, and they have terminated in the " Punch and Judy shows " now in use. *But there are two prominent features of the said séance which its plagiarists fail to copy ; the first, that it was held in a well-lighted room : the other that I, as medium, was before the curtain, and in full sight of all present.* I need hardly point out how idly-useless in a case like this would have been the indignities of rope-tying, sewing in a sack, &c. When the materializing mediums of to-day " go and do likewise," I shall cease to denounce their *séances* as more or less cunningly-contrived vehicles of deception.

· Concerning genuine materialization, I need hardly remind my readers that the carefully-conducted experiences of Mr. Crookes with Miss Cook were repaid by evidence giving undeniable certainty of the phenomenon. Other mediums might be named through whom well-attested manifestations of the kind have occurred. Why, then, should we be stunned with the foolish outcries against light, and against tests, fulminated by rabid enthusiasts who would exclude investigation and admit falsehood ? Why should *séances* be converted into puppet-shows, where greedily-venal impostors instal themselves as the showmen ? Why should spiritualism be made more and more a mockery and a by-word, whose reproach is such that its best friends are compelled, despite themselves, to shrink sorrowfully from the subject ? Why should weak-minded dupes be permitted to arouse the derision of the outer world by follies which make every reasoning spiritualist blush ? Let those of us who love the truth be up and doing. When the last of darkséance mediums has abandoned his or her vocation in order to set up as a third-rate conjuror, and the last puppet-box, alias cabinet, is demolished, or preserved in some convenient place, as a gauge by which posterity may estimate the credulity of certain of their fathers—when this has been accomplished the golden day of our cause's triumph may be accounted at hand.

CHAPTER IX.

I HAVE never yet beheld anything which could cause me to accept the asserted phenomenon of matter passing through matter. The instances witnessed by me (and they have been many), in which this was said to have occurred, could one and all be explained by less far-fetched theories. I do not say that the phenomenon is impossible. All through my life I have been cordially of the opinion of Arago, that " he who pronounces the world 'impossible' outside the domain of pure mathematics is a bold man." I simply ask, and I think the demand reasonable, that, if such feats be in very truth accomplished by spirits, the next live eels and lobsters they bring may be left imbedded in the re-integrated wall, instead of being brought through into the room where the circle is held. Then for the convincing of a sceptical world !

Or, perhaps, it would be better were the objects fetched inanimate. A block of ice imbedded in the wall, and " weeping itself away," would be a striking object. And how pleasant to find a ripened gooseberry or two coyly peeping from the plaster ! Pleasanter, certainly, than to be greeted with the disenchanting discovery that the articles in question had assuredly come from the pocket of the " medium." I recall an instance in which about half a pint of the above-named fruit was thrown on a table in the dark. " There," cried the " medium," " is not that a beautiful manifestation ? Don't you think it's perfectly astonishing ? " A burst of indignation ensued when the two other persons present " could find nothing astonishing in it." " What," said the wonder, " you think I had the berries in my pocket, do you ? " And to prove the honesty of all this wrath, the said pocket was turned inside out. Alas for the result! The " medium " had forgotten those little withered ends (the botanical name escapes me), which adhere to the gooseberry. At least a dozen of these were disentombed from the depths of that pocket. Was there no method of escape? Oh yes! Up came that ever-ready excuse, "Evil spirits must have placed them there."

Alas for the evil spirits! Surely as they do their marketing they laugh over the credulity of spiritualists. If a mother, whilst on earth, desired to bring her son eels or gooseberries from Covent Garden or a fishmonger's, she would hardly, in the first instance, *steal* the articles in question (though spirits are represented as doing so); and, in the second place, she certainly would not convey them to the boy in such a questionable manner that, to prevent his suspecting her of deception and falsehood, she would be driven to engage the services of some gifted Bedlamite who might bewilder the child with theories regarding " the disintegration of matter by spirit-aura," and the power another world possesses of passing rabbits, onions, &c., through the solid walls and locked doors of this.

Let me give an idea of how the bringing fruit, fish, &c., into a darkened room is often accomplished. The expectant circle, we will suppose, is seated round the table. The stream of harmony gushes forth as usual. Presently the " medium " (generally a lady —ladies' dresses offer such facilities for concealment,) feels, and announces, the presence of the " spirits." She commences to speculate as to what they will bring. " Let me see! At our last *séance* the dear spirits brought in some cabbages. Suppose they were to bring lilies of the valley * this time, how nice that would be. Oh, dear no! We must not ask for lilies of the valley. Let us think of something else. What would any of you like? "

Naturally a voice proceeds from some one in the circle, " *I* would like to have lilies of the valley."

The " medium " energetically repudiates the suggestion. " Per-

* Provided alway they are in season. The " spirits " never bring flowers which are out of season, or the products of distant lands.

haps the dear spirits could not bring them. Why *will* you ask for such out-of-the-way things ?"

" If they bring me lilies of the valley, I shall consider it a test."

The next instant a scattering sound is heard. A " spirit-voice " probably announces, " We have brought the lilies, since you wish for them so much." And, sure enough, on a light being struck the table is found strewed with the flowers in question. And the next issue of some spiritual journal describes, as a " good test," that " at Mrs. ——'s *séance* a few days ago, Mr. A—— wished for some lilies of the valley, which the spirits instantly brought." Such is a specimen of the suggestive methods by which " mediums " at times contrive to mould the wishes of the circle into accordance with theirs.

There are other ways of accomplishing the trick, and objects will even be produced after a strict investigation of the room, and the person of the asserted medium. Some years ago I knew of a person who was greatly favoured with phenomena of this kind. In more than one instance, after the most rigid scrutiny of her dress had been made, flowers, and even small branches of shrubs with the leaves attached, were brought—in total darkness, of course. A gentleman known to me arrived one evening too late for admittance to the mystic chamber where walls or windows were being de-materialized to allow of the passage of flowers and leaves. The circle terminated—the floral trophies were trium- phantly exhibited—and the " dear medium " was complimented in most honeyed terms. An aunt of the gentleman I have mentioned gave him one of the little " spirit-brought " branches to examine. Just at that moment the " dear medium " turned to speak to some one. As she did so the attention of the gentleman was drawn to a leaf hanging from the lower part of the red opera-cloak she wore. It corresponded exactly with the leaves on the twig he held in his hand. He caught at it, held up the cloak, and showed to all present that the " spirit-productions " had been concealed in the lining. It was then remembered that the " medium " (no longer " dear ") had, after being well searched, complained of feeling chilly, and had requested permission to put on the red opera-cloak which she had left (quite promiscuously, of course) in the hall. Her fee was paid; a cab was called; and she departed, leaving another exposure to go the rounds of society.*

The dark *séances* held for the rattling of tambourines, and the antics of pasteboard tubes, are made the vehicles of a deception which investigators may with ease prevent, unless confederates be present, and have seats next the "medium." Here is this trick, as to the *dark* circle born. The impostor B is seated between A and C. His left hand grasps the right hand of A, and his right hand the left hand of C. A series of violent twitchings follow, of course on the part of the medium. These end in all four hands being brought very close. Presently B suggests that, as it is warm, or for some other reason, it will be as well not to hold his entire hand, but simply the little finger. Should A and C hard-heartedly refuse, "the spirits" speedily declare them "inharmonious," and desire that their places may be taken by other members of the circle. Should they consent, the performance proceeds as follows. B approaches the hands of A and C still nearer. Suddenly a twitch more violent than the preceding ones unexpectedly releases one of the "medium's" hands, generally the right. The sitter from whom it was withdrawn gropes for it, and encounters what he supposes to be the finger that he previously held. There is no more twitching. The instruments begin to perform in lively style. *Instead of recapturing that little finger of B's right hand which he previously held, C has been given the thumb or forefinger of the hand whose little finger A grasps.* The momentary release of one hand enabled the "medium" to effect the change. When careful watching of the hands renders this trick impossible, the teeth are often resorted to; and in Amsterdam and Paris bitten relics of such *séances* may be seen.

Variations of the particular imposture in question have lately been devised. The said variations even dare "with their darkness

* Confederates play a great part in these deceptions. I have even known of cases where the servants of the house were bribed into acting as accomplices.

affront the light ; " a tiny ray of light, that is. As an example of the exposure of such frauds I make the following extracts from two letters written me in the spring of 1876 by an English correspondent. The first describes the performances of the asserted mediums ; the second gives proof of the trickery perpetrated.

"A green baize curtain was drawn across that corner of the room which formed the cabinet. Mr. —— stood in front of the curtain, and opened it after each manifestation. The younger boy was considered the most mediumistic, and the greater part of the phenomena took place with him alone. His coat was taken off, his hands were placed behind his back, and his shirt-sleeves sewn together about two inches above the button, and then sewn to his trousers. The elbows of his sleeves were also sewn together, and stitched to the back of his vest. He was then put in a bag made by the lady of the house, the strings of which were drawn tightly around his neck, and fastened to the chair-back. A rope was also tied round his legs, and the legs of the chair, and he was then lifted into the cabinet. A few seconds after the closing of the curtains the bell, tambourines, &c., which had been laid on his knees, commenced to sound. Rings taken from his lap were found in his pockets, on his fingers, and in his boots ; all within a few seconds. A jug of water and glasses were placed on his knee. Some of the sitters then thrust their hands between the curtains, and the glasses were given to them filled. A slate was put on the boy's knee. The sound of writing was heard, and on the slate's being examined writing was found.

"These things were repeated at each *séance*, and up to the last evening we all felt delighted. Towards the close of the *séance* in question . . . . five or six persons declare that they saw the boy's head move several times towards the wall, as though he struck it sideways with the hat" (placed on his head for the spirits to rap upon). "Of course several spoke, and wished both boys to be moved from the wall. This was done, and raps were again given ; but they were totally different from those heard a few moments before, and sounded exactly as though the boy knocked his hat against that of the brother sitting by his side. I need hardly tell you that we were not satisfied, and after the boy's denial that he *did* or *could* move his head were compelled to feel suspicious, and to doubt the genuineness of the other phenomena."

One of the sitters ultimately discovered that the whole of the said phenomena might be produced with the aid of a little manual dexterity, and, after no long practice, succeeded in conclusively demonstrating this. I wrote, making inquiry regarding the methods of accomplishing the feats, and received the subjoined reply :—

"March 27th, 1876.

"DEAR SIR,

"Your favour of the 14th came safely to hand. I informed Mr. M—— of your desire to know how he performed his tricks, and was requested by him to explain to you the *modus operandi.* He was secured in the same way as the boys (see above). He is then put into a bag ; the strings drawn round his neck, and the ends fastened to the chair-back against which he reclines. You can also tie cords round his legs below the knees.

" Whilst being put into the cabinet, or behind a curtain, he unbuttons one of his sleeves with the fingers of the other hand. He then *lowers* the arm as much as possible, and gets the sleeve and sewings *above* the elbow. The hand and arm can then, as you will easily see, be brought to the front, and, through the bag, take a bell or any such article from his lap, and ring it. If a tray be put in his lap, with a jug of water and glasses, he can easily pour the liquor from the jug into the glasses. With a little practice the glass may be worked by the hand up the bag as far as the mouth, and he may drink. He then lets it slide down into his lap. Rings laid in his lap are also worked up the bag by means of the fingers, until his mouth is reached. He then grasps the article between his teeth; passes his fingers through the neck of the bag; and, taking the ring from his mouth, puts it on his finger, or in his pocket. Mr. M—— did this repeatedly in *from nine to twelve seconds.* I think you will perceive from this that the feats in question, although they may appear to the uninitiated 'very wonderful,' and 'beyond human power to accomplish,' prove, like many other things, quite simple, when you comprehend *how* they are done."

Simple, indeed ! And absurdly simple, too, are certain other modes of imposture sometimes resorted to in the dark *séance.* The persons to be duped are ranged in a circle. Inside this circle sits the "medium ; " guitar, bells, &c., all well within reach. The extinguishing of the lights follows. The medium commences to clap his or her hands "with a steady, rhythmical beat." Guitar-strumming, bell-ringing, patting by " spirit-hands," and other performances of the kind follow. Yet the clapping of hands continues without a moment's intermission. The "test" was at first thought perfection ; and the guitars, &c., "went merry as marriage-bells," until some unduped investigator lit upon the awkward fact that " *the clapping of one hand on the cheek, the fore-*

*head, or any exposed part of the body, would produce exactly the
same sounds as the clapping of the palms, and leave the digits of the
other hand free to ‘ manifest.’ ”*

“ But oh dear no ! ” continues a small volume lately issued by
one of the conjuring firm over whom rabid spiritualists sing
pæans as “ the best of living mediums for the production of
strong physical manifestations.” “ But oh dear no ! To show the
impossibility of such a thing, one gentleman shall now be allowed to
hold the medium’s hands; still a bell shall ring, a guitar be
strummed, and possibly the gentleman holding the fair one shall
have his face fanned. How then can all this be accomplished ?
Simply thus : Miss X—— will pass a bell to a confederate’s
mouth (his hands being held), which bell he will shake as a
terrier does a rat, the while his boot operates upon the guitar-
strings and produces the thrumming; and the medium, with a fan
held between her teeth, will gently wave it in the face of him who
holds her hands.

“ Before I quit this subject,” continues our conjuror, “ I must
name how Miss X——’s business agent made an offer to me by
letters which I have now in my possession, that for a sum of
money the medium should expose the whole affair, as she was
not properly supported by the spiritualists; ‘ complicating ’ ”—I
suppose he means “ implicating ”—“ at least six big guns, the
F.R.S. people.   Miss X—— is now every night materializing,
and is *immense ;* another point I will give, she is in the RING of all
the best mediums in London, and gets letters every day that will
be big to work upon.” The managerial offer was not accepted
by me.

I desire, apropos of these and other professional jugglers, to
call attention to the persecution which my friend, Dr. Sexton, has
of late endured.   Not only have wrong-headed spiritualists
attacked him, because of his manful war on pretended mediums;
but his exposures of the carefully prepared tricks which conjurors
pass off on their audiences as reproductions of spiritual manifestations (they resemble the genuine phenomena about as closely as
an artichoke does a moss-rose) have drawn on him the wrath of

the whole sleight-of-hand fraternity, on account of the injury done
to their business, and consequently to that tender point of a
showman, the pocket.   Since these exposures, the jugglers have,
with steady malignity, done their worst to injure Dr. Sexton.   To
me it seems that the honest part which he has had courage to
play deserves to attract the sympathy and cordial support of all
worthy the name of spiritualist.

And now another variation of "phenomenal" trickery.   I was
once asked to visit a "boy" who obtained most wonderful phenomena *in the light.*   I went; and found that the degree of light
permitted was jealously restricted to the outside of the theatre of
operations.   A species of cabinet concealed the musical instruments, &c., to be operated upon.   Close to the entrance of this
the boy took his seat; and any revelation of what went on inside
the cabinet was prevented by a green baize curtain.   The boy's
arm when free could easily reach every article the recess contained.   I asked to be allowed to sit next the medium; and, being
a stranger to all present, save two persons who were like myself
lookers-on, my request was granted. · I was placed on the left
of the boy, who had now taken off his jacket; and from neck to
foot we were most carefully concealed from the view of the spectators by a heavy woollen shawl, the end of which was attached to
that green baize curtain I have described as hanging before the
entrance to the cabinet.   As will be observed, the boy had only
to get his right arm at liberty, to carry on a "cabinet performance" without fear of detection.   Of course, however, "tests"
were given, to prevent the possibility of his acting thus.   He
grasped my right arm with both his hands, and drawing it upon
his knee, began a series of twitchings, accompanied with pinchings
and pressures of the captive arm.   After about five minutes of
such treatment my arm was almost numbed.   His own right hand
continually shifted with great rapidity from my wrist to my elbow,
and *vice versâ.*   His left hand grasped my wrist, and with the
elbow of the same arm he would again and again press mine, until,
at length, I could hardly distinguish whether both hands were on
my arm, or whether I was not simply touched *by the elbow and one*

hand. Suddenly the bell in the cabinet was heard to ring. I distinctly felt the movement of the boy's body as he rang it. Then, with great rapidity, the right hand of the "medium" was *substituted for that left elbow which had been made to press my arm during the performance*. The audience asked me where the boy's hands were? I replied, as was the truth, that they grasped my arm; and a common "Oh! how wonderful!" was heard. My poor arm endured another series of twitchings and squeezings, and then I again felt the boy's left elbow pressing it, whilst his left hand grasped me near the wrist. Had I not been giving the strictest attention I should have believed that *both* his hands were on my arm. His right arm was now once more at liberty, and the bell a second time rang—the banjo being also sounded on this occasion. Then the "medium's" right hand again grasped me, and silence ensued. The trick was several times repeated. At last—my quiescence having in all probability given him courage—the "manifestations" became quite prolonged. It was again asked me, "Have you his hands?" No sooner said than the right hand darted back to that position on my arm where the left elbow had been doing duty for it. "At *this* moment I have," said I. Something in the tone of my voice must have aroused suspicion. The manifestations totally ceased—I was voted "not harmonious;" and the *séance* closed.

Thus far dark *séances* in the various phases of their development. There exists, however, a species of imposture which, strange to say, imperatively demands for its successful accomplishment a considerable degree of light. I allude to the pretended photographs of spirit-forms showered of late years on the spiritual public. The exposures of the fraudulent nature of many of these peculiar *cartes* have been so convincing that a reasoning man can put but little faith in the unexposed few. That they *may* be attributable to spirits, is the most one can say.

Baron Kirkup of Florence has had much experience with these productions, and the "mediums" who produce them. Here is what he writes me on the subject, Aug. 8, 1876: "I have preserved a specimen of each sham photo. There were four different scamps who forged them. They produced 'spirit-figures' in numbers. I believe all four to have been cheats, and I am certain that two were. It is my opinion that they used double glass negatives. Moreover, I have found out who posed for the spirits.

> "Your sincere friend,
>
> "Seymour Kirkup."

Amongst the photographs of this class in my possession are two taken by the notorious Buguet. Identically the same figure does duty as the "spirit-form" in each. It serves as the near relative (in one instance the father), of two natives of different countries; men who never saw or heard of each other. How many enthusiasts besides may have recognised a relation in the same dummy, Heaven only knows.

Certain words of the said Buguet deserve to be quoted. During the legal inquiry into his swindling transactions, the magistrate reproached him with having worked upon the credulity of a "certain portion of the public,"—*i.e.*, the spiritualists. "Monsieur," was the reply, "moi, je n'ai jamais cherché à faire rien croire à personne. Je me suis borné à flatter la manie des croyants. Au surplus, il n'y avait pas à les contredire. Une fois leurs idées arrêtées, ils n'en veulent plus démordre. Je n'avais donc qu'à dire comme eux." That is to say, "Sir, I have never tried to make any one believe anything. I have rather restrained than flattered the madness of the believers. Moreover, it was impossible to contradict them. Once their ideas were fixed nothing could make them relinquish those ideas. All that was necessary was for me to agree with whatever they said." The evident truth of the estimable photographer's words renders it wholly unnecessary to comment upon them.

From America comes the following explanation of the methods whereby "spirit-artists" contrive to extract ghosts from the camera. The author of the article is himself a professional photographer, and has evidently examined with care and keenness into the trickery which certain black sheep among his brethren employ for the deluding of the public. To give the whole of his description would occupy more space' than I can well afford, but I shall omit nothing which bears at all importantly on the subject. Here are our investigator's ideas of certain "spirit-photos" which fell in his way :—

"A number of queer monstrosities and nondescripts were also exhibited to us as the work of the spirits. Among these we examined a photograph in which the sitter's face came out black and the hair white, while the rest of the figure was normal ; the photograph of a gentleman without a head, a ghost having decapitated the negative, and a photograph of some person of the masculine gender, enveloped in a coil of ropes. 'Now, if it isn't spirits,' observed Mr. ——, 'I'd like to know what is it. It's contrary to all the chemical laws of photography.'

"We observed, however, that there were certain characteristics of uniformity about the whole collection of spirit pictures, which indubitably attested that their production was governed by chemical laws of some kind. A careful examination of the ghostly stock revealed the fact that the spirit figure in nine cases out of ten appeared *before* the figure of the sitter, and overlapped it ; and a further examination led to the discovery that in all cases where the figure appeared to be *behind* the sitter and embracing him, only the arms, shoulders, and head of the spectre were visible. There was no trace of flowing raiment behind the chair, no appearance of breast or bosom ; 'the Embracing Ghost' was invariably bodiless. In other cases where the figure appeared behind the sitter, but did not embrace him, it melted into air at a high altitude, never descending to the back of the chair. In one case we thought that the end of a lounge on which a ghost was lying, and which according to rules of perspective should have been at least twenty feet to the rear of the sitter, actually overlapped the figure of the latter. Indeed, in a large number of cases the perspective of these spirit pictures seemed all out of joint, so to speak—a fact which the medium would probably explain on the ground that spirits have a tendency to idiosyncrasy. We further observed that in the cases of spiritual embrace, above spoken of, the arms of the ghost were invariably either handless or shapeless ; the fingers of the hands were never visible ; they never clasped naturally ; and where the hands should join was marked by a shadowy blurr, even while the rest of the arms were strongly defined. This, if the work of a human being, would evince clumsiness or lack of shrewdness ; but who can account for the whims of spirits? An examination of the photograph previously alluded to, in which a figure appears hidden by a tangle of ropes, revealed to us the fact that the 'ropes' were simply cotton twine well photographed ; and that their apparent size by comparison with the figure, was owing to the fact that the pieces of twine and the figure were photographed with different focuses. On the whole the result of our investigation convinced us—

" Firstly. That spirits have nothing to do with the spirit photograph business at —— Street.

" Secondly. That the figures of the ghosts and those of the living sitters, although visible in the same picture, are the result of separate ' impressions.'

" Thirdly. That inasmuch as the spectre generally appears *in front* of the sitter, it is generally the last of two impressions taken separately on the plate, but developed together.

" Fourthly. That even in cases where the spirit appears to be in the rear of the sitter—embracing him, &c., it would actually appear in front of him, but for the fact that only its arms and head are ever produced.

" As a general rule, believers in spirit photography are people who know nothing of photography, although occasionally spiritualists with some inkling of the business will allow themselves to be duped by the most transparent frauds of this description. To no class of people is the old proverb : ' Convince a man against his will,' &c., more applicable ; and our remarks are in the present instance are rather intended for those whose ignorance of photography might lead them to believe in a very commonplace humbug. There are no more than half a dozen processes known to photographers by which spirit photographs may be manufactured—perhaps not that many ; but each of these processes is capable of numerous modifications, and every professional spirit photographer has his special modifications. But there is no trick known to these tricksters which an experienced photographer could not perform for the amusement of an audience with equal success. In order to give our readers some idea of the method in which these frauds are practised, it will be necessary to describe a part of the ordinary process of photography. The most important preparation of the glass plate for the negative is termed sensitizing ; and is effected as follows : The operator, holding the clean glass plate horizontally on his left hand, carefully pours upon it sufficient collodion—a preparation of gun-cotton dissolved in a mixture of ether and alcohol—to cover the whole surface, and leave thereon a thin transparent film when poured off. When this coating has settled to a gummy consistency, it is placed on an instrument called a dipper—a species of hook made of glass, porcelain or rubber—and deposited in a ' bath' containing a solution of nitrate of silver, where it is left for perhaps two minutes. The ' bath ' is generally a vertical glass vessel, flat-sided like a pocket flask, but uncovered. The plate is so placed in the bath, that no portion of the colodionized surface touches the sides of the vessel. When the plate is lifted out on the dipper, its face is covered with a creamy, opaque film, and it is then fully ' sensitized,' that is, prepared to receive impressions through the camera. This preparation must be completed in the dark room ; inasmuch as the plate is more or less sensitive from the moment of entering the bath, and exposure to light would ruin it. The ensuing part of the process, including the placing of the plate in the dark slide and carrying it to the camera, focusing, exposing and returning the plate to the dark room, has been witnessed by most people who have had a picture taken.

" After returning to the dark room the operator takes the plate from the slide, and pours over the surface—still covered with the white sensitive film—a solution of iron, called in photographic technicology the developer. This iron precipitates the silver ; here and there the creamy white of the film fades away, black shadows come forth, and the picture grows out from the pallid surface, first in pale shadows, which ultimately develop to strong reliefs of white and black, like the shadows on a wizard's mirror.

" The plate is liable to impressions from the moment of immersion in the nitrate of silver bath until the development of the picture is complete, so that at any intermediate stage of the negative-making process it is possible to produce ghosts on the picture, as we shall shortly explain. But even after the negative is made there are large opportunities for ghost manufacture during the making of the positive, which is printed from the negative on albumenized paper, rendered sensitive to light by immersion in a nitrate of silver solution. The sunlight acting through the glass negative on the sensitive paper makes the positive picture for the ' card-photograph.'

" There is considerable opportunity for humbug during the operation of ' retouching' the negative before printing. The term ' retouching' covers a multitude of means by which smoothness, clearness, transparency of shadows, strength of colour, &c., are given to prints, freckles removed, boils eliminated, scars obliterated, beauty bestowed, and the original of the portrait gracefully flattered to his heart's content. Further description of the process will not be essential to our purpose of showing that in the dark room, before exposure, in the operating room during exposure, in the dark room after exposure, in the development of the negative, in the retouching of the negative, and in printing from the negative, fraud may be successfully practised by spirit-mongers. Ghost pictures may also be taken in the ambrotype and ferrotype processes ; but the medium's opportunities are less numerous and promising of success, as the ambrotype is but a thin negative, taken on glass, and the ferrotype a negative on varnished sheet iron.

" Now for the process of Ghost Manufacture. The plate upon which one negative has been made may subsequently serve for scores of others, if carefully washed ; and in all photograph galleries numbers of old negatives are washed out from time to time and used afresh. The washing must be very thorough, else the old impression will come out faint and misty with the new one. It is consequently a common expression in photograph galleries, ' Wash these plates cleaner ; old impressions are coming out.' Well, some Eastern photographer had at one time lying in his dark room an old negative of a picture representing a fair girl in her snowy bridal dress, fleecy veil and fresh orange flowers—at least, we will so suppose. The dust of years had noiselessly enveloped the old negative with its ashy molecules ; the bridal dress had passed in fragments into the grimy bags of some great rag merchant ; and the very memory of the wearer had passed away like the fragrance of her bridal flowers from the musk-haunted atmosphere of fashionable society. So there was no more use for the old negative ; and they bade a boy wash it out. The glass was freed from dust and film and the shadowy presence that had dwelt there ; and the sunlight sparkled through it as through crystal. And it came to pass ere long that a bearded man came to have his picture taken ; and when it was developed by the strange magic of chemistry, behold the shadow presence had returned, fainter, indeed, but still lovely ; and it floated in pale light by the figure of the bearded stranger. Probably the careless apprentice was scolded for his carelessness, and a new plate procured ; but the strange picture, haunted by the gentle shadow, all in diaphanous robes of samite, and wreathed with ghostly flowers, was preserved by reason of its weird beauty. And one day the junior partner of the firm, while gazing upon it, suddenly slapped his thigh, and cried aloud, ' By G—d, Jim, let's go into the spirit-manufacturing business ! '

" By imperfect cleansing of the plates the most eerie effects can be produced. About a year and a half ago a poor Indiana photographer created a tremendous sensation by the production of spirit photographs in this manner, his success being in great part owing to the skill of a shrewd 'retoucher' in his employ, who utilized the shadows of dead negatives in a truly admirable manner. This fellow might have made a fortune had not the trickery been exposed a little too soon. The best of spirit photographs seem to have been made by various modifications of this process, portions of the old negatives being thoroughly washed out, so as to admit of proper adjustment. The knave's dupe is deceived by being allowed to handle and examine the apparently clean plate in the first instance, and afterwards to follow it through all its peregrinations. Whenever the ghost impression is thus made the spirit figure will appear behind the sitter unless, indeed, the old impression be so strong as to affect the development of the new. In brief we may say that all ghost impressions made before exposure—that is, before the plate is exposed in the camera—will come out apparently in the rear of the living figure ; and when the ghost figure is created subsequent to exposure, the spectre will seem to stand in front of the person photographed. As the spectres at ——'s lair almost invariably stand in front of the sitter, we must conclude that the ghost impression is almost invariably made subsequent to exposure. This is not rendered any more likely, however, from the fact that ——'s patrons are requested to bring their own plates with them, and mark them carefully, for we have already shown that the fraud may be practised in the dark room after sensitizing, before exposure, after exposure, or during exposure.

" By the old method above described, by which both an old and a new impression are together developed from the same plate, it is far easier to make good ghost pictures. Both the imperfectly washed-out ghost figure and the fresh impression are negative impressions, and produce good positives in printing. But the figure of a ghost impressed upon the sensitive plate by another negative, will produce a positive in development and a negative in printing ; so that in the card photograph the living figure would come out as a positive and the ghost as a negative. This will account for certain ghosts with black faces and white raiment, whose acquaintance we had the good fortune to make. Taking these things into consideration we must conclude that when —— produces ghosts subsequent to the preparation of the plate for exposure, the secret of his art lies in the manufacture of ghosts from transparent positives. Thus the ghosts become negatives in the new picture, and both figures will be printed as positives. This operation requires great judgment in focusing.

"While the plate is in the bath impressions may be made upon it, which will remain unperceived until the exposure has been made and the plate developed. A well-known photographer was not long since bothered considerably by finding that every plate dipped into a certain nitrate of silver bath in his dark room came out in developing with the letters ' P. Smith' across the face of the picture. It was finally discovered that a ray of light passing through a tiny crevice in the wall of the dark room struck the side of the glass bath on which the name of the maker was stamped in relief, and the letters were thus impressed on the face of the sensitive plate. With a glass bath and a concealed light wonderful frauds in the spirit line can be practised, and, by placing a transparent positive between the light and the plate in the bath, splendid ghosts could be made, even while the dupe is looking on in the belief that he cannot be fooled. We might dilate at great length on this use of the bath, but it will not be necessary. After exposure, the plate may be returned to the bath for a short time without fear of injuring the impression, and the ghost figure then impressed upon it.

"Another method is to hold up the sensitive plate (either before or after operating) for one or two seconds before a jet of gaslight, in the dark room, or even before the yellow-paned windows, as though to examine the coating of the plate, holding between it and the window or gaslight an old negative, transparent positive, or magic lantern transparency. Two or three seconds will suffice for the clearest of impressions ; and the looker-on would probably never dream of deception, supposing that the operator was simply examining the plate, ' to see if it was all right.' According to the distance between the two plates the ghost figure will be stronger or fainter. We witnessed last Thursday, a splendid operation of this kind at the Boston Gallery, in which two seconds sufficed for the production of a ghost figure by gaslight. By a clever device the sensitive plate may be impressed with the figure of a ghost while in the dark slide, on the way to or from the operating room, or even while in the camera itself. Indeed, twenty different varieties of deceptions may be practised during exposure. A common artifice is to place a microscopic picture within the camera box, so that by means of a small magnifying lens its image may be thrown upon the plate. Spectral effects may also be produced by covering the back of a sensitive plate with pieces of cut paper, and using artifices well known to re-touchers. The 'rope' picture, described in our account of the photographs, might have been produced by the adroit use of cotton twine, before or in the camera during exposure, or might have been produced by double printing. Extraordinary spectral effects, such as that of a man shaking hands with his own ghost, cutting off his own head, or followed by his own *doppel ganger*, may be produced by 'masking,' a process which it would take too long to describe here. There is scarcely any conceivable absurdity in portraiture which may not be accomplished by the camera; and the peculiarities of the business are so extraordinary, the opportunities for humbug so excellent, the methods and modifications of methods whereby spirit photographs may be manufactured so numerous, that it is hopeless for any person totally ignorant of photography to detect a fellow like —— in the act of fraud. Indeed, it often takes an expert in photography to detect certain classes of deception. Were we not limited by time and space in this article we could readily fill forty columns with an account of the many artifices practised by spirit-photo-graphers."

The length and thoroughness of the above leave neither space nor need for additions. I shall pass, therefore, to other subjects ; trusting that the ray of light thus thrown upon the mystery of the " spirit-artist's " operations will not be thrown in vain.

It would seem that the substantiality of " materialized forms " while outside the curtain, and the suddenness and totality of their disappearance when once more safely esconced within the depths of their " cabinet," have tempted admirers to seek for some solid memorial of these solid yet fleeting ghosts. One of the geniuses in question, we learn, after thoughtful consideration of a paraffin candle, suddenly started, and cried, "Eureka ! *I* have hit it." Forthwith his discovery was made public, and became popular. Mediums arose, who gave *séances*, the necessary adjuncts to which were tables with sliding leaves in the centre, pails of hot water, packets of paraffin, careful precautions against too-close scrutiny, dim light, an utter absence of tests, and, it would appear, *moulds of hands and feet, carefully packed in cotton-wool to prevent breakages.* The more than suspicious disclosures presented during such *séances* are past counting. In England "ugly green slippers" have been left on the carpet, and have turned out to be moulds taken from a foot which, if that of a spirit, was strangely enough the counterpart of the medium's. Other gatherings have resulted in paraffin moulds avowedly taken from a spirit-hand, which "spirit-hand" appeared on examination of the mould to have presented itself in shape of a plaster-cast. But the most striking story of the kind comes from America, and the events to which it has reference transpired among the spiritualists of New York.

A distinguished medium for paraffin mould effects gave a course of *séances* in that city. The first of the series was "on the whole, considered satisfactory," despite the perplexing fact that a piece of *dry* cotton-wool displayed itself within the mould spirits were supposed to have formed from the paraffin dissolved in boiling water, which a pail placed below the *séance* table contained.

Two days afterwards a second *séance* took place.

"About thirty people were present.* A small pine table was previously prepared by Mr. A——, with an opening across the centre, into which a board or leaf was so closely fitted, that, though it could be removed with one hand, it would require *both* to replace it. The pail containing the paraffin and water was sustained by one arm of a scale-beam, which was suspended from the frame of the table in such a way, that while the pail was under the table, the other arm, supporting the nicely balanced weights, was outside, and in full view of the audience, passing through a slot in the black glazed-muslin bag, which enclosed the table and its contents. The seams of the muslin bag were sewed by a lockstitch machine, and over the table were thrown blankets to exclude the light.

"Mr. A—— had some coloured paraffin which he desired to use, but it was declined. No light was allowed in the room, and only a moderate amount from an adjoining one, as the 'spirits' complained that the conditions were not favourable. Very soon a slight motion of the outside beam was increased to such a degree as to throw the weights from their place, which naturally attracted the gaze of all to this point, except that of Mr. A—— and two other gentlemen who were intent upon the fact that Mrs. —— frequently introduced her left hand under the blanket; and finally the motion became so attractive to *her*, that she rose many times,

* From a statement subscribed by seven leading New York spiritualists, and published in the *Spiritual Scientist* of March 30, 1876.

and leaned over the table to observe it, but *never* failed to pass her hand
under the blanket at the same time.

" The last time of this leaning over a violent motion to the outside
beam indicated the same to the pail within, and on the instant a light
' thud' was heard as of some substance dropping inside upon the carpet.
The left hand of Mrs. —— was withdrawn, and the blanket, previously
left rumpled, was now carelessly smoothed out, and it was soon indicated
that the work was finished. Upon removing the blanket Mr. A——
found the muslin pinned differently upon the top of table from the way
he had pinned it, and having, in the spot where the left hand had been
hidden, a *strained* appearance ; and *the middle board was found displaced.*
A paraffin mould was lying upon the bottom of the bag, a little under
the edge of the bowl."

However little the said paraffin mould may have been prized
by the spiritualists present at its production, they did not yet consider the evidence sufficient to warrant a verdict of fraud. But
testimony quickly accumulated.

" On Wednesday evening, as Mrs. A——, the medium, and her
husband were coming to a *séance* at the house of Mrs. H—— ; the
husband being quite in advance, and his wife next; Mrs. A——,
who was last, saw, in crossing the street, a paraffin mould lying
in the gutter, where the medium had just passed. She exclaimed,
' Why, there's a paraffin hand ! ' The medium, returning quickly,
crushed it, and both ladies picked up pieces from the fragments.
Mrs. —— scolded her husband for being so careless ' about
carrying that bag ; ' he ' ought to know that the top was liable to
spring open; and now perhaps there would not be paraffin enough
to form another mould to-night.' Mr. and Mrs. —— had, just
before leaving Mrs. A——'s house, denied that they had any
paraffin moulds with them."

The evening's *séance* duly came off. " Dr. H——, who occupied
a favourable position during the materializations of ' spirit-hands,'
&c., declared to Mrs. H—— and Mrs. S—— that he assuredly
saw *toes* three times, when the medium professed that the spirits
were showing hands. Present thirty people. Lights very dim."

On the Thursday some ladies who were talking with the medium
" saw the fingers of a paraffin mould protruding from beneath her
dress." They informed her of what they had discovered. " She

hastily concealed the mould, and declared them mistaken." The same evening a third *séance* was held. One of the sitters glanced beneath the table while "manifestations" were going on, and "saw the medium's foot manipulating the bell."

Saturday, March 18th, beheld the winding up of the series of *séances*, and the acquirement of final and conclusive evidence respecting the trickery practised. "A packet of paraffin designed for use at that evening's *séance* was received by Mr. M——. Taking it to an apothecary near by, he had it accurately weighed, and the weight, which was 11 lbs. 4 oz. avoirdupois, marked on the wrapper. Mrs. H—— and Mrs. S—— kept this packet sacredly until the evening, when it was shaved up in their presence, and before them, Mr. M——, and others, was placed in a pail, and hot water poured upon it. . . . The lights were required so low as to be of no avail in the back parlour, at the extreme rear of which sat the medium, facing her audience. No one was allowed within a semicircle of five or six feet from the table. The mould was soon declared finished, and on being quickly examined (by a novice, as it happened), another bit of *dry cotton-wool* was found within the orifice of the wrist; which Mr. A—— has, with the first, in his possession. Thirty-five people were present."

The paraffin in the pail was carefully collected. Mr. M—— took the package, and had it weighed on the same scales, when it balanced exactly at 11 lbs. 4 oz. avoirdupois, the same as before the *séance*. He also received the paraffin mould or glove from Mrs. H—— and Mrs. S——, and found its weight to be 2½ ozs. avoirdupois. The druggist performed the weighing in both instances.

"Mrs. A—— was unaccountably annoyed by bits of *cotton-wool* about her carpets, while the medium and her husband were with her.

"Upon Sunday, the 19th, Mrs. A—— saw the medium's stockings, worn the previous evening at Mrs. ——'s *séance*; at about two inches below the toe *they were cut across the sole, and lef open.*

"Each can draw his inferences from the facts we state. We

subscribe our names to verify what is attributed to us in this statement." (Here follow the seven names.)

How was a narrative like the above to be disposed of? The
inculpated medium, or rather her husband, contemptuously swept
it out of the way. " Most of the charges are too insignificant and
ridiculous to claim notice ! "

Into the voluminous correspondence and disputes which this
matter involved, and the desperate attempts of " veteran spiritualists " to whitewash the reputation of the inculpated Mrs. ——,
I think it unnecessary to enter. One demand, however, of the
believers who clung to her " through glory and shame " deserves
notice. " If not the work of spirits, how were the moulds produced ? "

" Agreeably to promise," says the *Boston Herald*, of April 9th,
1876, "one among the signers of the so-called *exposé* of Mrs.
H—— favours the *Herald* with his theory of producing paraffin
moulds. Briefly stated, he says the mould may be made before the
séance by dipping a mortal hand into wax. This mould may be
secreted in the pocket of the medium's dress. Aided by time and
darkness, the medium may break the thread at the seam of the
sack, and through an aperture thus formed let the mould slide to
the floor, after which she may sew up the broken seam. Taking
a small quantity of water from the bucket with a syringe or sponge,
to account for difference of weight, completes the job. There, now,
who may not be a moulding medium ? " (Who, indeed ?)

" If two mediums," says the *Spiritualist* of August 11th, 1876,
" would sit to get letters written by sceptics, regularly carried in
a few minutes between circles many miles apart, *as Baron Kirkup
of Florence once did*, it would be a most useful manifestation, and
a death-blow to the psychic force theory." Let us see what my
friend Baron Kirkup's own opinion now is of the means by which
his letters were carried. " You shall be free," he writes to me,
April 29th, 1876, "to make any use you like of what I shall tell
you."

The pseudo-manifestations which the *Spiritualist* values so
highly were, one and all, the results of conspiracy. "My

daughter," writes the Baron to me, May 4th, 1876, "married a stranger against my wishes. I took them into my house for a year, where they *performed* a correspondence, pretended to be by the direct agency of spirits ; and, stealing the said correspondence, deposited my letters in the tribunate to prove me insane. . . . . I have since learned much from my wife ; who for six years saw so much of the frauds of my daughter and her Italian friends, that she is not a spiritualist at all. She has explained many things to me which I thought it impossible could be trickery—the chief, and most frequent, being the responses of the table, whilst, *I supposed*, untouched. In the year 1871 I was favoured with materialization, and two ' spirits ' walked through my rooms, and shook hands with us. I have since found out who the persons were that enacted this comedy. . . . . . The conspirators were all Italians. My English and American friends were taken in like myself."

The various parties to this shameless fraud, by producing the letters which spirits were supposed to have carried, succeeded so far in their object as to have a keeper appointed over the Baron for a time. They also strove persistently to obtain the control of his property, and after two lawsuits he was forced into a compromise. " I found," he writes to me, " that I had spent all my ready money in the lawsuits, and I began to feel my situation getting dangerous. I had no resource but to accept a compromise. . . . My daughter and her husband have now agreed to sell me my liberty for a ransom, like the brigands of Calabria, and I have paid a part of my small fortune to save the rest. From the day they left my house I have heard or seen no more of spirits."

Despite the persecution and the cruel deceptions he has endured Baron Kirkup is yet a spiritualist. He repudiates, not the whole phenomena of spiritualism—but the fraudulent manifestations which he was deceived into believing genuine. " Some of my friends who were interested in the subject give it up," he tells the present writer, " as a total delusion. I do not. I have witnessed prodigies enough in twenty years. I have seen much, and so have millions of competent witnesses. It is the treachery of *sham* mediums that has been my bane."

Under such headings as "Correspondence with Spirits," "Delusions and Dupes," &c., the New York press has lately made itself very merry over the misdeeds of a "medium" who professed, as others still do, to answer sealed letters by spirit-aid.

"He respected, without knowing it, the Horatian maxim," says the *New York World,* "and wouldn't disturb a ghost on any ordinary occasion. With much propriety and patience he submitted the sealed envelopes containing these precious inquiries to the sweet influences of a kettle-spout until the steam opened them, and then he answered them himself with neatness and despatch. Being an illiterate man, and perhaps not imaginative, though benevolent, he kept a phrase-book, or complete celestial letter-writer, full of nice things to put into the answers, such as this :—'We shall journey along together my ("brother," "sister," or "love," as the case might be), with hands joined, one on either side of the curtain that falls between yours and mine.' Or this :—' I have walked with you upon the western side of life, and will soon meet you upon this.' Some hundreds of these tidbits he had carefully written out, ready for reference and use. . . . . What ought to be done to him ? It is too hard a question for us. We should rather like to leave it to his clients. . . . As we have said, there are thousands of letters. We can't print all of them; but surely in what we have given is matter for much and not wholly pleasing meditation on the world we live in."

The taste displayed in printing the names, and often the addresses, of those whose letters to the impostor had fallen into journalistic hands is certainly more than questionable. It must be confessed, though, that the letters themselves are curious. One smart Yankee addresses a deceased relative in the following business-like fashion :—

"Brother William,—We are engaged in making Nature's Hair Restorer. Will you give us your personal attention ? Inform me what is the best plan to adopt to make it pay a profit very soon. What shall I do to make my wife a happy believer in spiritualism ? "

Another correspondent makes bold to ask the spirit of Daniel Webster for legal advice regarding certain lawsuits against insurance companies. A third writes to his deceased wife to inquire whether he shall marry a Miss B———; if he may sell his farm, and go to Europe with his patent rails. "To all which queries," says *The World*, " the ' medium' annotates in the margin of the letter 'No.'"

Here this portion of my task must end. I might stretch this chapter to a much greater length by a few additional selections from the accounts of exposed fraud before me; but I am heartily tired of so uncongenial a task. Enough has been written and quoted in the foregoing pages to display the reality and magnitude of the evils which act as incubi to spiritualism. I have conceived it my duty to reveal their nature and to protest against their existence; but, while I wish the protest to be effective, and the revelations to the point, I would not have either cumbrous or diffuse.

Can *no* good thing come out of the spiritual Nazareth? Is our cause in its entirety made up of legerdemain accomplished under cover of darkness, of credulous dupes, of impostors ever on the watch to entrap such dupes; in short, of knavery and folly mixed as it pleases fate? Far from it. Let us turn from darkness into light, and, abandoning this study of the gloomy face of a cloud, cheer a little our depressed hearts in contemplating its silver lining.

CHAPTER X.

THE HIGHER ASPECTS OF SPIRITUALISM.

As I have in other portions of my work refrained from giving names, I shall adopt the same practice in my present chapter. There are, indeed, numerous reasons why the incidents about to be described should be veiled under partial obscurity. The persons concerned are, in most instances, opposed more or less strongly to their names being made public. It does not appear certain- that such publication would answer any useful purpose. I shall therefore preserve a strict incognito regarding the actors in these interesting dramas. It is my duty to add, however, that in every case, names, dates, and other testimony, are in my possession, to be made use of as necessity shall dictate. Nothing will find place in the ensuing pages but facts to whose verity witness after witness yet living can testify. Should any doubt be cast upon the truth of these narratives, I have at my command ample means of dispelling such doubt, and of proving that in every instance reality has been strictly adhered to. A faithful record, indeed, was the one thing necessary. In spiritualism above all subjects truth is stranger than fiction. The wonderful legends which credulous enthusiasts can construct with the aid of darkened rooms and puppet-shows, are as nothing compared to the *facts* which from time to time the spirit-world furnishes under conditions whose perfection of evidence renders doubt impossible.

The incident I commence with occurred in Hartford, Conn., some twenty-three or twenty-four years ago. I give the story as an answer to a question often asked. " Why," it is said, " should spirits visit us, and indicate an interest in those everyday trivialities of earthly life from which the grave parts them for ever? Is it not excessively undignified that eternity should be wasted thus?"

Undignified indeed, if we are to entertain the old, old myth—never taught by Christ—that death is a magician whose potent touch changes us with the rapidity of lightning from men and women to angels or fiends. What is earth to us in such a case? The golden crowns are on our foreheads—the golden lyres in our hands. And the past?—A disregarded dream. The future?—A peaceful slumber in the lap of beatified idleness—a lulling symphony of eternal song. What to us are the stumbles and the afflictions of brothers and sisters yet on earth? Let the darkness be never so deep in which they wander we have endless light. And shall we return, to cheer with whispers of affection, and assurances of brighter days, that pilgrimage which, long ago, we ourselves found so dreary and so long? Sanctified selfishness shudders at the thought. Rather let us wrap closer around us the spotless robes which mask the deformity of our minds, and, with Pharisaical ostentation, call God's attention to the praises we offer Him for having made us other than the worms of earth. The fact that we were once ourselves worms may be forgotten, with whatever else it is convenient to forget.

Such is Mrs. Grundy's heaven. The good old lady can be found with due regularity every Sabbath (unless it rains), seated primly in her cushioned pew, and drinking in with orthodox rapture the words of life which a fashionable preacher has found himself commissioned, in virtue of so many hundred pounds sterling per annum, to deliver to a thirsty flock. For Mrs. Grundy never pins her faith to anything that is not strictly orthodox, and in accordance with the way of the world. She comes of a very respectable family indeed. Eighteen centuries ago her great-great-grandfather made broad his phylactery, and enlarged the borders of his garments, and was called of men Rabbi, Rabbi, and loved the chief seat in the synagogue, and the uppermost room at feasts. He it was, and no other, whose saintly indignation against the iconoclast of Nazareth found vent in the cry, "This man eateth with publicans and sinners!" His wife, the venerated ancestress of the present Mrs. Grundy, doubtless drew her skirts shudderingly together whenever Mary Magdalen passed her; and may have remarked, on hearing of a certain incident of which all the world has heard, that had she been in the temple on the memorable morning in question, she would have felt it her duty to cast a stone. To come to more modern times, I am convinced that it was a worthy, though, doubtless, erring woman of the family who, on hearing that the steep path to heaven was common to herself and her footman, and that no carriage-road had been set apart for people of quality, nobly determined to become the martyr of her respectability, and not go to heaven at all.

But we must return to the Mrs. Grundy of the present age. In her the perfections of the whole race of Grundys have centred. A more estimable woman it would be impossible to find. Her creed is as orthodox as the most rigid of divines can demand. Her practice is equally exemplary with her precepts. She renounces the pomps and vanities of the world in a dress from Worth. Her prayer to be delivered from all uncharitableness is offered up by the same tongue which a few hours before talked scandal of some dear friend. Her favourite pastor tells her that the meek are blessed; she listens, assents, and goes home to scold her maid. Since she does all these things, and many more, she feels herself perfectly respectable and pious; and she sits, as I have said, in her pew on Sundays, gorgeous with false hair, a Parisian bonnet, and just a touch of rouge; and, in the nicest of falsetto voices, informs all whom it may concern that she

> " Wants to be an angel,
> And with the angels stand;
> A crown upon her forehead,
> A palm-branch in her hand."

One day she will awake and find it all a dream. As we have sown we reap. Death may be the golden gate of a world divinely beautiful, or the black portal of " a land as darkness itself, and where the light is as darkness," but it destroys nothing of the identity of earth. Rather would the great change seem, with a

revivifying touch, to brighten into fresh existence every faded
character on the blotted pages of memory. Such a keeping of
remembrance green may bring sorrow to some, but for the majority
of earth's children it must be the source of unspeakable joy.
What golden crown could glitter brightly enough to console the
mother, did she find heaven a jewel-bedecked prison, in whose
gates of pearl and jasper walls she must vainly search for one tiny
chink through which to catch a glimpse of the loved ones left
behind? Did she forget them, immortality would be a dream.
Her life was in the love she bore for her offspring. Destroy that
love, and her identity is destroyed. An angel may remain, fitted
for white raiment and endless psalms; but all of the woman is gone.

Let us thank God that in His universe this selfish heaven of
forgetfulness has no place. His love is over all His works, and
He would have His children's love, like His own, eternal. None
need tremble lest the darkness of oblivion shadow their dying bed.
Those who pass from this temporal state to an eternal one leave
only the dross of earthly life behind. The pure gold of affection
is still theirs, and from that affection they weave a bright chain of
communion with the loved of earth. That chain is in general
invisible to our darkened vision, but when at times a few links
become revealed, why should those who see them only afar off
complain that they seem trivial and slight? To the persons
intimately concerned in such revelation the apparent trivialities
may bear a value which the outside world can never estimate.
The circumstances of the communication are all in all. There are
hearts to which a commonplace word may say more than would all
the wisdom of Plato. Little everyday incidents may be connected
with that life from which the spirit has passed, the recallment of
which will do more to prove identity than would the most brilliant
description of the life to come. It is in these apparent trifles that
the greatest strength of spiritualism has lain. They are evidences
which it is impossible to doubt—arrows which cannot fail to be
barbed with conviction. Why then call that little which accomplishes so much? Why think undignified what contributes so
mightily to the victory of the truth?

For many years I have scrutinised anxiously, and treasured up with care, even the most trifling incidents testifying to the continuance of identity after death. The only supports of theories are facts. I select, therefore, from among the narratives in my possession, one or two which appear to me of the greatest interest. The events to which the first has reference occurred in 1852 or the following year, and the scene of their occurrence was, as I have said, Hartford, Conn., U.S.A.

At the time in question the medium who bears a principal part in the ensuing history was staying in Springfield, Mass., confined to his bed by a severe attack of illness. His medical man had just paid his customary visit. Hardly was the door closed upon the doctor, when a spirit made known its presence to his patient, and delivered the following message :—" You will take the afternoon train to Hartford. It is important for the present and future welfare of yourself, as well as for the advancement of the cause. Ask no questions, but do as we direct." The occurrence was made known to the family, and the medical man recalled and consulted. " Let him go," said he, on finding his patient determined to act in conformance with the message received. " His death will be on his own head." And the medium left, unconscious of the import of his journey, and not knowing what its end would be. As he got out at Hartford a stranger came up to him. " I never saw you but once," said this gentleman, " and then only for a moment; but I think you are Mr. ——." The other replied that he was indeed the person in question; and added, " I have come here to Hartford, but for what reason I am perfectly ignorant." " Strange !" said his interlocutor, " I was waiting here that I might take the next train to Springfield in quest of you." He then explained how a well-known and influential family had become desirous of investigating the subject of spiritualism, and were anxious for a visit from the very medium whose departure from Springfield had taken place under such peculiar circumstances. Here, then, was a foreshadowing of the object of the journey. What had yet to happen rested, however, in as much mystery as before.

After a pleasant drive the residence of the family alluded to came in view. The master of the house was by chance at the door just then, and thus gave the first welcome to a guest whom he had not expected before the morrow at the soonest. The medium entered the hall; and, as he did so, a sound resembling the rustling of a heavy silk dress struck on his ear. He naturally glanced round, and was surprised to see no one. Without, however, making any allusion to the incident, he passed on into one of the sitting-rooms. There he again heard the rustling of the dress, and was again unable to discover anything which might account for such a sound. It would seem that the surprise he felt was depicted in his look, for his host remarked, "You seem frightened. What has startled you?" Unwilling to make much of an affair which might, after all, prove explicable by quite ordinary means, the other replied that, having been very ill, his nervous system was undoubtedly out of order; but once reposed from the fatigue of the journey he would feel more at ease.

Hardly were the words uttered when, looking back to the hall, the medium saw standing there a bright, active-looking, little elderly lady, clad in a heavy dress of grey silk. Here then was an explanation of the apparent mystery. The visitor had heard the movements of this member of the household, but had missed catching sight of her until now.

Again the dress rustled. This time the sound was audible both to the medium and to his host. The latter inquired what such a rustling might mean. "Oh!" said his visitor, "it's caused by the dress of that elderly lady in the grey silk whom I see in the hall. Who may she be?" For the appearance was one of such perfect distinctness that he entertained not the slightest suspicion of the little old lady being other than a creature of flesh and blood.

The host made no reply to the question asked him, and the medium was diverted from any further remark on the subject by being presented to the small family circle. Dinner was announced. Once at table, it surprised the guest to see no such person as the lady in grey silk present. His curiosity became roused, and she now began seriously to occupy his thoughts.

As all were leaving the dining-room the rustling of a silk dress again made itself audible to the medium. This time nothing could be seen, but he very distinctly heard a voice utter the words, " I am displeased that a coffin should have been placed above mine. What is more, I won't have it."

This strange message was communicated to the head of the family and his wife. For a moment the pair stared at each other in mute astonishment, and then the gentleman broke silence. " The style of dress," said he, " we can perfectly identify, even to the peculiar colour, and heavy texture; but this regarding a coffin being placed on hers is at once absurd and incorrect." The perplexed medium could, of course, answer nothing. That speech on quitting the dining-room had been his first intimation as to the old lady of the grey silk having passed from earth, and he was not even aware in what relation she stood to his host.

An hour slipped by. Suddenly the self-same voice came once more, uttering precisely the same words. This time, however, it added, " What's more, S—— had no right to cut that tree down." Again the medium made known what he had heard. The master of the house seemed greatly perplexed. " Certainly," said he, " this is very strange. My brother S—— did cut down a tree which rather obstructed the view from the old homestead; and we all said at the time that the one who claims to speak to you would not have consented to his felling it had she been on earth. The rest of the message, however, is sheer nonsense."

Just before retiring the same communication was a third time given, and again the assertion as to the coffin was met by an unhesitating contradiction. The medium went to his room, feeling greatly depressed. Never before had an untrue message been received through him; and, even were the statement correct, such close attention on the part of a liberated spirit to the fact that another coffin had been placed above hers seemed ridiculously undignified. Golden crowns, spotless raiment, endless harpings, anything or everything was preferable to this. He thought of the occurrence through the whole of a sleepless night.

The morning arrived, and the medium made known to his host

how deeply the affair had affected him. The other replied that he was himself just as sorry, and added, "I am now going to convince you that if it were the spirit it purports to be, it is sadly mistaken. We will go together to the family vault, and you shall see that, even had we desired to do so, it would be impossible to place another coffin above hers." Host and guest at once proceeded to the cemetery. The sexton was sent for, since he had the key of the vault in question. He came: and proceeded to open the door. As he placed the key in the lock, however, he seemed to recollect something, and, turning round, said, in a half apologetic tone, "By the way, Mr. ——, as there was just a little room above Mrs. ——'s coffin, I have placed the coffin of L——'s baby there. I suppose it's all right, but perhaps I should have asked you first about it. I only did it yesterday."

Never did that medium forget the look with which his host turned to him, and said, "*My God, it is all true!*"

The same evening the spirit once more made known her presence. "Think not," ran the message now delivered, "that I would care were a pyramid of coffins to be piled on mine. I was anxious to convince you of my identity once and for ever— to make you sure that I am a living, reasoning being, and the same E—— that I always was. For that reason alone have I acted thus."

He to whom her visit was chiefly directed has since joined her in another world. His deeds were as noble as his nature, and his whole career was purity, unspotted by any taint of wrong. Some of the best of America's sons and daughters gathered around the bier of one whose life and death it was felt added another to the many proofs that

> "The actions of the just
> Smell sweet, and blossom in the dust."

Spiritualism was to him a glory and a joy. He had tested it, and knew it to be real. Yet he was never deluded into enthusiasm or easy credence. With the whole strength of his manly intellect did he winnow the wheat from the chaff, and, casting away whatsoever was worthless, hold firmly to the good and true. Now he re-joices in the reward of the course that he ran on earth, and, having "outsoared the shadow of our night," can behold clearly things which are dim to mortal eyes. A message communicated by him shortly after his departure from our world is so charac-teristic that I have determined to print extracts from it here. The remaining portions relate to family affairs, of which the medium through whom the message was received could by no possibility have known anything, and which served to relatives as excellent proofs of the identity of the author.

"Well, A——, it's the same old story, and whether we tell it on earth or from the eternal home it comes to just the same thing, and has exactly the same mystery attached to it. I had hoped to solve a little more of this, but, bless you, I rather feel that it is even now further than ever from me. I am confident the knowledge will eventually be mine; but will it benefit you, and those who are still on earth? Is it not rather a natural or spiritual influx adapted only to the actual condition of the identical spirit, and hence utterly unfitted for another? I am for the moment inclined to this view of the matter. I am no longer sur-prised at the lack of distinctness. From my point of view it is perfectly clear; but to make it so to others is quite another ques-tion. *I am, We are;* but the why and wherefore remain still enshrouded in the haze of the great unexplored future. It is, however, a great revelation to know that we exist, for existence betokens activity, and must include the development or unfolding of wisdom. All this is an incentive to well-doing in every stage of existence. I have seen those I loved, and the recognition was mutual; no hesitancy, no shadow of doubt. I have seen no Personal God. What I may see I know not. I lift up my thoughts in prayerful praise to a great and benign Creator; for I feel assured that a creative and harmoniously-constructed power does exist; but what that may be is not as yet made clear to me. I wait to be taught; but, in being taught, I must also ascertain why undevelopment stands side by side with a higher perfection;

known, as the two are, as Good and Evil. Does the same power produce both? This, and many questions of a like nature, I am asking just as I used to; only I hope now to have them made clear. If I can frame in clearly-to-be-understood language the replies I have, or rather the knowledge I gain, I will give them to you. Of one thing I am already certain; I am ———, all unchanged."

The following narrative was written for me by my dearly-valued friend Mrs. S. C. Hall, in answer to a request I had made that she would furnish me, if possible, with some well-attested incident which might constitute an addition to the " Lights " of my work.

"Several years ago, when some persons looked on spiritualism as a myth, others considered it a jest, others a snare of the evil one, and many wise and well loved friends entreated us to have nothing to do with it, or its ' prophets '—striving to convince us it was a peril to mind and soul—we for a very long time heard, saw, and listened, and doubted! but at last meeting with Daniel Home, and also with Miss Andrews, better known as ' L. M.,' we gradually became convinced of the existence of a great truth, clear and incontrovertible as the sun at noonday: and we felt it a delightful privilege to enjoy the society of both those ' unprofessional' mediums, at intervals, when they could escape from other friends.

" Mr. Home had loving domestic duties to attend to, but ' L. M.' was more at liberty, as she was not chained by them, and was not married until some time after the incident I am about to relate.

" One afternoon when Miss Andrews was our guest, I was sitting in the sunshine in our pleasant drawing-room in Ashley Place, accompanied by the sweet and gentle little woman, who had gained great reputation as a medium. As I have said, when first we met her, we had laughed at the wonderful things we had heard of ' L. M.,' and not even her beautiful hair, her soft eyes, and gentle plaintive voice had won us to put faith in her miraculous power : still she gained upon us, and the more we knew the more we loved her, and up to this very hour we have never lost faith in the fragile delicate woman whose faith in the righteous Lord has enabled her to bear physical suffering I could not attempt to describe. In those days she was in the enjoyment of better health than she has since known ; and I well remember that on that sunny morning we were recapitulating the enjoyments of the past evening, when the servant announced a gentleman of high repute in the literary world and whom we frequently met in fashionable as well as literary circles. I see no reason why I should not give his name— that of Colley Grattan is well known and much esteemed. He was the author of some works of much interest and value; and had been for some time Consul both at Antwerp and Boston, U.S.A.

" After the usual salutations he inquired—his laughing eyes fixed on my *mignonne* friend, whose pale face had become serious when he entered —' Well, mademoiselle ! have you had any visitors from the spirit world lately ? or have you been obliged to content yourself with us—poor miserable worldlings ?—come ! do not continue silent, but confess you have seen nothing ; heard nothing worth recording.'

" ' I see,' she said, ' a spirit standing beside you at this very moment, and her words drop from her lips apparently in letters of gold—she says her name is Emma ——.'   ' L. M.' spoke slowly, but, as she always did, distinctly—and the gentleman, Colley Grattan, sprang from his seat, and repeated, ' Emma—Emma —— ! say on.'

" He stood trembling before her. She continued—' She says she follows you to protect you often against yourself, in gratitude for the benevolence you and your wife showed her, when but for it she must have been sacrificed to the brutality of her husband—do you remember drawing her from the step of your hall door out of the rain one stormy night into your house—when she became insensible, and your wife folded her in her arms on her bosom, and you mulled the wine she poured into her lips ? Do you remember how you challenged him for his brutal cowardice ?' When ' L. M.' had said this, Mr. Grattan exclaimed, ' There—there—I cannot bear it—I must go, I must go.   Poor Emma ! poor sufferer ! that man, though a member of Parliament, was the greatest brute unhung— but I can hear no more now—Miss Andrews—I will never scoff again."

" Mr. Grattan stumbled out of the room. I followed him into the corridor and found him sitting on one of the sofas almost fainting.

" ' I daresay she may tell you more—but I cannot bear it ; that dear creature was my wife's dearest friend,' he exclaimed, ' but that fact which occurred soon after midnight outside our hall door was known only to my wife and myself.'

" When I returned to the drawing-room, ' She has followed him, for she feels it a duty,' she says, ' to help him sometimes.   Will you tell him that poor Emma —— died of cancer,' L. M. continued, ' he knows that, but he does not know that the cancer was caused by a blow inflicted by her husband ! '

" Two or three days after, Mr. Grattan's visit was repeated, but then ' L. M.' had gone home.

" He questioned me very closely to learn what she had said after he left the room, and was greatly struck when I told him that her death was caused by a ' blow inflicted by her husband.'   ' We knew,' he said, ' she died of cancer, but she never told us it was so produced.'

" ' Oblige me,' he added, ' when you next see Miss Andrews, by telling her she will never again hear me scoff at spiritualism.' "

If the following incident read like a romance the reader may be assured that it was at least a romance of reality, enacted in that most prosaic of all possible cities—London. A medium—who it matters not—had found himself, on the evening when the events in question came to pass, a guest at a party given in a country house on the outskirts of the modern Babylon. Suddenly, and without the least premonition, a spirit-voice spoke to him, bidding him at once leave, and return home. He obeyed. Passing along Piccadilly, and when almost in front of Apsley House, a miserable group arrested his gaze. Crouched against a wall, and almost hidden by the night and the obscurity of the position they had selected, were two most wretched figures. Their squalor and hideousness seemed scarcely to belong to earth. Indeed, the medium of whom I speak doubts to this day whether the figures whom he saw were real flesh and blood, or a phantasmagoria which spirits had created for purposes of their own. However, he halted, and looked at them; and a young man who was passing did the same. At that instant the spirit-voice again made itself heard. "Speak to the person beside you," ran the new mandate, "and on no account suffer him to escape you." The medium could conceive no reason for such a dictate; but, by way of obeying, he turned to the stranger with the remark,—" Is it not sad that such misery as this should exist in a wealthy city like London?" The other replied that it was indeed sad, and made a motion as if to continue his route. "You are going my way, I think," said his interlocutor. "Let us walk on together." The young man seemed embarrassed, and evidently wished to evade compliance; but the other was determined to carry out the directions he had received. The two, therefore, passed on, conversing in a desultory fashion, and arrived finally before the medium's lodgings. Again the voice spoke. "Invite him in," ran this third message. The medium turned to his companion: "You are not particularly pressed for time, I suppose?" said he. "Come in, and take some supper with me." The young man to whom the words were addressed started, and appeared greatly surprised. "Why do you invite me?" he questioned.

"No matter for that. Come in."

"But *why* ? "

" I will tell you afterwards. Come with me—we can talk more at our ease inside the house."

The stranger hesitated, reflected, and at last accepted the invitation given him. Once within the house, he continued anxiously to press the medium as to why he had asked him to supper. Not being as yet able to furnish any sufficient reason for having done so, the other at first evaded answering. He was speedily relieved from his perplexity, however. The spirit-voice once more spoke, and made a sufficiently strange communication. The medium addressed his companion : —

" You will go back to the city in the morning," he said. The other started from his seat.

" In heaven's name," said he, " who are you ? Tell me that— who are you ? "

" Never mind who I am. Go back to the city in the morning."

" But, if you know so much, you must know that it is impossible for me to go back."

" Not at all. Go just as usual, and all will be arranged."

The conversation continued for some time. The young man made clear those parts of his story—a sad narrative from first to last—which the spirit-voice had not revealed. What the difficulties were in which he had become involved need not be told. He at length agreed that he would return as usual next morning to his employment in the city ; and pledged his word to that effect. It was now late. The medium, therefore, offered his guest a bed on the sofa in the drawing-room for the night, which the other accepted. He left early in the morning, promising to return that evening, and take tea with his new acquaintance.

Hardly was he gone when the voice said, " He has not told you all." What the youth had kept back was then explained, and, armed with this new knowledge, the medium awaited the other's return. His guest was punctual ; and the two sat down at table together. After tea the conversation ran on the subject of the other's affairs, and the host suddenly remarked, " But you have not told me all."

"Oh yes!" was the reply. "Everything."

"No," said the medium, "you did not tell me that when I spoke to you yesterday evening you were about to commit suicide."

"For a moment the other seemed too astounded to reply. "'Great heaven!' said he when he had recovered speech, 'it is true. How you have discovered it I cannot by any possibility conceive; but last evening when you met me, *I was on my way to throw myself into the Thames.'*"

As I have in a former chapter remarked, it has given me much pleasure of late to notice a growing desire to obtain phenomena in the light. With Mrs. M. Sunderland Cooper, for instance, materialised hands and other manifestations are reported as witnessed "in the warm sunlight of a cloudless day." Such mediumship is the only one worth valuing. The slightest phenomenon regarding whose occurrence the proofs are complete, outweighs, in the estimation of all reasonable men, a whole conjuror's sabbath of dark *séances*.

In *Blackwood's Magazine* for March, 1876, appeared a remarkable article entitled "Powers of the Air;" the text for which was furnished by certain phenomena occurring in my presence, that had been described to the writer. As, however, the sketch given is decidedly incomplete, I have obtained from the lady to whom the article in question alludes an account, in her own words, of what she witnessed; and this I now design to offer to the reader, interspersing it with such extracts from *Blackwood* as may serve for commentaries and introduction.

The writer in Maga commences with an echo of the regrets to which Macaulay long ago gave utterance, regarding the small success which this world has had in piercing the mysteries of the next:—

"It is lamentable and discouraging," he or she says, "to reflect how little progress the human intellect has been able to make towards the solution of some questions among the most important that can occupy it. One of these questions, the existence or non-existence of spirit in the universe, was disputed between the Pharisees and Sadducees in the days of the apostles, has been disputed ever since, and, in these latter days, has separated disputants more widely than when the

argument was young. For although one must suppose that the
extreme of materialism had been reached by the Sadducees, who
denied the resurrection of the dead, and acknowledged the being of
neither angel nor spirit, it is certain that until the last century no
philosopher went so far in the opposite direction as to deny altogether
the existence of matter, and to affirm of spirit what the materialists
affirm of substance—namely, that it is alone sufficient to account for
everything in nature. Idealism, or the doctrine of the non-existence
of matter, has had very little success, because men can hardly be persuaded to discredit the evidence of their senses.

> " 'When Bishop Berkeley said there was no matter—
> And proved it—'twas no matter what he said;
> They say his system 'tis in vain to batter,
> Too subtle for the airiest human head;
> And yet who can believe it ? '

wrote one of our wittiest poets; and Materialism, or the doctrine of
the non-existence of spirit or soul, also finds it difficult to make converts, because men refuse to surrender an internal conviction that they
are in part immortal.

"Between idealism and materialism there have been very numerous
shades of opinion—more, probably, than I ever heard of, and far
more than I could presume to claim acquaintance with. I cannot
write philosophically about any; but about two doctrines, which are
more or less attracting attention at present, I should like to set down
a few words.

"The former of these is Spiritualism. We hear constantly that the
existence of innumerable spirits is easily and frequently made plain
to the senses; that our atmosphere is thick with spirits who, under
certain conditions, can be seen, heard and felt.

     *   *   *   *   *

"I will mention the last striking narrative that has come in my
way, not doubting that it will be found closely to resemble the majority of modern experiences in the same field.

"It happened that, a few months since, I was in a foreign city
where a well-known medium was also residing. He was frequently
to be seen in public; but I did not, during his stay, hear of any
appointed *séance*, or any spiritual manifestation in that city. After
his departure it chanced that I sojourned in the hotel where he had
been staying, and where many of those who had been his fellow-
guests still remained. A few days after my commencing my residence there, some other new-comer complained at dinner of noises
which disturbed his rest at night. 'Noises!' echoed half-a-dozen
voices; 'why, it is the quietest house in the city—notoriously so.'
The stranger didn't know: he could only say he heard people constantly moving about in the night, and the oddest sounds, as of things
thrown or dragged about, workmen at their work, persons shouting or

laughing at a little distance, and so on. At this there was quite an excitement, the majority of the hearers, jealous for the peaceful character of the house, protesting in earnest tones that the new-comer must be mistaken. He, however, was not going to be talked out of belief in the evidence of his senses; and the contention waxed warm, and might have become angry, had not an elderly lady interposed by asking the complainant if he did not inhabit a certain number on a certain flat? When he said that those were his number and *étage*, she answered quietly, ' Yes, I thought so. Those are the apartments which were inhabited last by Mr. ——' (the medium). ' I am not surprised at your hearing noises there.' Then a general conviction lighted on all the champions of the house. ' Oh, if it's that,' said they, ' of course it's another thing: those noises are different.' Little by little, then, it came to be mentioned how the great medium had really desired perfect quiet during his stay; but the spirits would not let him rest, and were always calling his attention* night and day; there used to be such curious sounds about those rooms! I ventured to observe that as the medium was now in another and a distant place, that was a reason why the spirits who were so fond of his company should *not* make noises in the hotel. But all the answer I got to this was, ' Yes, you would think so; but they are not quick to leave a place once they get used to it.' It certainly seemed to me that the conduct of the spirits would have been more consistent if they had not remained to make themselves disagreeable after he for whose sake they came had departed. And I thought but little more on the subject, these vulgar nocturnal disturbances not recommending spiritualism to my consideration at all.

"Some days later I and one or two more of the lately-arrived guests sat together in the *salon* conversing, when we were joined by a lady who had been resident in the house for two or three months. She happened to mention the medium, whereupon we asked whether she had known much about him while they were in the house together; and she said that she had been acquainted with him since the time of her coming thither, and that towards the end of his stay she had known him rather intimately. We asked whether she believed that the nightly noises had any connection with him, and she said she really could not tell; everything about the spiritual world was so strange that she did not know what to think. Had she ever witnessed any of these strange things? we asked. Well, yes; she had witnessed a great many strange things. Let me state in brief that she did not at first answer at all readily to our inquiries, but that she yielded by degrees to pressure, spoke after a time with less reserve, and finally became communicative. The substance of what she told was as follows:—The company in the house, knowing that they had a person of some celebrity among them, greatly desired to witness some manifestation of his power. They besought him to hold

* This is a slight exaggeration.—D. D. H.

séances. But this he persistently refused to do; saying that he was there for repose—repose, indeed, from those very *séances*, which had been wearing his nervous system more than he could endure. Howbeit, though this was his answer to the guests as a body, he had some few intimate acquaintances whom he invited occasionally to spend an evening with him, and to whom he would say that, although he *could* do nothing calculated to bring spirits to meet them, yet they must not be surprised at anything they might see, as spirits would present themselves unbidden sometimes, and be very demonstrative. The strange things which occurred at these reunions were a good deal talked about in whispers, and led the excluded portion of the guests to make strong efforts to obtain the *entrée* to the medium's rooms. Very few, however, succeeded in this. The lady who narrated these things made no endeavour to be admitted, but rather shrank from that which so many desired; being inclined to look on spiritualism as imposture, and having a great dislike to tricks and surprises. But a friend of hers who had been greatly impressed by what she had seen on her visits (being one of the *élite*) induced the medium to invite her, and then importuned her until she accepted the invitation."

The above account is slightly incorrect. The real circumstances of the introduction, and the phenomena which passed at the ensuing *séances*, are described for me as follows, by the lady to whom the *Blackwood* article alludes :—

"My first experience was as striking as unexpected. I had arrived at a hotel in one of the cities of continental Europe—an entire stranger. I found the absorbing topic of the drawing-room the strange phenomena witnessed at a recent private *séance* given by Mr. Home. I expressed a desire to converse with the great medium, which favour was accorded me, and eventuated in an invitation to be present at a *séance* to be held that evening.

"We were a party of seven, all strangers to myself, and all having met Mr. Home only within a few days. We sat about a large table, with the hands lying carelessly upon it, and chatted on indifferent subjects. At the end of perhaps a quarter of an hour a sensible vibration of the table was apparent, and shortly after several of the circle were startled by the sensation of being repeatedly touched where no hands were visible. Then came five distinct raps upon the table; supposed to be a call for the alphabet—whereupon, Mr. Home repeated the letters; the rappings being transferred to my knee, and in such rapid succession as to render it impossible to mark the letters indicated. There being apparently two influences, each striving for expression, Mr. Home requested that they would rap more slowly, and upon the table. All to no effect. At last he asked, 'Will you then reply upon the accordeon?' Immediately that instrument—which was lying upon the table—expanded, apparently of itself; giving out three clear, separate notes; supposed to indicate assent. The replies to questions were, for the remainder of the evening, all given by raps upon the woodwork of the instrument. With the consent of Mr. Home I put my hand under the table, requesting that it might be touched. Each finger of the open hand was touched in succession; and a hand giving the sensation of being as warm as my own was placed in the open palm. I quietly closed my fingers upon it; it remained quiescent for the space of perhaps a minute, and then—was gone— how, I cannot say. *It was not withdrawn,* nor did it appear to diminish gradually. Since then, I have, in an open and frequented thorough- fare, felt, whilst accompanied by Mr. Home, the same strange touch; the circumstances being such that he could by no contrivance, mechanical or otherwise, have succeeded in producing it.

"A request was rapped out that Mr. Home should take the accordeon. He accordingly took it in one hand, the end having the keys dropping almost to the floor; the music produced was beautiful beyond description, like the strains one sometimes hears in dreams, which can never be repeated, At Mr. Home's suggestion two lights were placed upon the floor, that we might watch the instrument, which continued to dilate and contract, and the keys to rise and fall with the music, without the intervention of any visible touch.

"When the music ceased Mr. Home withdrew his hand—the accordeon, still remaining open, moved slowly—as if by attraction— to the person seated beside him; against whose knee it rested, swaying like a balloon, during the remainder of the *séance.* From first to last the room was not only lighted, but well lighted.

"*By permission I put several mental questions, each of which was promptly and correctly answered; with the full names of friends and relatives deceased, and circumstances which could not have been known to any of those present; all, as I have stated, having been previous to the past twenty-four hours strangers to me.*

"Finally, Mr. Home, passing into a trance, described the personal appearance, and narrated correctly the incidents of the illness and death, of a relative of one of the party present.

"The following evening I was present by invitation of Mr. Home at the house of an artist friend, where the phenomena were somewhat different in character. The circle numbered as before seven—to my- self a new set of strangers. The first notable circumstance was that the table around which we had been seated for perhaps twenty minutes commenced slowly rising from the floor, with a swaying mo- tion like that of a boat riding upon the waves—six pairs of hands being upon the table—Mr. Home sitting a little out of the circle, with arms folded. When about a foot from the floor the table righted itself, and moved steadily upward—our hands resting upon it till it passed out of reach. It rose till within a foot of the ceiling, and then commenced slowly descending. The lady of the house sprang nervously forward to grasp a petroleum lamp which seemed in immi-

nent danger of sliding off the now slanting table—Mr. Home said
calmly, 'Do not be alarmed; no accident will happen;'—the table
came down with a bang, but not one of the numerous articles upon it
was disturbed. Again it rose within a foot of the ceiling, descending
this time as lightly as a feather. A third time it mounted with no
visible hand upon it, making its way back so gently that one might
have heard a pin drop as it touched the floor.

"Shortly after, several of the party saw hands moving along the
edge of the table. I confess I could not see them, although I could
distinctly feel their touch. Four successive times flowers were taken
from a vase and placed in my hand—how, I cannot say, the agency
was invisible. Once a hand holding a flower was placed upon my
forehead; the flower being repeatedly drawn backward and forward
over the face. A watch-chain worn by one of the party was repeatedly
pulled with such force as to cause the wearer to bend with the movement :—on the following day the links were found so stretched apart
as to have reduced the chain to pieces. All took place in full light.

" In the course of the evening an accordeon lying upon the floor
began discoursing beautiful music; in the midst of which a railroad
train rushed screaming by, winding up its salute with three piercing
shrieks. The music ceased abruptly, the accordeon took up the long
demoniac cry of the engine, with its three wild notes of warning, in
such a manner that one would have declared it an actual echo; then
the quiet, soothing melody was resumed, growing gradually more and
more faint, yet every note distinct, till it seemed to fade away in the
distance like the music of a retreating band.

" Presently the chair in which Mr. Home was seated was by an
invisible force moved slowly back, a distance of perhaps two feet,
placing him quite out of the circle. A moment after a hand appeared
on the knee of one of the party, distant about four feet from the
medium, a hand like that of a tall, powerful man; the fingers long,
the joints strong and large, the finger-ends bent slightly backward,
the fingers in constant motion, opening and shutting, as they lay upon
the knee, like a fan. This appearance remained from three to five
minutes I should say, although the time appeared to us much longer.
All rose, and gathered round, watching the phenomenon, Mr. Home
apparently as much interested as the others. When it disappeared no
one could say how it went; it did not fade out gradually, nor did it
glide away : we knew only that it was no longer there.

" Only a few of the prominent incidents of these two *séances* are here
given ; much that was interesting and striking was of too personal a
nature to be with propriety introduced.

" One occurrence impressed me very much. Mr. Home, whilst in a
trance, turned to me and said, 'There is a portrait of *his* mother.' I
made no reply; but my thought was, 'There is *no* portrait of her.'
Scarcely could the idea have taken form in my mind, when Mr. Home
said, 'Oh yes, there is a portrait.' I was determined to give no clue,
and I still said nothing; but I thought to myself, 'Strange as all the

rest has been, you are mistaken in this.' 'But we are not mistaken,' said Mr. Home instantly, as though in answer to my unexpressed thought; 'there is a picture of her with an open Bible upon her knee.' I then remembered that some thirty years before there *was* a picture taken of his mother, and, at his request, with her open Bible in her lap. Had Mr. Home made use of the word *picture* instead of *portrait* in the first instance the fact might have been at once recalled; but I was classing 'portrait' more as an oil painting. The picture in question had never been in my possession, and I had not seen it for many years. These circumstances, also, may help to account for the fact of its existence having faded from memory.

"It is impossible that Mr. Home can ever have seen the daguerreotype in question. Even had he seen it, however, it would have been equally impossible that he should have discovered the small, indistinctly-copied book there represented to be a Bible."

It is much to be regretted that various of the communications received at these *séances* were, as Mrs. ——— remarks, "of too private and personal a nature to be with propriety introduced here." This esoteric spiritualism, while furnishing the strongest of all possible proofs to those immediately concerned, remains, in general, by its circumstances and character, valueless to the outside world. There are few who have sufficient strength of mind to come forward, and, with the sure knowledge that the course they take will expose them to ridicule, misconception, and calumny, make public the evidence of man's immortality which has been granted to them. The greater honour then to that small band of noble men and women who, from a sense of duty, have gallantly dared the storm of popular prejudice, before which the sensitive and the timid recoil.

The secret nature of many communications, and the repugnance with which various persons whom these communications have convinced shrink from identifying themselves publicly with a cause so unpopular as spiritualism and defaced by so many abuses, should be held prominently in view by every critic who would deal impartially with the subject. They are points which the *Blackwood* writer seems somewhat to lose sight of in the following remarks :—

"I think it ought to be taken as proved that very many things have been, and are continually being, witnessed which are not traceable to any known terrestrial agency, yet which must proceed from rational beings. Once this is admitted, the existence of spirits will hardly be denied. This is something gained; but, against the materialist, not much. For the latter may still say: 'I don't care whether or not spirits may exist somewhere in nature; I say that there is no need of spirits to account for anything we know or experience.'

"I might here be reminded that he who believes these spiritual manifestations to be genuine, has the witness of the spirits themselves as to many of them being the souls of human beings who once lived on the earth. But I have not let slip the recollection of their testimony; I am only troubled with doubt concerning it; I think there is question of their credibility. The fondness of the spirits for darkened rooms "—(let me once more repeat that all the manifestations recorded in this and my concluding chapter took place *in full light*)—" their decidedly mysterious proceedings, their sparing and unsatisfactory communications, and the utter uselessness of many of their most startling deeds, are fatal to confidence. Thus spiritualism does not, I fear, prove that which many believers would be glad to prove; namely, that those who have preceded us on the earth certainly had souls— that there are spirits who influence and control matter—that matter is the creation of spirit."

If the occurrences which form the groundwork of the Maga article do not prove spirits to have control over matter, what can they be considered as proving? If the narrative with which my book concludes, does not show that those who preceded us on the earth certainly had souls, what hope is there of an immortality for man?

I am glad to notice, however, that the author of "Powers of the Air" is, in general, both liberal and thoughtful in his treatment of of the subject. The following remarks will commend themselves to all unprejudiced minds as, on the whole, just:—

"I have read sometimes of philosophical persons attending *séances* with the intention of testing the reality of the apparitions; but they would appear to have tested the media, not the spirits. The trials were as to whether the media were or were not impostors and mere practisers upon human credulity. But these philosophical persons, though they may have damaged the reputation of some of the mediums, have not succeeded in proving spiritualism itself to be mere imposture."

    *   *   *   *   *   *

"I ought to state that, although I appear to favour belief in spiritualism, I do so entirely in deference to what seems to me to be candid testimony. My natural bias did not prejudice me in its favour; and

I never in my life attended a *séance*. The evidence seems strong, and
has never been fairly rebutted. If we reject testimony simply because
it witnesses something disagreeable to us, or something that we arbi-
trarily pronounce to be false because it is extraordinary, how much
are we better than those opponents of Christianity who have decided
to reject the miracles of Scripture ' because they are contrary to experience ' ? We reasonably expect that the record of eye-witnesses
and contemporaries should have more weight than a philosophic idea
or axiom which a man may have taken into his mind. By the same
rule, if unimpeachable testimony of the existence of these spirits can
be adduced, we must not put it aside except on still stronger testimony
which can show the first to be mistaken."

That evidence could hardly be considered " unimpeachable "
which " still stronger testimony should show to be mistaken."
I dare assert, however, that " unimpeachable " is by no means too
strong a word to be applied to many of the facts which modern
spiritualism has placed on record. They have been tried by the
most searching scrutiny, and with the severest tests, and like gold
from the furnace they have come forth from the ordeal in all the
brightness of sterling truth. It is to these glorious gleams of the
light of another world that we may turn for consolation from the
blackness which at present overcasts our cause.

CHAPTER XI.

In the episode which furnishes a subject for this concluding chapter of my work I am fortunately able to give every name, date, and circumstance necessary for the complete authentication of the facts recorded. Those who have formed no idea, or but an imperfect one, of what a spiritual *séance* really is, may enlighten themselves by consulting the following narrative. They will find no magnifying of trifles into confirmation 'strong as Holy Writ;' no false glare of enthusiasm, no wealth of credulity, no want of tests. A simple statement of events is made, exactly as those events occurred. That the narrator to whom the spirit-world was thus unexpectedly brought so close should have been rendered happy with complete certainty of the existence of that world and the possibility of communion between its inhabitants and ourselves, was the natural result of the perfect evidence of identity which the loved ones whom she had lost accorded her.

The lady in question, and the author of the following account, gives me full permission to publish her name and address. I thank her much for the courageous course she has taken, impelled by a high sense of duty, which I could wish were more common than popular prejudices upon the subject of spiritualism have rendered it. She is Madame la Comtesse Caterina Lugano di Panigai, Via Jacopo da Diacceto, No. 8, Florence. As her narrative has a completeness and an interest to which no words of mine would add anything, I need say no more. It is the Countess who now speaks.

"The evening of July 7th, 1874, I had the good fortune to be present at a *séance* given by Mr. D. D. Home. His celebrity is so extended, and his position and high moral worth are so thoroughly recognised by a very large circle of friends, whose standing in society renders it impossible for even a breath of suspicion to rest upon their testimony, that any attempt to portray him here would be superfluous.

"We seated ourselves towards eight P.M. around a large table, belonging to the hotel where Mr. Home was staying. The persons present were the Marchioness Bartolomei Passerini, Mrs. Webster, the Chevalier Soffietti, Mr. Monnier, Mrs. and Mr. D. D. Home, and myself.

"The table about which we grouped ourselves stood in the centre of the drawing-room. In a corner of the apartment, and quite away from the company, was a second table, small and square in shape. Two wax candles stood on the table where we were seated; and on the other and smaller one was placed a petroleum lamp. The lamp and candles together rendered the room perfectly light.

"Madame Passerini and myself were on either side of Mr. Home; she to the right, I to the left. Whilst seating ourselves, and before Mr. Home had done so, a singular tremulous motion of the table became perceptible, to which I, who had placed my hand on the surface, called attention. The motion continued to increase until it was distinctly felt by all present. Then the table rose; first one side lifting itself from the ground, and then another, until this had been done in every direction. Rappings commenced, and were in some instances very loud. They sounded, not alone on the table, but in various parts of the room; on the floor, and even on our chairs. At last five distinct but tiny raps were heard directly under my hands. Mr. Home said that this was an indication of the alphabet being required, and commenced to repeat it; whilst another of the party wrote down the letters at which the rappings came. My astonishment may be conceived, when I found the name of Stella given in this manner. I was an utter stranger to Mr. and Mrs. Home. They had been but a few days in Florence, and had heard my name for the first time when an hour or two before a friend asked permission for me to be present at the *séance*. And now was given in this strange manner a name most precious to me—that of a dearly-loved child who, at the tender age of five years and ten months, had been torn from me after a few days of cruel suffering. Time had elapsed since her passing from earth, and in my dress there was nothing to indicate the mourning of my bereaved heart. I spoke; asking whether it could be that God in his mercy allowed the angel once so entirely and fondly mine, but now for ever freed from earth and its sorrows, to be near me. A perfect shower of gladsome little raps was the instant response. I then begged that, if it were indeed my child, her age at death might be given. It was at once rapped out correctly.

"My strained attention bent itself with all the eagerness of maternal love on those sounds—sounds which brought, as it were, faint echoes of the music of heaven to cheer my sad heart. Tears, that even the presence of strangers could not restrain, coursed plentifully down my cheeks. I thought myself in a dream, and feared every instant that I would awaken, and the celestial vision vanish, leaving only an aching void.

"The rappings continued, and the alphabet was again made use of. The message this time was, 'You must not weep, dear mamma.' At the same time the handkerchief that I had taken forth to dry my tears, and which now lay before me on the table, moved slowly to the table-edge, and was then drawn underneath. Whilst this was passing the form of my darling seemed to stand beside me. I could distinctly feel, as it were, the pressure of her body, and the folds of my silk dress were disturbed, and rustled so as to be heard by all present.

"But a few seconds had elapsed from the disappearance of the handkerchief when I felt what seemed the touch of a baby hand on my right knee. Almost instinctively I placed my own hand there. To my surprise the handkerchief was at once laid in it; and a little hand grasped mine, so perfectly corresponding to the hand of the tiny form which the grave had hidden from me that I felt my precious one and no other was beside me. Would the heart of every sorrow-stricken mother could be gladdened with a ray of the deep joy mine experienced then !

"I had not expected such a touch; I had not been told that I might experience it, and therefore it could by no possibility be the phantasm of an overwrought imagination.

"Mr. Home's name was, of course, one that I had heard before. I had heard of him; but had never read any details of his *séances*. On coming, therefore, to the one in question, my supposition was that we would be enshrouded in that utter darkness which I knew to be frequently demanded by those terming themselves mediums. Had I sat under such conditions the most palpable touch would have left no other impression on my mind than the suspicion of trickery. My disappointment was pleasant. I sat in a well-lighted room, and could make full use of my eyes. Already, within the short space of half an hour, I had heard sounds which could not have been imitated by a number of electric batteries combined; I had seen movements of the table that even the confederacy of half the persons present could not under the circumstances have accomplished; and now came this thrilling touch. I may state that when the table's movements were most active, Mr. Home, placing a light on the floor, not only invited, but urgently desired us to look under. So marked was the request, that even had curiosity not prompted us, good breeding would have necessitated compliance with the evident wish of our host. One and all obeyed, and saw the table lift from the floor, but nothing which could solve the mystery.

"There came another token of my darling's presence. On my left wrist—the one farthest from Mr. Home; whose hands, as the hands of all present, rested on the table, I felt the touch of tiny fingers. I looked, but saw nothing; although my eyes were strained on the spot where the pressure still continued. One of my lace sleeves was next gently grasped. All present saw this; and one of the party exclaimed, ' The Countess's sleeve is being pulled ! '

" Our attention would seem to have been over-concentrated. For the space of several minutes manifestations ceased, and all was as void of a spiritual presence as our ordinary everyday, prosaic life. We were roused by sounds proceeding from the smaller table, which I have mentioned as standing in the corner of the room. All present saw it move slowly from its place, and approach the table at which we sat.

" Again rappings made themselves heard, and a second name, also that of one very near and dear to me, was spelt out by means of the alphabet. An accordeon lay on the table. It did not belong to Mr. Home, but had been brought by one of the guests present. Mr. Home now desired me to take this instrument in one hand, that it might be seen whether the spirits could play upon it. Hardly had I touched the accordeon when it began to move; then sweet, long-drawn sounds issued from it; and finally a military air was played, *while I held the instrument, and could see that no other person touched it.*

" The alphabet was here called for. This time, instead of the usual rappings on the table, the message was communicated through distinct movements of my dress. The words were words of consolation and love, and their reference was to an incident known only to the nearest of my relatives, and which none of my fellow-guests at the *séance* in question could by any possibility have been acquainted with.

" Just after this communication had been made, my eyes rested for a moment on a most beautiful rose worn by Madame Passerini. I said mentally, ' If you are in reality the spirit you claim to be, I ask you to take that rose from Henrietta, and bring it to me.' The thought had hardly taken shape in my mind, when a hand, visible to every one present, the large, nervous hand of a man, grasped the rose, and disengaging it, brought it to me, and placed it in my fingers. This was not done in darkness, or in a dim light. The room was well lit, the hands of every person present rested on the table, and there hovered in the air before us a hand as perfect in form as human hand can be. Not only was it perfect in form, but it had shown its capability for physical action by the unfastening of the rose from the lace to which that rose was securely attached, and the carrying it a distance of two or three feet. And further, that action indicated the presence of an intelligence able to comprehend a mental request, for I had not uttered a word. I grant most willingly that all this is *strange*, but I affirm most solemnly that it is *true.* We were in presence of beings who could even read our thoughts. The names of those long since summoned from earth were given ; and the most hidden things connected with their earthly lives recapitulated. Not to me alone did these things happen, but to every one. In some instances there had even been forgetfulness on the part of the person addressed, and attendant circumstances were given that the incident might be recalled. Thus Mr. Home, passing into a trance, said to the Chevalier Soffietti, 'There is an old nurse of yours standing beside you—a negro woman.' The Chevalier could recall no such person. 'She says you ought not to forget her,' continued Mr. Home, 'for she saved your life when you were but three and a half years of age. You fell into a stream of water near a mill, and were just about to be drawn into a water-wheel when she rescued you.' Chevalier Soffietti now recalled the whole, and acknowledged the communication to be perfectly correct. He had been wholly unknown to Mr. Home till within three hours of the message being given, and not one of the remaining guests knew of the incident in question. I narrate this to show that others were like myself made happy by proofs of the continued existence of those dear to us. If, indeed, all these things be explainable by some hidden force or forces of nature, then God have pity on the shipwreck of our hopes of immortality. If they be dreams, then must our present also be a dream, and our future but that dream's continuation. Am I to believe that they were so many *ignes fatui*, leading only to destruction? Prove to me, or to any other present at that most memorable *séance*, that we were deluded, and I will prove to you that I have not written these words, and that you are not reading them.

"As I have said, Mr. Home passed into a trance. After the communication to Chevalier Soffietti he addressed himself to me, and gave facts which not only could he by no possibility have previously known, but which were in some instances unknown to any person in the world save myself. He told me he saw various members of my family. That he did in reality see them I am unable to affirm ; but that he gave me their names, and most accurately described them, I do affirm. 'Stella is present,' he said, ' and she says '— The words given need not be placed on record. To me they were most touching and precious—to the world they would be unmeaning. *I* understood them, and greatly do I thank God that in His mercy He permitted them to be given me: for they have made the burden of life seem lighter, and I can await now more patiently the joy of endless reunion with those I love.

"I *will*, however, give the conclusion of the message. My darling thus finished what she had to say: '*And I know, mamma, that you took the last pair of boots I wore, and hid them away with my little white dress in a box that you had ordered for the purpose. You locked them in that box, and when you are quite alone you take them out, and shed such sad, sad tears over them! This must not be, for Stella is not dead. I am living, and I love you. I am to tell you that you will have a very distinct proof of my presence, and that it will be given you to-morrow. You must not again open the drawer where the box is placed which contains what you call your treasures, until you hear distinct raps on the bureau.*'

"Not even my family knew anything of this box. I had kept the contents as to me most sacred relics; showing them to no one, and never by any chance alluding to their existence. Mothers who have been afflicted like me will alone be able to appreciate the sentiment by which I was guided.

"The *séance* ended. I naturally wished to thank Mr. Home for having been the means of giving me so great a joy. He refused to accept my thanks, and said that he was simply an investigator like others, and just as deeply interested in the thorough examination of the subject as I or my friends could be. The phenomena we had witnessed purported to be due to his presence; but he was, as we could all well testify, simply a passive agent; deep interest, or a strong desire for phenomena on his part, rather tending to prevent than to bring about manifestations.

"Everything had been foreign to my preconceived ideas. I had expected darkness, or, at the least, very little light; and some kind of dictatorial arrangement called 'conditions.' I was most agreeably disappointed. Mr. Home showed himself even more anxious for thorough investigation than were his guests. He was a confirmed invalid, and had just undergone a course of severe treatment. He suffered from a nervous paralysis, which rendered his limbs almost powerless. I think it well to mention these facts; having of late read and heard of some of the extraordinary theories whereby persons ignorant of the subject seek to show the world how the wonderful things occurring in Mr. Home's presence are accomplished. Mr. Home could not have moved a down pillow with his feet, and the large table at which we sat—and which, I may add, rose entirely from the ground more than once in the course of the evening—was an exceedingly heavy one. We all looked under the table when it became suspended in the air, and nothing whatever earthly was in contact with it. As to the hand all present saw being a stuffed glove, I shall believe that when I have become convinced that the hand I now write with is a stuffed glove also.

"I went home a happy woman. My prayers that night were the overflowings of a heart filled with gratitude to heaven, and the intensest joy. Sleep was banished from my eyelids; and the hours passed in a waking dream of delight. Ever and again my thoughts turned to the new proof of her presence that my darling had promised, and I busied myself with wondering speculations as to what that proof would be. I asked nothing more; for already my soul was satisfied beyond the possibility of doubt; but I felt, and rejoiced to feel, that some fresh token would be granted me; and so I tried to conquer my impatience, and to await the revelation with the calmness of assured hope.

"In the early morning I wrote a few words to a dearly-valued friend, asking her to come to me at once. She arrived; and as soon as we were together I began a recital of the marvels I had seen and heard. The half was not told when my friend pointed to the bureau, and said, 'Did you not hear rappings on that piece of furniture?' Instantly they were repeated. 'It is the signal,' I exclaimed, 'and it is there the box is hidden.' The key of that drawer of the bureau which contained my treasures was in my dressing-room. I ran to get it, and, unlocking the drawer, took out the box, which also was locked. With trembling fingers I turned the second key, and lifted the lid. The little boots—they are light summer ones—lay there, with the white silk elastic uppermost. *On the elastic of one boot was imprinted a perfect star, and in the centre of the star an eye.* The substance with which it is drawn is black. It has since faded slightly, but remains still thoroughly distinct. So mathematically perfect is the drawing that great skill and precision are necessary for an accurate copy to be taken. I have had an engraving made of it, which Mr. Home will give." (See opposite page.) "It is an exact *fac-simile* of that cherished token. At each of the six points there is, as will be seen, a letter. United, they form the name of my darling.

"I ordered my carriage at once, and drove to the hotel where Mr. Home was staying. Let me here state that not only had he never been within my house, but that up to the time of compiling this account—more than two years later—from my memoranda taken at that time, he has not even seen the house to my knowledge or his own. While I was showing him my little treasure—now doubly dear—manifestations again took place. Naturally I hoped and expected that they would proceed from the one whose life and love had now become so glorious a certainty to me. Instead, a singular medical receipt was given, and I was told to use it for my eyes. I had been long a sufferer through an inflammation of the eyelids, and was at that very time under medical treatment. I made use of the remedy thus strangely provided, and with most beneficial result; inasmuch as I experienced within only a few days a relief which celebrated oculists had failed to procure me during a long course of advice. Thus, apart from that inestimable and never-to-be-forgotten consolation which God, in His mercy, granted to my soul, I was physically benefited.

"I have decided to give these facts to the world from a deep sense of duty, and from that alone. They will answer, I hope, the 'Cui bono?' I have heard of. My darling's visit has come to me as a ray of the glory of that kingdom where there is neither parting nor sorrow, where all tears are wiped away, and God alone gives light. I have not belief, but certitude. The shadows of earth may gather darkly, but through them all pierces the clear splendour of that star which gleams where He who doeth all things well has in His love placed it, and lifting my eyes to the bright messenger I can say with a rejoicing heart—

"I THANK THEE, O LORD!"

APPENDIX.

" OUR FATHER."

BETWEEN two and three years ago I read in a Spiritualist publication, *Medium and Daybreak*, a short poem said to have been dictated by the spirit of Chatterton. There was true poetry in the composition, and memories were awakened in its perusal. It seemed a waif from the great ocean of thought, that had drifted down, and found a resting-place. I knew nothing of the medium, or his position in life, but I felt an irresistible desire to write to him. I reasoned thus :—If he is in reality a medium, my friendly counsels may be of use to him—at least, in teaching him to avoid certain quicksands where fond hopes have, before now, been engulfed. I also thought that, if he were not a medium, and himself possessed the talent of writing such a production as the one alluded to, it would be only doing right to encourage him in continuing to develop so beautiful a gift. A correspondence ensued, which terminated in his becoming a member of my household in the capacity of secretary. I have had most ample opportunity of studying the young man, and without hesitancy I affirm that I fully believe his poetic talent to be a direct inspiration. His gift is not under his control, and whether it be Chatterton who guides—and I can see no reason why it should not be the spirit it claims—I am well convinced the poetry is not the production of the medium.

The poem from which I am now about to make extracts was partly written when he came to me, and it is only very lately that the completion has been given. It purports, as will be seen, to be dictated by Chatterton through the medium, J. V——.

I.

" One shadow still upon my life is cast,
One fragment of the sorrows of the past :
The hated chain of memory links me yet
With days whose deeds I've striven to forget.
Wan from the gulf of Time they rise again—
The dead years : heavy with that weight of pain

Whose presence galled me to such bitter mirth,
When, in my misery, I walked the earth.

II.

" My birth in England was, and England gave
My hapless clay the shelter of the grave :
Would pity guide a pilgrim to that tomb ?
By time effaced, it shares the common doom ;
But Tully's skull was reared the Forum o'er,
And Cromwell's mould'ring frame a gibbet bore :—
If earth thus fail her mightiest dust to keep,
A pauper's bones could scarce in safety sleep ;
And branded so, 'twould seem, did worms receive
The all I, dying, to man's care could leave.

III.

" The deadliest stab it was that Fate could deal ;
The single wound my soul was formed to feel.
Secure I moved from every dart beside
In harness fashioned of despair and pride ;
And careless where my clay in death should dwell
As is the eaglet of his broken shell.
Had it been laid where birds their carols sing,
And fair flow'rs leap to greet the fairer spring ;
Or, on some field that slaughtered thousands saw,
The wild dog gorged, and filled the vulture's maw ;
Or journeyed slow the solemn aisle along
To where repose the happier sons of song ;—
Had it, where highways met, endured, unfelt,
Such shame as never was on Nero dealt ;
Had each bleached bone—proud fate !—beneath the surge
Mixed with the dust for which the sea makes dirge,
The rites assigned nor blame nor praise had won—
Earth had her earth, and I my life lived on.
Enough,—the Furies found a loathlier tomb,
And left me leprous with the pauper's doom.

IV.

" O Soul ! and can these trifles gall thee yet ?
Thy broken shackles wherefore not forget ?
Beneath the turf is laid now all the clay
That moved above it in my fleshly day ;
Empires since then have ended—mighty thrones
Are crumbled utterly as those few bones

That once a spirit and its woes locked fast,
And now are atoms o'er the earth's face cast :
The dust is utterly as Pindar's gone,
The soul, undying as the stars, burns on ;
And longings, quenchless as itself, doth nurse,
To pierce the mysteries of the universe."

A little further on the poem passes from the particular to the general,
and sketches as follows the obstructors of progress in the Past:—

"Such were the bigots whose fierce rage, of old,
Burdened the earth with horrors manifold—
Spending in slaughter half their fleshly day,
And seeming devils clothed awhile with clay.
'Tidings of love and peace' they preached, and came
Upon such mission armed with steel and flame :
A city razing for a dogma's sake
And answering reason with the ready stake.
In all lands bled their victims ; yet they still
Affirmed such slaughter as their Master's will ;
That—deep though flowed the sea of human blood,
Christ smiled applause, and Heaven their works held good ;
And louder, livelier, rang each seraph's lyre
When chain'd limbs writhed in the consuming fire.
Nor ceased with death the bigot's hate—he gave
The soul to other flames beyond the grave ;
Made hell of heretics the certain doom
And showed eternity a fiery tomb,
Where prisoned souls should endless horrors know,
While, pitiless, the Father watched their woe.
A fable 'twas by every Church received,—
A lie the holiest bosoms half believed ;
Till e'en the martyr, dying, smiled to think
His foes, departing, needs to woe must sink,
And hoped from heaven to watch by quenchless fire
The hands enwrapped that lit the funeral pyre.
Alas !—if bitter to mankind it prove
To vex with punishment the things they love,
How deep the woe that Deity would own
To list unceasing to His children's moan !—
To mark, still jarring with the seraph's strain,
The cry of spirits fixed in fiery pain,
And, glancing downward on their torment fell,
See Heaven grow tarnished with the smoke of Hell !
'Forgive them, Father,' Christ,—if Christ again
Could shine serene among the sons of men—

'Forgive them Lord,' would Jesu plead, ' who see
But passions—evil as their own—in Thee ;
They that, misguided, think the falsehood true
Thou, foe to sin, must loathe the sinner too ;
Who, when Truth beams the brightest, hold it night,
And, blind themselves, would give their fellows sight';
Forgive them, Father, if they have not known
Thy children's joys and sorrows are Thine own ;
That, wild as sweeps Eternity's wide sea,
Thy love, eclipseless, points a path to Thee ;
And every chastisement to error given
A balsam is that heals some soul for Heaven.' "

After various spirited and beautiful passages which I am reluctantly
compelled to omit, the creeds of humanity are considered in their
relation to the actual facts of spirit-life, and the view that opens on man
at his passing from this world to the next is thus described :—

" And what is't Constantines or Cæsars find ?
A judge relentless, or a father kind ?
They find with every action wrought below
Is linked some fragment of man's bliss or woe ;
That perfect in a moment none can be,
Nor hopeless any for eternity ;
They learn that of the thousand creeds of earth
Was none that all in error had its birth.
For, cheerful aye through Superstition's night
The glories break of Truth's undying light,
And ethics fair may through foul dogmas show
Like golden threads that in the dull rock glow.
The veriest bigot who a text can make
Pretence for all the torment of the stake,
From the same scripture draws command more pure
To clothe and aid the naked and the poor ;
The Turk, whose Koran's with uncleanness fraught,
That law yet rescues from the drunkard's fault ;
The Black, the Mongol, each could pick at need
True jewels from the dunghill of his creed—
Pearls radiant with a purity divine,
And cherished somewhat e'en by Vice's swine.
'Tis thus the various faiths of earth live on,
When far from earth their pioneers are gone ;
Though many an error mars the picture's grace
Some faint show hath it of the Father's face,
Some happy trait, by intuition caught,
Outweighs the lines with priestly falsehood fraught ;

Obscured and slight, that beauty still we view,
And half forget the worthless in the true."

There follows now what is assuredly the best portion of the whole
poem. In many lines of great force and interest the beliefs and actions
of the Israelites are described and criticized. I have read these stanzas
to various authors and divines of my acquaintance—including a bishop
of the Church—and even those who dissent most strongly from the views
unfolded agree that they have seldom heard a finer composition. I confess that I myself incline rather to the soft beauty of the concluding
part of the poem than to the tragic power here displayed, but the excellence of the lines is past question. The description, however, occupies
such space as quite to preclude my quoting it here; and it seems a pity
to mutilate it by extracts. I content myself, therefore, with quoting a
few lines which may serve as specimens of the many omitted. They are
from an apostrophe to the Deity regarding the actions of the Jews on
their entrance into Palestine.

"The cities wherein heathens had enjoyed
　Thy gifts, went down, and e'en the sites were void;
　Their masters' clay was cast in bloody graves,
　Their mistresses remained the murd'rers' slaves;
　From Dan to Gibeah the work was done,
　And Israel rested in the vineyards won.
　Of nations who their masters late had reigned
　The maids alone, to worse than death, remained.
　Their lust on these the people of the Lord
　Wreaked, when each male was smitten with the sword.
　For crimes thus vile were Hebrew pæans sung,
　For such have blissful shouts through Jewry rung:
　Her prophets praised Thee as a Sire who joyed
　To see Thy sons by other sons destroyed—
　Who grateful from Thy throne in Heaven looked down
　As rose the smoke from many a heathen town,
　And held that servant at the highest worth
　Whose sword most fearfully had scourged the earth.
　Such faith the wand'rers had—their scriptures still
　Bear record that Thy mandate was to kill;
　In solemn fashion is the story told
　Of murder to Thy glory done of old,
　And bright as Orient gems the verses glow
　That sing of Israel's triumphs o'er the foe.
　Skilled was each poet-prophet to impart
　The light that dwells within the minstrel's heart,
　But yet the glory to those pages given
　Was scarce a gleam that had its source in heaven."

The first part of " Our Father " ends by describing how the conceptions regarding the attributes of the Deity which the Hebrew has formed on earth are gradually abandoned by him on his entrance to a higher life. The " change that comes o'er the spirit of his dream" is summed up as follows :—

> " He finds, with each advance his soul may show,
> A brighter glory round the Godhead flow ;
> In spirit turns he to that heavenly ray
> And basks in all the splendour of the day,
> Then cries, enraptured, to the Sire above,
> ' No more I fear Thee, Lord, for Thou art Love ! ' "

The second part of the poem wants the tragic elevation of the first ; but this is amply compensated by its beauty, and depth of thought. Here is how the obscurement of Christianity by priestcraft is dealt with :—

> " The mightiest sceptre conqueror ever grasped
> That hand now wields which to the Cross was clasped ;
> With lordly diadems doth Earth adorn
> The brow that knew the piercing of the thorn ;
> And when in prayer her children's voices blend,
> Thy name, O Christ ! the loudest doth ascend :
> To Thee the incense floats of many a shrine,
> And nations hail Thee as a Prince divine.
>
> *   *   *   *   *   *
>
> Yet scarce the purple flung Thy form around
> Can hide the rankling of a secret wound,
> And though Earth's diadem doth weight it now
> Judæa's thorns were easier to Thy brow,
> Nor all the incense darkling in Thy praise
> May veil from man the sadness of Thy gaze.
> He knows Thee not, and sects with sects unite
> In anxious strife to shut Thee from his sight ;
> And souls who plead to see Thee as thou art
> Are shown some monster of the priestly heart—
> A Christ that never on the earth's face trod,
> A hybrid shape, with naught of man or God."

The mission of Christ then comes under consideration, and he is made to define it as follows :—

> " ' I come,' of old thou saidst, ' to give earth light,
> To guide the stumbling steps of man aright,
> And whilst this joy o'er others' years I cast
> In unshared sorrow must my own be pass'd :

Weary the path, and, when that path be trod,
'Tis mine in agony to pass to God :
O, bitter portion !—but my pity still
Can whisper blessings on the blind who kill ;
The love that stays me through the woe of death
Shall find expression with my parting breath,
And plead, as Hatred's roar my spirit stuns,
"Father, forgive, for they too are Thy sons ! " '
Such stooped on Palestine the Heavenly Dove :
His portion, poverty—his weapon, Love :
The olive branch of peace to man He bore,
And stretched that sceptre every nation o'er :
His parting smile was joy, his dying prayer
Breathed hope his murderers that joy might share.
If oft, whilst adding weary year to year,
Big from his eye would roll the burning tear,
His own woe never did such drops betray ;
'Twas that he yearned all tears to wipe away,
And bore—and gladly bore—the pangs of earth
That others' joy might from his pain have birth ;
His starry life a bright example, given
To point the erring to the peace of heaven."

Next we have a review of the corruptions which gradually crept into
the Church. It concludes with the following fine lines :—

" ' I bid ye love,' said Christ,—His Church's way
To read such Scripture was, ' He bids *Me* slay.'
Her dogmas shaped she human doubts to test,
And butchered rebels with a holy zest ;
And, lest the Hell she preached in myths had birth,
For ages strove to make a hell of earth :
The hideous stake she reared, and bleared the sun
With smoke from pyres where devilry was done ;
And still an unreal Satan cursed, nor knew
Herself was fouler than the Shape she drew.
The Heaven she promised was an arbour, blest
With all the languor of eternal rest,
Where lazy saints some droning psalm might suit
To match the thrillings of a golden lute ;
Or, journeying slow through never-ending spheres,
In blissful idlesse spend their wealth of years :
Their single task in concert palms to flaunt,
And, gathered round God's throne, Hosannas chant,
Prompt, should Hell's mouths send forth too weird a groan,
With anthems loud to hide the horrid tone.

> Alas, that Hell !—the terrors round it set
> Were such as ne'er in older Tophets met :
> Clasped to one burning bosom, son and sire
> Writhe hopelessly in never-slack'ning fire ;
> The air is flame,—the only language, cries
> Of tortured spirits howling blasphemies ;
> And, mingling with these sounds, the serpent's hiss
> Or demon's laugh floats wild from the abyss,
> And deathless fire is wrapped each heart around,
> And every brow with knotted snakes is bound ;
> Whilst livid Furies hang the sufferers o'er,
> And cry—'This torment is for evermore.'
> No tears are known—for how may tears be shed
> Whilst brow and brain seem charged with molten lead ?
> No tears are seen ; but each pale wretch his eye
> May lift despairing to a distant sky,
> And view, enthroned 'mid Paradise's glow,
> An unmoved Sire who coldly scans his woe ;
> And catch, as zephyrs bear them from above,
> The echoings of the anthem ' God is love.' "

" And Love Thou truly art !" proceeds the poet :

> " And Love Thou truly art !—nor ever gave
> As limit of that boundless love the Grave.
> I bow, and thank Thee, Father, that no sea
> Of flame and darkness shuts my soul from Thee :
> Wide are the heavens that of Thy glory tell,
> Yet all too narrow for the bigot's hell ;
> And still the chastisements Thou shapest prove
> Thy justice tempered with exceeding love ;
> A love that shall at length be understood
> When all of ill hath blossomed into good."

Here my extracts must cease. The conclusion is at least equal to anything given by me, but I can accord no more space ; and I trust, besides, that some brother spiritualists who can discern nobler things in spiritualism than dark *séances*, puppet-shows, and third-rate jugglery, will unite to find means whereby so beautiful a composition, and one that cannot fail to reflect honour on our cause, may be given to the world in its entirety. The fragments I have printed here will serve to indicate what the poem is as a whole, and I trust there remains enough elevation of sentiment amongst spiritualists to prevent that poem being lost.

PRINTED BY VIRTUE AND CO., LIMITED, CITY ROAD, LONDON.

CATALOGUE

OF

FINE-ART PUBLICATIONS

AND

WORKS IN GENERAL LITERATURE.

PUBLISHED BY

VIRTUE & CO., Limited, 26, IVY LANE,
PATERNOSTER ROW,
LONDON.

The Works in this List may be ordered of any Bookseller.

FINE-ART PUBLICATIONS.

Imperial 4to, with 20 Engravings on Steel, price 31s. 6d.

Pictures by Sir Edwin Landseer, R.A. With
Descriptions, and a Biographical Sketch of the Painter. By
JAMES DAFFORNE.

CONTENTS:

The Intruder.	War.
Breakfast Party.	The Marmozettes.
Naughty Boy.	Startled !
The Friends.	Friend in Suspense.
Highland Music.	Jack in Office.
High Life.	The Stag at Bay.
Low Life.	The Twa Dogs.
Death of the Stag.	Sleeping Bloodhound.
The Cavalier's Pets.	The Chieftain's Friends.
Peace.	Rout of Comus and his Band.

"Selected with judgment from the works of the great artist. Mr. Dafforne's
account of Landseer is full and interesting."—*Times.*

Royal 4to, handsomely bound in cloth gilt, with 16 Illustrations,
price 21s.

British Landscape Painters, from Samuel
Scott to David Cox. With a Preliminary Essay, and Biographical
Notices. By WILLIAM B. SCOTT, Author of "Half-hour Lectures
on Art," "The British School of Sculpture," "Life of Albert
Dürer," &c. Containing 16 large Engravings on Steel, from
Famous Pictures by Scott, Turner, Constable, Gainsborough,
Ward, Callcott, Stanfield, Creswick, Cox, and others.

"We have here an exquisite volume. Some of the most delightful landscapes of
our best English artists—the supreme masters of landscape painting—are selected
for reproduction, and the engravings are of the highest order of excellence."—
Daily News.
"Ward, Turner, Constable, Callcott, Danby, and Nasmyth, are all charmingly
represented, as are also Stanfield, Roberts, Hardwick, Creswick, and Cox, and it is
scarcely necessary to say that the engravings are beautifully executed."—*Morning
Post.*

Imperial 4to, elegantly bound, gilt edges, price 31s. 6d.

English Scenery.   By the Rev. J. G. Wood.   Illustrated by 21 Engravings on Steel from Pictures by—

Sam. Bough, R.S.A.	B. W. Leader.	P. Nasmyth, R.A.
David Cox.	J. Linnell.	J. M. W. Turner, R.A.
W. Evans.	J. C. Loutherbourg, R.A.	J. Ward, R.A.

ETC., ETC.

Imperial 4to, elegantly bound, with 16 Engravings on Steel,
price 21s.

British Portrait Painters, from Sir Peter Lely to James Sant. With Critical Descriptions, and Biographical Notices. By Edmund Ollier, Author of the "Doré Gallery," &c.

LIST OF ENGRAVINGS:

Sir Joshua Reynolds.	Sir Walter Scott, Bart.
The Duchess of Devonshire.	The Lady Dover.
La Belle Hamilton.	The Princess Charlotte.
Garrick and his Wife.	Morton, the Dramatist.
The Dowager Countess of Darnley.	Sir A. Hume, Bart.
Lady Hamilton.	Sir David Wilkie.
The Royal Princesses.	The Royal Sisters.
The Princess Amelia.	J. M. W. Turner, R.A.

"The engravings leave nothing to be desired; while the descriptive and historical notes, by Mr. Ollier, are far above the average letterpress of a fine-art volume."—*Times.*

Imperial 4to, with Engravings on Steel, price 21s.

Pictures by Sir Charles Eastlake, P.R.A.   With Descriptions, and a Biographical Sketch of the Painter. By W. Cosmo Monkhouse.

LIST OF ENGRAVINGS:

Haidée.	The Carrara Family.
Portrait of Napoleon I.	Christ Lamenting over Jerusalem.
An Italian Family.	The Sisters.
Pilgrims in Sight of Rome.	The Visit to the Nun.
Gaston de Foix.	The Good Samaritan.

Imperial 4to, handsomely bound, with Engravings on Steel,
price 21s.

Pictures by Sir A. W. Callcott, R.A.   With Descriptive Notices, and a Biographical Sketch of the Painter. By James Dafforne.

LIST OF ENGRAVINGS:

Crossing the Stream.	The Meadow.
The Benighted Traveller.	Waiting for the Boats.
The Benevolent Cottagers.	A Dutch Ferry.
Pool of the Thames.	Seashore in Holland.
The Wooden Bridge.	Entrance to Pisa from Leghorn.
The Old Pier at Littlehampton.	

Imperial 4to, elegantly bound, gilt edges, price 21s.

Home Life in England. By O. M. Wavertree.

Illustrated by Engravings on Steel after Pictures by the following Artists:—

W. Collins, R.A.	F. Goodall, R.A.	P. Nasmyth, R.A.
J. Constable, R.A.	W. H. Knight.	G. Smith.
T. S. Cooper, R.A.	F. R. Lee, R.A.	J. M. W. Turner, R.A.
Birket Foster.	J. Linnell.	T. Webster, R.A.

Imperial 4to, handsomely bound, with 13 Illustrations, price 21s.

Pictures by Clarkson Stanfield, R.A. With

Descriptive Notices, and a Biographical Sketch of the Painter. By James Dafforne.

LIST OF ENGRAVINGS:

Opening of London Bridge.	Ischia.
Royal Yacht off Mount St. Michael.	Vietri.
Portsmouth Harbour.	In the Gulf of Venice.
Battle of Trafalgar.	Wreck off Dover.
The Market-boat.	The Scheldt—Texel Island.
Venice.	Entrance to Portsmouth Harbour.
Lake Como.	

Imperial 4to, with 10 Engravings on Steel, price 21s.

Pictures by William Mulready, R.A. With

Descriptions, and a Biographical Sketch of the Painter. By James Dafforne.

CONTENTS:

The Wolf and the Lamb.	The Seven Ages of Man.
Fair-time.	Crossing the Ford.
The Negligent Boy.	Choosing the Wedding-Gown.
The Home-Expected.	The Butt—Shooting a Cherry.
The Last In.	Brother and Sister.

Imperial 4to, handsomely bound, with 9 Engravings on Steel, price 21s.

Pictures by John Phillip, R.A., Honorary

Member of the Royal Scottish Academy. With Descriptions and a Biographical Sketch of the Painter. By James Dafforne.

LIST OF PLATES:

The Gipsy.	The Fortune-teller.
The Spanish Letter-writer.	The Signal.
The Spanish Sisters.	Gipsy Musicians in Spain.
Spanish Contrabandistas.	The Wayside in Andalusia.
Scottish Lassies.	

Imperial 4to, with 13 Engravings on Steel, price 21s.

Pictures by William Etty, R.A. With Descriptions, and a Biographical Sketch of the Painter. By W. Cosmo Monkhouse.

LIST OF ILLUSTRATIONS:

Youth and Pleasure.	The Balcony.
The Coral Finders.	The Duet.
Cupid and Psyche.	A Persian Warrior.
Cupid and Psyche.	The Sepulchre.
The Dangerous Playmate.	The Penitent.
Bathers surprised by a Swan.	The Disciple.
The Brides of Venice.	

Imperial 4to, with 16 Engravings on Steel, price 21s.

Pictures by Italian Masters. With an Introductory Essay, and Notices of the Painters and Subjects engraved. By William B. Scott.

LIST OF ILLUSTRATIONS:

Madonna and Child.	The Daughter of Jerusalem.
Titian's Daughter.	Death of Peter Martyr.
Procession of the Virgin.	Dives.
Silence!	Europa.
S. Catherine.	The Magdalen.
Death of Cleopatra.	Judith with the Head of Holofernes.
The Woman of Samaria.	The Madonna.
Soldiers Gambling.	The Infant Christ.

Imperial 4to, with 9 Steel Engravings, price 16s.

Pictures by C. R. Leslie, R.A. With Descriptive Notices, and a Biographical Sketch of the Painter. By James Dafforne.

"A true picture-book, eloquently and practically pleading for picture-books, is this sumptuous volume. The engravings represent as worthy a selection of Leslie's works as any admirers of his refined genius could wish."—*Telegraph.*

Imperial 4to, handsomely bound in cloth gilt, with 11 Steel
Engravings, price 16s.

Pictures by Daniel Maclise, R.A. With Descriptions, and a Biographical Sketch of the Painter. By James Dafforne.

"Mr. Dafforne's volume is a worthy monument to the genius of Maclise."—*Bookseller.*

In folio, handsomely bound in cloth gilt, price £3 3s.

Gallery of Modern Sculpture. A Series of Steel Engravings. With Descriptions in Prose, and Poetical Illustrations, by J. Dafforne, T. K. Hervey, &c., preceded by an Historical and Critical Essay on Sculpture, Ancient and Modern.

Imperial 4to, cloth gilt, with 20 Steel Engravings, price 31s. 6d.

Pictures by Leslie and Maclise. Specimens of the
Works of these celebrated Artists. With Descriptive and Biographical Notices. By JAMES DAFFORNE.

"These two books are produced in the same manner, and a series of engravings from the works of a deceased master in his art, published in this style, appears to be exactly the right way to celebrate our leading artists as they pass from the stage. The memoirs of both artists are exceedingly well related."—*Academy.*

"The binding and get-up are most creditable, and Mr. Dafforne's pages descriptive of the pictures enhance the attraction of the book."—*Standard.*

Imperial 4to, handsomely bound in cloth gilt, with 15 Engravings on Steel, price 21s.

The Works of John Henry Foley, R.A. With
Descriptions, and a Biographical Sketch of the Painter. By W. COSMO MONKHOUSE.

LIST OF ENGRAVINGS:

Ino and Bacchus.	Goldsmith.
Egeria.	Lord Hardinge.
The Muse of Painting.	Helen Faucit.
The Mother.	Delhi.
Innocence.	Grief.
Asia.	The Tomb Revisited.
Caractacus.	Monument to General the Hon.
Hampden.	Robert Bruce.

Imperial 4to, handsomely bound in cloth gilt, with 20 Steel Engravings and 50 Woodcuts, price 21s.

The British School of Sculpture. With a Pre-
liminary Essay, and Notices of the Artists. By WILLIAM B. SCOTT, Author of "Our British Landscape Painters," "Life of Albert Dürer," &c.

"A resplendent drawing-room table-book. A handsome and artistic volume." —*Echo.*

"The volume contains twenty elaborate steel engravings, supplemented with numerous woodcuts. In a pictorial and literary view the book is remarkable, and has the rather unusual merit of being at once popular and trustworthy."—*Bookseller.*

"Let us give one glance to the exquisite genius which lends this great charm to Mr. Scott's volume. Many of the woodcuts from Flaxman's monumental reliefs are sufficiently delicate to give a fair idea of that genius. As we turn from one little group to another, finding in each a new version of that tale of sorrow which, of all tales, has been most outworn by the sculptor's art, what a singular variety and freshness in its rendering is set before us, what a truth to human feeling, what ever-present tenderness and elevation! Each of these woodcuts is a little poem from life, simplified and idealised by Flaxman's genius. Mr. Scott cannot write without showing an artist's feeling, and (what does not always co-exist with this) a genial sympathy for art of diverse aims and merits."—*Saturday Review.*

Imperial 4to, handsomely bound in cloth gilt, price £8 8s.

The Royal Gallery of Art. A Series of Engravings
from the private Collection of her Most Gracious Majesty the Queen. With Descriptive Letterpress by JAMES DAFFORNE.

By the gracious permission of her Majesty and of his Royal Highness the late Prince Consort, the present selection has been made from the very extensive collection of paintings at Windsor Castle, Buckingham Palace, and Osborne, where are treasured some of the finest works of the ancient and modern schools.

In Four Vols. folio, cloth extra, with 152 Steel Engravings,
price £8 8s.

The Vernon Gallery of British Art. Edited by
S. C. HALL, F.S.A. 152 Engravings, of the choicest pictures
by British Artists, in the Collection formed by the late Robert
Vernon, Esq., now in the National Gallery.

In Two Vols. imperial 4to, cloth extra, gilt edges, price £3 6s.

British Schools of Art. A Selection of Examples
engraved in Line, by eminent Artists. With descriptions by H.
MURRAY, F.S.A.

In Three Vols. royal 4to, price £8 8s.

National Gallery of British Pictures. Edited
by S. C. HALL, F.S.A. Containing 150 First-class Line Engravings of the Pictures in the Vernon Collection, with a Selection of
53 of the best Works of Modern Statuary.

The Vernon Gallery was presented by Robert Vernon, Esq., to the National
Gallery, by deed bearing date 22nd December, 1847. The Pictures are all of such a
nature as to be readily understood and appreciated, for the most part representing
subjects which appeal at once to the heart as well as the mind of all beholders.
By special permission, the Publishers were allowed to engrave the whole of these
Pictures. This has been done at an enormous cost, the best engravers and printers
having been employed to do justice to a work of so national and representative a
character.

In Two large Vols. folio, handsomely bound, price £5 5s.

Royal Gems from the Galleries of Europe,
Engraved after Pictures of the Great Masters. With Notices,
Biographical, Historical, and Descriptive, by S. C. HALL, Esq.,
F.S.A.

In folio, cloth extra, gilt edges, price £4 4s.

The Wilkie Gallery. A Selection of Engravings of
the best Paintings of Sir David Wilkie, R.A., including his
Spanish and Oriental Sketches, with Notices Biographical and
Critical, a Portrait of Wilkie, and a View of his Birthplace.

Imperial 4to, handsomely bound, price £5 5s.

The Green Vaults of Dresden. Illustrations of the
Choicest Works in that Museum of Art, in Chromo-lithography.
Edited by PROFESSOR GRUNER.

In Three Vols. imperial 4to, half-bound morocco, price £35.

The Pictures by the Old Masters in the

National Gallery, Photographed by SIGNOR L. CALDESI. With Letterpress Descriptions, Historical, Biographical, and Critical, by RALPH NICHOLSON WORNUM, Keeper and Secretary, National Gallery.

The National Gallery of Pictures, in point of careful selection of the specimens of the Old Masters which it contains, holds the highest rank among the public collections of Europe, whilst numerically its Art-treasures entitle it to be classed with the most celebrated of those which have been formed upon a like principle.

The letterpress descriptions are furnished by Mr. Ralph N. Wornum, the Keeper of the Gallery, who will adopt an historical classification of the Masters, a treatment which will combine the characteristics and chronology of Schools, with the incidents of individual biography, thus forming a guide to the history of painting, as represented by the National Collection, and furnishing ample means of intellectual enjoyment to persons of refined taste.

Imperial folio, handsomely bound in cloth, price £2 2s.

Frescoes by Raphael on the Ceiling of the

Stanza dell' Eliodoro in the Vatican. Drawn by NICCOLA CONSONI, and Engraved by LEWIS GRUNER and THEODORE LANGER. With Descriptions by LADY EASTLAKE.

In folio, cloth extra, gilt edges, price £3 3s.

Outline Engravings from Sculpture Paintings

and Designs by MICHAEL ANGELO BUONAROTTI. Reprinted from the original Plates.

One Vol. 4to, cloth extra, gilt edges, price 15s.

Cabinet Paintings in her Majesty's Private Collection

at Buckingham Palace. By JOHN LINNELL.

ILLUSTRATED WORKS OF HOME AND FOREIGN SCENERY.

Two Vols. demy 4to, cloth gilt, price 40s.

Coast Scenery and Watering-Places of Great
Britain. A Series of 125 Steel Engravings, from Drawings
by Harding, Creswick, Cooke, Bartlett, &c. Edited by W.
BEATTIE, M.D.

Two Vols. demy 4to, cloth gilt, price 40s.

Scotland. By W. BEATTIE, M.D. Illustrated in a Series
of 120 Steel Engravings after Drawings by Allom, Bartlett, and
M'Culloch.

Two Vols. demy 4to, cloth gilt, price 35s.

Ireland, its Scenery and Antiquities. 120 Steel
Engravings by W. H. Bartlett. With Descriptive Text by J.
STIRLING COYNE, N. P. WILLIS, &c.

Demy 4to, cloth gilt, price 25s.

Palestine (The Christian in); or, Scenes of
Sacred History, Historical and Descriptive. By HENRY STEBBING,
D.D., F.R.S. 80 Steel Engravings, from Drawings taken on the
Spot, by W. H. Bartlett.

Two Vols. demy 4to, cloth gilt, price 25s. each.

The Bosphorus and the Danube. "The Bosphorus,'
by Miss PARDOE, "The Danube" by W. BEATTIE, M.D. Illustrated with 168 Steel Engravings, from Drawings by W. H.
Bartlett.

Two Vols. demy 4to, cloth gilt, price 40s.

Piedmont and Italy, from the Alps to the
Tiber. With 138 Steel Engravings, after Designs by Harding, Pyne, Bartlett, Brockedon, &c. With Descriptions by DUDLEY COSTELLO.

Two Vols. demy 4to, cloth gilt, price 40s.

Switzerland. Illustrated in 108 Steel Engravings, after
Drawings by W. H. Bartlett. With Descriptions by W. BEATTIE, M.D.

Two Vols. demy 4to, cloth gilt, price 35s.

American Land, Lake, and River Scenery.
120 Steel Engravings, after Sketches by W. H. Bartlett. With Descriptions by N. P. WILLIS, Author of "Pencillings by the Way."

Two Vols. demy 4to, cloth gilt, price 50s.

Caledonia Illustrated. 170 Steel Engravings, from
Drawings by W. H. Bartlett, T. Allom, &c. With Descriptions by WILLIAM BEATTIE, M.D.

Two Vols. demy 4to, cloth gilt, price 35s.

Canadian Scenery. 118 Steel Engravings, after
Drawings by W. H. Bartlett. With Descriptions by N. P. WILLIS, Author of "Pencillings by the Way."

Two Vols. 4to, cloth extra, gilt edges, price 40s.

Passes of Alps. The Alps Illustrated, by which Italy
communicates with France, Switzerland, and Germany. Containing 150 Engraved Plates by WILLIAM BRACKEDON.

Fcap. 4to, neatly bound, with 210 Illustrations, price 21s.

The Stately Homes of England. By LLEWELLYNN
JEWITT, F.S.A., and S. C. HALL, F.S.A.

CONTENTS:

Alton Towers.	Alnwick Castle.	Haddon Hall.
Cobham Hall.	Hardwick Hall.	Hatfield House.
Mount Edgcumbe.	Arundel Castle.	Cassiobury.
Cothele.	Penshurst.	Chatsworth.
	Warwick Castle.	

2 Vols. Imperial 8vo, cloth, price 42s.

The Castles and Abbeys of England. By W.
BEATTIE, M.D. Illustrated with upwards of 200 Engravings on Steel and Wood. New Edition.

ART GIFTBOOKS AND PRIZES.

Small 4to, extensively Illustrated, price 12s.

Art Studies from Nature, as applied to Design.

For the use of Architects, Designers, and Manufacturers.

CONTENTS:

I.—The Adaptability of our Native Plants to the Purposes of Ornamental Art.
By EDWARD HULME, F.L.S.
II.—Seaweeds as Objects of Design. By J. S. MACKIE, Esq., F.G.S., F.S.A.
III.—The Crystals of Snow, as applied to the Purposes of Design. By JAMES
GLAISHER, Esq., F.R.S.
IV.—Symmetrical and Ornamental Forms of Organic Remains. By ROBERT
HUNT, F.R.S.

"Not one of the papers will be read by an intelligent manufacturer or designer
in almost any branch of ornamental business without affording suggestions which
will possess a money value in the market. The illustrations are numerous and
excellent."—*Standard.*

"A more apt or suggestive gift for the young artist or art-tradesman could not
be desired."—*Daily Telegraph.*

Small 4to, with 259 Wood Engravings, elegantly bound, price 12s.

Art Papers, or Rambles] of an Artist. By F. W.

FAIRHOLT, F.S.A.

Contents:—1. Among Old Books and in Old Places; 2. Grotesque Designs;
3. About Finger-rings; 4. Ancient Brooches and Dress Fastenings; Albert Durer
and his Works.

"Mr. Fairholt's knowledge and reading were extensive, his pencil facile and
accurate, and he possessed the pen of a ready writer. The volume is a pleasant
memorial of that skilful artist and intelligent archaeologist."—*Notes and Queries.*

Small 4to, with 133 Woodcut Illustrations, elegantly bound,
price 12s.

Art Rambles Abroad, or Homes and Haunts of

Foreign Artists. By FREDERICK WILLIAM FAIRHOLT, F.S.A.

Contents:—1. Haunts of Rubens and Vandyke; 2. Rambles in Belgium; 3.
Rembrandt's Studio; 4. The Country of Cuyp; 5. The Home of Paul Potter; 6.
The Dutch Genre-Painters; 7. Dutch Landscape and Flower-Painters; 8. Michael
Angelo's Home; 9. Raffaelle in Rome.

Small 4to, with 135 Engravings on Wood, price 15s.

Scenes and Characters of the Middle Ages.

By the Rev. EDWARD L. CUTTS, late Hon. Sec. of the Essex
Archaeological Society.

Fcap. 4to, cloth extra, with 20 Engravings on Steel, price 9s.

Picturesque Scenery in Ireland. Drawn by T.

CRESWICK, R.A. Accompanied by Descriptive Jottings, by a
Tourist.

Illustrated Books suitable for Presents and School Prizes.

THE CROWN LIBRARY.

An entirely New Series of Original Works of a Standard Character, suitable for Presents. Each Volume contains between 300 and 400 pages, crown 8vo, is Illustrated, handsomely printed, and neatly bound in cloth gilt, gilt edges.

The Price of each Volume is Five Shillings.

King's. Beeches: Stories of Old Chums. By Stephen J. Mackenna, Author of "Off Parade," "Plucky Fellows," &c., &c.

Contents:—Red Weskit's Mystification; A Bold Stroke for the Mastery; The Tug of War; A Happy Family; Temptation; A Birthday Memory; A Snake in the Grass; A Fish out of Water; A French Importation; "Billy the Boaster;" A Record of Glamour; "Soft Sawder;" Horace Salter's Adventure; An Awful Crisis; A Troublous Time at the Beeches.

"The stories are well told, and are redolent of schoolboy life."—*British Quarterly Review.*

"Another book for boys, and a very good one; the stories seem healthy, natural and spirited, and quite free from cant or priggishness."—*Graphic.*

Pioneers of the Christian Faith. By A. Gruar Forbes.

Contents:—The Beginning of the Gospel in many Lands; Eminent Christian Teachers of the earlier stages; Early Christianity in Britain; Introduction of Christianity into America; the Gospel in Ancient Gaul and Subsequent France; Introduction of the Gospel into Germany; the Reformation; Other Churches in other Lands; Modern Missions.

Six by Two: Stories of Old Schoolfellows. By Edith Dixon and Mary de Morgan.

Contents:—The French Girl at our School; A Ramble on the Rhine; Lilian and Lucy; How Nelly went to School; A Midnight Adventure; the Fault of the Roses.

"A bundle of fresh and pleasant reminiscences of schoolgirl days. . . . We can recommend them for holiday reading. Their illustrations are excellent."—*Times.*

"English girls will not the less like these pleasantly-written stories because they are about foreign school-life."—*Saturday Review.*

Told by the Waves: Stories in Nature. By Helen Zimmern, Author of "Stories in Precious Stones."

"Miss Zimmern writes with feeling, pathos, and a graceful and abundant fancy."—*Times.*

"A quaint and successful attempt to humanise external nature by endowing the whole family of mother earth with speech and intelligence."—*Daily Telegraph.*

"A volume of sweet poetical stories, as fanciful as they are fascinating."—*Graphic.*

Famous Books. Sketches in the Highways and Byways of English. By W. DAVENPORT ADAMS.

CONTENTS:

More's "Utopia."
Foxe's Book of Martyrs.
The First English Tragedy and Comedy.
Ascham's "Schoolmaster."
Sidney's "Arcadia."
Overbury's "Characters."
Quarles's "Emblems."

Browne's "Religio Medici."
Pepys' "Diary."
Selden's "Table Talk."
Steele's "Tatler."
Defoe's "Robinson Crusoe."
Chesterfield's "Letters."
Lamb's "Essays of Elia."

The Empires and Cities of Asia. By A. GRUAR FORBES.

Contents :—Topography, Languages, and Natural History; Turkey in Asia; Arabia; Persia; Russia in Asia; The Tartars; Britain in India; China; Japan; Conclusion.

"The topography, languages, and nations of Asia are severally treated, and their annals condensed, with wisdom and adequate knowledge."—*British Quarterly Review.*

Alice de Burgh: a Home Story for Girls. By LIZZIE JOYCE TOMLINSON.

The Children's Pleasure-Book: a Treasury of Original Stories, Biographies, Poems, Sunday Readings, &c. By W. H. G. KINGSTON, JEANIE HERING, W. BURNETT, the Author of "Poems written for a Child," the Author of "Brave Lisette," A. G. FORBES, HELEN ZIMMERN, and other Popular Authors of Children's Books.

The Sunday Pleasure-Book. Containing Stories told to Children.

In Crown 8vo, HANDSOMELY BOUND, 3s. 6d. each.

Adventures in the Ice. A Comprehensive Summary of Arctic Exploration, Discovery, and Adventure, including Experiences of Captain Penny, the Veteran Whaler, *now first published.* By JOHN TILLOTSON. With 4 Portraits and 14 other Illustrations.

Aunt Agnes; or, the Why and the Wherefore of Life. An Autobiography. By a Clergyman's Daughter. With 8 Illustrations.

Busy Hives Around Us (The). A Variety of Trips and Visits to the Mine, the Workshop, and the Factory. With Popular Notes on Materials, Processes, and Machines. With 7 Illustrations, by William Harvey and others, printed on Toned Paper.

Famous London Merchants. With Life-Portraits of George Peabody; Sir Richard Whittington; Sir Thomas Gresham; Sir Hugh Myddelton; Sir Josiah Child; Paterson, Founder of the Bank of England; Coutts, the Banker; and 17 others. By H. R. Fox Bourne.

Holiday Adventures; or the Strettons' Summer in Normandy. By Mrs. James Gambier. With 8 illustrations by Charles Altamont Doyle, printed on Toned Paper.

Habits of Good Society (The). A Handbook of Etiquette for Ladies and Gentlemen. With Thoughts, Hints, and Anecdotes concerning Social Observances, Nice Points of Taste and Good Manners, and the Art of making One's-self agreeable. The whole interspersed with humorous Illustrations of Social Predicaments, Remarks on the History and Changes of Fashion, and the Differences of English and Continental Etiquette. (Frontispiece.)

The press has pronounced this accurate, racy, and elegant volume a most complete and trustworthy book upon Social Etiquette.

Men who have Risen. A Book for Boys. With Eight Illustrations by Charles A. Doyle, printed on Toned Paper.

Including the graphic stories of the rise of the Peel Family, and the struggles of such men as Hugh Miller, Wilson the ornithologist, Smeaton the engineer, and Robert Stephenson.

Pilgrim's Progress (The). By John Bunyan. With 12 Illustrations by C. A. Doyle, printed on Toned Paper.

Pioneers of Civilisation. By the Author of "Lives of Eminent Men," &c. With Portraits of Dr. Livingstone, Captain Clapperton, William Penn, Captain Cook, Lord Robert Clive, Captain Flinders, Rev. Henry Martyn; and 10 other Page Illustrations.

Sandford and Merton. By Thomas Day. With Illustrations.

Sea and her famous Sailors (The). By Frank B. Goodrich. With 8 Illustrations, printed on Toned Paper.

Small Beginnings; or, the Way to Get On. With 8 Illustrations, printed on Toned Paper.

The Star of Hope and the Staff of Duty. Tales of Womanly Trials and Victories. With 8 Illustrations by Julian Portch, printed on Toned Paper.

Steady Aim (The). A Book of Examples and Encouragements. From Modern Biography. By W. H. Davenport Adams, Author of Famous Books. With 8 Illustrations by C. A. Doyle, printed on Toned paper.

Stories from English History during the Middle Ages. By Maria Hack. Revised by David Murray Smith, Author of "Tales of Chivalry and Romance," &c. With Illustrations.

Crown 8vo, handsomely bound, 3s. 6d.
Stories of the Flowers. By G. P. Dyer.

Watchers for the Dawn, and other Studies of Christian Character. By Mrs. W. R. Lloyd. With 8 Illustrations by James Godwin.

GENERAL LIST OF STANDARD AND OTHER WORKS.

Crown 8vo, price 5s.

Adams' (W. D.) Famous Books. Sketches in the Highways and Byways of English Literature.

Post 8vo, price 3s. 6d.

Adams' (W. D.) Steady Aim (The). A Book of Examples and Encouragements. From Modern Biography.

Post 8vo, price 3s. 6d.

Adventures in the Ice. A Comprehensive Summary of Arctic Exploration, Discovery, and Adventure, including Experiences of Captain Penny, the Veteran Whaler, *now first published.* By JOHN TILLOTSON. With 4 Portraits and 14 other Illustrations.

Two Vols. royal 8vo, Illustrated with Steel Engravings and Coloured Maps, price 45s.

America, Dr. C. Mackay's History of the United States.

Two Vols. demy 4to, cloth gilt, price 35s.

American Land, Lake, and River Scenery. 120 Steel Engravings, after Sketches by W. H. Bartlett. With Descriptions by N. P. WILLIS, Author of "Pencellings by the Way."

C

Small 4to, extensively Illustrated, price 12s.

Art Studies from Nature, as applied to Design.
For the use of Architects, Designers, and Manufacturers.

Small 4to, with 259 Wood Engravings, elegantly bound,
price 12s.

Art Papers, or Rambles of an Artist. By
F. W. FAIRHOLT, F.S.A.

Small 4to, with 133 Illustrations, elegantly bound, price 12s.

Art Rambles Abroad, or Homes and Haunts of
Foreign Artists.   By FREDERICK WILLIAM FAIRHOLT, F.S.A.

Small 4to, with numerous Engravings on Wood, price 12s.

Art Rambles at Home; or Homes, Works, and
Shrines of English Artists.   By FREDERICK WILLIAM FAIRHOLT,
F.S.A.

Imperial 4to, with Steel and Wood Engravings, price 31s. 6d.

Art Journal. In Yearly Volumes. Bound in cloth.

In Twenty-six Vols. uniformly half-bound, with nearly 900 choice
Engravings on Steel, and 5,000 original Woodcuts,
price £52.

Art Journal (The) from 1849 to 1874. The ART
JOURNAL is to the Art-world what the *Times* is to the metropolis.
From the first issue it has remained true to its avowed purpose,
and has been "*a Monthly record of the Fine Arts, the Industrial
Arts, and the Arts of Design and Manufacture ;*" and as these
different departments have been, and are always, entrusted to
those who are best acquainted with the matters to be treated, the
volumes of the ART JOURNAL really constitute a history in detail
of the progress of Art generally, illustrated by some thousands of
Engravings on Steel and Wood.

Art Journal Illustrated Catalogues.

THE GREAT INDUSTRIAL EXHIBITION OF 1851. Containing upwards of 1,400 Engravings on Wood, and Frontispiece on Steel. Price 21s. With additional Plates of Sculpture, 25s.

THE EXHIBITION OF ART-INDUSTRY IN DUBLIN, 1853. 10s. 6d.

THE EXHIBITION OF ART-INDUSTRY IN PARIS, 1855. 10s. 6d.

THE INTERNATIONAL EXHIBITION OF 1862. Illustrated with nearly 1,500 Engravings on Wood, and 12 on Steel. 21s.

THE PARIS UNIVERSAL EXHIBITION OF 1867. 21s.

THE PHILADELPHIA EXHIBITION OF 1876. Illustrated with 8 Engravings on Steel and 118 on Wood. Price 10s. 6d.

Illustrated with Maps and numerous Engravings, 4to, cloth, price 32s.

Barclay's (Rev. James) Complete and Universal

English Dictionary. Conformed to the present state of Science and Statistics. By B. B. WOODWARD, B.A. A Series of Supplemental Maps is also published, 1s. each Part.

Two Vols. royal 4to, with 45 Steel Engravings, price 48s.

Barnes's (Rev. Albert) Notes Explanatory and

Practical on the New Testament. Carefully Edited, with Original Headings and Improved Readings, by INGRAM COBBIN, M.A., and E. HENDERSON, D.D., and an Introduction by the Rev. H. STEBBING, D.D.

2 Vols. imperial 8vo, cloth, price 42s.

Beattie's (W., M.D.) The Castles and Abbeys

of England. Illustrated with upwards of 200 Engravings on Steel and Wood. New Edition.

Better Life (The). Small 4to, cloth extra, gilt edges,

price 6s.

Royal 4to, with Steel Plates, cloth, price 42s.

Bible (The Holy), Self-Interpreting. By the

Rev. JOHN BROWN.

c 2

Two Vols. 4to, cloth, price 55s.

Bible (The Holy). With Matthew Henry's

Commentary. Edited and Abridged by the Rev. E. BLOOMFIELD. Illustrated with Steel Plates.

Imperial 4to. In One Vol., morocco, £6 6s.; Two Vols., £7 7s.

Bible (The); with an Explanatory and Practical Com-

mentary. The OLD TESTAMENT, by the Rev. ROBERT JAMIESON, D.D. The NEW TESTAMENT, by the Rev. E. H. BICKERSTETH, M.A. With 40 Steel Engravings.

Fcap. 4to, handsome binding, price 5s.

Birthdays. Quotations in Prose and Verse. Selected

and Arranged by A LADY.

Burnet's History of the Reformation. Abridged

by the Author for the Use of Students. Post 8vo, 3s. 6d.

Burnet's History of his Own Times. Abridged by

the Author for the Use of Students. Post 8vo, 3s. 6d.

Two Vols. 4to, numerous Coloured Plates, price 52s. 6d.

Buffon's Natural History of Animals, Vege-

tables, and Minerals; including a General History of Man. Translated by W. SNELLIE, F.R.S.E.; with Additions by H. A. CHAMBERS, LL.D.

Crown 8vo, cloth gilt, 3s. 6d.

Bunyan's Pilgrim's Progress. With 12 Illustrations

by C. A. Doyle, printed on Toned Paper.

One Vol. royal 4to, cloth extra, 35s.

Bunyan's Pilgrim's Progress. Illustrated Edition.

With other Works by the same Author. Notes and Comments by various Divines, and numerous Engravings on Steel and Wood.

Royal 8vo, cloth, price 12s.

Bunyan's Holy War. Pictorial Edition. With

numerous Illustrations.

Four Vols. imperial 8vo, price 52s.

Bunyan's Entire Works. Edited, with Original
Introductions, Notes, and Memoir, by the Rev. H. STEBBING.
With Illustrations on Steel and Wood.

Royal 8vo, cloth, gilt edges, price 24s.

Burns's (Robert) Complete Works, Poems,
Songs, and Letters. With Notes and Life, by ALLAN CUNNING-
HAM, and a copious Glossary. Illustrated by 33 Engravings from
designs by Bartlett, Allom, and others, and Portrait.

Imperial 8vo, with 53 Steel Engravings, price 28s.

Byron. The Complete Poetical Works of Lord
Byron. Illustrated Edition. With Notes and a Memoir of the
Author.

Royal 4to, in cloth gilt, with 16 Illustrations, price 21s.

British Landscape Painters, from Samuel
Scott to David Cox. With a Preliminary Essay, and Biographical
Notices. By WILLIAM B. SCOTT, Author of "Half-Hour Lectures
on Art," "The British School of Sculpture," "Life of Albert
Dürer," &c. Containing 16 Large Engravings on Steel, from
Famous Pictures by Scott, Turner, Constable, Gainsborough,
Ward, Callcott, Stanfield, Creswick, Cox, and others.

Imperial 4to, elegantly bound, with 16 Engravings, price 21s.

British Portrait Painters, from Sir Peter Lely
to James Sant. With Critical Descriptions, and Biographical
Notices. By EDMUND OLLIER, Author of the "Doré Gallery," &c.

Imperial 4to, in cloth gilt, with 20 Steel Engravings and
50 Woodcuts, price 21s.

British School of Sculpture (The). With a Pre-
liminary Essay, and Notices of the Artists. By WILLIAM B.
SCOTT, Author of "Our British Landscape Painters," "Life of
Albert Dürer," &c.

8vo, plates, cloth, price 20s.

Brown's (T.) Manual of Modern Farriery;
together with Instructions in Hunting, Fishing, and Field Sports.

In crown 8vo, price 3s. 6d.

Busy Hives Around Us (The). A Variety of Trips and Visits to the Mine, the Workshop, and the Factory. With Popular Notes on Materials, Processes, and Machines. With 7 Illustrations, by William Harvey and others, printed on Toned Paper.

New Edition. In 1 Vol. 8vo, handsomely bound, price 10s. 6d.

Book of Ballads (The) Ancient and Modern. Containing Translations of Foreign Ballads. With many Illustrations.

Two Vols. demy 4to, cloth gilt, price 25s. each.

Bosphorus and the Danube (The). "The Bosphorus," by Miss PARDOE, "The Danube," by W. BEATTIE, M.D. Illustrated with 168 Steel Engravings, from Drawings by W. H. BARTLETT.

Imperial 4to, handsomely bound, with Engravings, price 21s.

Callcott (Sir A. W., R.A.) Pictures by. With Descriptive Notices, and a Biographical Sketch of the Painter. By JAMES DAFFORNE.

Two Vols. demy 4to, cloth gilt, price 50s.

Caledonia Illustrated. 170 Steel Engravings, from Drawings by W. H. Bartlett, T. Allom, &c. With Descriptions by WILLIAM BEATTIE, M.D.

Two Vols. demy 4to, cloth gilt, price 35s.

Canadian Scenery. 118 Steel Engravings, after Drawings by W. H. Bartlett. With Descriptions by N. P. WILLIS, Author of "Pencillings by the Way."

In 1 Vol. 8vo, cloth, price 8s. 6d.

Chess: Laws and Practice. Containing the Laws and History of the Game, together with an Analysis of the Openings, and a Treatise on End Games, by HOWARD STAUNTON and ROBERT B. WORMALD.

Small 4to, cloth extra, with numerous Illustrations, price 5s.

Children's Sunday Pleasure-Book (The). Containing Gospel and other Stories told to Children.

With 250 Illustrations, handsomely bound in cloth gilt, price 5s.

Children's Pleasure-Book (The): a Treasury of Original Stories, Biographies, Poems, Sunday Readings, &c. By W. H. G. KINGSTON, JEANIE HERING, W. BURNETT, the Author of "Poems written for a Child," the Author of "Brave Lisette," A. G. FORBES, HELEN ZIMMERN, and other Popular Authors of Children's Books.

Post 8vo, cloth, price 10s. 6d.

Cola's (P. R.) India: Undeveloped Wealth, and State Reproductive Works of.

Two Vols. demy 4to, cloth gilt, price 40s.

Coast Scenery and Watering-Places of Great Britain. A Series of 125 Steel Engravings, from Drawings by Harding, Creswick, Cooke, Bartlett, &c. Edited by W. BEATTIE, M.D.

Two Vols. imperial 8vo, bound in cloth, price 45s.

Copland's (Samuel) Agriculture, Ancient and Modern: its History, Principles, and Practice. Illustrated with Engravings on Steel and Wood.

Fcap. 8vo, cloth, Sixth Edition, revised, price 3s. 6d.

Cricket-Field (The). By the Rev. JAMES PYCROFT, B.A., Trinity College, Oxford. With a Portrait of W. G. Grace, Esq., NEW EDITION. Edited by C. W. ALCOCK.

4to, with a profusion of Coloured Plates, cloth, price 21s.

Culpepper's (Nicholas, M.D.) Complete Herbal and English Physician. With Rules for Compounding Medicines, according to the true System of Nature; forming a Complete Family Dispensary.

Small 4to, with 135 Engravings on Wood, price 15s.

Cutts' (E. L.) Scenes and Characters of the

Middle Ages. By the Rev. EDWARD L. CUTTS, late Hon. Sec. of the Essex Archæological Society.

Contents:—The Monks of the Middle Ages; The Hermits and Recluses of the Middle Ages; The Pilgrims of the Middle Ages; The Secular Clergy of the Middle Ages; The Minstrels of the Middle Ages; The Knights of the Middle Ages; The Merchants of the Middle Ages.

"A series of valuable papers. . . . A lucid text, terse and full of matter, excellently assists the illustrations, which of themselves would be a welcome boon to the antiquarian."—*Daily Telegraph.*

"The illustrations alone, taken as they are from some old rare manuscripts and other trustworthy sources, would make this volume extremely valuable."—*Post.*

Crown 8vo, cloth, gilt edges, price 3s. 6d.

Dale's (Rev. T.) A Life's Motto. Illustrated by

Biographical Examples. With a Frontispiece by J. D. Watson.

Imperial 4to, with Engravings on Steel, price 21s.

Eastlake (Sir Charles, P.R.A.) Pictures by.

With Descriptions, and a Biographical Sketch of the Painter. By W. COSMO MONKHOUSE.

Imperial 4to, with 13 Engravings on Steel, price 21s.

Etty (William, R.A.) Pictures by. With Descrip-

tions, and a Biographical Sketch of the Painter. By W. COSMO MONKHOUSE.

Crown 8vo, 320 pages, price 5s.

Election Manual (The): a Concise Digest of the

Law of Parliamentary Elections. By L. P. BRICKWOOD, M.A., and HERBERT CROFT, M.A., of the Inner Temple, Barristers-at-Law.

Small 4to, with 259 Wood Engravings, elegantly bound, price 12s.

Fairholt's (F. W., F.S.A.) Art Papers, or

Rambles of an Artist.

Small 4to, with 133 Woodcut Illustrations, price 12s.

Fairholt's (F. W., F.S.A.) Art Rambles

Abroad, or Homes and Haunts of Foreign Artists.

Small 4to, with numerous Engravings on Wood, price 12s.

Fairholt's (F. W., F.S.A.) Art Rambles at

Home; or, Homes, Works, and Shrines, of English Artists.

Post 8vo, cloth gilt, 3s. 6d.

Famous London Merchants. With Life-Portraits of
George Peabody; Sir Richard Whittington; Sir Thomas
Gresham; Sir Hugh Myddelton; Sir Josiah Child; Paterson,
Founder of the Bank of England; Coutts, the Banker; and
17 others. By H. R. FOX BOURNE.

Post 8vo, cloth gilt, 3s. 6d.

Fleetwood's (Rev. J., D.D.) Life of our Blessed
Lord and Saviour Jesus Christ. New Edition. With 8 Full-
page Illustrations.

4to, cloth, with gilt edges, price 30s.

Fleetwood's (Rev. J., D.D.) Life of Christ.
With an Essay by the Rev. H. STEBBING. To which are added
Bishop Hall's Meditation on the Love of Christ, and Bishop
Jeremy Taylor's Golden Grove and Worthy Communicant.
With 58 Steel Engravings.

In One handsome royal 4to Volume, cloth, price 28s.

Fletcher's (Rev. Alex., D.D.) Guide to Family
Devotion. Containing a Hymn, a Portion of Scripture, with
appropriate Devotional Reflections, a Prayer for every Morning
and Evening throughout the entire Year.

Two Vols. 16mo, cloth gilt, price 18s.

Fletcher's (Rev. Alex.) Scripture History, for
the Improvement of Youth. With 241 Engravings on Steel.

Two Vols. 16mo, cloth, price 20s.

Fletcher's (Rev. Alex.) Scripture Natural His-
tory. Profusely illustrated.

Crown 8vo, price 6s., with 8 Illustrations.

Forbes' (A. G.) Pioneers of the Christian Faith.
Contents :—The Beginning of the Gospel in many Lands; Eminent Christian
Teachers of the earlier stages; Early Christianity in Britain; Introduction of
Christianity into America; The Gospel in Ancient Gaul and subsequent France;
Introduction of the Gospel into Germany; The Reformation; Other Churches in
other Lands; Modern Missions.

Crown 8vo, price 5s.

Forbes' (A.G.) The Empires and Cities of Asia.
Contents:—Topography, Languages, and Natural History; Turkey in Asia; Arabia; Persia; Russia in Asia; The Tartars; Britain in India; China; Japan; Conclusion.

Foxe's Book of Martyrs. Being a History of Christian
Martyrdom from the Earliest Times. Carefully revised by the Rev. M. CROMBIE, M.A. 3s. 6d.

With 5 Engravings and Maps, two Vols. cloth, price 36s.

Gibbon's (Edward) History of the Decline and
Fall of the Roman Empire. With Memoir, and Additional Notes from the French of M. GUIZOT.

Crown 8vo, 3s. 6d.

Habits of Good Society (The). A Handbook of
Etiquette for Ladies and Gentlemen. With Thoughts, Hints, and Anecdotes concerning Social Observances, Nice Points of Taste and Good Manners, and the Art of making One's-self agreeable. The whole interspersed with humorous Illustrations of Social Predicaments, Remarks on the History and Changes of Fashion, and the Differences of English and Continental Etiquette.

With Illustrations, price 3s. 6d.

Hack's (Maria) Stories from English History
during the Middle Ages. Revised by DAVID MURRAY SMITH, Author of "Tales of Chivalry and Romance," &c.

4to, cloth, extra gilt, price 21s.

Howson's (J. S., D.D., Dean of Chester) The
River Dee: its Aspects and History. With 93 Illustrations on Wood, by ALFRED RIMMER.

Holiday Adventures; or, the Strettons' Sum-
mer in Normandy. By Mrs. JAMES GAMBIER. With 8 Illustrations by Charles Altamont Doyle, printed on Toned Paper. Price 3s. 6d.

Small 4to, with Wood Engravings, price 21s.

Hall's (S. C.) The Book of the Thames from
its Rise to its Fall.

Small 4to, handsomely bound, with numerous Illustrations,
price 21s.

Hall's (S. C.) A Book of Memories of Great
Men and Women of the Age, from Personal Acquaintance.

Two Vols. fcap. 4to, neatly bound, with 210 Illustrations,
price 21s. each.

Hall's (S. C., and L. Jewitt) The Stately Homes
of England.

Three Vols. royal 8vo, cloth extra, price 63s.

Hall's (S. C. and Mrs.) Ireland: its Scenery,
Character, &c. 48 Steel Plates and 500 Woodcuts.

Three Vols. demy 4to, price £5 5s.

History (The) of Hampshire. By B. B. Woodwood,
B.A., F.S.A., and the Rev. Theodore C. Wilks. With a
History of the Isle of Wight. By Charles Lockhart, Esq.
Illustrated by Steel Engravings after Original Views, Maps, &c.

Crown 8vo, price 2s.

Heraldry (The Manual of). Being a Concise Description of the Several Terms Used, and containing a Dictionary of
every Designation in the Science. Illustrated by 400 Engravings
on Wood.

Three Vols. crown 8vo, 31s. 6d.

Hering's (Jeanie) Through the Mist. By the
Author of "Truth will Out," "Garry," "Golden Days," &c., &c.

8vo, with 10 Engravings on Steel, cloth, price 15s.

Hemans's (Mrs.) Young Woman's Companion;
or, Female Instructor. A Summary of Useful Knowledge, calculated to form the Intellectual, the Moral, and the Domestic
Character. Interspersed with Interesting Tales, Biographies of
Illustrious Women, Hints on Education, Domestic Management,
Receipts, &c.

Four Vols. imperial 8vo, cloth gilt, price £4 4s.

Hume and Smollett's History of England.
With a Continuation to the year 1872, by Dr. E. H. Nolan.
108 Plates and Maps engraved on Steel.

One Vol. 8vo, price 16s.

Home's Lights and Shadows of Spiritualism.
By D. D. HOME.

Imperial 4to, with 16 Engravings on Steel, handsomely bound,
price 21s.

Italian Masters (Pictures by), Greater and
Lesser. With an Introductory Essay, and Notices of the Painters
and Subjects Engraved. By WILLIAM B. SCOTT.

Two Vols. demy 4to, cloth gilt, price 35s.

Ireland, its Scenery and Antiquities. 120 Steel
Engravings by W. H. Bartlett. With Descriptive Text by J.
STIRLING COYNE, N. P. WILLIS, &c.

Fcap. 4to, cloth extra, with 20 Engravings on Steel, price 9s.

Ireland, Picturesque Scenery in.   Drawn by
T. CRESWICK, R.A. Accompanied by Descriptive Jottings, by a
Tourist.

Post 8vo, cloth, price 10s. 6d.

India, Undeveloped Wealth, and Reproduc-
tive Works of. By P. R. COLA.

Three Vols. royal 8vo, cloth extra, price 63s.

Ireland: its Scenery, Character, &c.   By Mr.
and Mrs. S. C. HALL.   48 Steel Plates and 500 Woodcuts.

In Post 4to, with 6 Steel Engravings, price 5s.

Isle of Wight.   The only complete Road-Book of the
Isle of Wight. "Virtue's General Guide to the Isle of Wight,"
containing a Circuit Itinerary, and the Circumnavigation, together with the History and Topography of the Isle of Wight.

Jackson's Curiosities of the Pulpit and Pulpit
Literature, Memorabilia, Anecdotes, &c., of Celebrated Preachers,
from the Fourth Century of the Christian Era to the Present
Time. By THOMAS JACKSON, M.A., Prebendary of St. Paul's
Cathedral, and Rector of Stoke Newington, London. Price 3s. 6d.

Royal 8vo, cloth gilt, price 29s.

Josephus's (Flavius) Works.   With Essay by Rev.
H. STEBBING.   80 Woodcuts and 46 Steel Engravings.

Josephus's (Flavius) Works. Two Vols. post 8vo, 12s.

Crown 8vo, handsomely bound, gilt edges, price 6s.

Jameson's (Mrs.) A Commonplace Book of Thoughts, Memories, and Fancies, Original and Selected. By the Author of "Legends of the Madonna," "Sacred and Legendary Art," &c., &c. With Illustrations and Etchings.

Crown 8vo, Illustrated, 5s.

King's Beeches: Stories of Old Chums. By STEPHEN J. MACKENNA, Author of "Off Parade," "Plucky Fellows," &c., &c.

Imperial 4to, with 20 Engravings on Steel, price 31s. 6d.

Landseer (Sir Edwin, R.A.) Pictures by. With Descriptions, and a Biographical Sketch of the Painter. By JAMES DAFFORNE.

One Vol. 4to, cloth lettered, with 178 Illustrations, price 5s.

Langler's (J. R.) Pictorial Geography for Young Beginners. By JOHN R. LANGLER, B.A., F.R.G.S., Lecturer on Geography in the Training College, Westminster.

4to, with numerous Plates of Horses and Dogs, cloth, price 25s.

Lawrence's (Richard, V.S.) Complete Farrier and British Sportsman.

Imperial 4to, with 9 Steel Engravings, in cloth gilt, price 16s.

Leslie (C. R., R.A.) Pictures by. With Descriptive Notices, and a Biographical Sketch of the Painter. By JAMES DAFFORNE.

Imperial 4to, in cloth gilt, with 20 Steel Engravings, 31s. 6d.

Leslie and Maclise. Specimens of the Works of these celebrated Artists. With Descriptive and Biographical Notices. By JAMES DAFFORNE.

Crown 8vo, price 3s. 6d.

Life's Motto. By the Rev. T. PELHAM DALE, M.A. Illustrated by Biographical Examples. With a Frontispiece by J. D. Watson.

Imperial 4to, cloth gilt, with 11 Steel Engravings, price 16s.

Maclise (Daniel, R.A.) Pictures by. With Descriptions, and a Biographical Sketch of the Painter. By JAMES DAFFORNE.

Imperial 4to, with Engravings on Steel, price 21s.

Mulready (William, R.A.) Pictures by. With Descriptions, and a Biographical Sketch of the Painter. By JAMES DAFFORNE.

Men who have Risen. A Book for Boys. With Eight Illustrations by Charles A. Doyle, printed on Toned Paper. Post 8vo, price 3s. 6d.

Including the graphic stories of the rise of the Peel Family, and the struggles of such men as Hugh Miller, Wilson the ornithologist, Smeaton the engineer, and Robert Stephenson.

8vo, with 10 Engravings on Steel, price 15s.

Mavor's (J.) Young Man's Companion; or, Youth's Instructor. A Modern Compendium of Useful Knowledge, including Geography, Astronomy, History, Biography, Natural Philosophy, Commercial Affairs, &c.

1 Vol. crown 8vo, cloth lettered, price 10s. 6d.

Muddock's (J. E.) A Wingless Angel.

In Three handsome Vols. royal 4to, price £8 8s.

National Gallery of British Pictures. Edited by S. C. HALL, F.S.A. Containing about 150 First-class Line Engravings of the Pictures in the Vernon Collection, with a Selection of 53 of the best Works of Modern Statuary.

Three Vols. imperial 4to, half morocco, price, £35.

National Gallery Photographs of the Old Masters. By L. CALDESI. With descriptions by R. N. WORNUM.

Improved Edition, Edited by JOHN HAY, 4to, price 31s. 6d.

Nicholson's (P.) Carpenter's Guide. Being a Complete Book of Lines for Carpenters, Joiners, Cabinet Makers, and Workmen in General.

4to, price 18s.

Nicholson's Practical Treatise on Mensuration.
A Sequel to the " Carpenter's Guide."

Numerous Steel Engravings and Maps, Two Vols. royal 8vo, price 45s.

Nolan's (Dr.) History of the British Empire
in India and the East. From the Earliest Times to the Suppression of the Sepoy Mutiny in 1859.

Numerous Engravings and Maps, Two Vols. price 45s.

Nolan's (Dr.) History of the War against
Russia.

Illustrated with 26 Engravings on Steel, 4to, price 30s.

Nolan's (Dr.) History of the Liberators of Italy;
or, the Lives of General Garibaldi, Victor Emanuel, King of Italy, Count Cavour, and Napoleon III.

In Two Vols. imperial 4to, profusely illustrated, price 35s.

Our Sunday Book: A Treasury of Holy
Thoughts and Readings in Prose and Verse. Carefully selected for Family Reading on the Sabbath Day.

Demy 4to, cloth gilt, price 25s.

Palestine Illustrated; or, Scenes of Sacred
History, Historical and Descriptive. By HENRY STEBBING, D.D., F.R.S. 80 Steel Engravings, from Drawings taken on the Spot, by W. H. Bartlett.

One Vol. large 4to, cloth lettered, with 178 Illustrations, price 5s.

Pictorial Geography for Young Beginners.
By JOHN R. LANGLER, B.A., F.R.G.S., Lecturer on Geography in the Training College, Westminster.

In Crown Quarto, with 50 Illustrations, price 10s. 6d.

Picture and Incident from Bible Story. With
Letterpress Descriptions by DEAN STANLEY, Rev. SAMUEL COX, Rev. HENRY ALLON, and other eminent authors.

In demy 4to, with 160 Steel Engravings, price 45s. ;
or in Two Vols. price 50s.

Pictorial Table-Book (The). Containing a Selection
of Picturesque Scenery, Views of Historical and Romantic Ruins,
Portraits of Eminent Persons, &c., &c. With Descriptions by
JAMES DAFFORNE, Esq.

BY SAMUEL PLIMSOLL, M.P.

Demy 4to, with 58 Diagrams and other Illustrations printed in
Photography, price 14s.

Plimsoll's (S., M.P.) Our Seamen: an Appeal.
ALSO CHEAP EDITIONS, price 2s. 6d. and 6d.

Plimsoll's (S., M.P.) An Appeal on Behalf of
our Seamen. From the larger Work entitled "Our Seamen."
To which is added a Speech delivered in the House of Commons,
March 4, 1873, by Mr. Plimsoll. Also a Notice of a Speech
delivered at Leeds, Monday, March 16. Price 4d.

Plimsoll's (S., M.P.) A Bill to Provide for the
Survey of Certain Shipping, and to prevent Overloading. Pre-
pared and brought into the House of Commons by Mr. Plimsoll,
Mr. Horsman, and others. Price 4d.

Preliminary Report of the Royal Commission
on Unseaworthy Ships, an Analytical Index of the. Compiled
by JELINGER E. SYMONS, Lieutenant, Royal Navy. Price 2s. 6d.

"There are several ships that go to sea every year in such a condition as to be
dangerous to the lives of the people on board."—*Preliminary Report of Royal
Commission on Unseaworthy Ships*, p. 262.

Pioneers of Civilisation. By the Author of "Lives
of Eminent Men," &c. With Portraits of Dr. Livingstone,
Captain Clapperton, William Penn, Captain Cook, Lord Robert
Clive, Captain Flinders, Rev. Henry Martyn; and 10 other Page
Illustrations. Price 3s. 6d.

Pioneers of the Christian Faith. By A. GRUAR
FORBES. Price 5s.

Contents :—The Beginning of the Gospel in many Lands; Eminent Christian
Teachers of the earlier stages; Early Christianity in Britain; Introduction of
Christianity into America; The Gospel in Ancient Gaul and subsequent France;
Introduction of the Gospel into Germany; The Reformation; Other Churches in
other Lands : Modern Missions.

Fcap. 8vo, cloth, Sixth Edition, revised, price 3s. 6d.

Pycroft's (Rev. J.) The Cricket-Field. By the
Rev. JAMES PYCROFT, B.A., Trinity College, Oxford. With a
Portrait of W. G. Grace, Esq. Edited by C. W. ALCOCK.

Two Vols. demy 4to, cloth gilt, price 40s.

Piedmont and Italy, from the Alps to the
Tiber. With 138 Steel Engravings, after Designs by Harding,
Pyne, Bartlett, Brockedon, &c. With Descriptions by DUDLEY
COSTELLO.

One Vol. royal 8vo, price 35s.

Queens of England (The): Biographical
Sketches of the Queens Consort Reigning, from the Norman
Conquest to the Reign of Victoria. Edited by MARY HOWITT.

In Two Vols. 4to, cloth, gilt edges, price £2 12s. 6d.

Ramsay (Allan) and the Scottish Poets be-
fore Burns. Edited by CHARLES MACKAY, LL.D. Comprising
also Selections from Hector Macneil, William Hamilton, Robert
Ferguson, &c. Illustrated with 47 Engravings on Steel, after
Original Paintings by T. Clark, W. MacTaggart, Alexander
Johnston, James Drummond, J. B. McDonald, H. Cameron,
G. Hay, S. Bough, W. F. Vallance, &c.

In demy 8vo, cloth gilt, price 9s.

Rimmer's (Alfred) The Ancient Stone Crosses
of England. With 72 Illustrations.

New Edition, with 20 pages of Woodcuts, post 8vo, price 2s. 6d.

Rogers's (George A.) Art of Wood Carving (The).

In Quarto, with 72 superb Wood Engravings, price 21s.

Robertson's (H. R.) Life on the Upper Thames.
With Thirty-six full-page Illustrations.

In Two large Vols, folio, handsomely bound, price £5.

Royal Gems from the Galleries of Europe.
Engraved after Pictures of the Great Masters. With Notices,
Biographical, Historical, and Descriptive, by S. C. HALL, Esq.,
F.S.A.

D

Crown 8vo, price 3s. 6d.

Sandford and Merton. By THOMAS DAY. With Illustrations.

Crown 8vo, price 3s. 6d.

Small Beginnings; or, the Way to Get On. With 8 Illustrations, printed on Toned Paper.

Crown 8vo, price 3s. 6d.

Steady Aim (The). A Book of Examples and Encouragements. From Modern Biography. By W. H. DAVENPORT ADAMS, Author of "Famous Regiments of the British Army," &c. With 8 Illustrations by C. A. Doyle, printed on Toned Paper.

Crown 8vo, price 3s. 6d.

Stories from English History during the Middle Ages. By MARIA HACK. Revised by DAVID MURRAY SMITH, Author of "Tales of Chivalry and Romance," &c. With Illustrations.

Two Vols. imperial 8vo, cloth, price 45s.

Scotland, Dr. James Taylor's Pictorial History of, from the Roman Invasion to the Close of the Jacobite Rebellion, A.D. 79—1746. Illustrated with 79 Steel Engravings, from designs by W. H. Bartlett and others.

Two Vols. demy 4to, cloth gilt, price 40s.

Scotland (Illustrated). By W. BEATTIE, M.D. In a Series of 120 Steel Engravings after Drawings by Allom, Bartlett, and M'Culloch.

Imperial 4to, with 13 Illustrations on Steel, price 21s.

Stanfield (Clarkson, R.A.) Pictures by. With Descriptive Notices, and a Biographical Sketch of the Painter. By JAMES DAFFORNE.

Imperial 4to, in cloth gilt, price 21s.

Sculpture, the British School of. With a Preliminary Essay, and Notices of the Artists. By WILLIAM B. SCOTT, Author of "Our British Landscape Painters," "Life of Albert Dürer," &c.

In folio, handsomely bound, price £3 3s.

Sculpture Gallery, Modern.
A Series of Steel Engravings. With Descriptions in Prose, and Poetical Illustrations, by J. DAFFORNE, T. K. HERVEY, &c., preceded by an Historical and Critical Essay on Sculpture, Ancient and Modern.

Shakspere's Works.
New and Revised Edition of Knight's Pictorial Shakspere. With upwards of 1,000 Engraved Illustrations. Eight Vols. royal 8vo, handsomely bound in cloth, price £4 4s.

Six by Two: Stories of Old Schoolfellows.
By EDITH DIXON and MARY DE MORGAN. Price 5s.

Contents:—The French Girl at our School; A Ramble on the Rhine; Lilian and Lucy; How Nelly went to School; A Midnight Adventure; The Fault of the Roses.

Small 4to, cloth extra, with numerous Illustrations, price 5s.

Sunday Pleasure-Book.
Containing Gospel and other Stories told to Children.

In Two Vols. imperial 4to, profusely Illustrated, price 35s.

Sunday-Book: a Treasury of Holy Thoughts
and Readings in Prose and Verse. Carefully selected for Family Reading on the Sabbath Day.

Quarto, interleaved with blotting paper, price 2s. Annually.

Showell's Housekeeper's Account-Book for
1877. Exhibiting every Description of Expense likely to occur in a Family. With Tables, showing at One View the Amount expended Weekly, Quarterly, and during the Whole Year in every Department, and the Total Amount of Cash received and expended in One Year. Also—1. Selected Recipes. 2. Articles in Season. 3. A Word to Housekeepers. 4. Gardening.

Demy 8vo, with Portrait, price 5s.

Smith's (John) Erith: its Natural, Civil, and
Ecclesiastical History. By CHARLES JOHN SMITH, M.A., Christchurch, Oxford, late Archdeacon of Jamaica, Vicar of Erith.

Two Vols, demy 4to, cloth gilt, price 40s.

Switzerland.
Illustrated in 108 Steel Engravings, after Drawings by W. H. Bartlett. With Descriptions by W. BEATTIE, M.D.

Small crown 8vo, 3s. 6d.

Star of Hope and the Staff of Duty. Tales of
Womanly Trials and Victories. With 8 Illustrations by Julian
Portch, printed on Toned Paper.

Crown 8vo, limp cloth, second edition, price 4s.

Steel's Ready Reckoner for Farmers and
Auctioneers. New Tables for the Use of Auctioneers, Valuers,
Farmers, Hay and Straw Dealers, &c.; forming a Complete
Calendar and Ready Reckoner. By a RETIRED TENANT-FARMER.

Two Vols. imperial 8vo, cloth, price 45s.

Taylor's (Dr. James) Pictorial History of
Scotland, from the Roman Invasion to the Close of the Jacobite
Rebellion, A.D. 79—1746. Illustrated with 79 Steel Engravings,
from designs by W. H. Bartlett and others.

Crown 8vo, cloth extra, price 5s.

Tomlinson's (L. J.) Alice de Burgh: a Home
Story for Girls.

New Edition, Revised and Corrected, in Three Vols. price £3 15s.

Tomlinson's (Ch., F.R.S.) Cyclopædia of Useful
Arts, Mechanical and Chemical, Manufactures, Mining, and
Engineering. Illustrated by 63 Steel Plates and numerous
Wood Engravings.

Three Vols. royal 4to, cloth, price £4 14s. 6d.

Tredgold (Thomas) on the Steam Engine. In
Two Sections: 1. MARINE ENGINES; 2. LOCOMOTIVE AND STA-
TIONARY ENGINES. 1,000 pages of Text, and upwards of 220
Engravings; also 160 Woodcuts and Diagrams.

Demy 8vo, cloth, price 21s.

Timbs' Curiosities of London. New Edition,
corrected and enlarged.

In Four Vols. folio, with 152 Steel Engravings, price £8 8s.

Vernon Gallery of British Art (The). Edited
by S. C. HALL, F.S.A. 152 Engravings on Steel, of the
choicest pictures by British Artists, in the Collection formed by
the late Robert Vernon, Esq., now in the National Gallery.

Vicar of Wakefield (The). By OLIVER GOLDSMITH.

With 12 Full-page Illustrations, printed on Toned Paper. Post 8vo, price 3s. 6d.

Demy 4to, with 24 Steel Plates, and 14 valuable Plans, price 42s.

Walcott's (M. E. C.) The Ancient Church of

Scotland (Scoti-Monasticon), before the Union of the two Crowns. A History of all the Cathedral, Conventual, and Collegiate Churches and Hospitals of Scotland. With a copious Index and Table of Contents and List of Authorities. By MACKENZIE E. C. WALCOTT, B.D., F.S.A., Precentor and Prebendary of Chichester.

Watchers for the Dawn, and other Studies of

Christian Character. By Mrs. W. R. LLOYD. With 8 Illustrations by James Godwin, printed on Toned Paper. Post 8vo, price 3s. 6d.

In folio, cloth extra, gilt edges, price £4 4s.

Wilkie Gallery (The). A Selection of Engravings of

the best Paintings of Sir David Wilkie, R.A., including his Spanish and Oriental Sketches, with Notices Biographical and Critical, a Portrait of Wilkie, and a View of his Birthplace.

Imperial 16mo, handsomely bound, price 6s.

Wit and Pleasure. Seven Tales by Seven Authors.

With Seven Illustrations.

Yn gyflawn mewn 48 o Ranau, 1s. yr un, a phob Rhan yn cynnwys Cerflun Prydferth (in about 42 Parts, at 1s. each).

Y Bibl Cyssegrlan, sef yr Hen Destament a'r

Newydd. Gyda Sylwadau Eglurhaol ac Ymarferol ar bob Pennod. Gan y Parch. THOMAS REES, D.D.

DARLUN ANRHEGAWL RHAD.

Yn gyflawn mewn 21 o Ranau, 1s. yr un (in 21 Parts, at 1s. each).

Bywyd ein Harglwydd Iesu Grist (The Life

of our Lord Jesus Christ). Gan y Parch. JOHN FLEETWOOD, D.D. (Gwedi Ail-chwiliad a gofalus Ddiwygiad yn ol y Cynysgrif a argraphwyd yn 1768.) Gyda Rhagymadrodd gan y Parch. ARTHUR JONES, D.D. At hyn ychwanegir Bywydau yr Efeng-ylwyr a'r Apostolion.

DARLUN ANRHEGAWL RHAD.

Yn gyflawn mewn 21 o Ranau, am 1s. yr un, ynghyd â 22 o Gerfiadau hardd, a Darlun cyntefig o'r Awdwr (in 21 Parts, at 1s. each).

Taith y Pererin (Pilgrim's Progress). Gan JOHN BUNYAN. Yn cynnwys ei Drydedd Ran Wirioneddol, sef "Teithiau yr Annuwiol." Gyda Sylwadau Eglurhaol ganddo ef ei hun. Cyhoeddiad ROBERT PHILIP, Awdwr "Bywyd ac Amseran Bunyan," &c. Y Cyfieithiad a olygwyd gan y Parch. CALEB MORRIS, o Lundain.

ARGRAFFIAD NEWYDD A DIWYGIEDIG.

In 15 Parts, at 1s. each; or in Two Vols., price 18s.

Hanesyddiaeth Ysgrythyrol i Ieuengctyd (Scripture History for the Young). Gan y Parch. ALEXANDER FLETCHER. Y Cyfieithiad a olygwyd gan y Parch. CALEB MORRIS o Lundain. Yn addurnedig â Dau Gant a Deugain o Gerfiadau a Gwyneb-lun hardd.

Mae yr Argraffiad hwn yn gyflawn mewn Tri Rhifyn ar-bymtheg, pris 6c. yr un, yn addurnedig â Darlun ac a Cherfiadau eraill (in 18 Parts, at 6d. each).

YN Y SAESONEG YN UNIG.

Yn gyflawn mewn 25 o Ranau, 1s. yr un (in 25 Parts, at 1s. each).

Hanes Cymru, o'r Amseroedd Boreuaf hyd ei Chor-phoriad Diweddaf â Lloegr; gyda Sylwadau ar ei Daearyddiaeth, a Barddoniaeth, Traddodiadau, Crefydd, Celfyddydau, Moesau, a Chyfreithiau y Cymry. Gan B. B. WOODWARD, B.A. Wedi ei addurno a'i eglurhau â Lluniau o'r Lleoedd mwyaf nodedig, Hynafiaethau, Golygfeydd, &c.

Two Vols. super-royal 8vo, price 28s.

Woodward's (B. B.) History of Wales, from the Earliest Times to its Final Incorporation with England. Illustrated by Views of Remarkable Places, Antiquities, and Scenery.

Crown 8vo, price 5s.

Yeats' (Dr.) The Raw Materials of Commerce. With a List of Commercial Terms, and their Synonyms in several Languages.

Crown 8vo, price 5s.

Yeats' (Dr.) Skilled Labour applied to Produc- tion.

Crown 8vo, price 5s.

Yeats' (Dr.) Growth of Trade. 1500—1789.

Crown 8vo, price 5s.

Yeats' (Dr.) Modern Commerce. 1789—1872.

** These Volumes will be found to include every branch of Trade Education.

Also the following, price 7s. 6d. each.

Commercial Wall Charts. To Illustrate Lectures.

1. Historical Chart: showing the Rise, Progress, Culmination, and Decline of Commercial Nations, from 1500 B.C. to A.D. 1870.
2. Principal Caravan and other Routes of Eastern Commerce, Ancient and Modern.
3. The British Empire in 1873.

PC

०५

CPSIA information can be obtained
at www.ICGtesting.com
Printed in the USA
BVHW042148200920
589239BV00004B/79